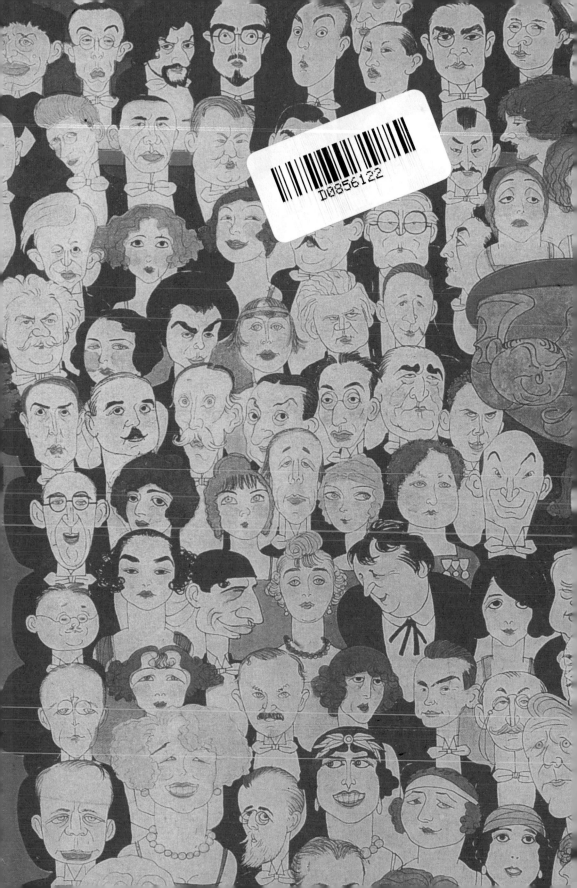

Otto Kahn

The University of North Carolina Press

Chapel Hill & London

Otto Kahn

Art, Money, & Modern Time

Theresa M. Collins

© 2002

The University of North Carolina Press

All rights reserved

Designed by Richard Hendel

Set in Baskerville and Didot

by Keystone Typesetting, Inc.

Manufactured in the United States of America

The paper in this book meets the guidelines for

permanence and durability of the Committee on

Production Guidelines for Book Longevity of the

Council on Library Resources.

Library of Congress Cataloging-in-Publication Data

Collins, Theresa M. (Theresa Mary), 1955–

Otto Kahn: art, money, and modern time /

Theresa M. Collins.

p. cm.

Based on the author's Ph.D. thesis, New York University, 1998.

Includes bibliographical references and index.

ISBN 0-8078-2696-0 (cloth: alk. paper)

1. Kahn, Otto Hermann, 1867–1934. 2. Bankers—United

States—Biography. 3. Philanthropists—United States—

Biography. 4. Art patronage—United States—History.

5. Art and industry—United States—History. I. Title.

HG2463.K34 C65   2002

361.7′4′092—dc21

[B] 2001059765

06 05 04 03 02   5 4 3 2 1

Endleaves: *Chauve Souris* curtain, by Ralph Barton

To Esther, come what might,

and to the memory of our mothers

Contents

Illustrations

Acknowledgments

So many of my family, friends, faculty, and colleagues have helped on this biography. On all accounts, I have enjoyed unwavering cooperation from the faculty at New York University, in particular from Thomas Bender, whose instructive discourses and meticulous readings kept improving my style, sharpening the analysis, and building new ideas. My memory of Vincent P. Carosso is etched in every page of this book as well as in every day of my academic life. In addition, my gratitude extends to several other fine scholars who read the manuscript in its entirety, understood its strengths, and pressed out many weaknesses: Richard Sylla, Mary Nolan, Stuart Stehlin, and Lisa Duggan of the NYU community; Sally Clarke and Janet Staiger of the University of Texas at Austin; and Townsend Ludington and Maury Klein, on behalf of the University of North Carolina Press. A most distinguished and generous colleague, Martin Bauml Duberman of the City University of New York, has given unstintingly of his time and friendship, while also leading me to trust my New York accent and find new ways of telling stories.

Among the individual archivists, librarians, and curators, I would like to thank Mary Anne Jensen and Andros Thomson, who assisted me as I plowed through the Kahn papers at Princeton University; Robert Tuggle, archivist of the Metropolitan Opera Archives, who was exceptionally helpful in directing me toward documents, and, along with John Pennino, in securing photographs; and Christine Nelson, along with the reading room staff, at the Pierpont Morgan Library, who exemplified curatorial collegiality.

Financial support was provided directly from the Faculty of Arts and Sciences at New York University, the Center for Philanthropy at the City University of New York, and the Lincoln Educational Foundation, but I wish to recognize the additional and indispensable support of public agencies and private foundations that have underwritten much of the scholarship I have referenced, and especially the long-term support that is necessary for scholarly, documentary editions.

From the earliest months of its conception to the present, this project has discovered a profound friend in John Ryan, whose hospitality, honesty, and outlook on the world all combined to catch glimpses of Otto Kahn that would have eluded me. I am grateful to him, and also to Lady Virginia Airlie, Elana Ryan, and the late Margaret Kahn Ryan, for the use of numerous photographs from their family albums. In addition, I owe a considerable debt to Christof Eberstadt, for his genealogical investigations of Kahn's siblings and ancestors; to Ernst Schulin, for his research pertaining to Lili Deutsch and Paul Kahn; to Priscilla Roberts, for her parallel and intersecting studies of the Kuhn, Loeb partners; to Jean Strouse, for her fresh take on the life of Pierpont Morgan and the biographical genre; to Dan Okrent, for a lively exchange concerning the Metropolitan Opera and Rockefeller Center; and to Ed Brunner, Greg Robinson, and George Chauncy, for finding several gems among the documentary sources.

The talented staff at the University of North Carolina Press made strikingly congenial collaborators. I am deeply appreciative of Sian Hunter, my principal editor, whose constancy, encouragement, skill, and wit put an easy order to the whole process. Eric Schramm, my copyeditor, contributed significantly to the manuscript, and Pamela Upton, my managing editor, will always be remembered for her efforts in tracking the transit of my manuscript in the days after September 11, 2001.

I am extraordinarily blessed by the counsel and affections of many good people who have seen me through the worst of times and cheered me toward the best: Lisa Collins Sliker, Mark and Christa Segal, Eli Zal, Lisa Gitelman, Gregory Jankunis, Cathy Moran Hajo, Sue Shapiro, Gregory Field, Aldo Salerno, Maria Vasaio, Jacqui Zambrano, Geoffrey Jones, Frances Truscott, Elaine Crane, Carl Prince, Anita Rapone, Gilbert Schrank, Steve Novak, Kathleen Hulser, Amy Gilfenbaum, Barry Thomson, Bill Collins, Gerry Kenney, Richard and Lynn Carlson, Jill Claster, Tamar March, and Osamu Doi. Above all, my public and private gratitude goes out to Esther Katz, tops and taps, for all her caring.

Otto Kahn

Locating Otto Kahn

Otto Hermann Kahn, a banker, was the most influential patron of the arts ever known to America. He brought a Golden Age to the Metropolitan Opera and the dancer Vaslav Nijinsky to America, and he steered Hart Crane toward his epic poem *The Bridge*. A Broadway angel, Kahn heard George Gershwin play "The Man I Love" and invested $10,000 in *Lady Be Good!* He also championed the civic virtues of art, and once told a New York City mayor that a piano in every apartment would do more to prevent crime than a policeman on every corner. Such sincerity was one reason for Margaret Anderson to admire Kahn. The *Little Review* co-founder remembered him as an uncommonly cultured millionaire and benefactor, with whom bohemian artistic and literary types would be willing to spend more than a little time, and not expect to feel completely bored or soiled as a result.[1]

A sophisticate of legendary, effervescent charm, Otto Kahn was cosmopolitan in every fiber of his being, a conservative with a flair for the new, sometimes considered the only capitalist of his era with a soul. He played a singularly significant role in the cultural history of his time, to the extent that he perfectly fit Zora Neale Hurston's term "Negrotarian," denoting humanitarian whites who supported talent striving for artistic recognition under the umbrella of the Harlem Renaissance. By other criteria, Kahn was a prominent symbol of high finance, a renowned partner of Kuhn, Loeb & Co., one of the great international banking houses of Wall Street that epitomized the marshaling of money and power in an age when cash, gold, and various idioms of business culture were the stock-in-trade of modernists. His attachment to the arts made Otto Kahn remarkable among monied men, and though it might have tested his tolerance for artistic revolt, three towering figures of the American literary canon who benefited from Kahn's largesse punned his name in their works. Hart Crane did it in *The Bridge*, as did Ezra Pound in his *Cantos* and Eugene O'Neill in *Marco Millions*. Each was most obviously borrowing from Coleridge's poem "Kubla Khan," and given the Great Khan's renown for introducing bank notes or paper money, swapping "Kahn" for "Khan" or "Chan" or "Kubla" would become a common enough practice. The *New York Times* did it when editorializing about Kahn's unsuccessful attempt to build a more modern Metropolitan Opera House, and a hint later worked itself into Nathanael West's novella *The Day of the Locust*, which reaches its climax at Kahn's Persian Palace Theatre.[2]

Citizen Kane quietly codified the trend. Like the Khan's palace in Coleridge's poem, the mansion of Charles Foster Kane was called Xanadu, "the world's largest private pleasure ground." As it happened, Otto Kahn's chateau on Long Island was the second largest private residence in America, and the opening sequence of *Kane* even included shots of it among the stock footage. Those two points weigh in favor of an argument made by one of the film's most careful students, that Kane's castle was more an amalgam of the ideal American millionaire's palace than strictly a copy of William Randolph Hearst's estate.[3] Yet a closer look at the script itself subtly indicates that Otto Kahn was yet another influence, quieter than Hearst, in associating the American millionaire with the legends of Xanadu.

Although Otto Kahn died in 1934, he was hardly forgotten by moviemakers. In 1919 he was a key influence in bringing Wall Street to finance Hollywood, and members of his banking house were board members at Paramount Pictures for many years after. When *Kane*'s screenwriter, Herman Mankiewicz, sat down to write the script, some specific memories of Otto Kahn came to life, too. In the 1920s, the early days of his career, "Mank" was an aspiring journalist and dramatist, and part of the celebrated Algonquin Hotel circle in New York. He picked up publicity work promoting dancer Isadora Duncan and Austrian theatrical producer Max Reinhardt, both of whom received Kahn's patronage. He also ventured a try at producing *Round the Town*, a revue that drew upon illustrious collaborators, but it failed, leaving Mankiewicz in debt. Otto Kahn helped him over the hump with a $2,500 loan. Afterward Mankiewicz headed west. His connection to

Otto Kahn on transatlantic crossing, 1920s. (Private collection)

Kahn likely eased his introduction at Paramount, where Mankiewicz swiftly became the highest-paid writer in the movies, reportedly making more than $40,000 his first year. Not long after, he encountered Kahn again, only to learn that the loan was not a gift: Kahn expected repayment if an artist later enjoyed commercial success. Mankiewicz, who was also a notorious gambler and always strapped for cash, could not convince his patron of sufficient ongoing hardship without revealing its real cause. The writer repaid the debt fully in installments.[4]

Thus Mankiewicz's personal perspective on great monied wealth came from many experiences, not only his personal relationship with Hearst. In all probability, in early 1940, when he was looking around for ideas while writing *Kane*, his memory of Kahn led him to lift a passage from Matthew Josephson's popular book *The Robber Barons* (1934), which told how Kahn's country estate was built on an artificial bluff to give it a view of Long Island Sound.[5] A trace of these remarks was written into the newsreel sequence of *Citizen Kane*, in which Xanadu is first described: "Here on the deserts of the gulf coast a private mountain was commissioned and privately built." While earlier versions of the script resembled Josephson's words even more closely, it would seem that his *Robber Barons* sat alongside Ferdinand Lundberg's *Imperial Hearst* on the screenwriter's bookshelf. Lundberg eventually sued Mankiewicz for plagiarism, but Josephson did not notice or did not care.[6]

The textual cross-references deserve exposition, not only because Hearst's castle, San Simeon, sits on a natural hill, but more deeply because any reader or writer of biography appreciates *Citizen Kane*. Obsessed with obituary and the human condition, the film's inconclusive grappling with different points of view makes a broadly relevant parable. More to the point, *Kane* belongs to a specific tradition of reportage, established and advanced in both the founding era of celebrity and the consolidating era of capitalism. It battles authority and authenticity, mixing facts with fictions that make saints and devils — or just sorry souls — out of the masters of industrial time. Surely, Otto Kahn belongs to the same tradition, but his place in *Citizen Kane* — so rapid, encoded, and easily overlooked — has other meanings. Much in the way historical memory is preserved, one must be told to find him there, and recognize how twists in consciousness, reality, and truth are lineaments of modernity.

Establishing the place of cinema among the arts is critical to this process. Thinking cinematically lends a different beginning and structure to biography. In the cinema no less than in the writing of biography or history, time, space, and logic do not, in Kristin Thompson's phrase, "fit together unproblematically." And as a method for reshaping narratives and themes, the cinematic metaphor goes beyond the heuristics of painted portraiture, allowing biography to maneuver and cross-cut between evidence, episodes, and perceptions so that Otto Kahn, international finance, and the modern arts in which he was involved all become one field of vision. Such thoughts put forth a dif-

Introduction

ferent means for the biographical genre to present, explain, and develop not only one life, but also the shifting silhouettes of modernity.[7]

Locating Otto Kahn is chancing upon a leitmotif. That aspect of the Kahn mystique was spoofed in a *New Yorker* piece by Rube Goldberg, which imagined how a tourist in the 1920s might cope with the dizzying possibility of seeing America's most celebrated banker-patron at every turn in a day about town. Kahn greets an opera singer at the Customs House, then shows up at the Ritz, and later sits among the first-nighters for the opening of a new revue. Everyone seems to be talking to or about Otto Kahn — his stockholdings, his travels, his art collection, his speeches, his theatrical underwriting. When Kahn is finally spotted at a late-night club, playing the kettledrum in a jazz band, the visitor can take no more. He is carted off to the mental ward at Bellevue Hospital: a conclusion that should worry any potential biographer of Kahn.[8]

Goldberg's fantasy found company in a few tuneful parodies concerning other aspects of the Kahn mystique. In Cole Porter's "Opera Star," a lampoon of soprano Maria Jeritza from 1925, the "opera vamp" betrays that the secrets of her success are passion and sex appeal, the kind she brings to the stage and to "the roles that I portray for Otto Kahn-o."[9] In 1927, Fanny Brice played a similar character, albeit one much lower on the ladder of success, who pokes fun at the exchange of sexual favors expected on the rise to stardom and asks:

> Is something the matter with Otto Kahn
> Or is something the matter with me?
> I wrote a note and told him what a star I would make.
> He sent it back and marked it "Opened by mistake."
> I'd even get fatter for Otto Kahn,
> As all prima donnas must be.
> I studied with Scotti, if you know what I mean.
> He said I had the finest diaphragm he had seen!
> And if my high C don't hand Otto a thrill,
> I think my tra-la-la will.

Whether worried about libel or other repercussions — perhaps from the possible allusion of "diaphragm" to birth control — the Victor Talking Machine Company expressed reservations about recording the song, prompting Brice to call Kahn to verify that it would not offend him. It did not.[10]

No such clearance was necessary for the Marx Brothers, who satirized Kahn in their 1928 musical *Animal Crackers* (two years before their movie of the same name). Set at the gala party of a wealthy Long Island doyenne, *Animal Crackers* parodies Kahn in the character of Roscoe W. Chandler, a millionaire art collector and legendary patron who is one of two honored guests (or attractions). The other is Captain Spaulding, the African explorer, played by Groucho Marx, who corners the wealthy Chandler and asks, "How would you like to finance a scientific expedition?" The request startles Chandler, for Spaulding wants him to pay for the "one thing that I've always wanted to do before I quit" — "Retire." Indeed, the spoof was not only of Kahn and the bewildering variety of petitions for his support, but also of the petitioning talent, whose ultimate desire was sufficient money to develop a genius or project with complete liberty. Before the scene ends with Groucho's classic line, "You go Uruguay and I'll go mine," the dialogue keeps spinning hilariously around other attributes of Kahn that were obvious to anyone with a bead of contemporary New York wit. Kahn's plans to build a new opera house, his opinions of art and money, and the schedules of busy men all get minced in rapid-fire lunacy.[11]

If some stories or sightings stand out better than others, the best are those neither easily found nor simply accounted. While researching the life of the renowned urban planner Robert Moses, for instance, Robert Caro discovered that Kahn was the lone "baron" to whom Moses deferred when constructing the Northern State Parkway. Although Moses built his reputation for being above corruption and proudly laid plans for building the parkway through the property of other millionaires, he backed off when the original route threatened to plow directly through the most prized amenity of Kahn's country estate: his golf course. Any hint of corruption stayed quiet for more than fifty years until Caro found some telling documents that unambiguously confirmed how Kahn had placed financial contributions into the coffers of Moses' Parkway Commission. That discovery ended Moses' cooperation with the biographer. It also sealed a portrait of Kahn. The modern aristocrat could, with the stroke of a millionaire's wand, successfully resist the enclosure of his property by the state. Otto Kahn had the power to make mountains, to move public works, to undermine the public good.[12]

All the same, he also created a legacy of pleasure. There was a peculiarly democratizing effect in Kahn's management of wealth and celebrity. For all the elitism, Otto Kahn's world was a playground for High

Kahn's Long Island estate, aerial view. (Long Island Studies Institute)

Bohemia—a place for kings and commoners—where lavish weekend romps might begin with guests being transported from Manhattan to Long Island on the banker's private yacht. Once commenced, some of the parties went all night. The 126-room chateau gave guests plenty of space to slip off, in private, so that dramatist Charles McArthur could pursue "boobish love antics" with Helen Hayes before "the open fire at Otto Kahn's," or so that publisher Horace Liveright might find himself propped against "a Kahn castle buttress" one morning, confessing his sexual impotence to writer Ben Hecht.[13] A few weekends were too irrepressibly raucous for the moral standards of Mrs. Otto Kahn, who stayed away from the bacchanalia whenever Alexander Woolcott's crowd gathered and was simply horrified by the antics of Harpo Marx. She thought that entire side of Kahn's life to be undignified, and she had a completely different conception of what an important banker should do and how he should behave.[14] As often as not, however, Kahn's entertainments stood firmly on formalities.

When Soviet filmmaker Sergei Eisenstein visited in 1930, for instance, he shot and then lost some photographs of Kahn's country place, but the meals made more lasting impressions. Years later there were still vivid memories of servants all about the table — their "hands appear from beyond the range of vision and simply paralyze your digestion." What he remembered best, though, was the artichoke, "the memorable, rhythmic sensation of confusion with the artichoke at Otto H.'s table!" Having been called away to the telephone while others ate their serving, Eisenstein returned to his seat of honor beside Kahn where he faced his first artichoke, not knowing how it should be eaten. In silent soliloquy, he wondered, "How, then, do millionaires eat artichokes? Only the soft, fleshy tender base? Or do they, like other mortals, have to suck out the fleshy bottoms of the separately torn-off leaves." He panicked "at the thought that I shall have to execute this operation . . . before the whole gathering . . . watching with folded arms to see how the Russian barbarian will get out of this tricky situation." A scene of impending death from *Ivan the Terrible* came to mind.[15]

The writer Klaus Mann penned another view. For him, Kahn's city palace on upper Fifth Avenue took its place among the pulse and roar and vistas of Manhattan, as part of the modern and American experience peculiar to New York: "There was something exciting and frightful about spending the afternoon with a bunch of penniless tramps — and then to rush home, to the Astor [Hotel], and change clothes for an opulent dinner party, say, at the palace of Otto H. Kahn." To Mann, another German, Kahn was more clearly an idiom of the grand bourgeoisie and the awkwardness of great wealth: "We were considerably impressed, not so much by his patronizing chat as the stunning display of Rembrandts and Mantegnas in his princely mansion. The millionaire, pleased by our awe, was all polite serenity and condescending blandness. . . . We never really felt at ease in his company. He had just too much money: the thought of it was faintly irritating. There are people who cannot help making insipid cracks about physical deformities in the presence of hunchbacks and midgets. Thus we were constantly tempted to discuss at the table of Otto H., the disquieting, indeed, untenable phenomenon of enormous wealth."[16]

One need not challenge Mann's impression, or apologize for Kahn, yet it would be fair to note that the art collection, like the day-to-day supervision of architects, designers, and house staff, was primarily the work of his wife, Addie. Even though the public always associated the collection with Kahn as head of household, and he did purchase much of it himself, the banker-patron was less intensely involved with the paintings and sculpture that decorated his houses than he was interested in the collaborative theatrical arts, of which painting and sculpture were part. However, the art in his palaces did stimulate conversation if not always wonderment. As Eisenstein gazed upon one painting, Kahn asked, "Do you recognize the brush?" Eisenstein could not. Kahn responded, "Only a Jew could paint a face so subtly!"—adding it was Rembrandt. The filmmaker, thinking, "Rembrandt is not a god in my pantheon," chose to "make a show, as if I were looking at El Greco," whose work he personally preferred. It made sense to flatter the patron. Eisenstein was en route to Hollywood, and a passport stamped with Kahn's approval would not hurt his career.[17]

One happens upon Kahn in so many places that the tracking itself can be as indulgent and intriguing as it is fun. His activities around town with literary communist Mike Gold, for example, would seem to reprise scenes of Heinrich Heine jaunting "famillionairely" with James Rothschild in the previous century. At other moments Kahn's life seemed to look ahead, with a view to traits more obviously characteristic of the twentieth century. Given how a subsidy for Jane Heap, co-editor of the *Little Review*, for instance, arrived exactly at the moment when Matthew Josephson published in its pages, the full extent of Kahn's patronage should hint at a multiplier effect, or networks and interdependencies, that both socialize and individualize Kahn's importance.[18]

A subject so widely found can be frustrating as well. If Klaus Mann thought Kahn had too much money and not enough essence, those keen on Kahn's biography might arrive at a similar conclusion when assessing the scope and amount of source material for him. Kahn appears with stunning frequency in a wide range of monographic literature, memoirs, and governmental hearings. Numerous biographical dictionaries and encyclopedias include him, and his death in 1934 was recorded in all the major newspapers and glossy magazines of the day. Two breezy biographies have since presented his fabled life for popular audiences: Mary Jane Matz's *The Many Lives of Otto Kahn* (1963) and John Kobler's *Otto the Magnificent* (1988). He was a major figure in *Our Crowd* (1967), Stephen Birmingham's study of New York's German Jewish elite, and any good history of Wall Street in the early twentieth century includes Otto Kahn as a partner of Kuhn, Loeb & Co., the investment house "second only to Morgan among private bankers, and second to none in railway banking" during the heyday of both.[19]

Inevitably, a search brings one to the enormous collection of his personal papers at Princeton University, a collection of some 250,000 items that is as much a magnet as it is an obstacle in locating Otto Kahn. Long ago, letters that would corroborate rumors of Kahn's extramarital transgressions were removed and destroyed, apparently upon the orders of the family during the early 1960s, as the collection was prepared for Matz's biography. The archives of his banking house are also missing. The extant documentation, meanwhile, is unevenly distributed chronologically. Most of the Kahn collection represents his later years, and almost nothing is left from before the Great War. An imaginative mind might associate this lacuna with the trajectory of modernity itself—marking 1914 as an apocalypse—and be content with the symbolism, except that such associative thinking also allows the unevenness of evidence to suggest something other than merely holes in the documentation. If Kahn's life is informed by, reflective of, and influential in the course of modernity, as I argue, the erasures as well as the evidence are indicative of how life is negotiated.

There is great gossip, for example, about the ladies in his life, which his own daughter freely admitted years after her father's death. But the absence of a locked letter book that once contained evidence of his affairs prevents us from prying or from seeing too clearly that the patron's sofa furnished a corner of the cultural marketplace. Such openly secret sexual affairs would be forever haunted by gossip. Only rarely does a witness speak bluntly of it, as actress Louise Brooks did, in describing party nights at Kahn's suite in the Ritz Hotel, where showgirls sparkling with ambition came for drinks and dalliances with very rich men, hoping it would lead to a movie contract. Just the same, hardly anyone touring Kahn's mansion in Manhattan—now a prestigious convent and school—goes away without hearing tales of how a semi-private staircase was his path in escorting young starlets to his bedroom for private entertainment. An air of suspicion ultimately suffuses Kahn's every encounter with attractive women. Any moment Kahn was alone with one is alive with interpretative possibilities, if not solid evidence, although that does not diminish our passions for looking.[20]

As great an interest is served by questions. Asking what, for example, results from Kahn's negotiations between private and public, one sees nothing indecent, immoral, or untidy about himself available to the public eye. He behaved mostly like the character in a novel by Maurice

Barrès who says, "You have to show people a smooth surface, give them only an appearance of yourself, be absent."[21] As we shall see, it was more comfortable for Kahn to let the art of his patronage disclose facets of modern eroticism. Concealment characterized his conduct in business as well, yet in both Kahn suggested a modicum of openness, which by comparison with other *haute financiers* seemed fresh and new.

This biography turns Kahn's catalog into a contemplative exercise. Moving the subject beyond random recognitions, but holding on to the thought that his ubiquity is also a clue to his interest and importance, there is a chance to introduce a large historical context. The scenes and settings in which this character acts connect a set of rarely combined themes in the generation from the *belle epoque* to the Great Depression. They may suggest a partial synthesis for an era too often divided by the Great War, not simply because that watershed was not the end of Kahn's life, but more broadly because Kahn's life intersects with numerous traditions that linger within modern transitions, and confound some "past-be-damned" assumptions of modernism.[22] His life mirrored and engaged the main transformations in world capitalism and the social architecture of western bourgeois culture. Within that matrix, one finds the nurturing of a specifically transatlantic cosmopolitanism that can be identified with the artistic impulses of Otto Kahn's patronage and the mystery of money for Otto Kahn's generation. If not clearly refracting the dominance of his class, or the many modernisms, or what Catherine R. Stimpson calls "the already messily large number of meanings attached to the word 'culture' itself," Otto Kahn nonetheless challenges us to treat such themes as culture, modernism, and class in a way that suggests coherence amidst contradictions.[23]

Retooling narrative biography to the task, this study takes the problem of totality and its parts as a central issue of a life in modern time. Kahn sought some coherence within art, money, and geopolitics, the forces that dominated his actions. Once his artistic interests are set alongside high finance, both indeed appear to be combinations and collaborations. His life also highlights the subject of intermediaries, a function of bankers and patrons alike, and more broadly it builds on the idea that actors in networks are important characters, as well as characteristics of modernity. If here such ideas ring more loudly than the usual cheers for Kahn's greatness, it is, I think, the only way to appreciate Otto Kahn, not as a catalog of actions, but rather a distinctly transatlantic life of cosmopolitanism, which foreshadows the history of globalization.

The resulting style is not nearly as neo-avant-garde as the desired effect for biography might suggest. True enough, at times readers may need to work through prose that is more impressionistic than sharp. But while I have repressed many urges to break some of the formalistic conventions in academic writing as well as formulaic biography, I remain steeped in the documentary tradition. There is also a conventional structure. A beginning, a middle, and an end correspond with Kahn's youth, adulthood, and seniority. Since the documents before 1914 are thin, but the life in those years is neither irrelevant nor erased in later stages, my approach to time is fluid even within a chronological arrangement. At several points the narrative unites montage with memory, or it combines sequence and simultaneity with flashback and juxtaposition. There are regular pauses to elaborate how the characters act within circles and webs, for Kahn is the prime subject—but not in isolation, lest we miss the intricacies or importance of his supporting role.

Mapping out this presence cannot be flat. It needs an eye for abstractions and symbols. Yet it must also account for concrete layers of circumstance and the signifying relevance of fact. Short of being the determining variables in either history or Otto Kahn's life, the structural shifts and economic circumstances of his time shaped both the mental and material world of modernity. So on the one hand, large trends find more personal expression than pure economic data or critical theory can express, while on the other, modernist sensibilities complicate the mission. Like liberalism or Jewishness or culture, the modern drifts through Kahn's world, without neat categories, seeming to be whatever one thinks it to be, for ideas of modern life, modernism, and modernization pose a constantly re-imaged reality. There is always more than one answer, another comment, the chance of no set pattern in the unifying and splintering. The modern strikes an arabesque of contradictions. If one direction refers to newness, unrest, and liberation, the other reaches toward imitation, persistence, and repression.

That said, a basic if not simple challenge is to move beyond dichotomies. One customary thought about Kahn has made him out to be the master of different personalities operating in separate worlds. As early as 1911, the *New York Times* described the contrasts in a "Man of

Steel and Velvet." Another New York daily was soon writing of "two Otto Kahns" — the Wall Street character, "cold, calm, courteous and impenetrable," and the "uptown" Otto Kahn, "supple, accommodating and urbane." *Time* later perpetuated the idea: "By day he was Otto Kahn the banker — shrewd, suave, sometimes ruthless. . . . After dark he was Otto Kahn, patron of arts, bon vivant, first nighter at opera and theatre." I take another view. When the financier and angel seemed to be incongruous identities, Otto Kahn was operating in multiple roles, and though his capacity to do so left many confused as to which was dominant, a good case can be made for their interaction.[24]

He rigidly separated neither daytime and nocturnal activities nor downtown and uptown interests in business and art. He could be shrewd in artistic matters, accommodating in business. Much of his patronage was also administered from his office in New York's downtown financial district, where he convened board meetings of the Metropolitan Opera Company and conducted a voluminous correspondence with creative talents. The seemingly anomalous decorum led Theatre Guild co-founder Lawrence Langner to remark that Kahn "habitually enlivened . . . [the] dull routine of making millions by interviewing at his office Metropolitan Opera divas, ballet dancers, painters and other glamorous souls who dispelled the gloom of Wall Street like rays of fitful sunlight." Even *Time* would marvel at how a text concerning monetary theory sat on his desk "side by side with a cello concerto."[25] Kahn was not alone in such practices during his time; he was only the best known. If few understood the interdependence between the banker and the patron, to some extent it appears that Kahn himself did. Otto Kahn was doing exactly what he thought a perfectly modern millionaire should do.

Positioning Otto Kahn among real and fictionalized millionaires amplifies our perspective. Understanding the modern millionaire is to understand fascinations with power, and several compasses are available for the task. While there is still no incontestable standard that will apply, there does seem to be a need to establish a type, and one rule of F. Scott Fitzgerald is pertinent: "Some instincts prepare us for unreality," for "even intelligent and impassioned reporters of life," says Fitzgerald, "have made the country of the rich as unreal as fairyland."[26] The estates of Otto Kahn in *Citizen Kane* remind us further of this warning. Almost by conditioning, one reaches for referential categories, looking to comparable lives — grouping, sorting, separating, and comparing. It is a widely exercised practice of study, and in *Kane*, when the newsreel editors are directed to show how Kane "was different from Ford? Or Hearst . . . or Rockefeller — or John Doe," it continues a tradition of public life coming to grips not only with the individual fortunes of capitalism, but also with clusters of cohorts who form and clash as socioeconomic elites, set trends in style and taste, and stand apart from John Doe or everyman. The *Christian Science Monitor* once did much the same, setting Kahn "in the front rank of that company that represented to the man in the street the capitalistic system." The so-called "man in the street" was intended to represent "everyman" on "Main Street," but it could also be the average denizen of Wall Street, as both "Main Street" and "Wall Street" were the perennial juxtapositions of community in advancing American capitalism.[27]

A better personification of Wall Street in this modern time was J. P. Morgan, a name that figures distinctly in Kahn's story. Although Kahn was thirty years younger than the elder Pierpont Morgan, he was born in the same year as the younger J. P. ("Jack") Morgan, with whom he shared numerous characteristics as a model of what Frederick Lewis Allen called "the Wall Street standard in dress and in deportment." They were always finely attired, sporting impeccably trimmed mustaches, and, as each owned city mansions and country estates (Kahn's spread on Long Island employed thirty-five live-in servants), they also practiced a few uniform activities in leisure, including a passion for golf. But all together, their expressed monied status reflected shared beliefs regarding the proper administration of wealth — what Europeans projected as bourgeois respectability, and what Americans determined was befitting wealth. Even so, while Otto Kahn was sometimes measured up to be "a small edition of J. P. Morgan," no two men could be more dissimilar. Morgan carried a tall, bulky body and looked and acted awkward in public. Kahn, shorter and slimmer, moved lithely in nearly every visible situation. He consequently enjoyed numerous social advantages that Morgan lacked, or did not value. Reasonably as important, though, were those similarities that betrayed differences. These worked against Kahn in geopolitics, where Otto Kahn and Jack Morgan were noted Anglophiles, yet Morgan's loyalty to British causes was never doubted as the German-born Kahn's would be. And there was no escape from the most basic difference between Jack Morgan and Otto Kahn: Morgan represented the apogee of the Yankee private international bank, his family having long ago set their roots in American soil; Kahn was foreign-born, a naturalized American, and part of the last cohesive generation in the German Jewish financial elite. Both men were scions of a new generation in their family-based, private international bank, but Otto Kahn was more the newcomer, as well as an outsider.[28]

Another shared, conflicted heritage was no simple matter. Both financiers attracted intense public scrutiny by champions and critics alike. Episodes in their business careers became allegories of economic power, woven into the general society as moral lessons through politics, journalism, and the arts. Their lives were interpreted alternatively as blessed or satanic, just or unfair, creative or destructive. Still, if public culture could imagine Wall Street as the source of economic evil and think negatively of the big businesses, that perception could also change — or be changed — and did change, as middle-class animosity toward giant firms and their Wall Street agents gradually moved toward accommodation during Kahn's career. Regulatory legislation, the corporate revolution, and a buffer of public relations counsel significantly helped to remove individuals from the direct line of public fire, yet with Otto Kahn the individual Wall Streeter was himself an agent of reshaping hostility into acceptance. Of course there were other progressive-minded business men of his generation, including several of his fellow partners in the banking house of Kuhn, Loeb. The exceptional quality of Kahn lay in the fact that it would be hard to find another financier who was so clearly influenced by theatricality as Otto Kahn when, with the tone of a stage critic, he denounced anti-business investigations as a pattern of cheap entertainments: "The appeal all too often is to the gallery, hungry for sensation" — or when, with the instincts of a drama coach, he identified effective techniques that financiers could muster to seem less defensive, reactive, or inflammatory. It effectively brought Otto Kahn to *juste-milieux* (points between two extremes).[29]

In short, Kahn perceived better ways to play his scenes. He pursued his role with thorough flair, forming cooperative solutions that not only mirrored the collaborative forms of opera and theater, his favored art forms, but also echoed the "community of interest" principles that were working to suppress the extremes of industrial and financial competition. It cannot be forgotten that Kuhn, Loeb's main business, the railroads, were about as quick as operas and theaters in discovering how useful good publicity could be. That would be notable if it only rubbed off on Otto Kahn. It is significant because, when it came to public relations, Kahn not only valued the advice of good counsel, he gave it too, and was himself a model of how one could go about modernizing and managing public impressions.

Other insights into this modern life are derived from geographical modeling. For example, like many of his time, Otto Kahn moved from smaller to larger cities as he expanded his own importance in the world. From the regionally important, medium-sized cities of his birth (Mannheim) and his first practical training (Karlsruhe), he went to Berlin, the financial and cultural capital of Germany and a major world city. In 1888 he arrived in London, the truly dominant world metropolis, the indisputable hub of international finance, and, if less commanding in cultural prestige than Paris, a cultural capital nonetheless. He became a British subject in 1893, but soon relocated to New York, an emerging world city.[30]

After joining Kuhn, Loeb, his spatial activities became faster and wider. He usually spent one-third of every year in Europe, but he also toured the American railroad systems that Kuhn, Loeb served. These trips gave Kahn a vast sense of the American continent, and the press coverage en route afforded him the chance to create a positive image of the Wall Street financier in the West. In addition, whether touring the nation himself or sponsoring the national tours of important theatrical events, Kahn's name was as much associated with aesthetic culture as it was with economic culture. In the meantime, his trips between New York and Washington, to meet a president or testify before Congress, underscored the dynamics between competing economic and political centers. Finally, following the movement of money itself, Kahn's financial interests and influence would spin from the hub of American and European capitals throughout the world, elaborating global interdependence in the last third of the nineteenth century and the first third of the twentieth century.

With all these movements Otto Kahn was representing the tempo, pace, and ranges of possibilities in modern space, time, and its most universal medium, money. But neither his comings and goings nor networks alone wholly suggests the images of the modernity that he created. To suggest the fuller range, we can locate Otto Kahn with a sense of place as well as space, and to this end the houses with which he was associated speak as symbols of his culture.

Probably his residences are the most obvious. His earliest country home was called Cedar Court, a set of twin mansions on 260 acres in the Normandie Heights section of Morristown, New Jersey, which actually belonged to Abraham Wolff, Kahn's father-in-law. It was here that the four children of Otto and Addie Kahn spent their early years, and, when elder daughter Maude made her debut in society, Enrico Caruso and Anna Pavlova performed. Cedar Court also stood in a community where the Kahns were concurrently assimilated and excluded, as Otto Kahn, a Jew, was barred from local social clubs, including the golf club adjacent to the property. Nor was he particularly welcome on the Millionaire Express, the special train that carried men of wealth between New York and Morristown.[31] Another dwelling, the Greco-Italian villa called St. Dunstan's in London's Regent's Park, was acquired in early 1912 amid rumors that Kahn meant to stand for Parliament. Instead of becoming the family's residence, St. Dunstan's became a domain of Kahn's philanthropic distinction when he loaned the villa to Sir Arthur Pearson's pioneering rehabilitation program for blinded soldiers and sailors during the Great War.[32]

Both St. Dunstan's and Cedar Court were razed by subsequent owners, but Kahn's two mansions in New York are still standing, although his family relinquished control of them not long after Kahn's death in 1934. As the Long Island estate passed through several owners, the acreage was subdivided into middle-class residences and a private golf club, while the mansion, its glamour and original opulence long gone, deteriorated seriously before becoming a site of locally regulated, privately financed preservation. During the real estate boom of the 1980s, developers failed in an attempt to restore the mansion and convert it into condominiums. In 1989 an anonymous Japanese buyer took title to the property, then let it back to the previous owner for alternative schemes of development under the name Oheka, an acronym for Otto Hermann Kahn. In this incarnation it takes bookings for weddings, fund-raisers, location photography, and the like, and, at the close of the twentieth century, there were plans to install a private health club — all meant to help fund the ongoing efforts of architectural restoration.[33]

Kahn's other famed residence in New York, built in Florentine Renaissance style between 1914 and 1918 at 1100 Fifth Avenue in Manhattan, directly across from the Carnegie mansion at Ninety-first Street, has been well maintained since its purchase by the Convent of the Sacred Heart in 1934. It has long since served as a school, gaining landmark status from the City of New York in 1970. Like the Long

Island house, 1100 Fifth Avenue is also available for weddings and special events, a trademark of the postmodern condition that should be considered alongside another: the fate of Kahn's house of business.[34]

Kuhn, Loeb & Co,, the once-venerable private banking partnership, passed into extinction during the 1980s. Having merged with Lehman Brothers in 1977, Kuhn, Loeb's identity was virtually lost in subsequent implosions and restructuring — to endure only in the annals of finance as an eminent investment house of the dynastic era. Founded in 1867, its indirect antecedents dated back to the general merchants' counting-house of the fifteenth century, when credit, foreign exchange, and banking were but a few of a merchant's many activities. Such business then shared the same address as the family, though separated from family living quarters. In the nineteenth century, with merchant banks gradually specializing from commercial to financial capitalism, and transforming networks of commercial credit and foreign exchanges into the world's preeminent facilities for long-term investment and lending, the house of business separated from the house of residence. By the time of Kuhn, Loeb's founding (and Otto Kahn's birth), banking houses had relocated to central business districts of towns and cities, but the firms were still family houses. The business identity stayed linked with the lineage of a larger kin group, even as the bourgeois family or smaller kin group came to dominate home life. By the 1890s the leading houses of London, Paris, and New York, complete with their ties to financial communities in Frankfurt, Amsterdam, and elsewhere, were the principal intermediaries for railroad, government, and, increasingly, industrial financing. As sons and sons-in-laws replenished the places of elder, retiring, or expired partners, the few leading houses resembled dynasties.

Otto Kahn was among the handful of young bankers who, between 1897 and 1902, became the third generation of Kuhn, Loeb partners. Along with Kahn, these included Mortimer L. Schiff, Felix M. Warburg, and Paul M. Warburg — the core of a generation intended to succeed Jacob H. Schiff, the senior partner under whose leadership the firm rose to rival J. P. Morgan & Co. as the leading investment bank in America. The new partners shared common traditions that linked them to the family-based, international investment bank by birth or marriage. Otto Kahn's father-in-law was a Kuhn, Loeb partner; Jacob Schiff and Paul Warburg were married to daughters of Solomon Loeb, a founder of the firm; Felix Warburg was married to a daughter of Jacob Schiff;

and Mortimer Schiff was the only son of Jacob Schiff. In addition, the Warburgs were brothers, and scions of M. M. Warburg & Co. in Hamburg, Germany.[35] Though by 1911 the firm had admitted one partner not related to other partners by blood or marriage, as late as 1933 Otto Kahn would say of Kuhn, Loeb & Co., "We are a family affair."[36]

Oddly enough, the basic business of Kuhn, Loeb was to finance soundly its organizational antithesis, the giant corporation, while the successful conduct of its partnership also included the preservation of an ancestral system. Though unlikely to have perceived this transformation, the house of finance that Otto Kahn knew and represented eventually became the kind of modern bureaucratic structure that Kuhn, Loeb had helped to pioneer for railroads and industrials. The transforming role of giant corporations as vehicles in a modernizing American economy, then, would ultimately sweep not only Kuhn, Loeb off the map of investment banking. With rare exception, all traditional financial houses would disappear. Successor firms might preserve a piece of the founding family name, common language may still refer to the banks as houses, and some of the investment functions repeat themselves, but contemporary investment banking structures, on the whole, are as different from the ancestral partnerships of Kahn's era as the industrial corporation was from the entrepreneurial firms of the early nineteenth century.

It is appropriate to discuss the social significance of investment banking as family enterprise, but choosing to highlight its history as a house affords an opportunity to establish and illuminate a long view of modernity. By acknowledging its antecedents in mercantile capitalism, one can position the merchant or private banking house on a continuum of transitions that runs from the mid-fifteenth century to the third quarter of the twentieth century, or, from the period that historians of Europe commonly call early modern to the currently fashionable conception of a post-modern era. If Otto Kahn's life and the period from 1867 to 1934 can be imagined as a prism of modernity's transitions, then the refractions bending with the house of Kuhn, Loeb may reveal some distinctive hues. Otto Kahn, his partners at Kuhn, Loeb, and their peers at other investment houses were agents of a capitalist system in transition — spatially, economically, politically, and socially. Historians see in this period a shift from a proprietary to corporate hegemony and, to the ultimate degree of human possibility, Kahn, his partners, and his peers were stewards of that transition. Bringing order from the reign of cutthroat competition, they were moderns in a sense not unlike that of architectural modernism, which tempered urban disorder. These financial capitalists among a few select others, such as the house of Morgan, "found a way to control and contain an explosive capitalist condition."[37]

A different set of contests and surprises were evident in Kahn's largesse. Otto Kahn would put palatial "cinemansions" and intimate art houses on the same cultural landscape: he helped to create the real estate empire of Paramount Pictures, while simultaneously supporting the venue that became the Little Carnegie Cinema. In like manner, he embraced both the Metropolitan Opera and the Provincetown Playhouse. One was a great temple, the other a tiny laboratory of performance; but if the Provincetown, in its cramped little quarters downtown, seemed the bohemian modernist, hellbent on striking a perfect contrast to, or revolt against, the grandeur, elitism, and tradition that epitomized the Metropolitan Opera, the differences between such enterprises should not overshadow their analogies. Highlight the likenesses among the egos and ambitions of theatrical talent, no matter the venue, or count the set designers the two institutions shared, then find *The Emperor Jones* on the boards of both, and it becomes clear that Otto Kahn was not alone in migrating between them. Look more closely and note that the two institutions were alike in ways that mirror some of the strongest themes in Kahn's life: each was being pulled by concurrent tensions concerning the international nature of art, the demand for national credibility, and the lofty standards attached to making New York a global capital for both culture and finance.

Nonetheless, one problem makes opera stand out among the modern arts. An art form of European origin — born of the Renaissance and nurtured by royal patrons — opera attracted both elite and popular audiences well into the twentieth century, but, despite ongoing popularity within its venues of live, recorded, and broadcast performance, opera became the definitive reference for middle- and upper-class elitism. With its broad public appeal eventually fading, numerous critics read the transformation as an outcropping of aristocratic ambitions among the bourgeoisie, whose modernity would seem controlled by the meshing of royal traditionalism and urban embourgeoisement, wherever symbols of the nineteenth century wealth survived in the twentieth. The majestic palaces of bourgeois barons, the dynastic traditions of banking houses, and grand opera, then, are one of a kind, and opera fell captive to newly wealthy patrons, needing validity for their status in social rank, who blindly copied the traditions of the aristocracy before them.[38]

Kahn's hand in this history suggests more nuances and variances. As millionaires of new social status, the *haute bourgeoisie* did emulate the aristocracy of Western European ancestry, with whom they also mixed and sometimes intermarried. Indeed, individual men of wealth but of common — even Jewish — ancestry could be elevated to the ranks of European nobility, and Otto Kahn would put his own hopes on that track for a while. All the same, recent scholarship points to greater diversity than previously appreciated in the ambitions, tastes, and displays of new wealth, for Germans differed from French and English or Italians, and all sorts of issues put businessmen of one industry at odds with their counterparts in another industry. Whether the question is economic protectionism, or definitions of liberalism, or desires for social integration, no generalization comes without caution. It might be easier if the *haute bourgeoisie* had been a narrower cohort, limited to captains of industry or international financiers — excluding heirs of wealth, professionals, and civil servants, or forgetting the women, who were important philanthropists, *salonists*, and reformers. However, while financiers as a group alone could individually add up to a diverse lot, they did most clearly emulate the aristocracy of Western Europe in varied forms and manners. At the same time, they also invented new traditions, revising the criteria of elitism in the more modern, cosmopolitan world environment. José Harris and Pat Thane have offered a compelling view of the paradox, jointly concluding that international financiers showed elements of aristocratic and bourgeois cultures that were "reducible to neither." The outcome was a pastiche of old and new, perhaps the most modern of all types, because one trait cohered *haute financiers* as a generalized breed: their most active participation in "a new kind of supranational socio-economic structure . . . that by the early twentieth century threatened to transcend and make obsolete the nineteenth-century boundaries of the nation and the state."[39]

The ambiguities of the bourgeoisie lead elsewhere. Only a few years before Dorothy Fields's enduring lyric, "If I never had a cent I'd be rich as Rockefeller," it was as popular in some circles to measure one's personal worth against that of Otto Kahn. "I am not Otto Kahn," complained Eugene O'Neill, when "seriously peeved" over delays in getting his due royalties from *The Emperor Jones*. In an earlier instance, it dis-

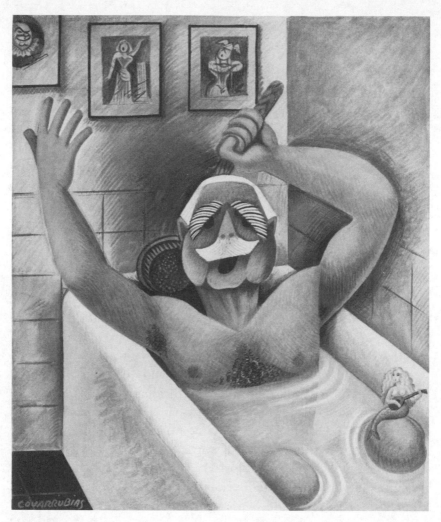

"Mr. Otto Kahn, the opera impresario and banker extraordinaire, tries out that famous bath-tub aria, 'You're an Old Smoothie.'" Caricature by Miguel Covarrubias, Vanity Fair, *October 1933. (Conde Nast Publications)*

pleased O'Neill to hear the patron had offered a small loan; "Either he's there for the big help or he isn't," the playwright grumbled.[40] Kahn's largesse regularly fell short of the many requests put upon him, or did not match the expectations and estimations of his riches. Luigi Pirandello was swept up by the buzz, in a good example, when Otto Kahn showed interest in bringing him to America and getting Paramount to buy his plays. Thinking Kahn was "one of the wealthiest

Introduction

persons in the world; they say he is the sixth richest," Pirandello figured, "if Otto Kahn . . . wants it . . . the deal should go through."[41] As it turned out, he was one of many who eventually realized that Otto Kahn alone would not make all his dreams come true. In the result, Otto Kahn would not only be famous as the greatest patron of art, but also at once synonymous with shortcomings of great wealth and insufficient largesse.

In addition, this patron, celebrated for backing arts that would lose money, clearly did not wish to back anything less than the best or most promising in art. His concern — or conceit — seemed less about losing money than losing prestige as a connoisseur. But other limits were also clear. Among them, Otto Kahn would never surrender all his wealth to art, or risk his reputation as the reliable, conservative trustee of high finance by flirting too openly with scandal — in art or business. He instead made compromises. Indeed, so did those who took Kahn's patronage, or came to feel that Kahn was one of the good guys on Wall Street — the rare capitalist with a soul. If many among the artists and intellectuals in Kahn's orbit might indict commercialism and rebel against bourgeois values, they were themselves operating in a market economy, full of ambition, wanting recognition, and willing to give and take. In that regard, the artists and their patron had much in common. A compromise cannot be made without a collaborator.

When another millionaire mockingly opined that Otto Kahn wanted "to meet all the important people in the world,"[42] it did seem as though he collected living talent like objects for a curiosity cabinet, to complement the masterpieces of European art that decorated his mansions, as a way to show off or feel self-important. A grander purpose would better account for the effect. Otto Kahn was reformulating the spatial breadth of the arts and their marketplaces. He did for the arts what August Belmont had done for cuisine: change the tastes and set the cultural pace of New York City, while at the same time elevating the city to the ranks of a global financial capital. More important, the artistic and financial exchange under Kahn's patronage ran in two directions. As he brought European geniuses to America, he also sent American talent to Europe, and his own character was itself something of an experiment in the tensions of foreignness and internationalism.

Here was a modernism of interrelations, blends, and hybrids, always looking forward with a foot also in the past. So if Otto Kahn could not write like a Joycean, he did subscribe to the legal defense of *Ulysses* in the United States and ordered a copy of the book for himself through Shakespeare and Company in Paris long before November 1930, when he accompanied James Joyce to a performance of *Guillaume Tell*. He was not a devotee of psychoanalysis either, yet he was for several decades an acquaintance and occasionally a benefactor of George Sylvester Viereck, who first interviewed Freud for American audiences. Nor was Kahn's modernity more than tangentially touched by the revelations of Albert Einstein. When Kahn testified before the Senate Banking Committee in 1933, for instance, he reached for an Einsteinian metaphor to express himself, and then had to admit overreaching his grasp, for he did not understand the theory.[43] However, the consistent factor in Kahn's modernity, right to the end, was optimism: all should work out well when the final curtain fell. That optimism of an incomplete Enlightenment, so important to him as a monied, cultured citizen, and as a Jew, was ultimately undermined and unfulfilled. Kahn's modernity emphasized the sweetness and light, but there was a dark side threatening, no more viciously than in the arrival of Hitlerism.[44]

Introduction

CHAPTER ONE

Foundations

Otto Kahn was hardly one to dwell on the details of his founding years. The few stories that he liked to tell were apportioned revelations, drawn from a handful of nested memories, and presented over and over to feature writers for the newspapers and magazines. Puffed and polished, these shaped the tale of Otto Hermann Kahn, the child who fathered the man of bourgeois respectability. Two lines of a plot intertwined like a double helix to determine how the well-dressed, well-mannered millionaire attained his credentials, comportment, and legitimacy. Along one thread, he was an "aristocrat by birth and breeding," the son of a prominent banker, "almost predestined to be a banker."[1] Along the other was his cultural capital. From an endowment jointly bestowed by his family and the city of his birth, Mannheim, Kahn's youth was steeped in respect for the arts and education. The civilizing edifice of aesthetic culture left him with vivid memories, clearer than those of anything Jewish.

Some of the details did noticeably change. For example, the character modeled upon Kahn in *Animal Crackers*—the aristocratic Roscoe W. Chandler—is discovered to actually be a rabbi-cantor from the old country (changed to a fish peddler in the film), and he will pay nearly any amount to keep it quiet. The joke, some say, satirized Kahn's religious ambivalence and assimilative strategies, but it may be emblematic of the opposite. During the 1920s Kahn was gradually revealing more of his Jewish identity than he had in earlier years. All along, however, any claim to categorical identities about his past or present would be complex.

Was he noble or middle class, an artist or a banker? With such hazy boundaries, one could (and society would) switch the variables and ask instead: artist or bourgeois, noble or American, German or Jew? Nor should any of these elements be considered too narrowly, without considering how easily Goethe and Heine translated into English, how Shakespeare came into the German canon, or how swiftly light switched between Rembrandt's *Holy Family* and families who owned Rembrandts, or, for that matter, how easily bank notes transformed from one currency into another (through gold). As important, we must also consider how much of the international style was founded upon the twin pillars of German embourgeoisement, *Bildung* ("how an individual is 'formed' or 'cultivated' within a social collectivity") and *Sittlichkeit* ("proper moral comportment").[2] One and all converged in Otto Kahn's German-Anglo-American synthesis of the emancipated Jew, and it constitutes a weighty cargo.

. . . .

FAMILY PORTRAITS

Otto Hermann Kahn entered the world on February 12, 1867, the third of five sons and fourth of eight children in an affluent household. All his grandparents were still alive except Michael Benedickt Kahn (1798–1861), his paternal grandfather, who as a young man had started a business in the wholesale trade and manufacture of feather-bedding, which was still prospering in 1867. None of Otto Kahn's versions of the family history mention that, before turning to business, this grandfather had trained to be a rabbi. It is unclear whether Kahn himself knew this about his grandfather, or, if he did, offered some casual remark that became the source of the Roscoe Chandler joke, but it was not the only forgotten or understated piece of Kahn's pedigree. Turning away from the rabbinate estranged Michael Kahn from the religious members of his family. He overcame the alienation through a good marriage in 1825 to Franziska Bäer (1809–92), the daughter of a popular innkeeper; together they worked to establish their business in the small farming community of Stebbach, forty miles from Mannheim. Otto Kahn later claimed to know little if anything about these grandparents, but chances are good that Franziska Kahn was literate and possessed at least rudimentary skills in arithmetic. She might have helped in weighing, measuring, counting, and bookkeeping. She probably also had domestic help for raising the children.[3]

The Kahns' featherbedding business careered through complicated

Foundations

times. Several larger economic factors were conducive to its development, including the piecemeal emancipation of Jews, a widespread
emancipation of peasants, and the easing toward free trade among the
many German states. Added into the mix was an all-inclusive commercial revolution, just on the cusp of industrialization, which brought improved techniques as well as yields to both land and livestock production, then stimulated the development of roads, harbors, and railways.

All of this disturbed traditional social relations, increasing the ranks
of landless peasants in need of work and money, but it also created
circumstances that allowed the Kahn firm to specialize without much
capitalization. The stuffing and stitching were initially done in their
own cottage; as the business grew, they would rely upon the putting-out
system — contracting and coordinating the labor of others who worked
from their own cottages. Then even after a formal factory was established, most of the work was done by hand, because technologies were
not nearly as important as market considerations to the featherbedding industry. It helped that featherbedding was neither a novelty nor
newly invented. Whether the merchandise was plain or fancy, hand-
made or machine-manufactured, mattresses, pillows, and comforters
were becoming necessities of modern contentment, both in domestic
life and in the military.[4]

A medley of traditions and transitions were further shaping the middle class, including inheritances, dowries, and sons to lead later generations of the firm. The firstborn was not always marked in the cradle as
the next head of the firm, nor was every son a good businessman, but
having five sons improved Michael and Franziska Kahn's chances to
apprentice some of their progeny in the business and to see at least one
or more installed in a leadership role. Law and custom further complicated the pattern of succession, or a family's transmission of wealth and
status. Because estates would be divided, siblings could figure on a fair
inheritance, but ultimately a legacy depended upon a father's will.
One's expectation for a fairly proportioned inheritance reinforced a
code of obedience to one's parents, and seeded some competition
among the children. Moreover, it meant a family's wealth could become diluted as it passed from one generation to the next. Sometimes
called the "Buddenbrooks dynamic," after a theme in Thomas Mann's
epic novel, the phenomenon is referred to in French as "*Il est plus facile
de faire l'argent que pour le garder*" (it's easier to make money than to
keep it), and in the American-tailored tradition, "Shirtsleeves to shirt-

sleeves in three generations"[5] — both pointing to a singular pattern, and an undercurrent of anxiety within the newly emerging middle classes. The comparison to *Buddenbrooks* best fits the Kahns, nonetheless, because it embeds the process in historical circumstances surrounding the revolutions of 1848.

When harvest failures in 1846–47 doubled the price of food, leaving many without the resources to pay their financial obligations, hunger riots and other forms of political unrest erupted. Everyone was affected, but not everyone suffered equally. As labor costs cheapened, the need for cash deepened, and thus the Kahns could procure feathers and labor at lower prices. Being a firm of modest capitalization, and apparently unburdened with debts, mortgages, or rents, their enterprise could withstand the worsening storm and come out better on the other side. Still, whatever steadiness was implied by their business's survival, the family's fate was not without danger. When revolutions swept through Europe and energized Germans in March 1848, the Kahns had three sons who were old enough to work in the business. They were also old enough to participate in revolutionary activities, which were seething with a particularly diverse, populist brand of upheaval in southwest Germany, a region already rife with democratic movements as news of revolution in France arrived on the last days of February 1848.

Within one week an assembly convened in Mannheim demanding a bill of rights. Spontaneous mass meetings and insurrections erupted in several cities, with strong popular support throughout the region. Although many expected the coming spring to bring revolution into full bloom, instead the southwest fell under siege with the arrival of Hessian troops until order was restored. Not long after, Germany's first national parliament convened as the Frankfurt Assembly; yet by autumn, as popular confidence in the assembly diminished, demonstrations resumed and the troops returned — first Prussians, then Hessians to relieve them. Order was again forcibly imposed. Then as soon as the occupying forces withdrew, popular associations mobilized once more, with local militia joining the democrats to establish provisional governments in Karlsruhe and Mannheim. The Prussians came back, engaged in heavy battles, and recaptured Mannheim in June 1849. The rest of the region was suppressed with similar force. These events, Otto Kahn later said, formed an inherited hatred for Prussian militarism, as he was "the son of a man who had fought in the revolution of 1848 against Prussian autocracy." His father, Bernhard (1827–1905), the eldest son of Michael and Franziska, seems to have been secretary for the *Volksvereins Stebbach*. Accordingly, he would have petitioned for freedoms of political association, among other liberal causes, and joined the provisional national committee of *Volksvereins*, a close network of organized democrats whose calls for a popular assembly at Offenburg was a prelude to the May 1849 revolution. Like many of the some 6,000 refugees of the revolution, Bernhard Kahn (1827–1905) was sentenced to death and escaped to America. He joined his younger brother, the middle son, Emil (born 1832), in Albany, New York, and apparently took up business related to their father's interests.[6]

The brothers were typical of many if not most of the Germans who emigrated to America before 1860. The majority of the 1.5 million German-born immigrants of their generation originated in the rural southern and southwestern German states. They settled in the mid-Atlantic and eastern north-central regions of the United States, often needing charity upon their arrival, then buying cheap farm land when able, and sometimes amassing capital after beginning as peddlers. The Kahn brothers, who arrived with the financial resources to establish themselves in business immediately and settled in urban America, were similar to approximately one-third of German immigrants, who were more likely to be urban dwellers than either Americans as a whole or Germans in their homeland. America's cities would change in consequence because a large, influential segment of the German American immigrants in the cities were affluent, well-educated liberals who immediately organized economic and cultural communities, establishing schools, clubs, newspapers, hospitals, musical societies, reading rooms, and recreational facilities. While strongest in New York City, these bilingual and German-speaking networks could be found in any city with a newly settled population of German immigrants. Their ties back to Europe were solid as well. German culture stayed dear and it eventually grew nearer, as amnesty was granted for the revolutionaries in their native land. That allowed condemned "Forty-Eighters" to travel between America and Germany for vacations and business, the education of their children, and various family obligations.[7]

It is as likely as not that Bernhard Kahn came to the United States in search of a haven rather than a homeland. He nonetheless became an American citizen in 1854, then took his first trip back to Germany no later than 1860. Whether he intended to visit or knew he would stay, during this visit he met and married Emma Eberstadt (1840–1906) and thereafter remained in Germany. Emil soon repatriated as well. By now, their father's business had relocated to Mannheim, the commercial center of Baden, where Michael Kahn was granted the rights of citizenship on July 29, 1851, and brought his family to live in April 1854. Two brothers, the second-born son Hermann (b. 1829) and the younger Leopold (b. 1841), remained engaged in their father's enterprise, which had also established its own factory and taken a leading position in the German featherbed industry. There was one notable setback, however, when a fire in 1858 destroyed the factory, the probable consequences of which were fairly significant. By the time Bernhard came home, his father had decided to rebuild and expand the plant rather than retire and live off his investments. This may have implied that he intended his sons to inherit the business and not merely his fortune, but also that perhaps there was not enough money to simply retire and live as well as the Kahns wanted. In addition, reconstruction and expansion after the fire would have diminished the family's capital; thus a more intense interest in angling for a legacy was likely in play when Bernhard Kahn and Emma Eberstadt were married.[8]

On the face of it, Emma Eberstadt made a perfectly good bride. She was a lively, pretty, talented woman, holding a cheerful though serious view of life, according to her favorite son. In all likeliness some romance developed between the future husband and wife, yet there was surely more to the courtship than starry-eyed attraction alone. These years saw arranged marriages drift out of style, if not practice; accordingly, family lore was more likely to record the affections than the arrangements when, as occurred often enough, a so-called surprise meeting between a potential couple was deliberately orchestrated by parents. The Kahn-Eberstadt case left a fairly suggestive hint of parental influence because, as family tradition tells it, Emma's father made Bernhard promise to stay in Mannheim before giving his daughter's hand. Ferdinand Eberstadt was motivated, they say, by love and parental attachment, yet the Kahns and Eberstadts would both benefit from keeping the couple nearby. The Kahns could tie Bernhard's impending inheritance to this marriage, which they considered a good one, and keep their eldest son around to care for his mother should she be widowed (which she was in 1861). The Eberstadts, in turn, might have thought the groom's future more secure if he were to stay in Mannheim. That was not the case when their daughter Elizabeth ("Betty") Eberstadt (1844–1931) married in 1867. She was allowed to make her married household in London with her husband George Lewis, an eminent English solicitor of Sephardic origin and friend of Edward, Prince of Wales. Another sister, Maria Johanna Eberstadt (1845–?), married in Mannheim in 1862 and emigrated to London. But in 1872, when the youngest Eberstadt sister, Bertha (1850–1913), married Emil Hirsch, a noted Mannheim corn wholesaler, hers seemed to be a match much like that of Bernhard and Emma, in that the Hirschs stayed in Mannheim.

The Kahn-Eberstadt union was itself an interesting alliance of complements rather than equals. Both families were new to Mannheim, but the Eberstadts were from Worms and therefore not as recently provincial as the Kahns, who, unlike the Eberstadts, were also not yet wealthy enough to support their sons in professions other than the family business. Perhaps too much should not be made of those differences, because, with the whole of the new bourgeoisie emerging rapidly, similarities of class, ethnicity, and politics could be more prominent than the differences. Indeed, the two families' similarities had likely brought them together before the betrothal of their children. Nevertheless, the differences still had an impact for Otto Kahn, whose mother had a more impressive lineage than his father. Emma Eberstadt's mother, Sarah Zelie Seligmann Eberstadt (1816–85), was the daughter of a merchant, descended from one of the first Jews to be a university-trained physician. Elsewhere in her family tree were the Anspachs, who may have been among the Court Jews, as Jewish financial advisers to the nobility of Central Europe were known; a niece from that family had married into the Parisian Rothschilds, but Sarah Zelie's own marriage was also one of regional distinction. Her husband, Falck "Ferdinand" Eberstadt (1808–88), came from a wealthy, patrician household, and the Eberstadts were one of the most cultured Jewish families of Worms, the city where they had lived since the seventeenth century.

Ferdinand Eberstadt was a principal in his father's textile and dry-goods wholesale house, but he was drawn to politics. In March 1849 he became mayor of Worms, perhaps the first Jewish mayor in any German state. He was also a democratic partisan who managed to survive the counterrevolution and served as mayor until 1852, though afterward Eberstadt's political life in Worms unraveled, presumably as right-wing reaction advanced. Returning to business he quarreled with his brother, then arranged to be bought out of the family firm. By the end of 1857, Ferdinand and Zelie Eberstadt had moved with their ten children to Mannheim, still the center of liberalism in Baden, where they opened a new firm. Their social, cultural, and political connections fast established the Eberstadts as one of the leading Jewish families in Mannheim. Ferdinand's ongoing political interests, and a financial stake in the local newspaper, *Neuen Badischen Landeszeitung*, would make it easier for Bernhard Kahn to resume his own political career. In a way, his marriage to Emma Eberstadt gave Bernhard Kahn the best of all benefits possible from the failed revolution. He became a citizen of Mannheim on September 5, 1860, six weeks before his marriage. Nonetheless, whether out of neglect, concern for his political safety, or doubt about his marriage, Bernhard Kahn kept his American citizenship for several more years.[9]

The death of Michael Kahn in 1861 brought the family to another turning point. When the estate was divided, Leopold and Hermann Kahn moved to Frankfurt, where they opened the banking house of Kahn & Co. Bernhard and Emil stayed in Mannheim, with Emil running the featherbedding factory while Bernhard specialized in the family's latest venture, the banking house of M. Kahn Söhn, established on August 11, 1867, only six months after the birth of Otto Kahn. By 1870 Bernhard Kahn was a Mannheimer of considerable standing, a member of many local organizations, and the owner of an elegant new residence in the stylish section of town. A few years later he became a city councilman, a position that he kept for better than two decades before retiring to a villa in Heidelberg as an untitled gentleman.

These first years of the new Reich brought official Jewish emancipation, along with pronounced swings toward populist anti-Semitism. It also brought German adherence to the international gold standard, as the empire entered an era of rapid industrialization, urbanization, and global expansion. Rural industries and populations remained important in Germany, and tariffs to protect products from foreign competition could help the featherbedding business; but so did the nature of that business, because featherbed manufacturers could produce smaller batches of high-quality goods and avoid the problems of overproduction. The more dynamic future lay beyond featherbedding, however. Mining, iron, steel, chemical, electrical, and engineering concerns, which signaled Germany's industrial emergence, all tended toward high capitalization and concentration, putting the banks in a compelling position while banking itself was undergoing its own organizational revolutions.

By the time of Otto Kahn's birth, investment functions and the public's appetite for speculation were growing both in breadth and depth, but market relations remained quite intertwined with social and economic bonds. Consider, for instance, the local manufacturer or wholesaler who kept his accounts with fellow townsman M. Kahn Söhn. Reading a newspaper, he would see the banker's advertised offering of shares in the debt of an American railroad. Given the uncertain nature of investments, the hopes for profit were coupled with trust in the middlemen, who issued, underwrote, and distributed bonds or stocks. A banker's good reputation could lessen the chance of folly and fraud. Something could go wrong at any time, just from the bad luck of an engineering disaster, for example, but financial setbacks that resulted from stupidity or dupery reached far beyond the balance sheet to impair the dignity of a firm, the confidence of investors, and the ability of industries to raise funds for expansion. And when monstrous disasters like the 1867 failure of the *Crédit Mobilier* made many faults obvious and infamous, confidence could be restored only with considerable effort. The bankers strong enough to survive also helped smooth over difficulties and were strengthened by the experience. Indeed, Bernhard Kahn's house not only survived the economic collapse in 1873, which occurred throughout Western Europe, America, and Russia, his bank endured the two decades of erratic economic swings that followed.

Private banks of mercantile origins were meanwhile transforming the world's preeminent facilities for long-term investment. A few of the leaders had been Court Jews during the age of absolutism. Most renowned among them were Rothschilds, who originated in Frankfurt, established branches throughout Europe, and hired representatives in countries beyond the continent wherever investment activities were significant. Yet even as the Rothschilds came to the top of international finance, and to symbolize Europe's greatest multimillionaires, several new structures of the nineteenth century were emerging to accumulate and distribute capital more diversely and extensively than private banks alone. These included the share-holding company, or joint-stock company, in the expansion of which Bernhard Kahn participated concurrent with the operations of M. Kahn Söhn, as he took co-founding stakes in the Reinische Hypothekenbank (1871) and the Deutsche Unionsbank (1873). Another structure of financial innovation, the syndicate, was similar to the stock company in that it distributed the risk and lessened the impact of failure, allowing the more secure underwriting of business too large for one bank to handle alone. Unlike a stock company, a syndicate need not be permanent or chartered; it officially lasts only as long as the business at hand. However, because one good syndicate operation could bring an invitation to work with the same group in another offering, there was significant stability within syndicate groups, which helped to regulate the ethics of associates. It also created the impression of cabals and conspiracies, as financial power tended to concentrate among a few great banks and their privileged fraternity.

Bernhard Kahn's banking career mirrored these dynamics of finance without him rising into the ranks of the upper echelon. Other joint-stock and private banks were bigger and, on the face of it, more conspicuously important. Kahn's house was likely engaged in commercial banking, handling the occasional distribution of bonds and securities in smaller lots, and no evidence as yet suggests that his bank directly participated in underwriting syndicates. While smaller firms managed to carry on with their own meaningful roles, there were acknowledged leaders of high finance at that time, and Bernhard Kahn was not among them. Even in Mannheim, the *bankhaus* founded in 1836 by Seligmann Landenburg (1797–1873) was more prominent. The Eberstadts had brought Bernhard Kahn closer to the better circles of European finance, but he was still the son of a *Handelsmann in Landprodukten*, a commercial man dealing in agricultural products, and the base of banking operations for Bernhard Kahn was neither the traditional banking center of Germany (Frankfurt) nor its newly emerging financial center (Berlin). His father's position would ultimately affect the place of Otto Kahn within the world of international finance.

· · · ·

BUILDING A CHARACTER

All together, the process through which Kahn came to be "an aristocrat by birth and breeding" may be one of purposeful compression, with the Kahns more clearly burghers, or bourgeois, and parvenu at that. They were not so unusual. The bourgeoisie often forgot their origins as commoners, or hid them behind desires for social approval, for it was beneficial to forget, especially as the distance between themselves and the aristocracy became bridgeable. Rather than debate aristocratic pretensions exclusively, though, it is better to picture the Kahns in contrast to the philistine — that anathema of mid-century bourgeois mentality, who made everything useful and nothing beautiful, only dull, shallow, self-satisfied signs of a new civilization that was inherently short on humanist goals, aesthetic achievements, and concern for human needs. The Kahns and Eberstadts epitomized an alternative model — a refined and cultured bourgeoisie, as confident in businesses as they were committed to culture, which was as much a part of family life as the children.

The city of Mannheim itself furnished a conducive environment for the shared aims of economic and cultural leadership. It was a young city, chartered in 1607, and twice destroyed by wars of the seventeenth century, then rebuilt by successive electors of the Palatinate, who made Mannheim a Baroque court seat and a center for performing arts. Royal patronage was a magnet for conductors, musicians, and composers, coalescing as the Mannheim School, whose symphonic writing and orchestration influenced Haydn and Mozart. The Mannheim Nationaltheater, another site of city pride, opened in 1778 to house the oldest professional orchestra in Europe. The city also saw the premiere of Friedrich Schiller's revolutionary play *Die Räuber* (The Robbers) in 1782, and it was a stop on Hector Berlioz's triumphant tour of Belgium and Germany in 1842–43. During Kahn's youth, Mannheim, primarily a residential town, remained famous for its cultural life, yet was well on its way to becoming an important industrial and transportation center. This was due in part to Mannheim's location at the convergence of the Rhine and Neckar Rivers, where the city's harbor could be optimized by canals and so developed advantages over those of other Rhenish towns.[10]

Otto Kahn grew up in the most fashionable section of town, within a few minute's walk from the Nationaltheater — an institution more prominent in his upbringing than any religious affiliation. Kahn always maintained he had no childhood memories of Judaic practices, even on the holiest days, but was initiated instead into the rituals of art. Some of the city's most influential musicians were hired to teach the Kahn children, all of whom started musical training early. Although it was his brother Robert who showed signs of being a prodigy, Otto learned to play the violin, cello, and piano. At around eleven years of age, he was taken to his first opera, Wagner's *Tristan und Isolde*, which, true to his parents' expectations, fascinated him. The family also had connections to the opera company: Bernhard Kahn, a baritone with perfect pitch, was a benefactor, and Kahn's parents were both close friends of its conductor.

Proud to be connoisseurs with the highest standards of taste, the Kahns were a better class of amateurs — an educated audience that took serious pride in their knowledge of music and literature. As if to underscore the point, Otto Kahn liked to convey disapproval for an elder banker, seated near him in the audience at that first operatic experience, who "fidgeted restlessly through the first act," then fell asleep during the second and snored. An attentive posture was more becoming, as theaters and concert halls would permit the bourgeoisie to demonstrate values of citizenry and individual cultivation. These were also places, beyond the *bourse* or banking house, where Jews could mix with the larger society, and art crowds attracted a good many Jewish patrons. This reality signified multiple trends, including a decline in aristocratic patronage, the need for fresh money, and the fact that new audiences led to new groupings and venues of participation, such as private recitals and literary *conversaziones* in homes of the well-to-do, where musicians and artists mixed with politicians, intellectuals, and writers along with their hosts. Kahn's aunt, Bertha Hirsch, for instance, hosted what was considered the best *salon* of Mannheim. If the gatherings in Kahn's own household were second-tier by comparison, they were bright and lively nonetheless. In either household, a nonstop parade of social celebrities, talent, and entertainment could change one's status within a wider social structure. Emancipated, assimilating Jews remained outsiders, but *salons* of the highest quality could entice non-Jews into homes of Jewish ancestry.[11]

As a matter of course, no outward Jewishness was evidenced in the Kahn household or its entertainments. The Kahns were assimilated and irreligious, a conventional type among affluent German Jews who, in Irving Katz's phrase, "attempted to join the German cultural tradition into which they were newly initiated and contribute to it." They did not need to convert to Christianity for Judaic traditions to collapse, but neither did they need to completely quitclaim to a Jewish identity in order to think themselves German through and through. In the end, Kahn's parents were laid to rest in a Jewish cemetery that was later defiled by the Nazis. History ultimately reversed what assimilating families like the Kahns expected from liberal modernity when they spoke German, a bit of French, but never Hebrew or Yiddish, and they took the German word of greatest importance to be *Bildung*—an ideal presumed to offer fulfillment and social redemption for Jews as German citizens and individuals of cultural distinction. That meant more than money, although money was both a factor in developing *Bildung*, and an old stigma for Jews.[12]

Integrative success was not without its dangers, of course. It became the grist for anti-Semitic mills, and depictions of Jews as social climbers, using any means at hand to dominate, pollute, infect, or debilitate were always lurking around the corner. The Germany of Kahn's youth was fraught with such conflict, and in hindsight, after the 1930s, the pull toward *Bildung* would be widely criticized as a delusional "one-sided love affair." Jews embraced Germanness while Germans held out against Jews. In Kahn's childhood the ultimate winner of this clash was less obvious than the immediate struggle, and a family as comfortable as the Kahns would stay confident in their hopes of progress. Enrolling Otto Kahn and his brothers at gymnasium brought another milestone. A secondary school for classical education, preparatory for entrance to university, the gymnasium was a domain of privilege, a haven of humanistic learning in a rapidly modernizing world. As it was also the preferred education for sons of Mannheim's leading Jews, the gymnasium indicated an attitude as much as a change, moving away from the pragmatically oriented education of Jewish sons that was typical of the earlier nineteenth century. By 1875, when the Jews were little more than 8 percent of Mannheim's population, they accounted for 28 percent of gymnasium students, a disproportionate ratio that continued for the remainder of the century.[13]

A number of explanations lay behind such data. The least lofty, perhaps, was the advantage earned after six years of attendance — gymnasium students were then exempted from the standard three years of conscripted military service and could instead enlist for one year as a volunteer. Kahn himself enjoyed this privilege when he served with the Hussar unit in Mainz. Rationalizing the exemption was the educational demands and career objectives of gymnasium students, whose lengthy course of studies was a step toward professional careers in law, medicine, and education. Not incidentally, these same professions traditionally barred Jewish participation, and were thus a testing ground for universal emancipation. But there was another attraction. An assumption that gymnasium students were smart made a classical, secular education fit well with the hosting, viewing, and sponsorship of an aesthetic curriculum in his family life. These would all merge in support of bourgeois enlightenment. Possessing a knowledge higher than commerce was proof of one's cultured worth.

What rubbed against the ideal could also undermine the foundational tenets of bourgeois power. If business culture was inherently dull, then the need to work in business could be as undignified as idleness. On the other hand, cultivating the rewards of business could also jeopardize the real basis of embourgeoisement — the ability to make monied wealth. Such inevitably crossed purposes came to a climax for Otto Kahn during the early 1880s as he neared sixteen years of age; his parents awakened to their need for a son with practical training. The duty fell decidedly upon Otto. His own hopes were to become a writer, and he had secretly composed poems and plays in free verse, which the adult Otto Kahn would call "juvenile rubbish," having long before internalized the humiliation of his talent at this crucial junction in the building of his character. With subtle variations in the legend, Kahn's parents "discovered his opus" — including one or two five-act plays — then "summoned the youthful Otto to bring his manuscripts to a family conference," and condemned rather than commended his talent. In one version, his mother is said to have worried that none of her sons was prepared "to take charge of the family affairs," and determined business was better suited for the talents of Otto. In another, his father played the disciplinarian and "threw the whole lot of poems and dramas into the fire." Yet one more account has the obedient boy thrusting his own pages into the flames. A consoling father then advised Kahn to combine banking and the arts in one career, or pursue literature after he had made a success of business. In all the variants, the denouement always brought a graceful resolution in which trauma was denied. "Without resenting his parents decision . . . [Kahn] made two resolutions: (1) to make money, to be successful; (2) to employ his success to foster the consciousness of art and to give material encouragement to art." Thus Otto Kahn invented a goal that he could conquer.[14]

Some stories are nested too thickly to go without comment, and Kahn's could be a page from a *Bildungsroman* (a novel of personal cultivation and development, such as Goethe's *Wilhelm Meister*). It was all the more difficult because it meant that Otto Kahn would not be allowed to follow in his own brothers' footsteps. Franz Michael Kahn (1861–1904), the eldest child, had already left home, headed for the legal profession and judicial scholarship. A man of wide and deep studies, his doctoral thesis examined the history of women's hereditary rights in Roman antiquity, and thereafter he published several highly regarded works on international private law. Robert August Kahn (1865–1951), the second-born son and his mother's favorite, had the *hofkapellmeisters* of Mannheim Nationaltheater to train him before going to the Royal Academy of Music in Berlin in 1882. Every imaginable connection of the family was brought forth in support of his career, including consideration from conductor Hermann Levi and composer Josef Rheinberger. Yet another door opened in 1886 when Johannes Brahms visited Mannheim. Either Bertha Hirsch or Helen Hecht (a cousin of Emma Kahn) hosted a reception where an introduction was arranged for Robert to meet the famed composer. He later followed Brahms to Vienna, and before long Robert would become a notable composer of chamber and vocal music. His first orchestral work premiered in Berlin in 1890, and he taught at the *Hochschule fur Musik* from 1893 until his retirement in 1930.[15]

With these older brothers as symbols of how successful the Kahns had become in ethno-occupational terms, what then should be made of the third son, Otto, being withdrawn from the gymnasium and tossed back into the world of filthy lucre, which tainted bourgeois wealth generally and Jews so fiercely? The answers would be clearer if one knew exactly in what direction the family's financial accounts were shifting, yet surely the options might have changed if one of the elder brothers had been inclined toward business or if Otto Kahn had been a parental favorite. But one must still wonder: if the boy's writings were indeed composed secretly, before his parents discovered them, then when did that practice begin? And why would he not write openly? Did an ongoing critique by family members already indicate that he would be put to work in banking? Did he write in secret rebellion until he could no longer deny his destiny as the son who was to sustain the family drive for fiduciary wealth? There were unspoken memories, undoubtedly painful, in confronting parental will and a harsh lesson in connoisseurship.

This much also was true when Kahn entered banking — he would not go broke for art. Whether he lacked talent or loved money more, Otto Kahn accepted an art world organized around the principle of genius, then found his way to collaborate — knowing he was not a genius. To some degree his support for emerging artists would give others the

The Kahn brothers, ca. 1877. Left to right: Felix, Franz, Paul, Otto, and Robert. (Private collection)

encouragement that he had missed, and foster the artistic rebellious-ness that Kahn also missed; but when he funded geniuses who bought a typewriter, paid the rent, or traveled with Kahn's money, the patron could partake in the creative process without being pummeled by criti-cism of the kind that had undermined his own youthful aspirations. He would keep something alive of his own poetry, too, when later penning domestic rhymes that were fun to write and adored by his children. Every now and then he coupled the child and father with the celebrity, as he did with a verse for his young daughter Margaret ("Nin"):

Foundations

The gent you see depicted here
Is well known as a financier
The men who our papers edit
Give him considerable credit:
He's hailed as a speaker of renown,
He wears the late Maecenas' crown
He spurns the tawdriness of fame
He shuns publicity's acclaim.
Far sweeter than the flattering din.
Counts he the term "Father to Nin."

At sixty years of age, he could also still recite a "fragment from one of my youthful doggerel-ballads."[16]

As important, Kahn's tale strikes two parallel themes of bourgeois ideology. Along one, a self-fulfillment animates personality—if ideals and reality collide, reconciliations are possible. Along the other, the myth of bourgeois confidence is rife with trepidation. Looking ahead at the fate of Kahn's family wealth illustrates the latter, as well as one of the missing links in his story, for as these heirs of urban capitalism were cohorts of a generation in the liberal epoch, they etched a baseline in the accumulation and restructuring of family-based wealth.

None of Bernhard and Emma Kahn's offspring would succeed their father at the helm of M. Kahn Söhn, and Otto Kahn, the only life-long banker among them, would never be a banker in Mannheim. The financial fate of the other children varied, although each had an allowance from inherited money. One sister, Elisabeth Franziska "Lili" (1869–1940?), became a famous *salonist* in Berlin. The trusted mistress-friend of Walther Rathenau, she was the wife of Felix Deutsch (1858–1928), a top manager at Allegemeine Elektrizitäts Gesellschaft (AEG), and second only to Otto Kahn as the wealthiest sibling. Otto's brother Robert, the eldest surviving son after the death of Franz Michael in 1904, was probably the third-most secure financially. He earned a salary from teaching, along with royalties and performance fees, in addition to his inherited income. The rest of the siblings had one trait in common. Each was more dependent upon the Bernhard Kahn inheritance, the Deutsch circles of Berlin, and/or the benevolence of their wealthiest sibling, Otto. These included Clara Maria (1863–1922), whose husband, Paul Simon Jonas (1850–1916), was an attorney in Berlin who moved in circles that included Otto Brahm, the famed director of the

Deutsches Theater. Paul Friedrich (1870–1947), the third brother, trained as a lawyer and worked briefly as a secretary to playwright Gerhart Hauptmann (1862–1946), but most of his livelihood depended upon employment or contacts at AEG, and he occasionally required supplementary aid from Otto. Likewise, when the twice-married youngest sibling, Hedwig (1876–1950), mother of British actress Ellen Pollock, struggled to collect alimony from her second husband, she also showed signs of insufficient independent wealth. The fourth brother, Felix Paul (1873–1950), a life-long bachelor and accomplished amateur violinist, was the most compatible with and financially dependent upon Otto in New York. Felix started in banking, then emigrated to the United States before the First World War, where he both scouted and represented several of Otto's motion picture interests. He sat on the board of directors of the Famous Players Lasky Corporation, a forerunner of Paramount Pictures.[17]

Otto Kahn, in turn, was the sibling least dependent on either his Mannheim roots or the Deutschs' circles or other family connections from the past. Financial and familial advantages gave him a good start, but his own fortune depended largely upon a good marriage in America. There would be no great banking house bearing his personal name; the difference between "Kahn" and "Kuhn" in Kuhn, Loeb is a big one. When the public later thought Kahn to be a man of unlimited wealth, it could not readily see how his familial wealth had dissipated. Otto Kahn himself would have good reasons not to think of it.

What little Kahn told others of his banking apprenticeship simply emphasized affirmation. Customarily, a banker-in-training began with the basics — clerking in a house friendly to his father, then moving from one firm to another as a sort of journeyman before settling with one house for the remainder of his career. Kahn spent three years with Veit L. Homburger in Karlsruhe, the seat of Badenese government, then, after one year away in military service with the Hussars, he went next to Berlin to work for a year with Marcus & Volkmar.[18] Both were relatively smaller houses of limited scope, with not much to boast other than a neat little story of how Kahn was first promoted. In scenes reminiscent of old-world scribblers and clerks, we are introduced to the newcomer, young Otto Kahn, "cleaning the inkwells of the other clerks, running out to buy sausages, beer, and . . . being kicked around in a manner calculated to cure any symptoms of swell-headedness." As registered by one author, Kahn thought the clerkship "useful, salutary training, for it taught discipline and order. One must learn to obey before he is fit to command. It instilled a proper sense of one's place and emphasized that the most humble duties must be performed conscientiously and without any loss of self-respect." Such an outlook had its rewards, Kahn figured: "I suppose I must have wiped the inkwells fairly satisfactorily, for it was not long before I was promoted and had another novitiate to clean my inkwell and fetch my lunch."[19]

The stitch of this embroidery is obvious and thick: work hard and get ahead. It hints of other stories, including that of the office boy in *H.M.S. Pinafore* who so perfectly polished the entry-door handle and ultimately became "the Ruler of the Queen's Navee." It was also a tale to help Kahn cross boundaries. He could be both a self-made man and born of wealth. In a 1924 speech to Harvard-trained businessmen, Kahn switched his proficiency for cleaning inkwells to licking stamps, but either prop would have worked in bonding the first generation of elite university-trained businessmen to their countinghouse heritage. Soon after, Waldo Frank, writing for the *New Yorker*, saw more than an "efficiency-confession" in Kahn's parable: "In licking stamps, Otto Kahn was not more industrious, not more intelligent than others: he was more artistic."[20]

He was also quite ambitious. In 1888, stepping happily into higher realms of international finance, he secured a position with Deutsche Bank at its London subsidiary, the most important foreign office of one of the largest German banks. London, the unrivaled financial center of the globe, offered a most promising place for the social advancement of financiers. Kahn carried a number of advantages not only for entry into "the City," London's famous financial district, but also to join England's gentlemanly elite tradition. On one hand, *Bildung*, the "knighthood of modernity," and *Sittlichkeit*, or "respectability," helped his transitions, partly because "The German Idea" had been taken up by Coleridge and Carlyle. On the other hand, German Jewish immigrants had special cultural status among Anglo-Jewry, for unlike the typical Jewish immigrant of Eastern European origin, German Jews came from monied wealth, cultured backgrounds, and secular educations, and they had already apprenticed in trade and commerce. Even more to Kahn's liking, both the landed classes of English nobility and parliamentary ranks became increasingly open to men of acquired wealth during the late Victorian era. Indeed, financiers (German-born

Jews among them) secured nobility more rapidly and in greater number than industrialists.[21] A prosperous segment of wealthy Jewry, especially financiers from the City, gradually found opportunities for political office, ennoblement, and intermarriage with Gentiles in England. They also had a niche in smart society, due mainly to the disposition of Edward, Prince of Wales, who counted a good number of prominent Jews within his entourage. Among them was George Henry Lewis (1833–1911), the high-society solicitor who had married Kahn's aunt, Betty Eberstadt. Lewis was knighted in 1892 and elevated to a baronetcy in 1905.[22]

The Lewis household made Oscar Wilde's London also Otto Kahn's London, gay, satiric, and romantic. A costumed epicycle of *dramatis personae* and artistic wealth opened to him. Kahn chanced upon a crowd for whom art was the secret of life. He found the best of light opera, new drama, and literary entrepreneurship, along with beautiful women and the latest gossip.[23] He discovered a passion for Ibsen and Shakespeare, so much in vogue then on the London stage, and he read Thomas Carlyle and Walter Pater, further polishing his sense of heroism, art, and beauty. He loved being around the pacesetters, and as the Lewises knew nearly every future contributor to the *Yellow Book*, the illustrated quarterly of new artistic literature, Kahn grew acquainted with the poet and novelist Richard Le Gallienne, whose future daughter, Eva, the actress and founder of the Civic Repertory Theatre in New York, would one day benefit from Kahn's patronage. Years later Kahn would also recall a casual encounter with Elizabeth Robins at an 1892 gathering, when she reigned as London's leading lady of Ibsenian drama: "You came with Mr. Heinneman [Ibsen's publisher in England], whom I knew, and we exchanged a few words — I was hungry for more. I was young and quite insignificant. You were very young, very good looking, by no means insignificant, and in my eyes, rather a romantic figure."[24] Whether his flattery was flirtation or not, or whether Kahn knew that Robins or, for that matter, Eva Le Gallienne were both lesbians, it probably would not have diminished his attraction to their beauty.

Otto Kahn moved admiringly among London's smart set, later remembering these years as "the most impressionable period of my life."[25] Neither a stranger nor a luminary, but star-struck, he was once again the novitiate, licking something other than stamps. The stage, the city, the manor seemed within reach of a single goal — the English

Otto Kahn. He donned a crisp sartorial style, switched his citizenship, and changed his patterns of speech. A German accent lilted through British inflections thereafter, making the origins of his dialect more difficult to detect. In most ways, Kahn adopted the elegance of the sophisticates around him — an elegance that became Kahn's armor, for it gave him a means to live conservatively on the edge of scandal. As for secrecy, Kahn could observe its best practitioner: Sir George Lewis. Of the solicitor who so adeptly managed the legitimacy of royal sins, the Crown Prince Edward supposedly said, "He is the one man in England who should write his memoirs, but of course he never can." Added into the mix was tolerance. When Oscar Wilde prepared Elizabeth Robins for her introduction to Lewis, he offered this cryptic assurance: "Oh, he knows all about us — and forgives us."[26]

Kahn meanwhile advanced in his banking career, where he also wanted to be one of the pacesetters. He was promoted to vice-manager, then arranged to move up and beyond, making a step that took him away from Deutsche Bank and England almost as soon as he became a British subject on July 15, 1893. In that same summer, Kahn headed for New York on a temporary assignment with Speyer & Co. and with one goal in mind. He wanted to make the best of a good opportunity to work for one of the truly great dynastic financial firms of the time.[27]

• • • •

THE NEW YORK GRID

The Speyers had been bankers in Frankfurt since 1644, and were even wealthier than the Rothschilds in 1800. A triumvirate of firms was formed in Frankfurt, London, and New York, with the New York house, established in 1837, quickly forging a premier position in German American finance. Soon after the brothers Philip and Gustavus Speyer arrived from Frankfurt to take charge, the house became a distributor of American railway securities in Europe, then a leader in the European distribution of U.S. government securities during the Civil War. In 1878 it reorganized to deal exclusively in underwriting and distributing securities. Meanwhile a London house opened in 1862 under the management of Leo Bonn (1850–1929), another son of Frankfurt who continued with the firm when the reins passed to Edgar Speyer (1862–1932), a New Yorker who was educated abroad and barely five years older than Otto Kahn.[28]

Moving over to the Speyers came at the right time for Kahn. If Kahn was to be a star, a partnership with Speyer would set him high in the firmament of international banking houses, and at slightly more than twenty-six years of age, it was nearly time for Kahn to settle down. So he took the chance of going to New York in hopes that it would lead to a partnership, preferably with the Speyer house in London, for which he had several reasons to prefer to New York. Though New York was second only to London as a world financial center, and great money could be made in America, Kahn's arrival coincided with the beginning of a long, severe depression, which dampened his chances of making a great fortune. His family ties in New York were also noticeably weak. Every German seemed to have an uncle in America, and Kahn was no exception, but his New York uncle, Edward F. Eberstadt, was not someone of highly valued associations. This Eberstadt left Germany in dishonor during the 1870s after killing a man in a duel, and shame seemed to follow his quarrelsome nature. He was twice mentioned in the *New York Times* during the 1880s — once for assaulting a man and his son in the financial district, and then for refusing to pay his tailor's bill. He also had liaisons with showgirls, one resulting in an illegitimate son.[29]

Nevertheless, Kahn's opportunities in New York were generically better than other cities to which London's capitalists were regularly dispatched, such as Buenos Aires or Hong Kong. The New World's greatest city was already a world capital of music, and for some, its multimillion dollar Metropolitan Opera House topped the city's list of cultural bragging rights. For others the city's musicality was better evidenced in the New York Philharmonic, Brooklyn Philharmonic, or the Oratio Society, and it was better heard at any one of several premier concert halls, or at one of the several less grand houses of grand opera. As with any great city, New York's cultural offerings were both flawed and fine — the debate itself was a sign of greatness. But New York measured up to greatness by another gauge as well. It received the leading talents of musical Europe. In the early 1890s alone, Tchaikovsky was present for the opening of Carnegie Hall, and Dvořák came to lead the New York Conservatory of Music. Overall, the city was strong on symphonies and opera, weak in ballet and dramatic theater, neither a complete imitation of nor yet a serious competitor to European artistic centers. The city's definition of aesthetic culture was developing on its own terms, and was uniquely modern in its embrace of breakneck speed.

Distinct among American cities, Manhattan alone had 210,000 German-born residents in 1890, and New York's ambitious *Kleindeutsch-*

Foundations

land had made the city more like Paris, Berlin, or London than Boston or Philadelphia or Chicago — in other words, more a part of Europe. It was not hard for Kahn to find his bearings in this modern cityscape. But if the German imprint cut even more deeply in New York than in London, and for that matter more in America than in England, the foreign element of upper-class German Americans had less direct consequence on the shape of so-called fashionable society. The backbone of New York's musical body was German, for instance, and perhaps on account of the fact, many among the Yankee elite in New York felt threatened by and resentful of the Germans, who appeared superior in their knowledge of high culture. And because so large a number of Jews were represented among the German-born, it is impossible to state surely how much of the ethnic rivalries been Germans and Yankees found its roots in anti-Semitism. Elite New Yorkers of non-German ancestry had this in common with the British of the same period — they thought of Germans first as Jews. What finally made New York less likable for Kahn's taste, perhaps, was its lack of the precise aristocratic traditions per se, and the fact that New York's fashionable society was also more exclusive of Jews than Kahn's crowd in London. The rush of freedom that he felt as an Englishman contracted in New York. Since America's non-Jewish elites were industrial and financial capitalists of self-sufficient means, they were less dependent upon cash infusions from Jews than the British aristocracy. America's non-Jewish elites were also less secure in their own hereditary leadership, and further conflicted by the expectations for new wealth in a new nation and democratic society. Excluding Jews helped to invent cohesion among non-Jewish millionaires, and to secure their own sense of class distinction.

Still, the rules were bent slightly on Wall Street. New York's investment banking elite in the 1890s was divided into two classes: German Jewish (founded by immigrants) and Yankee (founded by New Englanders). Both groups actually emerged similarly. They were family partnerships and private banks (as distinguished from chartered corporations), often growing from antebellum, mercantile roots toward finance. Having flourished while meeting the financial demands of the U.S. government during the Civil War, and surviving the panic of 1873, they had extensive ties abroad and were able to meet the capital requirements for American railroads. In the hierarchy of American private banking during the 1890s, Yankee or German Jewish, the Morgan partnerships were indisputably in first place, while the German Jewish houses showed greater mobility (or instability) among the leaders: Kuhn, Loeb & Co. was displacing Speyer & Co. at the top, while one rung down there were backsliders as well as climbers, such as the Seligmans and the Lehmans, respectively.[30]

When meeting the great capital needs of railroads required it, the Jewish and Yankee houses collaborated, occasionally in syndicates that drew upon their mutual access to capital abroad, but mainly by conducting their business affairs with extreme courtesy. Regardless of ethnic ancestry, the best houses of Wall Street took healthy pride in their self-regulatory, gentlemanly codes of behavior. Beyond the financial district, however, these masks went off. In clubs, resorts, ballrooms, and country enclaves, the same Gentiles with whom they conducted business daily treated New York's German Jews as *bête noires*. New York's German Jewish elite responded by forming a separate elite—"Our Crowd," as it was known—which would never feel comfortable to Otto Kahn. More German than English, a bit like a ghetto of older times, it felt too Jewish and insular to him. A religiously ambivalent man, Kahn might have felt like an outsider among "Our Crowd," even though, as in England, America's Jewish elite included apostates as well as religious traditionalists. The bigger problem for Kahn was likely that their entertainments seemed dull by comparison with what he had known in London. The Schiffs, for example, would stay home on Friday nights, see the Seligmans on Saturdays, and dine with the Loebs on Sundays. Week after week, their unvarying patterns lacked the spontaneity to which Kahn was accustomed and drawn. Furthermore, although everyone seemed to have some musical training and civic initiative—music and politics also being the pride of this crowd—Kahn likely thought that his own experience and networks were superior. That offered advantages, of course, when parents looked him over as a prospective groom for their unmarried daughters, but it was also off-putting. Kahn's self-consciously superior identification with British society made him something of a snob.

As it turned out, Kahn's banking career in New York added up to more and less than he expected. The Speyer house was muddled by internal conflict over the course of generational succession. Leadership was passing to James G. Speyer (1861–1941), one of the richest bankers in the world, who, like his younger brother, Edgar, was born in New York, raised and educated in Frankfurt, then trained with the family's European houses. Meanwhile, the New York house had no family member at its head. It was run by an able partner, William B. Bonn (1843–1910), who had joined the house during the 1870s and had good reason to feel untroubled by the prospect of one day stepping aside for a namesake of the firm, since his own brother played a similar custodial role at the Speyer house in London. That would change when Edgar and James Speyer came of age — except it worked out differently than all the rules of gentlemanly capitalism would have predicted. James Speyer returned to New York in 1885, at once clashing with Bonn. Within fifteen years James not only managed to irreconcilably alienate the most experienced partners in his firm, but he and Edgar lost their footing for cooperation with the leading bankers of Wall Street and London. Communications within the Morgan firms, for instance, expressed "the best opinion" of the Speyer houses in 1880, when the Bonn brothers' were in charge; their estimate turned decidedly unfavorable after James and Edgar rose to seniority. Perhaps the shift occurred most resolutely in 1896, when the Speyer house in London stood with rivals to challenge Morgan leadership in reorganizing the Baltimore & Ohio Railroad, but eventually the Morgan houses would no longer want to do business with the Speyers, and Pierpont Morgan would stand in the way of James's social ambitions.[31] For his own and similar reasons, Jacob Schiff at Kuhn, Loeb fell into the same fold as the Speyers' detractors. But in the short run, the dislike for James Speyer not only spelled trouble for the house; it also pushed Kahn's career toward the equivalent of limbo. Advancement was difficult and Kahn, a little fish in the big pond, was not getting any partnership offers to lead him back to London. He desperately needed a good way out, and he found it in his marriage to Addie Wolff in January 1896.

Like his father before him, Otto Kahn made a favorable match. Addie was a daughter of German-born Abraham Wolff (1839–1900), a widower with no sons and two daughters who came to New York around 1860 with enough capital to establish an importing house. Early on he shared a residence at 39 East Thirty-first Street with his cousin Samuel Wolff. Together with yet other distant cousins, they co-founded the enterprise known as Kuhn, Loeb & Co. in February 1867, where the principal partners, Abraham Kuhn and Solomon Loeb, were also brothers-in-laws, self-made men, and new to the field of banking. Kuhn had come from Bavaria in 1839, peddled for a living until he opened a store in Lafayette, Indiana, and then moved on to become a drygoods merchant and clothing manufacturer in Cincinnati. By 1850, a penni-less Loeb arrived from Worms (his visa signed by the mayor, Ferdinand Eberstadt), and he joined the Cincinnati business with Kuhn and his partners. During the Civil War they supplied blankets and uniforms to the Union Army, making enough of a profit to retire in New York—except Loeb, who at barely forty years of age was not yet ready to rest idly. Instead he brought Abraham Kuhn together with a few supportive partners and opened their private bank at 31 Nassau Street in 1867. With Kuhn dropping back from active involvement in 1869 and Sam-uel Wolff withdrawing in 1872, the day-to-day management was left mainly in the hands of Loeb, whose own sons were not yet old enough to secure generational succession.

Abraham Wolff was one of two new partners to join the firm in 1875. The other was Jacob H. Schiff, a short man who cast a long shadow and eventually took charge, while Wolff remained helpful "so far as the active direction of the firm and its policies were concerned."[32] Their daughters were childhood friends, and the house at 33 West Fifty-seventh Street in which the Wolff girls were raised had been owned by Schiff before he acquired a larger mansion on Fifth Avenue during the 1880s. Addie's father, always a step behind and below the senior part-ner, had served happily for decades, leaving Schiff to oblige loyally, if reluctantly, when in 1896 Wolff asked that his new son-in-law, Otto, become a partner in the bank.

For the time being, Otto and Addie Kahn were off to Europe on a year-long grand tour. The honeymoon gave Kahn time to catch his breath, redesign his plans, and adjust to married life. He was still a British subject and perhaps did not feel rooted in New York, while Addie was irresistibly attracted to the circles that accepted Kahn in Europe. She had been educated abroad, enjoyed Europe, and was fur-ther seduced by European charms during their honeymoon. In discuss-ing the goals of their marriage, the newlyweds decided to live perma-nently in England, although that goal would need to be delayed until Kahn had made enough money in New York, which they presumed should take about ten years. What Kahn meanwhile would have to endure as a partner at Kuhn, Loeb was not a happy prospect. He likely knew that Jacob Schiff was not bowled over by the idea of Kahn's part-nership. Three months after their marriage, Schiff entrusted his opin-ions to Ernest Cassel: "As conditions now stand I probably must follow Wolff's wishes and agree that his son-in-law, Mr. Kahn, shall enter into

Foundations

our firm, unpleasant as it may be to me. I do not want to have Wolff feel badly about it as he has always been a good friend to me. He told me he would be very unhappy if his eldest son-in-law should not become his successor."[33]

Whatever reasons stood behind Schiff's reluctance, none of the prevailing explanations are particularly convincing. Neither Kahn's religious ambivalence nor his artistic alliances make credible excuses. Jacob Schiff tolerated exactly the same in many close friends and associates, including his confidant Ernest Cassel, one of the most reputable German-born Jewish financiers in England, who had recently become the friend and financial adviser of Edward, Prince of Wales.[34] From a strictly business point of view, though, Kahn was a transplant from the Speyer house, and if he actually intended his stay in America to be temporary, there were several more reasons for Schiff to resist his partnership. Inasmuch as William Bonn was one of Schiff's favorite friends, Kuhn, Loeb's senior had heard enough over the years to conclude that the decisions of Bonn and two other partners to eventually quit the house were "due to James Speyer's deficiencies of character." Because Schiff did not like Speyer, Kahn's association with that house was one strike against him, but Kuhn, Loeb's senior might also have questioned whether it was wise to train and trade secrets with a partner who might return to Europe, perhaps to work with the Speyer house after all.[35] In any case, Kuhn, Loeb had no foreign branches to which Kahn might be dispatched, and there was already one partner who was only committed to the firm for the short term: James Loeb intended to leave banking immediately after the death of his father, Solomon Loeb.[36]

But Schiff also possessed a deeper rivalry, going back to his hometown of Frankfurt, that had major implications for his opinion of Otto Kahn. In everything about his career, experience, and associates, Jacob Schiff wanted to claim a destiny appropriate to his family's pedigree. He was the proud descendant of a distinguished rabbinical family, with roots that were older than the Speyers and older than the Rothschilds, who neighbored the Schiffs in the old Judengasse of Frankfurt in the eighteenth century. The Rothschilds and the Speyers had since become the wealthier families; still, Schiff thought his was the better stock, especially with regard to Judaic commitments. Against enormous odds, New York had given him a chance to close the gap in terms of financial distinction. William Bonn, another son of Frankfurt, had aided Schiff's move in that direction by opening his home to the new

Englishman in New York: Kahn on horseback, ca. 1896.
(© Museum of the City of New York)

immigrant and then helping him found a brokerage firm in 1867. By
1872, Schiff was already an American citizen, a member of the New
York Chamber of Commerce, and soon on to other things. Making his
way back to Germany, a job opened for him at the London & Hanseatic
Bank in Hamburg, where he would represent M. M. Warburg & Co.
briefly in 1873, until familial responsibilities called him back to Frank-

furt. Next, Abraham Kuhn presented him the opportunity to join Kuhn, Loeb. Schiff accepted, entered the firm on January 1, 1875, and a few months later married Therese Loeb, a daughter of Solomon Loeb and niece of Abraham Kuhn.

Although Solomon Loeb remained senior for another decade, Schiff began to take charge long before becoming senior himself in 1885. Along the way, Kuhn, Loeb advanced toward a dominant position in railroad financing. On that even Pierpont Morgan would agree, but while the meteoric rise of Kuhn, Loeb under Jacob Schiff may be indisputable, there have been some persistent questions concerning exactly how he managed to pilot the relatively obscure firm to such dominance so quickly. One compelling clue to the answer was left among the notes of Cyrus Adler, Schiff's friend and authorized biographer: "Schiff was concerned with the financing of nearly all the important railroads in the East, which were not personally owned by families." In other words, he turned the weaknesses of others into Kuhn, Loeb's strength. In addition, Schiff forged friendships and cultivated business alliances with important European financiers who were themselves largely independent, that is, not already committed to the Morgans, Speyers, or other established houses. These associations included Eduard Noetzlin of the Banque de Paris et des Pays Bas, and Robert Fleming of the American Scottish Investment Company, a pioneer of investment trusts. The most valued of his contacts in England was Ernest Cassel, with whom Schiff corresponded on a weekly basis for forty years and who was one of his dearest friends. Schiff became their expert on American affairs, and Kuhn, Loeb became the bankers behind the Louisville & Nashville and the Pennsylvania railroads, as well as the Texas & St. Louis in the Cotton Belt (later part of the St. Louis Southwestern).[37]

In time Schiff's ambition for his own dynasty would affect Kahn most directly, for Kuhn, Loeb was coming to another generational conjunction when Kahn arrived. As of 1891, Schiff and Abraham Wolff were the only really active partners, and by mid-decade new plans and options for the future began to unfold. In 1894, James Loeb came on board reluctantly as the one of Solomon Loeb's two sons to enter banking (brother Morris escaped into the world of academe as a chemist). Solomon Loeb's nephew Louis A. Heinshiemer was also elevated to partner in 1894; he had worked for the firm since the late 1870s and was getting on in years. Meanwhile, Jacob Schiff went about grooming his own only son, Mortimer, for entry into and eventual leadership of

Kuhn, Loeb. When he complained about giving a partnership to Otto Kahn in 1896, Schiff added, "As soon as Mortie will be a few years older I hope to be able to retire from active work. . . . I also hope that Morti will get the whole business into his hands." Mortimer Schiff joined the partnership on January 1, 1900, by which time two marital alliances had been forged between Kuhn, Loeb and the Warburgs, the most distinguished banking family of Hamburg. Jacob Schiff's daughter Frieda married Felix M. Warburg on March 19, 1895, and after their honeymoon Felix entered his father-in-law's firm. Addie Wolff was one of the bridesmaids at the wedding — where Paul Warburg, best man and older brother of the groom, met Nina Loeb, the maid of honor and youngest daughter of Solomon Loeb (also Jacob Schiff's sister-in-law). Paul Warburg and Nina Loeb married the next year, and, after living abroad for a few more years, Paul Warburg became a Kuhn, Loeb partner in 1901.[38]

Sized up against Schiff's other pickings, Otto Kahn was a familial outsider and a relative newcomer to the wealth elite. He could not be expected to bring comparable *yichos* (Yiddish for hereditary distinction) to a firm that sorely needed its dynastic traditions strengthened if it was to be one of the leaders of international finance by the terms decided in the nineteenth century. Although many respected German Jewish banking houses of New York had founders who started as penniless immigrants and peddlers, there was another group, represented principally by August Belmont Company, as well as Speyer & Co., which had begun as extensions of established European concerns. Jacob Schiff could be classified somewhere between these two groups. Spared the indignity of peddling and storekeeping, he had sufficient capital, connections, and ambition to enter finance immediately. He possessed the talent to be a great banker, but initially lacked the wealth and status of a Speyer or Rothschild, and he headed a firm that had come relatively recently from these other, more humble origins. Jacob Schiff was not an upstart, but while he was on the rise he looked down on Otto Kahn, whose ancestral distinction was mostly matrilineal and therefore inferior not only to Schiff's, but also to that of the Warburg patrilineage, which predated the seventeenth century. In any event, if Otto Kahn did not quite add up to what Schiff wanted in a partner, he did have enough *yichos* and *Sittlichkeit* to avoid the rags and go straight to the riches. Besides, in America, there were distinct advantages to being a self-made aristocrat.[39]

Foundations

CHAPTER TWO

Metropolitan Scenes in the Harriman Cycle

On the rise in what Maxim Gorky would call the "City of Mammon" (1906) — the New World metropolis — Otto Kahn cruised toward special achievements in a time of booming prosperity. The long economic downswing that began in 1893 suddenly turned upward in 1897, catapulting the fortunes of great financiers and industrialists, but Kahn's ambitions were also served as fully by other factors. For one, Kahn had come to New York via England, possessing a command of the English language and able to use his British credentials as uniquely "acceptable social passports"[1] for crossing the boundaries of fashionable society. A few cognitive connections from his boyhood in Mannheim would help his adjustment to Manhattan as well. Though Kahn's hometown did not front on the ocean or open to the world and stand as the gateway to a continent, Mannheim was a port town, and its parallel streets were named with letters and numbers, as were the streets of New York. As important as anything, the Anglo-German Otto Kahn possessed great sensibilities when it came to understanding how New York was embedded in transatlantic cosmopolitanism. The American city best able to reference, reject, translate, emulate, and contrast Old World influences, New York was also rising to compete, cooperate, and integrate with the economic and artistic life of Europe's capitals.

Prosperity and self-possession went hand in hand for New York's wealthiest elites, and to some extent that dictated why, by the end of the 1890s, Kahn's father-in-law wasted no time in building Cedar Court, a country residence to crown his career. Wolff began assembling the land in Morristown in 1897, around the time his first grandchild, Maude Emily, was born to Otto and Addie Kahn in July. The well-known New York architectural firm of Carrère and Hastings designed its buildings and gardens, drawing up a pair of adjoined villas that Wolff wanted to accommodate himself, his two daughters, their husbands, and all his future grandchildren. By the turn of the century, his family was living at the new estate, and Wolff could feel that his domestic and business households were both settled into pleasant routines. Then, on October 1, 1900, having spent the morning at Kuhn, Loeb, he attended a luncheon organized by Schiff for Lord Revelstoke and a group of financial people before catching the four o'clock express for Morristown, where he dined at home and suffered a fatal heart attack. A few days later, his funeral at Manhattan's prestigious Temple Emanu-El drew 2,000 people, including orphans from asylums to which Wolff had contributed. Nearly the whole of Wolff's estate was willed in trusts to his daughters and their children, some yet to be born. Kahn was named a trustee but inherited only the privileges of being Addie's husband and a partner in Kuhn, Loeb, where he still served at the pleasure of Jacob Schiff.[2]

What Kahn lacked at the banking house, he could not expect. He would never be a Schiff or a Warburg or a favorite of the senior partner. His one great advantage was a camaraderie with E. H. Harriman (1848–1909), a new client and ally, whose business made great money and not a little trouble for the firm. The opening of the twentieth century brought an unprecedented wave of industrial consolidations; it was in this period that Harriman became stunningly famous for rebuilding the Union Pacific Railroad, uniting its system with the Southern Pacific, then catalyzing a stock panic on Wall Street. He also cofounded the allegedly monopolistic Northern Securities Company and exercised power in numerous other rail concerns, so that it seemed overnight a national railroad empire had come into being under his control. Meanwhile, Harriman rather dangerously courted hostility from businessmen and politicians who maligned his methods and manners. But Otto Kahn defended Harriman and more readily discerned his admirable qualities. Those perceptions, along with how Kahn acted upon them, were among the major reasons for Kahn's success on Wall Street.

In the absence of diaries or memoirs by either man, one important source illuminates them both in Kahn's voice. After Harriman's death,

Otto and Addie Kahn with their first-born child, Maude, ca. 1898. (Private collection)

Kahn molded his mentor's image in a speech before the Finance Forum in New York on January 25, 1911, which he later printed and circulated as a pamphlet and included in two volumes of his own collected writings. The text helped to seed a historiography of appreciation for Harriman, deftly furbishing him with the image of a flawed hero and genius instead of a reckless robber baron.[3] However, Kahn's speech also signaled the mature beginnings of his own public relations and methods of impression management. And, as important, Kahn's memories of Harriman offered vivid hints of Otto Kahn himself, whose stride alongside Harriman also suggests a special arrangement in the transition to Kahn's middle years as a banker-patron.

As the new year of 1897 approached, Kahn and Felix Warburg were slated to join Kuhn, Loeb & Co., while Harriman, a man of Schiff's age but little previous acquaintance, had recently crept into the firm's highest affairs, appearing to disrupt its work in reorganizing the Union Pacific Railroad (UP), a colossal business. Begun as a mixed promotion of private and public interests, the UP met the Central Pacific in 1869, its last spike of construction giving America one of the more defining pictures of manifest destiny, if not postbellum unity, as the rail system now reached California. The UP also turned out to be the shame of the Gilded Age, a prototype of plundering, and the playground of Jay Gould, which rightly or wrongly made a compelling story of capitalist rascals and thieves but also a target for corporate reform impulses. By the depression of 1893–97, however, the whole dreary state of the U.S. rail sector seemed evident in the condition of the UP, as the corporation dropped into receivership and separate receivers took major branches out of the system. No reorganization plan short of foreclosure was in the offing by mid-1895, although its bonded debt to the federal government ($52 million with back interest) would begin to mature in November 1895. As one proposal after another faltered and refunding bills stood mired in Congress, Jacob Schiff was asked to take on the reorganization that autumn.[4]

Out of caution and courtesy, Schiff first paid a call of competitive civility upon J. P. Morgan, a member of the earlier reorganization committee, to be sure that Morgan did not have plans of his own for the railroad. Schiff then canceled a trip to Mexico and went to work on the UP, tasting the potential for great exaltation should he succeed. The difference between this and his everyday business was deep-felt. "Meeting the continuing financial requirements of enterprises was profitable and important business," according to historian Vincent Carosso, but "it did not garner the prestige and esteem of extraordinary accomplishments," which in turn attracted wide public notice as well as better clients.[5] Saving the UP was an uncommon opportunity, and Schiff savored its blue-ribbon potential. By October 1895 he had a plan that would satisfy a majority of shareholding interests, whereby a syndicate led by Kuhn, Loeb would provide $15 million for capital restructuring in exchange for $6 million of preferred stock. The remaining obstacle was Washington, and the government's assent would have to wait through the election of 1896, but the end seemed near in December, as the legislature appeared ready to take a cash bid in the range of $30 million to foreclose the debt. Optimistic over the likelihood of a cash settlement with the government, Schiff crowed about his firm's prowess, writing privately, "We have — what I believe has never been done before in financial history — secured within three days subscriptions for practically the entire $40,000,000 which we shall require in case we shall have to buy the property under a Government foreclosure."[6]

After more than a year of steady work, Schiff remained guardedly braced for success. The caution proved wise because, toward the end of 1896, he somehow detected a breeze of trouble. Not even Schiff could remember for sure what had made him guess that someone was interfering — whether it was the petty grievance of a minor shareholder, the quiver in a congressman's confidence, or an adverse comment in the press. Yet something in the air tipped him toward concern, and his hunch sent Schiff directly to Pierpont Morgan, inquiring whether he had turned against Kuhn, Loeb's plan. Morgan vowed he had not and promised to help pinpoint the source of trouble. A few weeks later Morgan reported, "It's that little fellow Harriman," whom Schiff barely knew. They had met as early as 1884, briefly, under favorable circumstances, when Harriman won approval from the Amsterdam bankers who spoke for Dutch investors in the Illinois Central. Like most of Wall Street, including Kahn (who first laid eyes on Harriman in 1894), Schiff knew only of Harriman's "moderate degree of importance" as chair of the finance committee for the Illinois Central Railroad, whose "credit was of the highest." Pierpont Morgan, on the other hand, knew Harriman better. They were both original box owners at the Metropolitan Opera and occasionally had disagreeable encounters in business. After Harriman wrested a railroad away from Morgan control in 1886, Morgan called it "the Dubuque, Sioux City steal." When they nearly tussled again during the reorganization of the Erie Railroad in 1894, cables between the Morgan houses in London and New York sounded cries of a new battle approaching: "Harriman still very bitter will resort to any means," "anticipate active hostility. He is a great fighter . . . we must beat Harriman." Harriman's opposition to the Erie matter faded, but Morgan's opinion of him did not. "Watch him carefully," he warned Schiff.[7]

Reasonably suspicious, if not fully prepared for the iron will of his opponent, Schiff arranged to meet with his new competitor and soon learned that Harriman had the upper hand. He could beat Schiff with a bid backed by Illinois Central bonds at 3 percent—a full point lower than rates available to Kuhn, Loeb. Schiff proceeded to sort out the tangle, finding that Harriman's intention was to take the UP at any price, but he was also perceptibly amenable to doing business with Kuhn, Loeb. By February, Harriman agreed to let the reorganization committee proceed in exchange for Schiff's promise to give him a future in the company's management. Their compromise marked the beginning of a new tack. As Kahn remembered it, Harriman would start coming to Kuhn, Loeb with proposals for other business within a few months. More significant, by year's end, when the board of directors of the reconstituted UP convened, E. H. Harriman and Otto Kahn were the two conspicuous newcomers to a group where almost everyone else was previously connected with the property.[8]

What happened during the next ten years was unexpected for Harriman, modestly foreseeable for Kuhn, Loeb & Co., and not wholly unexpected for Kahn. Harriman, a late bloomer, had displayed nothing in his previous fifty years to enable anyone to predict his emergence as the "new colossus of roads" during the final dash of his career. By 1897, however, Kuhn, Loeb was America's leading specialist in railroad securities and the principal banker for the Pennsylvania Railroad and the Union Pacific, as well as several rail properties in which the Gould estate held substantial interests. Kahn, in turn, was very ambitiously situated at the center of Kuhn, Loeb's work.[9] Yet it is impossible to say exactly why Jacob Schiff put one brand-new junior on the Union Pacific board rather than another such as Felix Warburg, who had also recently become a partner. Perhaps Kahn's abilities in banking were better evident from the start. Perhaps Abraham Wolff wanted to see Kahn installed as a railroad director, so Wolff could mentor him toward succession, both as a railroad financier and a lesser partner to Jacob Schiff. It was nonetheless a test of competence for Kahn, with the senior Schiff also sitting on the board in direct supervision and always assessing whether the new junior was up to the job. On the other hand, Schiff could use Kahn to gain some distance from Harriman, a pesky and as yet unproven financial associate, for it did not take long for people to notice what Kahn described as Harriman's "undisguised authoritativeness." Since Jacob Schiff was himself given to mood swings and fits of temper, it left Kahn caught between the two difficult personalities.

Kahn protected himself by pleasing the client and finding harmony within the discordance.[10]

Though Kahn and Harriman were roughly twenty years apart in age, they enjoyed several similarities. Kahn stood only three inches taller than the 5'4" Harriman, making them rather unlikely giants. They had both left school before graduating, married well, and found their first appointments as railroad directors through the aid of their fathers-in-law. They both needed constant stimulation, expended relentless energy, and, during their dozen years of close association (until Harriman's death in September 1909), moved from comparative obscurity to distinct fame. There the resemblance would seem to end. All the suavity that Kahn possessed and prized was lacking in Harriman, and few if any of the artistic elements that so enlivened Kahn were obvious in Harriman. One confounding factor, though, brought them to a common place: they shared the otherness of outsiders and newcomers.

The sociability that governed New York's high society and America's plutocracy put Otto Kahn and E. H. Harriman noticeably in between. Kahn was an odd combination in the non-American Jew, whose German *bildung* blended with the style of an English gentleman. Because Harriman, however, had an ancestry perfectly suited for either antebellum or Gilded Age circles, it should have insured his inclusion in New York's high society. His maternal lineage listed Stuyvesants, Bleeckers, and Neilsons—all founding families of Dutch and English settlements on the east and west of the Hudson River. His paternal grandfather came from London in 1795, prospered in the general commission business, and owned a residence on Broome Street near Broadway, where much of New York's wealth congregated in the early nineteenth century. Harriman also made a good marriage in wedding Mary Averell, daughter of a respectable family from the St. Lawrence region. All the same, two twists of fate reduced the estate into which Harriman was born. The first, a fire, if not the panic of 1837, destroyed a good amount of the family's property and wealth. Second, Harriman was born on the poor side of what remained a family with wealth. His father's ministry was the odd financial failure among Episcopalians, and Harriman's childhood poverty left him to make the family fortune anew. His final estate of $70 million was thus not strictly parvenu, but rather a fortune in recovery.[11]

Harriman's particulars would be less interesting if he had been strictly a newcomer or an absolute outcast, but his Wall Street career also started with more ambition than prestige, and that would forever mark him. After public schooling in Jersey City, he attended the Trinity School in Manhattan on a clergyman's discount, only to leave without graduating in 1862. When he headed to work on Wall Street, he started as an office boy, then advanced to a "pad-shover" or message clerk, before borrowed funds from his uncle, the merchant Oliver Harriman, brought him a seat on the New York Stock Exchange and his own brokerage house in 1870. Early on, Harriman earned a two-dollar commission with every hundred-share deal, and picked up the derisive pedigree of a "two-dollar broker." But bigger deals and clients of good quality followed. Along the way he made money for some of the more socially prominent investors, including Stuyvesant Fish. Fish was a distant cousin who would seem to have seen Harriman for what he was: a poor relation due some social acceptance as a birthright, or because his money-making skills could temporarily cloud over certain traits that made him less than completely equal. In other words, Harriman was admissible enough for the Union Club and the Racquet Club, but not completely suitable for the *beau monde*.

These preconditions placed Harriman at a point of flux and tension where polite, fashionable, and smart circles were changing. He fell in with the right people, their clubs and summer resorts, yet Harriman ultimately received the subtle snub of a type more obvious to the one who spurns than the one rebuffed. He never quite made it among the crème de la crème, whether it be New York's nouveau riche (the fashionable set of the Vanderbilt-Astor vintage) or older circles of wealth (the polite society of Washington Square, Hudson Valley, and the like). The nuance was relevant for what Otto Kahn encountered among New York's monied elites. As many millionaires as New York produced (an estimated 1,368 in 1892), money clustered in social enclaves — at times overlapping, at times exclusive, but always competing and changing. Money or birthright alone could not buy entry into polite New York, fashionable balls, or the smart set. Indeed, one could be disqualified for having too much money or not enough, for being recent money, a fortune still in the making, or, as the reigning *grande dame* declared, for being "vulgar in speech and appearance." And being Jewish, of course, provided the clearest grounds for exclusion. These were the most cohesive values in the amalgam of New York's plutocracy during the entire nineteenth century.[12]

What likely kept Harriman from rising to the top was less his self-proclaimed lack of ambition for social success than the implicit rejection of him by the social elites, which came as he tended to break many rules of gentlemanly capitalism. While financiers of the higher ranks strived for a community of interest, Harriman thrived, Kahn said, on the "harmony of conflicting interests." He repeatedly clashed with the better families and men of the monied elite, including Stuyvesant Fish, his boss at the Illinois Central, who had opened many doors to New York's social life for him, yet had difficulty accepting Harriman as a peer. Harriman's business encounters with Morgan would not help him socially, either. Neither would his protestations at the Metropolitan Opera when, along with Jay Gould, he was one of ten stockholders who legally challenged the amount of their assessment, and kept using their boxes while they refused to pay. Legally correct but socially inept, Harriman was labeled a welcher. The former "pad-shover" was not much better than a peddler with millions. This does not mean a Harriman daughter ever went without a debutante's ball, or that anything less than self-assurance showed when Harriman claimed to lack real interest in fashionable society. But neither does it mean that fashionable society had much interest in welcoming Harriman himself to *beau monde* New York, if only because he was missing, in Kahn's words, both "the faculty of attracting men in general" and "the faculty of placing veneer over his domineering traits."[13]

Never one to gossip about such sensitive matters for the record, Kahn did report that late in Harriman's life, he "used to say that the fact that he had been born and bred in New York . . . had mitigated against his recognition." Kahn rationalized that "it was the old story of the prophet having little honor in his own country." He also would see Harriman lacking "eloquence . . . tact or magnetism" — some of the very traits, of course, that Kahn used so effectively among New Yorkers of wealth. And although Kahn did sometimes "plead with him" to try "less combative, more gentle methods," he eventually realized that Harriman was "stiff-necked to a fault," a man "purposely creating obstacles for himself," quite probably "for the mere sport of overcoming them." That brought Kahn to think of Harriman as he might think of an artist. Drawing an analogy between the client and "what Whistler called 'the gentle art of making enemies' " was Kahn's way of evoking an ideal of inner necessity in Harriman, the man whom Kahn remembered as saying, "I can work only in my own way. I cannot make myself different, nor act in a way foreign to me. . . . I simply cannot achieve anything if I try to compromise with my nature."[14] Kahn likened the soul of the artist to that of the capitalist-entrepreneur—and found in Harriman a mission like Kahn's own. Maestros and masters, artists and capitalists, were neither completely different nor autonomous; genius was genius in Kahn's double mirror. A later biographer would admire Harriman as the artist of details rearranged. In Kahn's prose of praise, it was the "boldness and accuracy of his conceptions and visions" that helped Harriman accomplish "things that seemed utterly improbably of realization." He was "a born fighting genius" who "planned for a generation ahead."[15]

Aside from admiration, another of Kahn's personal strengths was one that worked particularly well with Harriman. While Kahn's abilities as a listener and negotiator proved useful both in business and the arts generally, his ability to follow partly articulated ideas was crucial in his dealings with Harriman, whose excitable mind was, by most accounts, given to lateral thinking and leaps of verbal expression. Day to day, face to face, and in written correspondence, Harriman rambled incessantly. Speaking beyond the speed of a telegraph, he compressed complexities. "His mind worked so rapidly," Kahn wrote, "his thoughts crowded upon him at such a rate, that his words would not come anywhere near keeping pace with the workings of his brain. . . . He raced for the points he wanted to make, taking short cuts of thought and expression, expecting the bewildered listener to keep up with the chase. . . . Not infrequently he was but half understood, or not at all understood, by those who had not, through prolonged association, acquired the faculty of reading his mental shorthand." Maybe music prepared Kahn to follow the variations as Harriman thought aloud. But as he kept up— translating the forceful *and* incomprehensible Harriman, Kahn helped make him intellectually accessible. In its most practical application, Kahn's assistance would make the client's conversational exchanges easier for Jacob Schiff, who was also struggling with deafness.[16]

Both Kahn and Schiff grew to appreciate Harriman's prophetic genius, which also meant that Kahn could later look back with superiority when counting himself among those few who understood the sense in Harriman's "pretty wild talk" for 1897–98, after a tour of the UP system filled him with forecasts for prosperity. At the time, Harriman wanted $25 million to reunite, massively rebuild, and improve the UP system. He also personally bought "all of the UP common stock that he could accumulate," leaving doubtful critics to think him a reckless speculator, because the stock "was considered to have little intrinsic value" so soon after the reorganization. Even Kahn "took it with a large grain of salt."[17] But as Harriman's ideas turned out to be valid, the excitement that followed was comparable to what Kahn would feel for the artistic avant-garde. Being a good Carlylian (with regard to heroes) and aesthetic elitist (in understanding how great art invariably breaks traditions), Kahn elevated the prophet of prosperity and America's railroad revival to the heaven of culture-heroes. A pride similar to finding and ordaining Harriman (or the difficult modern) would reappear, for instance, when Kahn consecrated the American cultural scene with the arts of European modernism. Meanwhile, the negotiating rules that Kahn learned from Harriman would become modal representations, if not always models in the higher narrative of how Kahn dealt with artistic temperaments and the capitalist spirit. These lessons, moderately more advanced than the stamp-licking stories of his apprenticeship, could be as simple as knowing it was better to argue a point in the cool of a summer morning rather than the heat of the afternoon. At the next level, Kahn learned about winning, improbable odds, biding time, and battle will. Kahn could play conciliator to the conqueror, junior to the senior, making a name for himself in various supporting and leading roles.

If the extent to which Harriman worked miracles on the UP has been both mythologized and revised, there is no mistaking the importance of his career to Otto Kahn or to the history both of Kuhn, Loeb and Wall Street. Harriman took command of the UP, pouring all his energies and intellect into a system that was actually in good shape to start, and as good as any other road in the West. The new owners had gotten a bargain, not a steal. In order to succeed, they needed to upgrade, modernize, and reassemble everything, optimize costs, and redirect operations toward greater hauls at lower rates. In Harriman's opinion, they also needed to control the Chicago, Burlington, & Quincy (CB&Q) — for its access to the East through Chicago. The obstacle was James J. Hill and J. P. Morgan, who acquired the CB&Q under the auspices of the Northern Pacific Railroad, then refused to share it, which in 1901 led Harriman and Schiff to initiate combat — going for control of the Northern Pacific itself. They began quietly buying enormous quantities of Northern Pacific stock, along the way stirring up short-speculators who were unaware of the plot but attracted by the stock's rising price. When Hill learned what was happening, a wave of retaliatory buying commenced under Morgan's guidance, until the price per share rose from $90 to $1,000 and the stock was cornered. With none left to buy, the short-traders were unable to cover themselves. May 9 brought a wild panic. Speculators liquidated collateral stocks in the largest single-day decline on Wall Street since 1803, shaking the stability of American securities trading while also bringing ghosts of the Gilded Age back to life in the new century.

In the end, Harriman failed to gain control, because Schiff tactfully stopped his drive at the eleventh hour. When the so-called "Battle of the Giants" ceased, the combatants rescued victimized brokers, then settled their own differences through a merger, forming the Northern Securities Company on November 12, 1901. During the final phase of its organization, a financial journalist offered a passing glimpse of Otto Kahn, one of the "lieutenants" who successfully carried out "the yeoman work of the negotiations." Hardly prescient of Kahn's future fame, it was an accurate statement of his subordinate status, for junior partners at Kuhn, Loeb mainly stayed in Schiff's shadow during these eventful years. The senior decided all serious matters. He faced the press, making periodic comments about the financial outlook in Europe and United States. He also answered any difficult questions of accountability, which arose when Harriman went head-to-head with James Hill, and with many mounting criticisms of Wall Street's money power. When a 1905 joint committee of the Senate and Assembly of the State of New York convened to publicly question the ethics of Wall Street and the control exercised by investment bankers, Schiff and Harriman testified at the hearings, not Otto Kahn (although his name appeared in the record inconsequentially, and sometimes mistakenly as "Kuhn").[18]

Subordinate status was a trade-off. It allowed junior partners the freedom to start families and move into new residences. They went about establishing themselves in civic, charitable, social, and cultural activities. But these were not leisurely times. All Kuhn, Loeb partners were undeniably engrossed in the firm's snowballing business, making millions in the process. The fees and commissions to the house ranged between 2.5 and 10 percent of the underwriting, depending on the ease or difficulty of an offering. As the principal banker for some of the largest railroad systems in America, Schiff's house was a great one for New York, enjoying close relations to the National City Bank and the Rockefeller interests along with Harriman, relations that were as financially potent as they were publicly suspect. Kuhn, Loeb was soon considered to be one of six alleged key players in the interlocking concentration of American banking power. By May 1903 the partnership had moved its headquarters to the upper floors of 52 William Street, at the corner of Pine Street. A new, wholly owned, twenty-story structure that was tall for its time, the building was at once both emblematic of the bank's standing while also much larger than the bank's current staffing needs. Most of the building was leased to tenants, including two floors to Guthrie, Cravath and Henderson, the law firm that represented nearly all of Kuhn, Loeb's business.

Meanwhile, aside from its work with the Union Pacific, the bank was financing the Pennsylvania Railroad system with more than $200 million over the period 1901–5, enabling that entity to construct tunnels under the Hudson and East Rivers, expand the lines on Long Island, and otherwise modernize. In addition to the Missouri Pacific and Baltimore & Ohio, among many more steam rail interests, Kuhn, Loeb was also active in the development of traction enterprises (or street railways). In 1902 it underwrote the $30 million, newly formed Metropolitan Securities Company, an investment trust controlling most of the surface rail transit in Manhattan and the Bronx; the trust collapsed calamitously in 1907, leaving an embarrassed Schiff to say that his own conscientious scruples had been undermined by the lack thereof on the part of the company's dominant figures, Thomas Fortune Ryan and William C. Whitney. More laudable for the house, however, was Kuhn, Loeb's role in attracting Americans to foreign investment. It sold German (1900) and Swedish (1904) treasury bills in the United States, and also gained worldwide acclaim for financing Japan. Discussions of the latter began in London during Japan's war with Russia and would entail the distribution of issues on both sides of the Atlantic, including a $75 million war bond in the United States—the first American loan to Japan. As for industrial financing, Kuhn, Loeb's services were available to Westinghouse, the American Smelters' Securities Company, and many syndicates led by others, including the Morgan-led U.S. Steel consolidation (1901).[19]

Kahn's assignments among the myriad transactions were primarily clustered in the rail sector, although he also served as a trustee of the Equitable Trust Company and was the partner-in-charge of Kuhn, Loeb's interests with regard to New York's electrified Third Avenue Railway. Often, his work at Kuhn, Loeb was demanding enough for him to stay overnight in the city—at the family-owned townhouse on Sixty-eighth Street—yet not so busy or exhausting to leave him without the time or energy to go out in the evenings. The weekends, however, were mainly devoted to his children in Morristown, and one month after the death of Abraham Wolff, Addie was pregnant with their second child, Margaret Dorothy, born on July 4, 1901. The first son, Gilbert Sherburne, arrived on July 18, 1903, and the youngest of the brood, Roger Wolff, was born on October 19, 1907.

Over the years, family life (and domestic staff) shifted its location at intervals. Sometimes this meant staying at the townhouse in New York, and one such occasion bore unexpected consequences on February 3, 1905, when fire destroyed a wing of the Morristown residence. Otherwise, the family regularly spent summers in the Adirondacks or Maine, with Kahn coming along for part of the vacations. As the children became old enough for foreign travel, Addie took them to Europe, where they would join their father, who was regularly spending up to one-third of any year in Europe for business. None of the children suffered from health problems, but before Kahn turned forty a string of other significant people in his family died. Back in Germany, the death of his eldest brother in 1904 was followed by the death of his father in 1905 and his mother in 1906. In addition, Addie's sister Clara died from complications in childbirth in August 1903, leaving no heirs other than her husband, Henri P. Wertheim. Adding Abraham Wolff into the sequence, it would seem that while this cycle of deaths intersected with Kahn's own experience in fatherhood, pushing him further along toward the position of a familial patriarch, it was all occurring on a timetable quite inconsistent with events at Kuhn, Loeb, where playing the subordinate ran contrary to Kahn's ambitions. His first chance for individual renown arrived by a complicated route, through the Metropolitan Opera rather than Kuhn, Loeb.[20]

· · · ·

INTO THE LIMELIGHT

In no other part of his world was Kahn more characteristically at home without actually belonging. The Metropolitan Opera was a house divided, officially, between the owners of the building and the several

New York's Metropolitan Opera, at Broadway between Thirty-ninth and Fortieth Streets. (Library of Congress)

operating companies that over the years leased the house and presented the performances. Unofficially, other divisions evidenced a larger domain, where critics and widely held convictions could branch out in various directions or get gnarled in distinct controversies concerning singers, conductors, and audiences, as well as the repertory and the hall itself. Other divisions were ethnic. Historically, there were Jews among the talent and management of the operating company, none among the owners of the house, and none among the owners of the operating company.

That changed in 1903, when an ethnically mixed board of directors for the operating company came into being as the Conried Metropolitan Opera Company (CMOC). It was the brainchild of Henry Morgenthau, another Mannheim-born Manhattanite who helped the Austrian-born impresario Heinrich Conried secure a new lease on the opera house. Conried initially found enthusiastic backing from the likes of Jacob Schiff, Daniel Guggenheim, and Henry Ickelheimer. Yet Morgenthau knew this roster stood little chance of winning the Metropolitan's lease—it sounded too German and Jewish. So he marshaled assistance from a scion of American-bred capitalism, James Hazen Hyde, one of the "younger social leaders," who attracted sponsorship from members of the Vanderbilt, Goelet, Whitney, and similar clans. Hyde also invited Otto Kahn to sit on the founding board of the CMOC, which opened the opera house on November 23, 1903, with *Rigoletto*, featuring the debut of tenor Enrico Caruso. Hyde then proceeded to consolidate control. He eventually alienated Morgenthau, who resigned, leaving Kahn and later James Speyer as the only Jews among the directors of the operating company.[21]

Straightaway, Kahn went on the executive committee, stepping into several new roles at once. Neither the protégé of an elder man nor socially corralled within the boundaries of the German Jewish crowd, he raced toward the fulfillment of *Bildung* in a modern frame, self-consciously mixing with a new generation of wealthy New Yorkers who were cosmopolitan, serious about aesthetics, and challenging the plutocratic imbalance at the opera house, though with hands that were hardly free. Numerous rights were retained by the Metropolitan Opera Real Estate Company (MORECO), which owned the house. For every New York season—running from November to March—MORECO included a demand for "all first-class artists," and a limit on the number of German operas (apparently having grown tired of the cerebral demands of Wagner). There was also an ironclad claim to the ring of boxes—the Diamond Horseshoe—where bejeweled high society reigned in immensely publicized, self-involved performances of their own.[22]

The importance of Hyde to Kahn's success cannot be easily glossed. Hyde's father had founded the Equitable Life Assurance Company (ELAS), a leading institution for savings and investment, and when his father died in 1899, the twenty-three-year-old Hyde became the company's first vice president. He had inherited the controlling block of ELAS stock, which was held in trust until he reached the age of thirty, but the legacy allowed Hyde to make a meteoric rise in the financial world. Becoming chairman of the Equitable's executive committee and finance committee in 1902, he wielded considerable power over a complex investment portfolio, and he became acquainted with Kahn through numerous Wall Street syndicates and directorships. Hyde was wealthier, younger, and newer to business culture than Kahn, but he was also a kindred spirit with regard to aesthetic culture. For every bit of the cultured Edwardian in Kahn there was a match of Harvard-educated

Francophilia in Hyde. They were like-minded opera enthusiasts and serious art lovers who adored Paris and the theater and were out to fashion an enclave of high society, "The Smart Set," which would think of itself as neither stupid nor banal. But their bonding was strengthened by yet another factor, for Kahn and Hyde had recently each become heirs of different sorts: Hyde had the legacy coming in trust from his father's death, and Kahn was trustee for Abraham Wolff's estate. Hyde also enlarged the social sphere of Mr. and Mrs. Otto H. Kahn.[23]

Then, no sooner than the second opera season (1904–5), Kahn's new friend headed for a downfall. What began as a personal, internal struggle between Hyde and the ELAS president expanded into a contest among millionaire capitalists for control of the company's assets — totaling more than $400 million. It soon developed into a public scandal, as blazing newspaper headlines and cruel cartoons accompanied the disclosure of questionable practices, including the allegation that in January 1905 Hyde reached into the Equitable till to pay for his fancy-dress "Versailles" ball at Sherry's Restaurant. (Addie Kahn, but not Otto, was on the guest list for Hyde's costume spectacle.) Even before becoming a scandal, and perhaps one of the factors facilitating the eruption of a public investigation, the party made Hyde a victim of his own success. When *Metropolitan Magazine* christened Hyde's party "the most memorable ball given in the memory of living New Yorkers," *grande dame* Caroline Astor felt he had eclipsed the reputation of her own ball of that same month. Hyde himself suspected that Kate Davis Pulitzer had set the sparks, because she had not been invited. How far such rivalry went in accelerating Hyde's troubles has long been the stuff of society gossip, but in any case Hyde's blurry distinction between private and corporate wealth began to make headlines in conjunction with the struggle to control the Equitable. It all erupted in an investigation of the entire insurance industry and Wall Street, leading to a series of comprehensive reforms that marked the dawn of a new regulatory era.[24]

Besides leaving a vivid fable of millionaire splendor and a blueprint or governmental supervision, the whole episode scorched James Hyde, who felt his character and lifestyle egregiously attacked. Making matters more interesting, he also felt himself the victim of duplicity at the hand of E. H. Harriman, who was one of several parties contending for control of the Equitable. Hyde in turn impetuously sold his entire ELAS stock to Thomas Fortune Ryan near the end of 1905. The trans-

*E. H. Harriman and his daughters, dressed for James Hazen Hyde's ball,
1905. (© Museum of the City of New York)*

action signaled his defeat at the Equitable, but it also left him with $2.5 million in cash. Awash in liquidity, the fatherless Hyde then turned to the financier Otto Kahn for investment advice. Much later, when nearly everyone was down, he would thank Kahn for the soundness of his portfolio.[25]

At the end of 1905 Hyde stepped away from the flash fires of American progressivism and notoriety. He inspired the character of Freddie Van Dam in Upton Sinclair's novel of New York society, *The Metropolis* (1908), but by the time that book was published, Hyde was already removed from New York's metropolitan scenes and living primarily in Paris. He stayed active in New York's cultural enterprises for a while, voting via proxies and advising through correspondents, but his departure instantly widened Kahn's avenue for advance at the Metropolitan. It also gave Kahn a friend and cultural liaison in Paris, where Hyde organized a committee of American patrons to back Gabriel Astruc's Théâtre des Champs-Elysées, and where Kuhn, Loeb made history in 1906 as the first New York investment house to float an American bond directly on the Bourse.[26]

The events leading to Hyde's expatriation presented important lessons for Kahn. He would need to tread carefully if not timidly on America's metropolitan scene. The dandy or the fashion plate risked no less effigy than the money lord or capitalist in America, and it was doubly dangerous to be at once an art lover and a money manager. If the mere invitation for Kahn to join the Metropolitan board had already caused some in his business world to intimate that such activity would distract Kahn from business, no young banker concerned with his reputation could ignore the censure launched at Hyde when, for instance, the *Evening Post* warned: "Large responsibility ill becomes a social butterfly." Furthermore, the arts of modernity could bait ill tempers. While New York's rejection of Wagnerian modernity was notable in this regard, the Hyde episode revealed a more general tendency to ridicule or reject cosmopolitanism, painting it as snobbish, effeminate, or, worst of all, *French* ("the 'shirt-sleeved' people of this country . . . can stand an Anglo American, but they cannot comprehend a French-American," scoffed one commentary). Poking at foreignness was not uncommon in clashes of class, cosmopolitanism, and cultural nationalism, yet if Kahn felt secure that he could hide his own Francophilia behind his credentials as an Anglophile, that armor was thin and transparent. His social rivals as well as his aesthetic allies also knew him to be a Jew, and the mix of cosmopolitan and Jew could be lethal.[27]

In 1906 Kahn made long strides toward leadership at both the Metropolitan and another heralded focus for patronage among New York's wealthiest — the New Theatre. An idea proposed by Conried, it sought to emulate the *Comédie Française* and drew much of its financial support from men behind the Met, who each contributed $50,000 to the original capitalization. Born of the same genealogy as the Met, the manners and negotiations were similar at the New Theatre, except here Kahn more clearly stood as a leader among founders. Deeply interested in the project, he aligned with the few backers who knew anything about theater and who, while not Jewish, were outsiders among the mainstream of New York society because they were aesthetically sophisticated.

In any event, it took more than one "stormy meeting" for the New Theatre founders to hammer out their own policy with regard to the exclusion and participation of Jews. A rumpus set loose when Clarence Mackay, the president of Commercial Cable Company and a Catholic, offered an incorporation plan that could unwittingly "let all the Jews in town into the thing." The fear was clear: "They would swamp it in no time and work us all out," according to one of the co-founders, Eliot Gregory, a writer who enjoyed solid social standing and kept a running chronicle of the events for Hyde. When "the Jew question came up point blank . . . before Kahn," at a later meeting, attorney Paul Cravath insisted, "We might as well face this Jew question now as later." Kahn replied, "Gentleman, I have not the same prejudice against Jews as I am one. But I agree for the success of this enterprise it will be better to have only one or two boxes sold to Jews." That cleared things up for the moment. "Schiff and Speyer and Kahn will be the three Jews," said Gregory, "and we will stop there. Firm." Morgenthau, another prominent Jew in organizing the New Theatre, had already left in a fit of temper because Conried was pushed aside.[28]

Speyer's tenure was also short lived, much to Kahn's delight, as his former boss committed one *coup de grace* after another, then found himself in a frost and resigned in a huff. No one begged or desired his return, but as the incorporation proceeded without him, Speyer became "wild to get back" and kept "running to Kahn every day to ask . . . to be taken back." The best Kahn would offer him was a box, rather than a directorship, and box owners had no artistic authority. When Pierpont Morgan joined the board, it sealed Speyer's fate with the New Theatre ("J.P. coming in keeps Speyer out," Gregory reported to Hyde). But instead of putting an end to Speyer's pleas, he kept "going-on like mad" about his treatment, and sent his wife to vent at "people's teas" ("bursting to tears and saying J. P. M. has been trying to injure J. S.'s position"). As Gregory relayed all this to Hyde, he said, "The truth is the little fool has been caught in his own trap." By now, it was "all over town [that] J. P. said he 'he would not serve on any board with him.' " Speyer was unable to see that there was nothing "to gain by telling people so."[29]

Kahn was golden by comparison. Back at the Met, that meant a combination of money well spent, fancy footwork, turning the other cheek, and a bit of backstabbing, especially when it came to Conried, who took the brunt of blame for whatever complaints emerged ("The Met Real Estate gentlemen seem to *hate* him," wrote Gregory of Conried). Kahn took advantage of the situation, leaving Conried unprotected while reserving the role of conciliator for himself so that he could emerge as the executive spokesman of the performing company. In truth, Kahn also benefited from the fact that MORECO's directors were, in Gregory's words, "as musical as four blue apes," although they need not have deferred to his musical superiority explicitly for Kahn to give them a sense that their opera was offering the finest artistic choices. He also laid before them a list of concrete accomplishments that buoyed their pride and satisfied their expectations. The performing company offered thirty different operas during the 1905–6 season, meaning that no subscriber had to see the same opera twice. In addition, receipts for the season broke all company records, while subscriptions for the next were coming in "a landslide." Through it all, indeed, Otto Kahn would use his own money to grease the machine and ease the concerns of other stockholders. In that regard, the turning point came while the opera company was in California on tour in 1906. All the traveling sets and costumes, along with the advance sales of its bookings, were lost in the San Francisco earthquake and fire. It was then that Otto Kahn became an artistic angel. Within a week of the disaster, the CMOC executive committee met at Kahn's townhouse, where he produced an emergency letter of credit in the amount of $75,000.[30]

All told, by January 1907 and the approach of his fortieth birthday, Kahn's ascension as a culture broker had been fairly steady and smooth. There had been good and bad publicity for the Met. The bad included a brief skirmish with impropriety in November 1906 when Caruso reportedly squeezed the buttocks of a lady while visiting the Central Park Zoo. The good carried the world's most popular singer through a triumphant season nonetheless. The 1906–7 season also celebrated the Metropolitan Opera debut of American soprano Geraldine Farrar, a beauty who remained with the company for sixteen seasons, adored by the public and publicity managers. As she prepared to star in the Met's first production of Puccini's *Madama Butterfly*, there were also plans underway for the composer to visit New York. In January 1907, Kahn was serving on the committee to fête Puccini, though he was not one of Kahn's favorite composers.[31] Then, with so much blue sky on the cultural horizon, a case of censorship accompanying the American premiere of Richard Strauss's *Salome* on January 22, 1907, gave Kahn his first important crisis as a patron. During church-going hours the previous Sunday, Conried had opened a dress rehearsal of the opera to the stockholders; in other words, he hosted a performance without the high society gowns, entrances, and distractions that normally occupied the *grande dames*, nobs, and swells in the boxes. This audience could thus give more than its customary attention to the opera, and its first encounter with the work brought no small amount of shock: not so much from Strauss's music or the Dance of the Seven Veils or the suggestion of incest in the plot, but rather all these, combined and undiluted, coming to a climax with the decollated head of John the Baptist cradled by Salome in uncompromising lust. That sent Louisa Morgan Satterlee reeling to her father, J. P. Morgan, who, in a display of moral outrage, ended the Met's run of performances after opening night.

Kahn's reaction was more reasonable than rash. The cancellation posed financial problems for the performing company, whose sudden loss of $30,000 in advance sales so soon after the San Francisco disaster was reason enough for Kahn to oppose the hasty closing. He would as well feel compelled to defend the opera on artistic grounds. Even though *Tribune* critic Henry E. Krehbiel deplored its "ugly music," New York's reputation as a host to serious art was also at stake. The Met's rejection of *Salome* sharply offended Strauss, and response or non-response to the MORECO order thus risked Kahn's social and cultural capital in New York as well as in Europe. Kahn, who cared about such things, chose to respond. Artistic and social success rather than sheer musical and theatrical rebellion was foremost on his mind (even if a popular production of Wagner's *Parsifal* that premiered on a Christmas Eve suggested a mild insurgence was necessary for success — in that instance, ministers condemned the depiction of Christ's Last Supper).[32]

Salome further tested the social limits of artistic expression. Disliking the ban as much as the quarrel, Kahn was particularly taken aback because Morgan had personally consented to the production at a meeting with him the previous summer. In January 1907, however, Kahn and the producing company lacked the freedom, power, and will to demand the modernist moment at the Met. Daring to dispute Pierpont Morgan and the MORECO board could lead to the end of their lease, but short of eviction, a row at this moment could obstruct Kahn's private ambitions. A member of the CMOC executive committee, he was not the major stockholder or yet in the position to act as the board's chief executive, and he would want to become both in the near future. He nonetheless improvised a defense for the opera, leading the CMOC board through a spate of phone calls and impromptu meetings, then drafting a letter for their joint signature.

Instructive of Kahn's compromises, the letter itself distilled a mix-

Olive Fremstad in the U.S. premiere of Salome. *(Metropolitan Opera Archives)*

ture of dignified outrage and superior aesthetic judgment. Seeking the points of widest appeal and validity, Kahn pandered to the conventional in this instance, choosing to assert the supremacy of music over lyrical content, performance, and all other elements; in other words, he momentarily abandoned the inclusiveness that Kahn might otherwise have advocated in mixed genres of art. He also tried to sidestep the decadence controversy, and with it the stigma of the late Oscar Wilde, author of the original play, whose sodomy conviction twelve years earlier still tainted his works for decent society. While "not concerned [with] defending Oscar Wilde's text," Kahn's letter declared that its critics were seeking "hidden motives, meanings and imaginations in no way apparent from the text." In so many words, Kahn tried to neutralize Wilde without condemning him. Then, finally getting to the business at hand, the CMOC proposed to tame the production, so that the head of John the Baptist would be kept offstage in subsequent performances: "Except for one short moment, it would be entirely hidden from the view of the audience."[33]

A little censorship in art, as in business, seemed better than losing the whole show. It was a compromise that Kahn could live with and would employ again, notably with Nijinsky, and also with his own Jewishness, but in this instance it did not work. *Salome* remained forbidden at the Met as long as Pierpont Morgan was alive.[34] Kahn's own strategy for advancing an eclectic, aesthetic avant-garde was meanwhile evident in his partial acceptance of defeat. Still burning to restore the opera, his executive committee resolved on March 1 that *Salome* would be given the following season. The committee surrendered their resolve a few weeks later, in Kahn's absence; then a bare quorum of the board overruled objections from Kahn, Hyde, and Gregory in June, "owing to the objections made by the directors of the Met. Opera & Real Estate Co." Afterward, Kahn would stay the battle rather than bolt, massage the situation, and broker three competing groups that were claiming cultural leadership at the opera. One was the morally indignant crusaders against indecency. Another was the ostentatious parade of high society. And the third consisted of those who were moved not only by the music but also, in the words of W. J. Henderson, critic for the *Sun*, by the sense that "the nineteenth century was closing with something like midsummer madness in art." For this last group, "when Art had turned for her inspiration to the asylum, the brothel, and the pesthouse, it was . . . a new renaissance. Strauss was our musical Maeterlinck, our tonal Ibsen." If asked to pick one as his cohort, Kahn undoubtedly chose the "new renaissance." He considered his own ascendency to be part of its program. The avant-garde arts that George Mosse has claimed "broke with past traditions but did not really menace respectability" would be characteristic of Kahn's patronage.[35]

Less than one month after his battle with the *Salome* censors, Kahn found himself in a strangely comparable position, defending another prophet whose head was also very nearly a trophy. Past and future frontiers of private and political capitalism set up the conflict. An invasive public reflex broke loose between 1901 and 1913, bringing storms and floods of investigations that challenged the concentration of economic power in America's new century and asserted the regulatory powers of government. From the antitrust suit filed against the Northern Securities Company in 1902 to the Supreme Court's dissolution of the Union Pacific in 1912, and the federal investigation of the "money-trust" in the same year, a good portion of negative public opinion fell upon Harriman and Kuhn, Loeb together. Midway through the period, an intense investigation by the Interstate Commerce Commission (ICC) targeted the Harriman railroads quite exclusively. It ultimately led Kahn, the senior Schiff, and other financiers to think that Harriman was unfairly becoming a scapegoat.[36]

The investigation put Otto Kahn on the witness stand during the winter of 1906–7. This was his first subpoenaed, sworn testimony of public note. Coming so close to Kahn's debut in the ICC hearings, the *Salome* episode was more than an overture. The aesthetic crisis and political critique jointly secured his dual role of banker-patron. Without one, the other would have been incomplete. Kahn emerged as a master of the revels and the money. Both parts were interdependent and inseparable from what Kahn offered the new century.

Harriman, who preceded Kahn on the stand, fared badly, for "he always made an indifferent witness, being impatient and rather resentful and defiant under examination," as Kahn later said. But this made Kahn's appearance doubly impressive in contrast. Holding the stand for six hours while the government questioned him on the propriety of UP stock and bond issuances, or how Kuhn, Loeb acquired the Southern Pacific for Harriman, Kahn kept his answers to the particular. Steering clear of loose generalizations and comparisons, he was such a good pupil of his own instinct and legal counsel, that, wrote the *Herald*, "to the lawyers and those who were hearing Mr. Kahn for the first time, this was all very amazing." Kahn looked and sounded good, definite, and reasoned, showing a talent for clarity that led the press to marvel over his "alertness of manner" and "wonderful knowledge of railroad conditions and values." He also inserted pragmatic reassurances of the bankers' ethics and, for the moment, asserted the private bankers' right to conceal the members of a syndicate list. Defense of the latter position would work its way to the U.S. Supreme Court, where it was upheld. Not without consequence, he also photographed well, and his picture appeared twice on the front page of the *Daily Tribune*. In one, Kahn sits calmly on the witness stand, a step below the panel of commissioners on his right, facing a room crowded with observers. In another he poses in full frontal view, buttoned in a double-breasted topcoat, clasping a walking stick, with his eyes fixed directly on the lens and his shoes glistening as much as his top hat — though not perhaps as brightly as his testimony, which received favorable editorials from the dailies.[37]

Kahn performed so well partly because he had been long waiting for this moment; being held in the background was contrary to his ambitions. Mostly he thrived on the excitement of public performance, the accomplishment of the moment, and the pride in knowing that he and the senior Schiff had regained some ground against the image of a menacing Wall Street, while they also articulated the higher principles of financial practice and secured the terrain for private control. However, more than all this was involved in the presentation. The ICC investigators were in pursuit of documentation, numbers, and testimony that could discredit the capitalists. With the whole of Progressive Era inquiry, it was a kind of peep-show naturalism. Such investigations and performances would later become set pieces of American regulatory ambivalence, but their newness during the early twentieth century came in an emerging routine of modernity with regard to publicity, trust, and the expressions of monied values. A wider figurative language was being made with regard to money itself. Cyclical, circular, hoarded, and hustled, as good as gold or a pound-sterling note, money could be substance and function, a storehouse of values, a filthy passion. Theorized, valorized, universal, and mysterious — money was conspicuous and concealed. It was always contiguous and kinetic. In the modern world, moving in a time quickened by rails and wires, money had its own electric convertibility, and its accounting had architectonic qualities on the order of the printed typeface (though the "modernness" of double-entry booking has yet to rival discussion of the Gutenberg press). Money was the most potent nexus of the entire bourgeois modernity, including the emerging public discourse in which Kahn made himself known and felt.[38]

The ICC probe marked only the beginning for Otto Kahn. He would thereafter step into public hearings many times. Near the end of his life, when the discursive mode of American legislators and regulation

Metropolitan Scenes

was in crises and climax, Kahn's mark lay at center stage. In 1907, though, the impression given in Kahn's public performance suggested that he made an art of this forum. Gracefully eager, he could articulate banking principles clearly and practically. He looked both fresh and classic. He calmed heated questions. Young and smart, a promising discovery, Otto Kahn was part of a new generation.

. . . .

A STORE OF STRENGTH

Kahn's acclaim in the ICC affair did not hinder his ascendency as a broker of New York's cultural affairs. In 1908, he took charge as president and chairman of the newly reorganized Metropolitan Opera Company, from which Conried had been ousted (and, incidentally, James Speyer was absented). Kahn's unmistakable, methodical hand in managing the downfall of Conried had meanwhile betrayed his graceful knack for executing unpleasantries and exploiting another's weakness. Unpopular with members of both opera boards, Conried became a scapegoat for the *Salome* debacle, as Kahn blamed the ban jointly on Morgan's religiosity and Conried's "clumsiness" — for having "tactlessly called the dress rehearsal" and invited "tout New York" during church-going hours. He promptly began to escort Conried toward retirement. The path began at the New Theatre, where, according to Eliot Gregory, Kahn was said to have "stolen [Conried's] idea, taken his land, chucked out his friends . . . and at the same time kept him in a good humor." Completely mannered in this capacity, Kahn talked to Conried "like a father-in-law . . . until the poor Herr Directeur was reduced to tearful pulp." A key word in the report, "poor," conveyed Kahn's pity as well as Conried's poverty, and spoke to another aspect of Kahn's shrewdness: Conried was out of money and Kahn traded financial advice for the impresario's concessions. Eventually Kahn eliminated him from the Metropolitan Opera as well. In early 1908 he "first hinted" to Conried that his contract might not be renewed. The impresario exploded with numerous financial demands and threatened to rally his supporters, but Kahn pressed back, implying that resignation was better than termination. He offered a payout of $75,000, which the impresario accepted; then he resigned for reasons of poor health and, said Gregory, to "save his vanity and his face."[39]

Kahn moved with stiff resolve. Drawn to the limelight, expecting to find social acceptance in the process, he sought both by becoming the majority stockholder of the opera's performing company, as well as New York's most heralded patron of the arts. The particulars of his strategy included excellence on stage and a ready guarantee to help the financially turbulent Metropolitan, combined with patience and discretion (even appeasement) in the face of opposition to his ambition and his Jewishness. In one instance, when the founders' crowd at the New Theatre drew in a member of the Kountze clan, who had "not been nice [to Kahn] at Morristown," Gregory noticed Kahn's characteristic response: he "acted as usual like a gentleman and put aside his personal feelings." Kahn bided his time and suffered degradation, all the while sticking around and working toward more positive experiences and greater power. Eventually he would lunch with Kountze at the pleasure of Mrs. William K. Vanderbilt, a *grande dame* who became Kahn's friendly ambassador for the cause of reviving *Salome*. In 1908 she tried unsuccessfully to turn J. P. Morgan around toward lifting the ban. Meanwhile, suave compliance with the ongoing suppression of *Salome*, along with the termination of Conried, worked toward reassuring the MORECO board, which was about to concede additional rights to Kahn's board in a new lease. With Conried gone, the performing company's directors, rather than its impresario, gained the right to choose and supervise the opera's artistic management, and the lease was not only lengthened from three to five years, but renewal became automatic unless one of the parties were to give warning five years in advance.[40]

The etiquette of the house otherwise went undisturbed. It unsettled no one, for instance, that Otto Kahn did not agitate to buy a box of his own, since Jews were unwelcome as box owners, and only minimally tolerated as renters. Even after purchasing Box Fourteen for himself in 1917, Kahn judiciously preferred to continue sitting in the Director's Box rather than an owned stall. A further means for contenting his co-directors involved several games of male congeniality on the edges of propriety—a subject that Gregory loved to divulge. For instance, adding J. J. Astor to the board of directors pleased one wing of the competing families among New York's high society, and Astor, who cared little about opera, would not challenge the artistic ideas of the other directors. He was mainly there to enjoy "great opportunities for pinching ballet-girls," which his fellow directors were happy to accommodate. In another instance Gregory cheerfully crackled about the winks and smiles "between the lines," when Kahn's regime gave directors the right to bring one lady to their box for tea during matinees. Catering to such whims and fancies, which Kahn shared, worked in tandem with other ways for Kahn to keep everyone trouble-free and happy with the opera and its administration. He was willing to pay the bills, reaching into his own purse to cover the company's deficits, along the way accumulating favors like notes of credit to be tactfully called in when a battle needed it. Thus, having guaranteed to offset losses of $95,806 in 1907–8, Kahn possessed sufficient leverage to fight for Gustav Mahler's appointment as conductor, for after Mahler visited the Met with great critical success in early 1908, Kahn had "at once jumped at the idea of putting him at the head at the Opera." The idea met with resistance from his board, however. They generally wanted "to work away from the German atmosphere and the Jew (Mahler is a J.)," said Gregory. They nonetheless accepted a compromise from Kahn: in the 1908–9 season, Mahler would conduct the Met's German operas, Arturo Toscanini would conduct the French and Italian, and the newly appointed general manager would be Giulio Gatti-Casazza, from La Scala, Milan.[41]

At the bottom line, Kahn could view each gesture of tolerance as a step toward acceptance. That is often the case in pathbreaking. The same could not be said of his wife, whose social route apparently was not ascending as rapidly. Just as Kahn was consolidating power over New York's cultural life, the couple "went backward" in their social career, and by mid-1908, Gregory opined, "Kahn is beginning to find out some of the sorrows of being too much in the limelight, and I fear his troubles are only beginning." Publicity was coming at a faster clip — in notices about the New Theatre and the opera, along with stories about Wall Street. Perhaps the rise was too fast and bright; perhaps Addie was unable to do as well in her own sphere — except Gregory focused the blame on her: "She is 'impossible' for any social purposes having that worst of all defects '*débineure*'" (he likely meant *débineuse* or *débineur*, French slang for "slanderer" or "detractor").[42] His choice of terms could have had many inferences, but plainly Addie was not catching on with the right people. Before long, she would want to leave New York and settle in England, where her social life was better. The lengthy vacations abroad each year intensified that desire.

The whole family took lavish European tours, some as long as four months in duration. One, in 1909, saw the Kahns book six suites on a North German Lloyd liner from New York to Cherbourg, then proceed to Paris by private train car, then on to "the watering places in France" among various other destinations, including Frankfurt, where Kahn took an hour-long flight in "Count Zeppelin's airship." He loved the adventure; Addie watched from the ground. It was that kind of proximity that characterized their married life. Typically, when the family took a house for their stay abroad, recalled one daughter, "we'd all arrive with everything . . . father would take one look at it, say, 'it's too boring,' and he would then go off and see some marvelous thing."[43]

According to her admirers, who emphasize Addie's intellect, she had "a charming, gracious personality as well as unerring taste and mental distinction." Bookish, controlled, and aloof, even in later years when she was better engaged in public cultural activism, Addie shied away from publicity. But in this earlier period, while she was preoccupied with managing the various households, a few important diversions occupied her. A practiced sculptress, Addie selected most of the paintings and sculpture in the family's collection; she was always more studied about these matters than her husband, as well as a discriminating and versatile collector who had a better ear for languages. Their respective interests and knowledge did overlap nicely in music, however, and the couple could be seen together at operas and symphonies in New York and abroad. For all their time apart and his independence, the Kahns jointly hosted dinners for distinguished guests, including one for Gustav and Alma Mahler in New York, at which Addie appeared "wearing a white satin dress with white slippers and strings of pearls nearly to the floor." Their meal was capped with an outing to some "dreary proletarian building" on Broadway, in search of a seance, recalled Alma Mahler. Addie was also on hand to receive Gatti-Casazza in Paris when Kahn offered him the job of artistic director at the Met.[44]

However stark the contrasts, Addie and Otto Kahn had tacit understandings in their personal arrangements. The man to whom her father had given her hand was entrusted to manage Addie's money. She was devoted to the marriage and Kahn was loyal in his way, controlling his extramarital activities enough to keep Addie protected from public humiliation. He was also an avid reader, a charming talker, handsome, and never a dull companion. Moreover, as America's elite became Europeanized, and *salon* styles of entertaining took shape, it was Otto Kahn who brought the couple into contact with the world's movers, positioning them for social success on new terms. Still and all, when Hyde's retreat from New York gave Kahn more room to maneuver, it closed one of Addie's circuits of parties and balls. She depended upon her husband to open doors and establish social communities, but she liked the proper, aristocratic life almost exclusively, while he felt more comfortable with bohemian revelries and the "midsummer madness in art." There was one final similarity of note, however. Addie and Otto were both nonpracticing Jews who practiced at being non-Jews. They jointly vowed to make Christians of their children, all of whom were subsequently christened as Episcopalians. Moreover, the Kahns increasingly exempted themselves from the social networks of "Our Crowd," which risked further isolation among the elites, since New York's real non-Jews were not waiting with open arms either.

As partners and parents, Otto and Addie were not without their conflicts. There was a refreshingly boyish energy that made Kahn irresistible to the children, though apparently this was not something Addie wholly admired. In the early years of their marriage, she spent more time with the children than he did. However much of the child rearing was left to governesses and tutors or fencing and riding instructors, the limits set in the household's decorum became identified with Addie's rules. She was remembered as a stickler for minor social details, and "very strict about anything that was a convention," but also as ultimately forgiving, because, like Kahn, or under his influence, she was also "extraordinarily tolerant and understanding" about the larger issues in the children's lives, and eventually accepting of their adolescent and later rebellions. Nonetheless, when the brood was young, family life was always more colorful and exciting whenever Kahn was around. The household's tight manners and propriety could unravel in gales of giggles. He took the children on high-speed carriage rides, made indelicate jokes about diarrhea, and, if no guests were around, played unpretentiously at dinner.[45] Behind the anecdotes of his various antics was a father-hero-God in rebellion — his outbursts of Dionysian vitality added comedy and adventure to the heavier curriculum of cultivation. Addie seemed a dour contrast when playing the advisory role expected of wife and mother, though no one was more fastidious, punctual, and meticulous than Kahn himself, and that struck some balance in the mix of authoritarian and ruffian.

It does, however, seem that Otto and Addie's minds likely were in agreement with regard to the family's future when, upon returning to New York in the autumn of 1909, Kahn was handed a series of tests. Addie had probably begun to remind him, now that he was well past his fortieth birthday, that they were not progressing toward their goal of living abroad, where perhaps their sons should be educated. The discussion had further resonance because E. H. Harriman had died in September while the Kahns were still abroad, which could certainly have an impact on Kahn's career at Kuhn, Loeb. The New York cultural season, meanwhile, was something of a roller coaster in 1909 as well. At its low point, the New Theatre was a bust, and it fell upon Kahn to figure out what should be done. He had assured some of the founders there would be no financial risks, only chances of great honor, but the hall was too big, the acoustics were bad, and the selection of plays awfully weak. It all added up to high costs in terms of both money and reputation. For years afterward, the New Theatre stood as a symbol of art theater gone wrong in America. And while critics blamed everyone from the architects to the millionaire sponsors and the artistic director, it was primarily Kahn who stood in the breach. Taking over the bills and mortgage, he reorganized the house, which for the moment he turned into an experiment with popularly priced opera, under the auspices of a gentleman's club.[46]

The Met also had its problems. The silver lining, if there was one, came with the ascension of Toscanini as conductor in the production of *Tristan und Isolde*, which Mahler had considered to be his signature piece in 1908–9. By the autumn of 1909, the Met had lost Mahler to the New York Philharmonic, where he would not have to share the podium. Mahler carried with him some antipathy for Kahn, as the two had probably clashed over money when Kahn's executive committee took a relatively hard stand on the conductor's contract.[47] But overall, the Metropolitan Opera Company was "cheerfully losing $10,000 a week and giving excellent opera" in return, as Gregory blithely put it, while Kahn covered the losses. These amounted to roughly $200,000 in 1908–9 and $250,000 in 1909–10. Whereas Kahn told the public that the Metropolitan Opera would make art its priority "without any thought to pecuniary benefit," and he received cheers from the arts chroniclers in exchange, he was not undisturbed by the deficits. Behind the scenes he worked doggedly to balance the opera's artistic integrity with its account books.[48]

There seemed to be only one major obstacle: Oscar Hammerstein's Manhattan Opera House, a rival company perched on Broadway between Thirty-fourth and Thirty-fifth Streets since December 1906, which in Kahn's view upset the bidding for talent and audience, as well as Kahn's efforts to rationalize excess capacity within America's operatic marketplace. Hammerstein's company offered more contemporary opera, including recent French works to which it and not the Met owned the rights, and also made its seats available at lower prices than the Met. Hammerstein, a German-born self-made impresario (whom Gregory called "a crooked Jew with no backing") displayed real talent for packaging shows, cashing in on the earlier publicity for *Salome* by producing it successfully in 1909. On the other hand, Hammerstein had financial difficulties, too, and that made him vulnerable when Kahn's board decided to buy him out. A deal, signed at Kahn's townhouse in April 1910, gave Hammerstein $1.2 million in exchange for his agreement to refrain from producing opera in New York, Boston, Philadelphia, and Chicago for an entire decade. Hammerstein soon challenged the covenant, alleging a violation of the Sherman Antitrust Act, but the courts ruled that opera was not interstate trade or commerce, and Hammerstein died before resuming operatic productions in America. Kahn never admitted wrongdoing in winning the battle. Nor did he give much weight to the idea that he and a battery of Wall Street interests and expensive lawyers had crushed Hammerstein. New York, all the same, lost an impresario who offered world-class stars and a socially mixed opera house — where great opera held sway over grand society, and ordinary attire brushed shoulders with haute couture. Without remorse, Kahn mostly felt confident that he could not only achieve these same goals, but also bring aesthethic modernism to the Met.[49]

The traits that Jost Hermand has observed among leaders of the commercialized avant-garde in turn-of-the-century Germany apply quite well to the American scenes played by Otto Kahn at the Met. It was "bourgeois modernism" to claim aesthetic leadership and grandeur at once. This was not a revolutionary aesthetic avant-garde, but rather an amalgamation between *l'art pour l'art* and wealth holders who wanted to be "culturally as well as economically up-to-date."[50] Otto Kahn cast his lot with the elites of New York. He wanted acceptance within America's self-fashioned aristocracy. He wanted to be the guiding force behind America's premiere operatic facility. Within a decade Kahn commented that these had been his high-brow years. It would take longer for Kahn to regret more fully the compromises made within the Met.

By 1910 Otto Kahn was a full-fledged celebrity millionaire. Helped by art dealer Joseph Duveen, his record-breaking $500,000 purchase of Frans Hals's *Family Group* (1648) bested Pierpont Morgan's bid at a Christie's auction in London in March of that year, and the sale received wide publicity as the highest price ever paid for a work of art. The New York newspapers announced that Anna Pavlova and Mikhail Mordkin had danced at one of Addie's entertainments, and Kahn's entries had taken blue ribbons at the Bar Harbor horse show. Increasingly, the dailies began to count Kahn among the "Future Kings of Finance," distinguishing him from other Wall Streeters, because the average reader knew Kahn first on favorable terms as a patron of the arts. The public was also about to hear more of Kahn's progressive opinions concerning public regulation, which he liked to say was here to stay and would bring "change for the better" if "corporations, by meeting authorities half way, can promote a spirit of cooperation which will make regulation a protection instead of a menace."[51]

A transcontinental train tour in the autumn of 1910 went further toward establishing Kahn as a likable character out West. Though he privately thought western populism to be "as rabid as ever," his public remarks were more reserved. When interviewed on the steps of his rail car, Kahn articulated eastern money reassurances, making good efforts to encourage more congenial relations between the railroads and the public. In Denver, he preached that capital, "more versatile than water," runs not merely downhill, but when confronted with contentious, "pernicious legislation," "it can go anywhere and does."[52] One wonders if Kahn thought himself to be as fluid. Indeed, on this same trip Kahn mourned the loss of his mentor and client, for the daily business of railroad financing could grow monotonous without Harriman's genius to fascinate him. He was probably bothered as much in realizing that, whether or not journalists counted Kahn among the best suited to lead Wall Street, the weight of Jacob Schiff's supervision, partiality, and temper could keep Kahn saddled indefinitely. As the American public awakened to Otto Kahn — "Man of Steel and Velvet," Wall Streeter, and Maecenas — Kahn, like his wife, became restless, wanting more.

The piece missing from the puzzle seemed nearly in hand during the autumn of 1911. While visiting England for the coronation of George V, Kahn was to become the "first political promotion" of Max Aitken (later Baron Beaverbrook), a Canadian-born financier and political climber who had emigrated to England, befriended Bonar Law (the future prime minister), and in the second general election of 1910 become a Unionist member of Parliament. During the coronation festivities, the newly knighted Aitken conceived of a plan, or deal, whereby Kahn would become the Unionist MP from Manchester's Gorton division (a working-class district) and also buy the financially distressed *Daily Express*, a half-penny Unionist newspaper owned by C. Arthur Pearson. For Kahn it promised be the ultimate assimilation, short of religious conversion. His ideal ambitions could be fulfilled by a seat in Parliament and ennoblement. Plenty of men from the City had followed this course, some of them German-born Jews. In the same stroke, Addie's desire to live abroad would be satisfied. By year's end Kahn confided to Aitken that he had "practically concluded to follow your advice and example." In January he leased St. Dunstan's, a former home of Henry Hucks Gibbs (First Lord Aldenham), a director of the Bank of England.[53]

Kahn also rented an office in the same building that quartered Aitken, and he tended an offer for the *Daily Express* (putting £30,000 at Aitken's disposal pending final approval). A visit to Manchester proved additionally promising, after which Kahn contributed £100 toward the expense of election preparations. Even so, Kahn approached this English future warily. The whole plan was a case of one foreign-born newcomer leading another up the ladder of politics toward ennoblement, but there was a catch: Kahn wanted his candidacy and transition to be without a contest or unexpected surprises. The chance that he might leave the super-rich security of America and Kuhn, Loeb only to face defeat in a British election haunted him. Downward mobility was the last thing he wanted and his sister, Lili Deutsch — who noted, "Otto is tortured by terrible ambition" — advised him to stay in America, pointing out that a "Parliamentary seat . . . is far too uncertain." Kahn heeded the advice in his own fashion, by insisting the campaign present no risk of failure, and delaying his final decision.[54]

He had negotiations with Kuhn, Loeb to plan. New York would not be abandoned impulsively. Because Kahn intentionally discussed none of these English affairs with his Kuhn, Loeb partners, he also demanded no publicity about his candidacy until the time was right. Realizing on February 1 that "my plans as to settling in London are getting . . . rumored about in the City," he reminded Aitken to delay the announcement. A similar message went to J. W. D. Barron, party secretary in Gorton, who, without Kahn's knowledge, had just shipped him a handful of recent news items related to the candidacy, and more were forthcoming. At face value, the earliest reports appeared editorially sympathetic to Conservatives, stirring no direct criticism, except they did mistakenly think Kahn was Canadian when he was still a British subject, and his surname became twisted into the odd appellation, "Khan Kahn." What really chilled Kahn's nerves was a front-page story in the *Manchester Weekly Citizen*, a Socialist paper with Labour leanings, that dripped with derision about Kahn's candidacy. Calling it a foreign invasion, here his name also became "Khan Kahu," which could have been a phonetic play on a word for the proboscis monkey ("kahau"), and therefore an anti-Semitic stereotype. In any case, reading it weakened Kahn's faith in a successful, dignified campaign, and immediately led him to question the vulnerability of a Jew of German origin in standing for Parliament. Aitken assured him, "I do not think that attacks on Jews have the slightest weight in England," adding that "the suggestion of German origin will not do any real harm." "England is a tolerant country," he continued; "intolerance will only make you political friends."[55]

Otto Kahn saw things differently than the Canadian-born Christian. A few weeks later, back in what he called New York's "realms of haute finance," Kahn reminded himself (and Aitken) that his Kuhn, Loeb partnership was "no mean position that I shall have to give up." If Aitken held any "doubt whether I should be able to make a real and thoroughly satisfying success in British politics," Kahn asked, "I shall be grateful indeed if you would tell me so very frankly." Aitken badly wanted Kahn's backing for the *Daily Express* and replied by cable, "I think you will win constituency . . . even if you lost . . . you would get position. I realize your strength in New York and wont lightly urge you to throw it over. Can you delay decision."[56]

By now the New York press was covering Kahn's prospective candidacy, and Jacob Schiff quite likely made a tempting counteroffer to keep Kahn with Kuhn, Loeb. The senior was himself still unwilling to retire, but he would not want the inevitable succession of his own son to come up short-handed, and the firm could ill afford the loss of another partner at the time. Death had taken Louis Heinshiemer in 1909; Paul Warburg was gravitating toward politics and monetary theory (in 1914 he would resign to join the Federal Reserve Board); and, as ever, Felix Warburg was more interested in philanthropy than banking. In addition, by now Jacob Schiff had to value the fact that, of all the partners, Kahn possessed the best public relations instincts, a prized talent considering the intensive public scrutiny being cast upon America's socalled "Money Trust," which would soon be investigated by federal legislators. Kahn was also the partner in charge of such delicate situations as the Union Pacific (facing antitrust prosecution), the Missouri Pacific (undergoing complex reorganization), and New York's Metropolitan Street Railway (in receivership). Nor was it uncommon for fellow bankers to consult him before granting their own interviews with the press, or turning to squash some reckless rumor among Wall Street brokers. Kahn's memories of E. H. Harriman and talents for relating them were still to be valued, too, since the deceased Harriman was still quite alive in the discourse not only of legislators and regulators, but also of social scientists, including William Z. Ripley of Harvard University and Werner Sombart, a leading sociologist of the German Historical School. In weighing the prospect of Kahn's resignation, Schiff undoubtedly thought first of the firm's endurance, then had to admit that this junior partner was needed.[57]

"Strongest pressure being brought to bear upon me to stick to my big position here," Kahn cabled Aitken on February 26. "The situation here, and with it my own views have undergone a very material change since my return." Aitken conveyed frustration in a telegraphed reply: "Change your plans would considerably embarrass me and others more important . . . you can hardly afford it." Under these circumstances, an auditor's report providing details about the nearly bankrupt *Daily Express* led Kahn to say, "My business judgment rebels against dropping money into what looks like a bottomless pit." Then by April, Kahn was clearer: "I shall be giving up too much here, if I go to England, to take the jump blindly and without having a pretty accurate and well defined notion as to where I shall land." Aitken urged him to expect "intangibles." In this instance, Otto Kahn would not. Feeling duty-bound to Aitken and his political friends in England, Kahn continued to grant modest financial support for the Gorton division, and allowed the use of his name until an alternate candidate emerged, but by early 1913 Kahn's withdrawal was known among Unionist Party leadership, and by August 1913 he was definitely out of the running for the Gorton seat.[58] In the end, Kahn remained a partner of Kuhn, Loeb.

Visible and rooted in many metropolitan scenes, Otto Kahn was now a man in his mid-forties. With gray creeping into his still full head of hair, by contemporary standards of Wall Street seniority he was also still young and positioned for further distinction. One new mansion went under construction on Fifth Avenue, and he bought Long Island property for a country estate to replace Morristown. He was also renovating

St. Dunstan's for a home in London—if he could not deliver the life-style of an English lord, dual residence would give him and Addie the next best thing. His speech on Harriman in early 1911 had been published in English, French, and Chinese, and Kahn began to branch out further in public relations, making statements on economic, civic, and cultural matters. His cultural activism stayed in the news through various gestures, including one that put $1,000 worth of tickets to the Century Opera into the hands of schoolchildren. If not every act of patronage—or cultural industrialism—found publicity, it was increasingly known that Kahn was likely to pay the salary of a Henry Street Settlement worker, cover the tuition of a slum-child with a promising voice, or advise the Music School Settlement on fund-raising. On a wider scale, the (Italian) Cines Company and the Thanhouser Film Corporation tempted his interest, while the Mutual Film Company and the Reliance Motion Picture Company attracted his investment. He also erased the red ink from Walter Damrosch's opera *Cyrano*, and held directorships on the boards of the Chicago Opera Company and Boston Opera Company as well as the Met, although in 1913, at Kahn's instigation, he and other board members of the Metropolitan Opera Company would sell their Chicago Opera shares in a deal that kept the Chicago company "west of the Allegheny Mountains" to protect the Met in the East. Looking across the Atlantic, his role as a cultural liaison grew stronger throughout Europe. He promised to bring Max Reinhardt's acclaimed production of *The Miracle* to Madison Square Garden, and entertained ideas for giving Reinhardt a permanent festival theater in New York, although Kahn was also unlikely to promote another grand theatrical construction so soon after the New Theatre had failed. Meanwhile, he became an honorary director of Covent Garden, and occasionally looked after American investments for Aitken and Rudyard Kipling. In addition, he sat on the founding council of L'Institute Français Aux États-Unis, was treasurer of the Museum of French Art on Madison Avenue at Forty-seventh Street, and joined the international committee of patronage that backed Gabriel Astruc's Le Théâtre des Champs-Elysées in Paris—where Stravinsky's *Le Sacre du Printemps* premiered on May 29, 1913.[59]

There are several ways of seeing Otto Kahn at this juncture, the montage above being only one. From his vantage point, if not seeing himself as the man who would acquire both a portrait of Giuliano de Medici by Botticelli and the honor of being America's Medici,[60]

Kahn surely saw his activities as routes to progress and positive change. Whatever his shortfalls, Otto Kahn was in a place inconceivable twenty years earlier, when high society in New York was unthinkable without the dominance of Caroline Astor or Pierpont Morgan. Both were now dead, and Kahn had shown the social promise for progress in the new century. A foreign-born, monied Jew could find and keep his dignity, survive the many cockfights (colloquial and canonical) of Wall Street, society, and aesthetics, and become one of the so-called better men of business and modernity, and therefore entrusted to shape monied values. Good taste, Anglo manners, and his sense of public opinion helped as much as money. But his personal ascendence aside, his progress in these years suggests the ultimate extent of transatlantic integration. From this view, Otto Kahn had become a unique emissary of art, capital, and metropolitanism. He had come to represent the marketplace of world cities — an expansive metropolitan culture carried outward on the tracks of railway systems, the wires of news services, and the shipping lanes of the Atlantic. Kahn emerged as a leading actor in courts of opinion and law if not of the nobles. He had adjusted to a network of friends and enemies — sometimes friendly enemies — who were constantly encountering and evaluating each other, and always performing.

If not fully content, Otto Kahn was satisfied in his discontent. Looking forward toward seniority, proud of himself and *La Belle Epoque*, he fairly well mastered his social performance. He also began an application for American naturalization in 1914. The transition made sense from a number of viewpoints. He had been in the United States for more than two decades, and all of his Kuhn, Loeb partners, as well as his wife and his children, were Americans. After British ennoblement eluded Kahn, there were also careerist advantages to American naturalization. Kahn wanted to influence public opinion and the political economy. If he could not do it in England, why not in America?

CHAPTER THREE

Rupture and Renewal

On a European tour since mid-June, Addie Kahn arrived in London on the night of August 6, 1914, having made a hurried exodus from the continent newly torn by war. Traveling without her husband, who had sailed for New York on July 10, she maneuvered the four Kahn children and twelve servants through a harrowing Channel crossing. She also managed to keep in tow sixty-five trunks of possessions, some containing valuable jewels, furs, and silver, but left behind two automobiles that were confiscated in France. Once in London, Addie paused, thinking it "unwise [to] go [on a] poor crowded boat." While other frenzied American tourists tried to steam home from every port, she would do nothing rash in "getting accommodation." Instead she spent the next days cabling rounds of inquiries and news. Some verified the well-being of family members and friends. One told her husband that the Ballets Russes would be "available surely" for the United States "unless war interferes." She did keep trying to get home, yet Mrs. Otto Kahn also declined passage on three different ships within one week, purportedly because each lacked what she perceived to be sufficient cabin space for her party and luggage.[1]

Such demands and expectations were normal for a woman of her class and customs. But with every stock and foreign exchange market closed, and the whole of high-seas shipping in a complete jumble, Addie Kahn's attitude raised the bristles at Morgan, Grenfell on Broad Street, where many Americans of wealth were helped in booking passage home. E. C. Grenfell, Morgan's senior resident in London, indicated that Mrs. Kahn's demands for comfort were inappropriate. Though he assured her husband they were attempting "to help her in every way," Grenfell remarked, "She evidently appreciates the advantage of having a comfortable house here," and, with a hint of reprimand, noted, "We are all sympathizing with the large number of your compatriots who are stranded on the Continent and enduring real privations."[2]

This vignette, while idiosyncratic, offers tantalizing signs of something more general. Consider Amy Lowell, the American imagist-poet and essayist-lecturer. She shipped her automobile through to Boston in the opening weeks of the war and, like Addie Kahn, stayed over in London for a while longer before heading home. During the same weeks music critic and photographer Carl Van Vechten left a Venetian vase and a pottery bowl at his hotel in Paris and "departed for Florence . . . with no faint notion that I should not be coming back to Paris." His objects d'arts eventually arrived in New York, having shattered during shipment.[3] These are more than merely anecdotes about bourgeois complacency at the beginnings of a war that many had thought would be brief. The scenarios of baggage, rescue, and cosmopolitan expectations are emblematic of displacements in a war that closed the nineteenth century and gave birth to different perceptions of internationalism.

Two important signs of the crisis may be extracted from Otto Kahn's story. For one, there was a questioning of Kahn's citizenry and loyalty. Grenfell's remark about "compatriots" would at first seem confused. Did he think Kahn was an American? Soon, all the Morgan houses would more directly exploit ambiguities of Kahn's identity, often taking them to be symptoms of treachery, yet in the war's earliest moments a pattern was already present — as when elsewhere Grenfell muttered about "German Jewish acquaintances" who "infested this office to get special accommodation," and were "abusing England behind our backs while properly obsequious here."[4] The veneer of gentlemanly competition would buckle quickly, beginning a play within the play, with the Morgans (the Allies' banker) set against all the German Jewish houses, and Kuhn, Loeb taking an awkwardly neutral position until America entered the war. These times of radically reconstituted geopolitics left many of Kahn's cosmopolitan privileges impaired but, suspended in between the constellations of enemy, alien, and Jewish identities, he kept faith with the cosmopolitanism of the *Belle Epoque*, believing the war to be an aberration rather than an end.

The *beau monde* that Kahn knew and wanted slipped over a precipice from which, Kahn had to believe, it could be pulled back. For this reason, Kahn's negotiations to bring the Ballets Russes to America were important, because Kahn wanted bridges of continuity. When the war began he was involved with plans to import Max Reinhardt's wordless spectacle, *The Miracle*, for a limited run at Madison Square Garden. There was also talk about arranging a visit to America for Gordon Craig, Britain's renowned theatrical theorist, director, and designer. Of these three prospects, only Diaghilev's ballets actually made it to the United States during the war. Craig never came to America, and by the time Reinhardt's masterpiece arrived in 1924, more than twelve years had passed since its world premiere. That the cultural weight of theatrical modernism in America fell disproportionately upon Diaghilev's ballet gives but a hint of the discontinuities in Kahn's aesthetic curriculum, yet at the same time, we shall see, the very act of bringing aesthetic modernism to America during the war was also a way for Kahn to find continuities and renewals.[5] More than the finest jewel of this patron's crown, the Ballets Russes represented a continuous thread of transcultural collaboration. When the war split Kahn's world and identity into pieces, the theater offered meaningful representations of the synthesis that Kahn sought for himself, the world, and its cosmopolitan capitals.

. . . .

FINDING HIS COURSE, 1914–1915

Before anyone fully realized what had begun, chaos was the order of the day. Uptown and downtown, nothing about Kahn's New York was neutral. Nor had any previous experience of modernity so thoroughly underscored the simultaneity, interdependence, or disorder of the modern world. That any opera season in New York got underway at all was a wonder considering the confusion, but, like Addie Kahn's luggage, keeping the Met's blue-ribbon status in world opera was a measure of Otto Kahn's priorities.

With German troops holding Belgium and marching on French soil, some of the Metropolitan's directors preferred to immediately cancel the German repertory. Kahn seems to have convinced them it was not worth the high price of buying up the contracts with German artists, none of which provided for cancellation in case of war. Moreover, an uninterrupted opera season made it possible to dream that art would escape the ravages of war, that steadiness could continue amid the crises. Though opera companies in Boston and Chicago were forced to cancel their seasons entirely, the 1914–15 season went on in New York. The Met was in better financial shape than other American opera companies, but its continuity also involved nonfinancial resources, including its successful efforts to free two of the Met's tenors, Albert Reise (a German national) and Dinh Gilly (a French national), who had been captured by French and Austrian forces, respectively. Another diplomatic problem sprang from patriotic clashes between the singers, many of whom were European nationals, and in early October the board of the Metropolitan Opera Company ordered that "none of the artists should give out interviews in connection with the war."[6]

Downtown, Wall Street made a great commitment to stability that autumn as well, even though the stock exchanges were closed. As historian Vincent Carosso tells it, with the City of New York about to see $80 million in outstanding obligations mature on European markets, there was "widespread suspicion that the United States, a debtor nation, would not meet its international obligations." The suspense concluded with a notable finale. More than six dozen New York banks and trust companies, co-managed by J. P. Morgan and Kuhn, Loeb, brought out New York City's $100 million refunding gold notes of 1914. That demonstration of America's financial maturity validated the leadership of New York's financial community. It also showed how sturdy the guard against default could be, and implied a discipline that would both influence the prosecution of war and prefigure the hard line taken in America's postwar policy toward Europe's debts.[7]

The modern world war was instantly changing the status quo among creditor and debtor nations and among the premier private banks. At least once before the war, for instance, Mortimer Schiff concluded that Kuhn, Loeb was better organized for business on the European continent than the Morgans. Even without foreign branches or a partner equal in stature to Morgan's E. C. Grenfell (a director of the Bank of England since 1905), Kuhn, Loeb had a finely geared mechanism in London through Sir Ernest Cassel and superior ties to German-based capital through the Warburgs; it was also pioneering the multilateral linking of New York and Paris with wider world investment markets. U.S. railroads were Kuhn, Loeb's bread and butter, but making new markets for the direct placement of foreign securities had become characteristic of the firm's extraordinary business. It was evident at the war's beginning in the firm's plans to offer an American issue for

HAPAG, the Hamburg American Line of Albert Ballin. The war unraveled that business and more.[8]

At first news of the war, surprise and regret overcame all the partners at Kuhn, Loeb. Each had to confront his moral allegiances — to nation, homeland, family, friendship, and business. A solidly pro-Allied camp formed among Kahn, Mortimer Schiff, and Jerome Hanauer. They would constitute an ineffective majority, since the German allegiances of Jacob Schiff along with Felix Warburg, in the minority, would instead set Kuhn, Loeb's course, if it came to that. Behind them all at first was hope that the war would end quickly enough to let the firm's opinions go unnoticed by the public. In late autumn such hope was lost when Jacob Schiff's sympathies were published in the *New York Times*, then carried by international wire to newspapers in Europe. The genie had slipped out of the bottle. In the final movement of his long career, Schiff urged a negotiated peace among the belligerents and a return to the antebellum balance of European power. He also pledged the neutrality of his firm for the war's duration.[9]

Aggravated and concerned, Kahn would not contradict his senior in the press. He instead turned privately to his own important friends for support and damage control. Max Aitken would see to it that the British press knew of Kahn's support for the Allies. Kahn also trusted his friend to believe that "I cannot control Mr. Schiff's feelings and utterances," indicating an awareness that his senior's opinion was "being criticized by the Germans, and it certainly cannot be pleasing to the English." Aitken concurred, "On nearly every side I hear criticisms."[10] Indeed, everyone who cared knew this already and worried about the consequences. It was bad business from start to finish. Neutrality was the one position bound to produce the most enemies. Bowled over to find his best access to American capital blocked, Max Warburg looked badly within the kaiser's entourage, and Warburg's inability to raise capital in the United States during the war ultimately became inextricable from the German tragedy of defeat. Meanwhile, Schiff's course could not but accelerate a reversal of fortunes for Sir Ernest Cassel, the most successful Anglo-German newcomer of the Edwardian years, who was very nearly paralyzed by his alien-enemy birth. On the American side of the Atlantic, most of Wall Street held pro-Allied sentiments, but overall, the charade of gentlemanly capitalism lost much of its charm. Ethnicity and allegiances became acutely defined elements of identity and belligerence.

Rupture and Renewal

There was much sorting out to be done. In December 1914, Kahn asked Lord Victor Paget "whether one, who is of German birth and bearing a German name, however genuine my love for England and my sympathy with her cause, would be welcome in England." Knowing the answer to his own question, Kahn anticipated "some unpleasantness" and stayed stateside. He also postponed final paperwork for his American citizenship, fearing that his "actions or motives in giving up my British nationality during the war might be misunderstood." Preserving the core of his cosmopolitanism required enormous discretion. Before the end of 1914, for example, Kahn was asked to lend his name in support of New York–born banker and broker Jules S. Bache, who was expelled from the Travelers Club in Paris for having remarked, "The Germans would take Paris in three weeks." Kahn declined to get involved "in this painful episode," explaining that "it would be indelicate for one of German birth and bearing a German name, however sincere his sympathies and good wishes for France (as mine are), to interfere in any way." The sudden limitations were evident as Kahn concluded, "Mr. Bache's own cause would not be served by the presence of any such names on the list."[11]

Benefactions made a more significant tool in renewing trust. The publicity surrounding the use of his house in Regent's Park as a home for blinded soldiers and sailors, for example, meant that when that model rehabilitation facility was mentioned in the press and professional journals, or amongst royals, Kahn's name and charity received due gratitude and courtesy. The gesture served an additional purpose, for it inserted Otto Kahn among those who supported charities for the blind. These circles long included Jacob Schiff and Felix Warburg as prominent benefactors. Otto Kahn thus brought himself to a place where he could engage his opposing partners on the issues of war and humanitarianism. Changing the senior Schiff's mind and policy offered the best chance, and formed the central challenge, in what Kahn could do for the Allied cause.[12]

Jacob Schiff strained to blame neither side, knowing all the while that he could no more easily "side against my own native country" than "against my own parents." He professed, and honestly possessed, some compassion for all the belligerents, except the anti-Semitic tsarist government that he had opposed with financial diplomacy for more than a decade. Schiff's priority was a swift and fair peace. He did not rush to promote Germany "in the role of a world conqueror," thinking instead that a victorious Germany would inevitably be "a menace not only to her immediate neighbors, but to the entire globe."[13]

For all their disagreement, there was some ground for concordance between Kahn and his senior. Both men had kin in England and Germany as well as France who were vulnerable to conscription, harassment, and deprivation, and meanwhile confused about why their New York relations seemed to desert them. In addition, the Kuhn, Loeb partners found themselves reviled in the German press, because German-born expatriates were expected to help the homeland. Schiff also had feelings that Kahn admitted of himself—"honest and deep anger and grief" at seeing "Germany and England-France, the three countries of Europe which the world most needs . . . tearing one another to pieces in senseless fury." And both men were among the first to differentiate between governments and their peoples when condemning the belligerents. Kahn, ever the negotiator, hoped that somewhere among these common elements he might maneuver Jacob Schiff closer to aiding the Allied cause.[14]

Kahn likewise desired "a speedy end to this awful war" during its first year. At best he wanted "the triumph and glory of England" and its Allies, but he would be satisfied if Germany could "rise to the moral heroism of taking the first step towards dispelling the dreadful misery" and speak "not of victorious peace, but of righteous peace." He still felt that way in the spring of 1915, when Kahn privately went on record in a provocative exchange of confidential letters with his brother-in-law Felix Deutsch. A determined German patriot, Deutsch argued that Germany had been peace-abiding for forty-four years, and could justify its invasion of Belgium and the naval blockade; it could also reprove the British for using troops from Turkey and India, and chastise America for supplying armaments that prolonged the war. Kahn rejected most of it. Instead, he "freely, in some respects even bluntly," blamed Germany's Junkers and jingoists, the "deification of sheer might," and its naval build-up for "a needless war wantonly started." In addition, he warned that his own views reflected "the great majority of thinking people in America."[15]

As copies of the correspondence moved around his family circle, no support or praise for Kahn came from Mannheim, where Allied airships flew overhead "every night to watch the big factories, all of which . . . turn out nothing but supplies." An aunt there delicately concluded that Kahn was poorly "informed about the German situation." His brother Paul, writing from Greece, referred Kahn to Thomas Mann's essays for a better perspective on "how radically the ethical views in Germany differ from the ideals of the French Revolution." Undeterred by such rebuffs, Kahn began to circulate copies of his correspondence with Deutsch among a wider circle of well-chosen readers. Eventually his letter came out in the press, which reportedly got hold of it from censors, although other means were available and Kahn had some desire to see it leaked. The epistolary lent a small way for Kahn to contribute to the philosophical debate, for he felt yet unable to make his opinions public and still pursue hopes of changing Kuhn, Loeb's course.[16]

No less difficult for Kahn was the deterioration of goodwill from the Morgan houses, and the consolidation of their power. Unified in their pro-Allied position, they negotiated most of the French and British credits, coordinated Allied purchases in the United States, and took the lead in repatriating foreign-held American securities during Wilsonian neutrality. In consequence, the assets of J. P. Morgan & Co. better than doubled between December 1914 and December 1917.[17] Its meteoric rise brought a newly confident disdain for Kuhn, Loeb that went hand-in-hand with the Morgans' role in gathering intelligence for the Allies. From the first days of war, the Morgan partners set themselves solidly against the "German Jew element" in the United States, opposing its proposals for peace talks, its role in public opinion, and subverting its potential for raising German loans or procuring strategic goods. The Morgans and many within the British government tended to view Kuhn, Loeb as the enemy, an agent of the enemy, or an enemy sympathizer, and treated the firm's members with corresponding suspicion.[18]

True enough, Morgan partners felt their intelligence was quality stuff. They procured information discreetly from available sources, occasionally making a direct examination of Kuhn, Loeb partners, and while many allegations indeed lacked substance, if the result of the Morgans' surveillance concluded there was no cause for worry, they would not purposely foment undue hysteria. Such was the case in late 1915, when it was feared that Jacob Schiff, a director of Western Union, might have access to confidential messages. On the other hand, on those occasions that the Morgans' investigations confirmed suspicions about Kuhn, Loeb, whether true or not, it came with an air of authority—their enmity was strengthened by assumptions of veracity. The situation was one in which, if Kahn seemed believable, other remarks and actions suggested fundamental distrust on both sides. The relations eventually became so duplicitous and hostile that no Warburg, Schiff, or Kahn escaped some smear from a Morgan partner. By 1919, Jack Morgan remarked that he would have been happy to see Otto Kahn "shut in Gaol."[19]

Longstanding tenets in the Morgans' business conduct further complicated matters. Since Pierpont Morgan had died in 1913, his heir as senior and namesake, Jack Morgan, was proving himself "able in a measure to take Father's place." In addition, since the panic of 1907, when Pierpont Morgan stood as the banker of last resort, the Morgans believed that "it has been a good thing . . . that the country in these days got the habit of turning to us." Anyone challenging that position was a threat. It followed that the Morgans should lead all business in which they were involved, including Allied finances, and all Allied finances should in turn be coordinated fully and solely by the Morgans. Not that they took every piece of business, but they expected the right of first refusal as well as the authority of approval. Furthermore, the current Morgan cohort was not only decidedly Anglophilic (a fact deeply resented by the French), their few direct relations with German concerns, including Dresdner Bank, were of relatively new vintage. The Morgan firms were not heavily invested in Germany financially or culturally, nor were they interested in anything short of decisive victory for England. Making it easier to reject all things German, many of their German banking competitors were also Jewish, and to Jack Morgan in particular, a Jew was first and always a Jew. That applied to Kahn, in the earliest weeks of the war, as Morgan politely referred to him as "a German-Hebrew friend of mine, a partner of Kuhn, Loeb & Co."[20]

Generally, when Jack Morgan called a Jew his friend, he was motivated by expedience. The Jew was an expendable species of friendship, especially if the Jew had German connections during the war. No friendship better illustrates this fact than Jack Morgan's acquaintance with Sir Ernest Cassel. Writing to his father in 1903, Jack Morgan reported, "Sir E. Cassel has rather drawn towards us lately and this may be a good thing as all Egyptian business is practically in his hands and . . . he is not anxious to go on doing business indefinitely." Undoubtedly appreciating that Cassel had no male heirs, the younger Morgan concluded, "There might very likely be a . . . good connection" in the making. Two years later, while jointly considering the introduction of Thomas Edison's storage battery in England, Jack Morgan went to see the inventor in West Orange, New Jersey, where Edison, a man with anti-Semitic biases, likely expressed concerned that Cassel was a Jew, and Morgan "was able to reassure his mind." In the years after, Cassel and the Morgans cooperated on matters of Alaskan development and Chicago traction, among other business interests. As late as 1913, their relations were cordial enough that Cassel would invite Jack Morgan to join his shooting party.[21]

Yet missing from the picture is how Morgan's opinion of Cassel differed from relations with the Speyers, and how together these influenced the Morgan firms in their conduct toward Kuhn, Loeb, and then ultimately Otto Kahn. In 1905 the Speyer houses were the subject of discussion in one of the most unlikely places, when the Morgans joined Kuhn, Loeb in handling a $100 million convertible bond for the Pennsylvania Railroad. That by itself was, in Jack Morgan's eyes, "all rather amusing in view of the history of business since 1901." The comment fit the circumstance, no less on account of residual enmity from Schiff's attempt to corner the Northern Pacific for Harriman than because Schiff, who needed the Speyers for Pennsylvania financing in 1901 and 1903, was now freely talking about "the advantages of being free from Speyers in the most open possible manner." Thereafter, as the Morgan houses did draw closer to Kuhn, Loeb, the rapprochement with Schiff better reflected the policies of Pierpont Morgan than his son. In 1906 the latter grumbled that Kuhn, Loeb's "pleasant little ways" left him "very much inclined to dissociate" from the business of jointly financing the Pennsylvania Railroad, although he knew the Morgan senior would "feel otherwise." Schiff at any rate proved to be steadily cooperative in relations with Morgan, during the panic of 1907 and in organizing the American Group for investments in China (1909–13). In the meantime the Morgans managed to stay at arms length from the Speyer houses. As Jack Morgan drew nearer to seniority, he said of the Speyers: "You cannot rely upon them [to] carry out their agreements if they can at any time break them to their advantage." The Morgan houses preferred to forsake business that involved "people [of] that character."[22]

This long history played a part, as did the war itself, but something else — aside from the decidedly pro-German declarations of James Speyer — made it easier to convince the Morgans that all of New York's

German Jewish houses were snipers' nests of the enemy. Whatever anti-Semitic feelings Pierpont Morgan harbored, the best scholarship on the Morgans during Pierpont's tenure uncovers nothing as unequivocal in tone or temper as the evidence left by his son, whose anti-Semitism was more subtle before the war but also more discernible, when, for instance, he remarked casually to George W. Perkins in 1908, "If we are going on with business, some of us will have to turn Jew ... so you might as well choose your surgeon now."[23] With such preexisting attitudes ready to flourish, the Morgans would regularly blame Kuhn, Loeb for some misfortune during the war. In one famous fit of blunt temper, after the *Lusitania* went down, Jack Morgan literally made an indignant "turn on his heel" and refused to speak with Jacob Schiff. After Schiff left the room, Morgan took hold of himself, and thought aloud, "I went a little far. I suppose I ought to apologize?" His partner, Dwight Morrow, hurriedly scripted a note, recalling Ezekiel 36:22, and handed the words to his senior: " 'Not for thy sake, but for thy name's sake, O House of Israel!' " Morgan knew what he had to do. Self-assuredly in the role of God, he "reached for his hat, and hurried across to Kuhn, Loeb & Co. to apologize to Mr. Schiff."[24] That contented Schiff, but Kahn was growing increasingly irritated with the Morgan houses. In August 1915, when Morgan and Kuhn, Loeb joined in converting American railroad debts from the French franc to dollar securities, Jacob Schiff tried to smooth things over, telling Kahn that the "Morgans have been very nice in this matter and appear to have acted straightforward and decently, as is their wont with us."[25]

It was clear to all at Kuhn, Loeb that neutrality only encouraged a Morgan monopoly. And it did nothing to discourage the impression in America that the firm was pro-German. Also, after the *Lusitania*, the weight of Schiff's doubts about German guiltlessness grew heavier. Everything included, the senior was rethinking which course was best for the firm, while Kahn and Mortimer Schiff were continually advocating change in a pro-Allied direction. By mid-September 1915, when the Anglo-French financial mission arrived in New York to negotiate a blockbuster loan for the Allies, it seemed quite possible that Kuhn, Loeb would join in the underwriting. At least that was the impression given by Kahn and Mortimer Schiff, who whirled into the parley, with Ernest Cassel at their side, and assured Lord Reading, the head of the commission, that an American loan could be issued on more liberal terms than the Morgans advised. (The commission arrived expecting to raise $1 billion; the Morgans proposed $250 million; the compromise was $500 million.) Kahn, Cassel, and the younger Schiff were meanwhile awaiting Kuhn, Loeb's official commitment to underwriting the loan, and they never got it. Jacob Schiff refused because some of the loan was earmarked for the Russian allies. He could not aid the tsarist regime that persecuted Jews, and Lord Reading could not exclude Russia from the proceeds of the loan. Drawing his junior partners into a dramatic meeting, the senior Schiff announced, "I cannot sacrifice my profoundest convictions for the sake of whatever business advantage. I cannot stultify myself by aiding those, who in bitter enmity, have tortured my people and will continue to do so." He continued, "I know your objections and counter arguments and criticisms. They do not and cannot affect my conclusion. This is a matter between myself and my conscience, and no one but I myself can solve it for me. You are younger men. Some of you do not feel as I do on what I consider the morally controlling element of the question. I cannot have many more years to live. The future of the firm is yours. Realizing my duty by the firm and by you, I have gone to the limits of what I can sanction."[26]

His decision was irrevocable and inauspicious. Kuhn, Loeb lost its chance to at once mend fences with the Morgans and the Allied governments, to break the Morgan monopoly, and to help Cassel, who went home to find his membership in the Privy Council challenged under the British Nationality and Status of Aliens Act. This all ran very deep. The partners who stood in waiting to succeed Jacob Schiff coped with anxieties not present at the house of Morgan, where generational succession had occurred in 1913. The war certainly challenged the Morgans, but with nothing like the internal divisions underway at Kuhn, Loeb. The younger generation — men approximately fifty years of age — had neither come to power nor could bring their firm into war-related financing. Furthermore, instead of easing tensions, the Anglo-French loan intensified friction and suspicions — between the financial houses, and between bankers and governments. The loan came out in October 1915 without official support from any of the leading German houses; individual partners with pro-Allied sympathies stepped forward to participate, nonetheless. Kahn took a personal subscription of $100,000. Mortimer Schiff participated as an individual as well, and Cassel, the largest individual subscriber from England, contributed $2.5 million. Germany decried the betrayal of them all.[27]

At the same time, the whole affair unsettled the Morgan houses in America, England, and France. At $500 million, the Anglo-French loan of 1915 was the largest foreign bond as yet issued in the United States, if not J.P. Morgan's finest hour. The loan was extraordinarily difficult to market and came up short in public sales, in part due to its unpopularity among Irish and German partisans, but its drab performance also marked a significant turn in the Allies' opinion of the Morgans. They were already frustrated with their banker's inability to raise sufficient capital on favorable terms, growing resentful of Morgan profits, and henceforth became more vocal in their complaints. Meanwhile, the Morgan partners harbored resentment toward those whose interference had infringed upon their exclusive authority. From the Morgans' viewpoint, the issue was too large, so its sorry showing originated with the meddling of Kahn and Mortimer Schiff. It was easier to dump a disproportionate share of their frustrations on the German Jews, since these were not the parties with whom the Morgans would need to negotiate in future Allied financing. But hardly the last would be heard of the bitterness. As the Morgan firms ascended and became "the most important investment banking group in the world," their hostility toward the German Jews contributed to the immovable animosity of the postbellum status quo.[28]

. . . .

REUNITING STATES, 1915–1917

With its hands tied in Allied financing, its bindings with German houses severed, and the leading Anglo-German houses undermined, Kuhn, Loeb's standing had been alarmingly compromised. Kahn coped with the situation, in part, by finding novel alternatives that would permit him new avenues and agencies without abandoning the firm. A notable instance came fresh on the heels of the Anglo-French loan, in the founding of the American International Corporation (AIC), a $50 million investment conglomerate. Incorporated in November 1915, the AIC launched an unparalleled commitment, setting out to capture opportunities that arose during the war for American capital abroad. Encouraging the United States to "think internationally" and take a giant step toward the coexistence of New York and London as world financial centers, the vision was so forward-looking that the AIC was, in a manner of speaking, avant-garde. It aligned many of the leading names in American trade, transportation, finance, industry, and engineering, including Armour & Co., General Electric, International Nickel, Anaconda, American Telegraph & Telephone, Westinghouse, W. R. Grace & Co., the Robert Dollar Company, and Stone and Webster among them.[29]

American International Corporation was also more than just the brainchild of its founding chairman, Frank A. Vanderlip, president of the National City Bank. The original idea for the new company emerged collaboratively, from Vanderlip, Kahn, and Cassel. During the latter's visit to New York in September 1915, Cassel had predicted that "for a number of years to come the United States will have the only fund of capital in the world for world development. . . . The opportunities that this situation presents promise something quite without parallel." For Kahn's part, 1915 had been a year spent searching for a means to conduct war-related business that was technically neutral. By August, he and Mortimer Schiff had persuaded their senior to finance American companies whose exports might aid the Allies. Kahn was additionally looking at ways for Kuhn, Loeb to pick up the slack in South America, where European capitalists were hastily liquidating holdings. He had in mind an investment agency to enlarge American exports, encourage direct foreign investment, and promote trade in foreign securities. This would appeal to the pro-American convictions of Jacob Schiff, and align nicely with what Vanderlip and Cassel were thinking.

Vanderlip took Kahn's idea further, getting public credit for organizing a company that could reach global proportions and complement the new foreign branch operations of National City Bank. Vanderlip also sensed that Kuhn, Loeb wanted "a predominating influence in the company" in exchange for its investment of $2 million (including Cassel's stake) in the AIC, which Kahn leveraged on the board of directors and executive committee. Kahn, whose influence at the AIC incidentally outlasted that of Vanderlip, was also decisive in choosing the AIC name from a list that included "United Nations Corporation." Within one year of its organization, the AIC had received 1,230 remarkably diverse propositions for business, driving Kahn wild with enthusiasm over the possibilities. The company had contracts to construct waterworks and sewerage systems in Uruguay, a subsidiary Latin-American Corporation, and a vice president to represent its interests in Petrograd. The AIC also bought the Pacific Mail Steamship Company (jointly with W. R. Grace), the New York Shipbuilding Company in Camden,

New Jersey, and controlling interest in the International Mercantile Marine Company. In addition, it acquired a machine tool manufacturer, Allied Machinery Company, with offices in France, Switzerland, and Russia.[30] All this bustle was underway without participation from J. P. Morgan & Co., which had declined involvement in the AIC venture. Kahn could therefore operate beyond the control and supervision of his competitor, while using the AIC to entertain business with Allied governments and put Kuhn, Loeb back on course as an intermediary for international industrial investments. More generally, the whole project fit perfectly with Kahn's ongoing march toward a new public definition of himself as an American international. That progression turned Paris and New York into joint hubs of his struggle to regain lost ground in both finance and the arts.

Paris posed a distinct set of problems and opportunities. These were partially evident in James Hyde's mournful report from the spring of 1915 after seeing "what remains of the cathedral [at Rheims]." The German assault on the cathedral had become widely synonymous with modern barbarism, leaving Parisian conservatives to charge that the German military offensive continued prewar subversion: the total undermining of French culture by Germans, Wagnerites, and modernists. Enemy-alien consciousness combined to transform the cosmopolitanism of art and modernity into obscenity and sedition. In the same stretch, the war swept individual artists and their patrons into economic dilemmas. As galleries, theaters, and salons closed, knocking out many of the venues and networks for artistic production and exchange, New York, a so-called neutral city, became a haven in the storm, and Otto Kahn became a key escort in opening the American marketplace as an alternative to Europe.[31]

"Business is driving me pretty hard," wrote Kahn on March 4, 1915; "it has not yet succeeded, however, in drying up the springs of my interest in and enthusiasm for art and beauty, and it never will if I can help it." Two days earlier it had been announced that he was putting the Century Theatre (formerly the New Theatre) at the disposal of Isadora Duncan, who had recently denounced the rich from the stage of the Metropolitan Opera, and again won the hearts of her admirers. Two months later Kahn became responsible for the debts from her Century programs (the ones not paid by other admirers, including Frank A. Vanderlip). He then helped Duncan sail with her girl-pupils for Europe. In June he also advanced $3,000 toward the new Washington Square Players, which put forth contemporary American drama as well as European work of high artistic value. By autumn, Kahn saw little room for additional undertakings, saying, "The theatrical game is being enormously overdone, several new theatres for 'intellectuals' have sprung up besides the Washington Square Players, the Russian Ballet is coming here for the first time, a French season with several first rate actors and actresses will take place, and almost every virtuoso in the world who is not fighting will be in New York this winter."[32] Kahn, of course, was helping to make all this happen with amazing simultaneity. He was also overstating his case. One great virtuoso not in uniform, Arturo Toscanini, was not coming back to New York, and Kahn already knew it. Another, Russian dancer Vaslav Nijinsky, had been scheduled to open with the Ballets Russes in New York in January, but he was put under "open arrest" in Budapest in September 1915.

Getting the star dancer released and sponsoring the ballet's tours in America would forever make Otto Kahn world-famous. He paid the company's debts, insisted the star was necessary for a successful tour, and arbitrated arguments of a personal as well as artistic nature among Diaghilev, Nijinsky, and Gatti-Casazza. Nine years after *Salome*, Kahn was better prepared for a *succès scandale*. While he chided censors "not able to distinguish art from lubricity" in *L'Après-midi d'un faune*, he also suppressed the masturbatory climax of Nijinsky's choreographic poem. "America is saved," Diaghilev declared sarcastically, although this same compromise had been made in Paris, London, and elsewhere since the world premiere. In addition, Kahn assembled a first-class publicity team that included young Edward Bernays (soon a wartime propagandist for the U.S. Committee on Public Information and later a leading public relations consultant). The publicity team effectively promoted the dance company and, in the process, preserved Kahn's esteemed place in the public eye.[33]

The Ballets Russes allowed Kahn to express himself in two meaningful ways. First, he challenged the New World to receive "nothing less than new art." Playing the high priest of culture, he was consecrating the soil of artistic modernism in America, which meant preparing American audiences to expand their expectations. By definition, new art must be seen from a different viewpoint, but collaborative art adds another challenge by asking its audiences to see both the whole and the interactions of complexities. Kahn encouraged the public to recognize

Vaslav Nijinsky in La Spectre de la Rose. *(Photograph by Herman Mishkin;*
Metropolitan Opera Archives)

the combination as a lesson of life — in this case, to see great choreography working with "great painters like Bakst and great composers like Stravinsky, in its combination of music, color, rhythm and movement." The cultural weight of his remarks may be abstracted — from the particulars of art to the society more generally and internationally — to suggest the ideal totality that Kahn sought.[34]

Second, Kahn used the Ballets Russes to fashion a comeback for cosmopolitanism and the avant-garde. At the same time he was moving himself toward a joint resolution of cultural, diplomatic, and financial exchange. A different form of brokerage, the Ballets Russes was comparable to his contemporary interest in the AIC. In both, Kahn fostered activities that, in his view, the United States needed for world leadership. And while the AIC took up foreign investment when European capital was being diverted by the war, Kahn the patron pumped money into Diaghilev's financially unstable ballet when its European patrons were also overwhelmed by the war. The AIC and the Ballets Russes each played another similar role in bridging the past and future. The expansionist goals of the AIC were patterned on the past, the present, and the future — on prewar precedents, as well as opportunities created by the war, and projections for the postwar world. Diaghilev's Ballets Russes occupied an analogous place, as critic-historians Lynn Garafola and Kenneth E. Silver both conclude: the wartime encounters with the avant-garde produced a model of the modernist ethnic mix or "stateless present."[35]

In this sense, the most striking subtheme in Kahn's project with Ballets Russes relates to how Kahn made Nijinsky's release a *cause célèbre* of the Great War. Colleagues abroad rallied support, while Kahn pleaded a case for the neutrality of art to the Austrian ambassador in Washington. A gala benefit in Paris for the British Red Cross helped to raise further interest. As Lady Ripon, the Duke of Alba, King Alfonso of Spain, and similarly eminent persons joined the campaign to free Nijinsky, Kahn went to work on the American secretary of state, Robert Lansing, convincing him to intervene in the case. Kahn was then allowed to guide American intelligence through informal talks between the U.S. ambassador in Vienna and the local aristocracy. By the end of February 1916, Countess Greffuhle apparently contacted the Emperor Franz Josef directly, and Nijinsky was released. Offering his gratitude to an Austrian aristocrat, Kahn promised "the considerate act of the

Austro-Hungarian Government" would be acknowledged by the American people.[36]

This was an internationalist episode from start to finish. Otto Kahn was reconstructing the *beau monde* of international art, which had meant so much to the prewar status quo. He was making a fresh start for his German-born self among the French. Renewing liaisons with continental patrons and the French Ministry des Beaux Arts, in turn, produced a burst of official French music and drama in New York, which was intended in part to sway American public opinion toward the French and entry into the war. Most notably for the new moderns, Kahn brought Jacques Copeau's Théâtre du Vieux-Colombier to New York. One of the more influential forces in twentieth-century theater, and notably one that looked to the past for inspiration in renewing traditions of simplicity, Kahn had seen the troupe perform on the Left Bank during its 1913 inaugural season. It had since been forced to disperse on account of the war, and offered no productions during 1915 or 1916, so the chance to reconvene in New York figured prominently in the continuity and survival of Théâtre du Vieux-Colombier. In exchange, Copeau gave New York two seasons (1917–19) of theater with literary merit. Although the first season did not draw well, the critical successes brought an invitation from Kahn to return. As important, the first season saw Copeau venture downtown to catch the bill of the newly established Provincetown Players, where his own dramatic theories, as well as Kahn's patronage, would have great weight for American theatrical modernism.[37]

Otto Kahn had returned to his job of seeding the garden of internationalism. Most particularly, he had gained new esteem in France, where respect for the Morgan bank was waning and Jack Morgan wanted Kahn's ascendency stopped. Upon hearing that Kahn might guarantee funds for the Comédie-Française to visit America, Morgan instructed Herman Harjes of the Paris house to "approach [the] Minister of Public Instruction and Beaux Arts on the subject." He was instructed to communicate "that [Clarence] Mackay would have more advantages in New York than any group of which [Lucien] Bonheur [founder and director of the Théâtre Français des États-Unis in New York] and Kahn were chief movers." Harjes took Morgan's message "to the proper authority," getting a noncommitted pledge to "be guided by your suggestion which is much appreciated."[38]

At the same time, a different set of concerns was forthcoming from

Kahn's acquaintances who lived or traveled in war-torn Europe. After a summer spent on "the Old Continent," one of the Metropolitan Opera's administrators returned telling stories full of horror about Europe, "a mad-house soaked with blood." Another arts broker, the former director of the Boston Opera Company, Henry Russell, wrote of his own efforts to arrange Diaghilev's tour, insisting, "You in America have not a notion of the difficulties and dangers to which an Englishman is exposed in traveling. . . . Frontiers are closed without notification and the last time I met Diaghileff [*sic*] in Rapelle I was held at the French Frontier on my return . . . and I was not allowed to communicate for 24 hours." As 1915 closed, a friend in England wrote, Europeans "are fed up with the war," but nearly everyone's attention had shifted from art and literature to death and destruction. The distance between neutral America and the European war was demarcated more precisely by Henry Russell at the beginning of 1916: "The season in America is not the sort of thing one can talk about over here just now." Kahn weighed New York's social and cultural offerings in comparison, then privately acknowledged, "New York is very busy and very gay — much too gay, considering the appalling tragedy which is being enacted in Europe." He could be genuinely proud of his artistic benefaction, yet had to admit it was "a trifling" in "the tremendous drama of this war."[39] The mobilization of military troops mattered more than reconvening theatrical troupes. Thinking probably of the carnage at Verdun in May 1916, he wrote, "Even art, so noble and in ordinary circumstances a serious thing, does not matter now." The unprecedented American economic boom, meanwhile, gave Kahn "a feeling almost as of shame." (He wrote: "America is reveling in prosperity . . . whilst the blood of Frenchmen is flowing in streams.") However much Kahn believed that "one of the most effective ways to bring nations nearer to each other is to spread the knowledge of and understanding for each other's art," the war had a way of draining his joy.[40]

Past prestige guaranteed nothing either. Even at a distance, Kahn was vulnerable to the same forces that ostracized some of the most prominent members of Anglo-Jewry of the Edwardian era. Both Ernest Cassel and Edgar Speyer had been role models of acculturation as well as business associates for Kahn, and they were now being dragged through a mire of scurrilous allegations. It gave Kahn cause for continued concern about his own reputation in England,

and in trying to silence whatever questioning was ongoing, Kahn offered another complex defense of himself in correspondence with Max Aitken, who had been elevated to the baronetcy as Lord Beaverbrook. Since Aitken was already convinced of Kahn's loyalties, the letter was probably intended for circulation among other well-placed persons whom Kahn hoped to persuade. But these were such strange times; Kahn would not rule out the possibility that even his friend "might imagine . . . because I happen to be of German extraction . . . I could be other than heart and soul for the British cause."[41]

The situation on Wall Street would only redouble his frustration, since appeals for financing kept arriving from Max Warburg in Germany, and Kahn was naturally nervous that one might wear down Schiff's resistance. But Allied financing was also moving in newly diversified directions, while Kuhn, Loeb was still left out of it. In May 1916 the Morgan house headed the first public offering of the American Foreign Securities Company (amounting to nearly $100 million in fresh funds for France), and in August it led another powerful banking group with a $250 million loan to Great Britain and Ireland. Tired of watching such advances by the house of Morgan, in August 1916 Kahn was additionally humiliated, when two partners of the rival firm interviewed him with regard to a rumor that Kuhn, Loeb was secretly working to buy the Vanadium Company, so the German government could "stop thereby delivery . . . to the allied countries." Face to face, the questioning was an excruciatingly polite "formality," in which Morgan partners Edward R. Stettinius and Dwight Morrow assured him that they "did not for a moment believe the story was true."[42]

The rumor in any case was as false as the etiquette on both sides of the interrogation was thin. And Otto Kahn was also keeping secrets of a different kind than the Morgan partners would suspect. Unknown to them, he had found fresh energy in the smart, new idea of issuing a five-year bond in the amount of $50 million for the City of Paris. Brilliant in its simplicity and fusions, the loan was the first Parisian financing of its kind to be made outside of France. Because none of the proceeds were intended for war-related purposes, Kuhn, Loeb could offer the loan without abandoning neutrality. It did not match the magnitude of the 1915 Anglo-French loan, nor equal the volume of Kuhn, Loeb's railroad financings, but it still exemplified the workings of a premier investment house, and Jacob Schiff not only approved, he also realized the business would "guard our standing and prestige as a great American international house."[43]

Kahn supervised the distribution of allotment letters for the Paris bond on the last Friday of September while the senior Schiff and his son were away on vacation. Enjoying the command as much as the outcome, he was all aglow on the following Monday, after the loan had been oversubscribed by better than a three-to-one ratio. "I have never been so happy at the conclusion of business," he wrote, "as I am at this public association of my firm with the City of Paris." Calling it "the most popular businesses we have ever done," he bragged about "its dramatic unexpectedness, its terms, its boldness, its object" and how "everything attracted favorable comment." High on his list of favorable comments were those from friends who were pleased to see the Morgans' jurisdiction challenged: "In the many congratulations which we received, there was noticeable an undertone of resentment against the Morgan monopoly and of satisfaction and relief, not only because France is popular, but because Morgans are unpopular."[44]

Negotiations began right away to finance other French cities, giving a further boost to Kahn's reputation as a benefactor of France, which would soon contribute to his first decoration by the French government. He plainly understood these municipal loans could help squash any doubts about his support for the Allies, but in the shorter run, his finest hour precipitated an uninvited consequence for Kahn's designs. News of the municipal financing instantly led Max Warburg to propose that Kuhn, Loeb should now issue loans to Hamburg, Frankfurt, and Berlin. Jacob Schiff was inclined to do it, and Kahn could offer no effective argument to stop them. As events moved quickly, by the first week of October, Warburg guaranteed the money would not be used for military purposes, and the Hamburg house awaited the final "terms . . . to close [the] business." Kahn was sweating and disheartened, expecting the deal to go through, when a German U-boat sank five vessels off the coast of Nantucket on October 8, 1916. Afterward Kuhn, Loeb cabled Hamburg: "Matter must be postponed for present."[45]

Meanwhile, the Morgan houses were reacting to their rival's moves. The first word of the Paris loan disturbed the London firm more than New York (whose partners sarcastically quipped, "We are delighted . . . to have Germans in America lend money to the Allies"). That dismissive tone soon enough turned serious. In the wake of the offering, the

Morgan partners, resentful of their rival's good publicity, began pressing a haze over every ray of Kuhn, Loeb's iridescence. In New York they snapped, "The issue was small enough to be easily absorbed by the banking community, . . . which was naturally glad to assist Kuhn, Loeb & Co. in the only real operation they have had since the War began." They blasted Kuhn, Loeb's ethics, too, alleging that "all such methods of which Pine Street [Kuhn, Loeb] is past-master were adopted" to boast the loan. Figuring that slick tricks were the loan's secret success, nothing more, they concluded it was oversubscribed because Kuhn, Loeb had told institutions that "if they wished to secure allotment, say $250,000, they better subscribe for several million dollars."[46] The sum of all these remonstrations at any rate indicated repressed anger. What was not said meant as much as what was said. Kuhn, Loeb did for France what the Morgans said could not be done: it issued an unsecured loan with *succès d'estime* in the United States, bringing new credits to France, the Ally most aggrieved by the Morgans' preferential treatment of British needs. The Morgans could accept it once, not twice, even though they were not yet aware that Kahn and Mortimer Schiff were set to bring out additional French offerings.

During the whole of October and November 1916, the Morgans were setting up their own municipal group for England, France, and Belgium, while Kahn and Mortimer Schiff were "anxious to proceed" with a $60 million offering for the cities of Bordeaux, Lyons, and Marseilles. There was also still a possibility that Kuhn, Loeb would finance German cities. These three paths of action collided with a fourth on November 28, 1916, when the Federal Reserve Board warned that "the interest of the country" was incompatible with investment in foreign treasury bills. That made December especially cold for American financial markets, as the Fed's warning "proved quite effective in calling a halt" to foreign loans.[47] All together, it produced a gnarled mess of ill will.

In mid-November, the Morgans learned of the Bordeaux, Lyons, and Marseilles financing. The development was considered a threat, not only to its own municipal group, but to the whole of Allied financing. During the weeks since the Paris deal, said one Morgan partner, "many in the Street" felt that Kuhn, Loeb had "broken through" the Morgans' lock on Allied financing, and the door was open for others to follow. Mostly, the Allies' banker was furious because France had tugged at the linchpin of Morgans' coordinated war-financing by

Rupture and Renewal

seeking independent bankers.[48] When on Saturday morning, November 18, Kuhn, Loeb officially advised the Morgans that negotiations for the three French cities would close on the same day, the Allies' banker moved promptly in an attempt to put down the deal, deciding to surprise the French minister of finance, Alexandre Ribot, with the news that Kuhn, Loeb was planning to finance German municipalities. Ribot immediately declared that it "could not be tolerated." Indeed, neither Kahn nor Mortimer Schiff had whispered a word to the French about the negotiations with Hamburg, until Monday, November 20, when they met with French officials to iron things out. Everyone in the room wanted the French loan to proceed and no one wanted financing for Germany, but Kuhn, Loeb's juniors had no authority to guarantee that there would be no German loans. They gambled nonetheless, saying that "under existing circumstances there is no likelihood of Kuhn, Loeb & Co. undertaking the placing here of any German municipal or other bonds." It was the best they could offer until November 24, when President Wilson unofficially counseled Kuhn, Loeb that "our relations with Germany are now in a very unsatisfactory and doubtful state, and that it would be most unwise at this time to risk a loan."[49] The offering of the Bordeaux-Lyons-Marseilles bonds had begun on the previous day.

With Wilson's words dimming the likelihood of a German loan, Kuhn, Loeb's future relations with the French momentarily seemed secured, until other trouble followed. November 28, the closing day of the Three Cities syndicate, also brought the Federal Reserve's warning, undercutting demand for all foreign issues. The disturbance was felt throughout short-term foreign securities markets, and it depressed the trading price on the Bordeaux-Lyons-Marseilles bonds, of course, but having sponsored so little by way of recent foreign securities, the impact upon Kuhn, Loeb was slight. The same could not be said of its effects upon the Morgan houses, for this event would topple British confidence in the Allies' banker.[50]

Every Morgan partner damned one person — Paul M. Warburg of the Federal Reserve Board. Closely tied to his Germanness, Warburg held a powerful position in affecting American policy. He desired neither an American declaration of war against Germany nor the unmitigated defeat of his homeland, and he was keen on doing what he could to bring peace in Europe, which loomed large after Wilson's reelection. The president himself wanted to tighten foreign credit in order to pressure the British, who were expected to frustrate his proposal for a peace conference, which Wilson incidentally was writing when he sent word to Kuhn, Loeb about financing the German cities. Nevertheless, it was not the president who was torched in Morgan cables that week. In exchanges with Jack Morgan, who was in London, Henry P. Davison alluded to Warburg as "a man in Washington whom we believe is doing everything he can to thwart the financial endeavors of the Allies." Jack Morgan replied, "It may be necessary to come out in public attack on the German-Jews and their influence with the Government." Davison counseled otherwise: "Any attempt along this line would be futile as well as harmful." Preferring instead for the Morgans to sound their alarm using private channels, so that various "authorities should know that there are evidences of increased activity in German propaganda," he also conveyed a sense that "there is something impending, just what it is I cannot determine." He guessed "it is in the direction of an important Peace movement" with the German Jews "actively and force-fully" backing it. A few days later the Morgan partners in New York added Kahn and Mortimer Schiff to the foci of their distrust: "[They] are outspoken for the Allies, but just where they really stand is hard to know."[51]

• • • •

WARRING TOWARD PEACE, 1917–1918

Rather than ask, "Which side are you on?," it would be better to ask, "Which sides are you on?," "Who believes you?," and "When loyalties conflict, which wins?" Such questions speak against Kahn's proclamations of unambiguous loyalties, but give a better impression of the actual turmoil. And while it is fitting to ask whether the Morgans subordinated French interests in favor of the British, or, simply, if the Morgan house in America put its own interests ahead of everyone during the war, one must also question whether Otto Kahn was any less motivated by self-interest than the Morgan partners. The bottom line was the sum of many financial and emotional factors. Kuhn, Loeb's neutrality and the Morgans' attitude toward German Jews obstructed Kahn's agenda, yet the Morgans' Anglophilia allowed Kahn to make inroads into new French business. And the French themselves were not any less disposed to use Kuhn, Loeb in leveraging better treatment from the Morgans than Kahn was ready to use the French (culturally and financially) to secure his place in the cosmopolitan world. Finally, if it was hoped that the French municipal loans would break the Morgans' monopoly, the end result was both more and less than Kahn expected. Kuhn, Loeb's business in France precipitated the worst crisis in the Morgans' relations with that nation to date, and the Allies' banker momentarily entertained the idea of leaving the French to "do their own purchasing." Calmer reactions reigned instead, as the Morgan partners decided to "keep our temper" and "serve France at whatever cost of humiliation or trouble." For the time being, they would "refrain from any present hint of real feelings," leaving ample room for festering resentment.[52] The possibility of future retaliation was wide open.

In that future, Otto Kahn would be an American of the most cosmopolitan sort—more the urbane New Yorker than typically American. Yet regardless of his citizenship, birth identity was doubly branded upon him. Perhaps Kahn took some solace in knowing that Ernest Cassel had been forced to leave Paris during the Franco-Prussian War. In this sense the Great War was only the more thorough breakdown in the transnational idiom of Kahn's modern times. All the same, Kahn was in uncharted territory—trapped between the identities of self, naturalized citizenship, and his community of descent. Through all, his goal stayed fixed on reembedding himself in the transatlantic world.

When Otto Kahn acquired American citizenship on the eve of America's entry into the war, it brought him the right to manage his own portfolio in two respects. With one hand he could better control his own financial resources. Had Kahn remained a subject of England, the new British denaturalization law might have returned him to German citizenry; then, as a German national when America entered the war, Kahn would have needed to surrender his American investments to the U.S. Alien Property Custodian, which Americanized the financial stake of Germans in the United States. The other hand was more visible. Feeling safer in American citizenship, Kahn reached toward a renewed public life. He soon went out to speak on the war-rally circuit, where, under the umbrella of national unity, he took up a number of themes. Among them, he conceded a permanent place for trade unions in industrial life. Acknowledging "high and noble" values in socialist doctrine, he granted that socialists could indeed be American patriots, while he also condemned the extremes—from "the militant Bolsheveki in our midst" to "the myth of a Rich Man's war." Along the way, whenever one of his speeches dealt with issues of class conflict, or national efficiency, Otto Kahn pitched his case for revising America's income tax system. He was an early and long-term opponent of exorbitant inheritance and capital gains taxes. In any event, whether he was making calls to arms, or to pocketbooks in support of Liberty Loans, there was one special concern in all of Kahn's wartime speeches — he unambiguously helped the cause of wartime unity by speaking for and to persons of German birth or ancestry in the Allied nations.[53]

He preached to hearts that were twisted in pain over the thought of warring with their German families or traditions. Kahn was speaking not as a voice of the U.S. government, but rather as a private citizen whose government valued his rhetoric, publicized it, and understood it to be more persuasive, coming "from me — born in Germany," than if it had come from an American without cultural ties to Germany. So long as America was at war not with the German people but with the German state and military, as Wilson himself had declared, Kahn could movingly allude to a longer odyssey. The shared ideals that remained fixed in his own marrow, as the son of a father who "stood in arms against Prussian oppression, for liberal ideas," led Kahn to promise that the Allies would "rescue Germany" — the real Germany of Luther, Goethe, Schiller, and Kant, which just thirty years earlier, he said, everyone admired and envied as a place of quickening energies, creative abilities, material achievement, and social progress. The sentiments and sensitivities of German identity, he likewise acknowledged, could not be captured by accepted notions as simple as the hyphenated "German-American," a term Kahn used only reluctantly, knowing it was inappropriate unless the "widely divergent interests and traditions" among Bavarians, Saxons, and Prussians, as well as the Jews, were understood as part of the "German" identity. With that echo of American pride in its own multirooted civilization, Kahn intended to plant a seed of further thought, hoping that "British friends and allies" would understand "that Americans of German antecedents can hate the fiendish mania which is Prussianism."[54]

As yet, when Kahn used himself as an example, he did not identify himself as a Jew. His speeches touched upon the differences between Russian and German Jews, and the identity crises of German nationalists who were Jews, without connecting these matters with his own heritage and identity. If this made it easier for Kahn to present himself as a favored son to those of German descent in America, even so, his Jewishness was likely the weightier determinant of Kahn's fate, especially among those who were unable to distinguish between the German and the Jew, or seek another alternative. Morgan would call Kahn a "German-Jew" or "German-Hebrew," not a Hun, and even among Kahn's friendlier acquaintances, one in Britain concluded that any and all of the honor earned from Kahn's service to the Allied cause could be dismissed because "his ancestors pitched their tents on the wrong side of the Jordan."[55] We must wonder, then, what Kahn was actually seeking in June 1917, when he finally bought shares and a box from MORECO. The standard notion is that Kahn finally decided to crack this portion of MORECO's anti-Semitic wall. Yet consider his ambivalence as a Jew over the long term; consider Kahn's decision to buy a box not as a privilege extended by MORECO, but rather as a choice made by Kahn himself; and consider the time. Was he not seeking acceptance in multiple identities — not as a Jew but rather as an American cosmopolitan, who presently saw Germanness to be the matter in higher relief?

Four days after America entered the war, Kahn wrote to President Wilson on the subject of German opera, saying that his board was "confronted with the question whether Opera in German sung by German artists shall continue to be given at the Metropolitan Opera House during the war." The patrons of the house were more divided now than in 1914, and it was clearly getting harder to preserve the internationalism of art. Wilson sent an ambivalent response, trusting "the good sense and moderation of the Directors of the Metropolitan Opera Company not to take any extreme or unnecessary action." That said enough for Otto Kahn. For the time being, the Metropolitan's board of directors would conclude "its duty — barring unforeseen events — [is] to continue its international repertoire as heretofore."[56] Not that Otto Kahn shunned the use of art for political purposes. He used the Metropolitan Opera House to speak out against kaiserism at a Liberty Loan rally, and, working with Aitken, he was probably instrumental in getting the Allies to commission a war film by D. W. Griffith.[57] At the outset of American belligerency, when he defended the continuation of German opera, it was likely with an understanding that a German artistic presence was consistent with his rhetoric about the inherent honor of the old Germany and its aesthetic traditions.

Such logic held sway only until too many Met directors saw it another way. In October 1917, the new season was about to begin when Clarence Mackay causally asked, "Has anything been decided in regard to giving German Opera at the Metropolitan this year?" One of the more musically minded and financially dependable directors, Mackay had been away all summer, neither thinking about the opera season nor available when Kahn gently polled the board members in New York on this question, and quietly decided the matter in discussions between himself and Gatti-Casazza without a quorum of the board. Now the opera season was only one month off, German operas were scheduled, and Mackay indicated that he had a problem with the inclusion of the German repertory. Calling this a question of "great delicacy and complexity," Kahn offered to talk privately with him about the issues or convene the directors to discuss the subject, whichever Mackay preferred. They spoke privately, exchanged further correspondence, then scheduled a meeting of the directors. Along the way, Mackay weighed his love for Wagner against his patriotism, ultimately concluding it was un-American to have German opera at the Met with the United States "at war with Germany." He went "squarely on record as against it" by the end of October, and the Metropolitan board followed.[58]

The resulting policy officially removed the German language rather than German music from the Met's offerings. That stood at odds with Kahn's pleas to the Austrian ambassador during the Nijinsky campaign, and it contrasted specifically with the policy at Covent Garden in London, where the German opera repertory continued throughout the war. However, if banning the German language exclusively let the Met's board members seem to be good Paterians—protecting music, the highest form or art—it also implied support for the policy at the New York Philharmonic, where German music was offered for the duration of the war. In a related matter, Kahn probably acceded with difficulty when the Metropolitan board commissioned a translation of Wagner's *Parsifal*. Kahn, who frowned on opera in translation, likely felt vindicated when the production was mounted in February 1919 and one critic jested that the text was better understood in German. In any case, carrying out the policy and politicizing the Met left public opinion divided; dropping German operas from the 1917–18 season immediately sparked a lawsuit by contralto Margarete Ober, a native of Berlin, for infringement of her contract; and the extra vocal demands of the substitute season inevitably strained the voices of other leading performers, including Enrico Caruso and Geraldine Farrar. The house was further politicized in 1918 when the U.S. national anthem was played before performances. The next season began with Caruso and the company singing the Allies' anthems between acts of Saint-Saens's

Samson et Delila. By then, the chorus had been weeded of four Germans and two Austrians, victims as much of their enemy-alien status as their articulation of pro-German sentiments. Though impossible to say exactly where Kahn stood within all this, the absence of German opera did afford greater opportunities for French works at the Met, which suited Kahn's other interests. Throughout, he was mainly waiting for the war's end to make New York and all the other culture capitals neutral cities once again.[59]

The setback to Kahn's aesthetic curriculum paled by comparison to the obstacles hindering his other ambitions. He hopelessly wanted to play a greater role among statesmen. By now his firm was joined in the great movement to finance the war, and Kahn stepped forth in support of the publicity campaigns. But Jacob Schiff was Kuhn, Loeb's point man with the various Liberty Loan committees, and Kahn had little or no intellectual inclination to command the leftover, back-office work. He ached instead for the opportunity to go "on some kind of official or semi-official mission" commensurate with his know-how and experience. Instead he found "little encouragement on the part of our governmental authorities except for military or Red Cross purposes." Meanwhile, throughout 1917, he thought about projects for France after the war, entertaining ideas for the AIC to work in navigation, harbor development, and shipbuilding, as he also tried to get the French government to lobby for "a small commission" from America to consider "the matter of reconstruction and kindred questions" — undoubtedly wanting himself appointed to it.[60]

Some encouraging words arrived in November 1917, when Paul Cravath, serving as legal adviser to the Inter-Ally Council in London, wrote, "I shall not be surprised to hear any day of your coming over on some official meeting." Nothing happened. At best, Kahn did get a meeting with President Wilson, of whom he later privately remarked, "When he wants to know, he asks. When he does not ask he does not care to know. . . . When he does not care, he stops at a siding and whistles for the other mind to approach." If that meant Kahn could not advise this president, it did not mean he had run out of resources for promoting himself. He continued to deliver patriotic speeches on the home front. One given in January 1918 discussed "the commissions now dealing with economic affairs" as well as the "serious and complex problems [that] must be solved . . . while the nation is at war and in the period of reconstruction and adjustment." Implying his appropriate involvement in solving the issues that "will set in with the coming of peace," Kahn seemed to be seeking public support for his own appointment. He had also grown tired of the pulpit, saying privately, "It is a nuisance to make these long and tedious trips" when, undoubtedly, a trip abroad would have been more exciting. Weary of waiting, he finally went to Europe during the summer of 1918, entirely in a private capacity.[61]

When he returned to America, Kahn tempted Wilson once more with a confidential letter summarizing his activities abroad. Others have emphasized the enclosure with this letter, which contained intelligence pertaining to an uprising of the Spartacus League, a German-based faction of social revolutionaries opposed to the war. The less sensational elements of his report were fundamentally more meaningful for Kahn. These included discussion of improved French ports and work presently underway by the U.S. Army that he thought could "form the basis of a permanent structure." If Kahn did not want to direct such improvements himself, he conveyed sufficient expertise for one or another important job. On the other hand, he also indicated — ever politely — that the American government had no practical sense of what he could effectively do. General Pershing had asked Kahn to meet secretly with Germans in Switzerland who might support surrender or peace, but Kahn had declined to go. Lest the president question Kahn's loyalty, he painstakingly explained that someone as famous as himself could neither travel secretly nor reach out to German nationals abroad, for it would "lay my actions, intentions and attitude open to misconstruction." Most important for Kahn to impress upon Wilson were the characteristics that brought Pershing to seek him out in the first place: a "knowledge of several languages and other personal qualifications," including "my international acquaintanceship and my banking relations."[62]

These qualities were not, in the end, sufficiently appreciated by official policymakers. Whatever the reason — and perhaps it was mainly Kahn's proximity to Paul Warburg, whose Germanness kept him from serving a second term on the Federal Reserve Board — Otto Kahn was offered no officially sanctioned role in representing America abroad. He did become chairman of the Military Entertainment Council Advisory Board; but he wanted much more and thought himself qualified to do much more.

CHAPTER FOUR

Seniority without Authority

"Now we face a different world." With these words to Max Warburg on August 26, 1919, Jacob Schiff proposed they should set aside events of the last few years and get on with the business that the war had distorted. It was no less odd because world conditions that had isolated Schiff and Warburg during the war now made it necessary for them to evaluate every question on a day-to-day basis. International financiers preferred long term orientations toward stability. Less obvious, perhaps, were the ultimate consequences of this war of unanticipated length and unfathomable cost, though at the end of 1915 Schiff grasped the possibility that, having fought to the point of unconditional surrender, the peace would be "the harbinger of another war in the near or distant future, bloodier than the present." In the event that men like Schiff and Warburg did not yet realize they were living in a world between wars as well as after one, they were aware that Germany, international bankers, and German-associated Jews were in the throes of acute identity confusion.[1]

The question as to why internationalism fared so badly after the war may be as old as the Treaty of Versailles, which Kahn claimed was also the answer. The peace treaties left him "sore at heart and sickened," immediately replacing Germany in Kahn's reasoning about what was wrong with the world.[2] But Kahn's story puts an accent on yet another point. Where every former adversary was unable or unwilling to collaborate, what they lacked were often qualities that Kahn had in abundance, and that would make him seem uniquely qualified to negotiate some of the more controversial issues of the postwar era. Imagine what role he might have assumed in negotiations between former belligerents. Otto Kahn was now an American, and one who, in the words of a Hungarian reporter, was "a true Schöngeist," or beautiful spirit, "which is met in America only rarely." He had been decorated in France (Chevalier, Legion of Honor), in Spain (Knight, Order of Charles III), and in Italy (Commander, Order of the Crown). Kahn also understood the languages of continental Europe better than many Americans, including some key representatives appointed by the Morgans or official Washington.[3]

His own experience during the war aside, there was no legitimate reason for Otto Kahn to think his isolation would extend into the postwar era. Except in all important matters, timing is everything. The war and the so-called peace had changed the times. While the damage to his name had been significantly controlled, no gossip entirely dies away if many people voice it, and Kahn would continue to struggle against the Anglo-Saxon rejection of German and Jewish self.[4] The sources of that rejection closely aligned another fatal clause in postwar governance — the rivalry between Kahn and the Morgan houses. The Morgans' attitude toward Kahn mirrored the wider punitive legacies of war, to some degree controlled them, and impeded a more collaborative postbellum era, which also sanctioned anti-Semitism. This is not to fix all of Kahn's shortcomings on the Morgan firms. "Such obvious conflicts of unmistakable good with unmistakable evil can only supply the crude drama of villain and hero," as George Bernard Shaw once wrote.[5]

Otto Kahn had additional problems — being an outsider within Kuhn, Loeb, reluctant to rebel, and ambivalent about giving a scrappy fight, he was as much inhibited by his own investment in the codes of gentlemanly conduct and conflicted by his cosmopolitan loyalties. However strong his desire to resume an esteemed place in all the formerly belligerent countries, Kahn would not, for instance, abandon his Anglophilia in favor of Francophilia or Mittleuropa. In addition, being a Jew as much as being a German and a financier drew more outward hostility after the war than he expected or readily admitted. His own sense of importance posed further problems. As the international press found him to be an accessible and amiable voice, it inflated Kahn's status in international affairs. The problem was, perhaps, that Kahn believed his press at a time when he was largely powerless, no less on the world stage than within Kuhn, Loeb, where his co-senior kept the firm from the aggressive pursuit of foreign investment opportunities that Kahn initially advocated.

After Jacob Schiff died on September 25, 1920, the succession at Kuhn, Loeb configured quite differently from what the former senior had earlier intended. The firm was short on partners, since Paul Warburg did not return after his resignation from the Federal Reserve Board in 1918. Felix Warburg was still devoted chiefly to philanthropic interests, and had little to do with the business, while Jerome Hanauer worked hard but lacked *yichos* (hereditary distinction) as well as family connections with anyone at Kuhn, Loeb, until his son-in-law, Lewis Strauss, joined the firm a few years later.[6] That left Mortimer Schiff and Otto Kahn as the only serious contenders for seniority. Schiff was unquestionably the heir, but Kahn was too important to stand in the shadow, and they would not reprise the roles played earlier by the father of one and the father-in-law of the other. An unusual agreement resulted whereby Kahn took less of the profits, lacked decisive authority, and publicly claimed the title of co-senior.

An additional personal context should be established before taking up any of the above subjects and themes. Kahn, who turned fifty-two in 1919, was contending with warnings of his own mortality. He had fainted at a banquet in Chicago six years earlier; he suffered a serious stroke in 1921. As he began two months of recuperation at Evian in mid-year, it became clear to Kahn that seniority had arrived with a double setback. The ravaged state of world affairs found a mirror in his body and psyche, leaving Kahn to confide, "There is little satisfaction in knowing that the world at large is a good deal more out of joint than I am personally." In any event, he refused to let either to vacate his identity, or deny his vitality. A few months later, he was back in New York, "this nerve-wearing, rushing city of stress," claiming to have recovered. Kahn was always ultra-private and vain about his ailments, but high blood pressure and chest pains continued to bother him — the signs of the heart condition that would ultimately kill him.[7]

It may be that when Kahn's biological clock chimed the late hour, he reacted as if dawn were speeding him to work. He refused to slow down. He moved harder and faster in pursuit of wholeness, optimism, and the recovery rather than the decline of transnational relations. In that regard, Kahn's patronage gave him room to act and earn respect, bringing just enough satisfaction and fame to feel himself moving toward fulfillment. But Kahn also had an uncanny way of being at once ahead of his time and yet out of date. He was ahead of his time in thoughts on "international unanimity," envisioning the coexistence of

A caricature, "intended to be Good-Natured," by Miguel Covarrubias,
Vanity Fair, *1925. (Conde Nast Publications)*

world capitals rather than the supremacy of one financial center. He
was also ahead of his time in modulating the snobbishness of wealth
and art. "I am not a 'high-brow' (though I admit I used to be one),"
said Kahn in 1919, when he praised the People's Theatre, a movement
begun by New York's labor unions. And he was ahead of his time in
stating that "private enterprise in America cannot by itself accomplish"
what was needed either for the financial recovery of Europe or the

Seniority without Authority

sustenance of arts. In 1919 Otto Kahn thought it better to maintain the administrative apparatus in Washington that could coordinate much-needed postwar intergovernmental loans. In addition, he advocated the creation of "a Federal Department of Fine Arts, such as exists in many European countries."[8]

Still and all, in an era of ready-made clothing, Otto Kahn never wore anything off the rack. When he partied among the Greenwich Village bohemians, Kahn dressed religiously in Savile Row suits, and his boots, made by the best craftsman in New York, were nearly always covered by the most immaculate spats. When fashionable American moderns wore tuxedos, he donned full evening wear. Always looking well appointed and civilized, his elegance also could nonetheless seem, as Eisenstein once said of Pirandello, a little too proper and nineteenth century for the world after the war.[9] The point speaks to more than the clothes. Kahn carried much over from the nineteenth century, including his bonds with *Bildung*, the insignia of *mécène*, and a loyalty for the values learned in Pater and Carlyle. These mainstays seemed flexible enough for him in the 1920s. In an unfamiliar world, they helped Kahn find strains of sweetness and light, progress, enlightenment, and a faith in solutions to problems. Unable to control the outcome, only three outcomes seemed possible: reconciliation, destruction, or the absence of ending. Ever the optimist, Kahn counted on reconciliation.

· · · ·

MISSING STAKES AND SUPPORTING ROLES

In November 1915, Jack Morgan had concluded there were "certain racial characteristics and habits of mind which I believe always work, and always will work, to prevent a Jew from being entirely great, no matter how clever he is." That system of values was again evident, a few years later, when he summarily dismissed a candidate for the governing board of Harvard University by saying, "The Jew is always a Jew first and an American second." Another candidate went down for being a papist.[10] In world affairs it would follow that Morgan and his cohorts could continue treating all Jews as captives of their co-religionists, the Germans as adversaries, and the French as strange. They also carried forward the belief that only one house should lead New York and London into the postwar world, where the Morgans' position as the world's most prominent bankers was matched by their resolute resistance to the idea that leadership would be better shared. A pattern was emerging in 1919. When Kahn learned that the Morgans, "our friends at the corner of Wall Street," were seeking to replace Kuhn, Loeb in refunding the French cities, he found it "interesting but hardly surprising."[11] In this case, and during negotiations in 1922 with the Paris, Lyons, and Mediterranean Railroad, Kuhn, Loeb secured business the Morgans wanted and felt they deserved. Along the way, the Morgan partners developed a definite animosity for Otto Kahn personally. They spread rumors about Kahn secretly financing Germany during the war, and a secret operative, who was hired to prove it, also tried to worry Kahn that a clerical error in Britain had voided his American citizenship.[12]

Such behavior was more than retribution for wartime grievances. It boarded on an obsession. Yet the ethnic politics, personal grudges, and petty smears were complicated by Kahn himself, who was convinced a wiser course for settling the affairs of Europe would be to rescue modernity, not destroy Germany. On the cultural front, as early as August 1919 he began working to restore German opera at the Metropolitan, urging Gatti-Casazza to get the rights to recent works of Richard Strauss, Franz Schreker, and Erich Wolfgang Korngold. By November 1921, when Austrian diva Maria Jeritza debuted with the company in Korngold's *Die tote Stadt*, both she and the score were well received.[13] Nevertheless, the restoration of cultural ties lacked counterparts in nearly every other aspect of Kahn's internationalist agenda. He believed not only that Germany's economic health would be in the best interests of the former Allies, but also that a stable Germany posed both a bulwark against Bolshevism and a probable agent for the industrial development of Russia. Kahn was forward-looking enough in November 1919 to proclaim the need for a humanitarian loan from the U.S. government to all European nations in distress — with a special understanding for the need to ease Germany's pain in its first winter after the war. His position on Allied debts to the United States, in addition, favored dealing with them "on broad, farsighted and liberally constructive lines."[14]

Kahn used numerous channels to promote his views. He wrote and spoke tirelessly on international relations. He was a founding director of the Council on Foreign Relations, and his proposals for adjusting the Allied debts to America shared headlines with those made by J. P. Morgan. He golfed with President Warren Harding and conferred with him on domestic as well as foreign economic matters. He also briefed old New Yorkers such as Bainbridge Colby and Charles Evans Hughes when each was secretary of state, and he contributed significantly to the financial health of the Republican Party.[15] None of this, however, gained a place for Kahn and his firm at the postwar negotiating tables. The Morgan partners resolutely defended their supremacy in this realm, locked him out of high-level policy making, and effectively marginalized Kahn, even as he grew more popular and otherwise more annoying to Morgans.

Seeking to regain the kind of extraordinary European business that Kuhn, Loeb once knew, Kahn quietly aligned with French, British, and German financial associates who resented Morgan dominance, and thought the Morgan strategy was neither a fait accompli nor well conceived. He occasionally implied that Kuhn, Loeb could "take American leadership" in issuing German Reparation bonds "either alone or with Morgans," and he allegedly complained when Jack Morgan became the sole representative of American private banks on the Loan Committee to assemble in Paris in May 1922 — hinting that the team should have included himself. Such tactics only left the Morgans itching to "get all our friends in line to . . . counteract the strenuous efforts of our adversaries." When Morgan partner Thomas Lamont, former U.S. Treasury representative at the 1919 peace negotiations, described Kahn's assertiveness as "the campaign of the Chosen People against the Christians," he advised "a most discreet course in picking up all of these loose ends."[16]

Frictions at Kuhn, Loeb toughened the going. Even so, Kahn had gotten off to a good start in the direction of aggressive foreign investment. In 1920 Kuhn, Loeb and the Guaranty Trust Corporation of New York jointly purchased 125,000 shares of the equity capital in Austria's Creditanstalt — Austria's leading bank, Central Europe's most internationalist bank, and a major concern of the Viennese Rothschilds. Creditanstalt and the Rothschilds subsequently invested $125,000 in Paul Warburg's new International Acceptance Bank, which was backed by Kuhn, Loeb and the AIC as well. By the following April, Kahn was eyeing further opportunities in Central Europe, and wrestling with "skeptical associates" in his firm, whom he found needing assurance that "we shall not be blackening our fair name and doing a deed of reckless irresponsibility by being the instrumentality to entice good American dollars into Czech-Slovakia." On that matter he achieved some success, as Kuhn, Loeb's offerings in 1922 included $14 million in bonds for the Czechoslovak Republic, and a $7.5 million mortgage loan for the

City of Greater Prague. The same year saw additional French offerings amounting to $30 million for the Paris, Lyons, and Mediterranean Railroad and $25 million for the Department of Seine. All the same, when it came to "placing or keeping capital on the European continent," as Kahn wanted, during the 1920s it was more characteristic for Kuhn, Loeb to hesitate than to proceed. In May 1922 Kahn recommended that the cash-starved Max Warburg do what Kahn himself was doing—"Keep on suggesting things," despite the "lack of receptiveness" among American financiers "toward various Central European proposals." "Sooner or later—maybe sooner," he continued, "something is bound to materialize."[17]

Events were clearly shaping expectations. At that time, hyperinflation was already gripping Austria with as much severity as the more infamous inflationary calamity that climaxed in Germany in 1923. A meager U.S. market for foreign securities spelled caution for American investors. Yet another cause for Kuhn, Loeb's timidity (and Kahn's frustration) sat specifically with Mortimer Schiff, whose father always questioned his son's capacity to do the job that he was born to do. Little ever changed in the elder Schiff's temperament, which early on faulted Mortimer's "tendency to be too hasty and independent in his judgment" and "not always ready to go as deeply into details as is necessary."[18] Since the war had also divided them, and the son was a less devout Jew than his parent, such assessments were among many unresolved issues to merge with all the emotional intensities of bereavement when seniority came to Mortimer Schiff. His training brought neither the necessary confidence nor experience for making bold decisions, and instead left him haunted by the years of chronic chastening. Soon enough, Kuhn, Loeb's new senior overidentified with the financial conservatism, unquestioned authority, and notions of gentlemanly competition that had distinguished his father's ways of business. Expecting obeisance from his own partners, while tendering deference to the Morgans, the result was institutional hesitation for Kuhn, Loeb that stymied the bolder Otto Kahn, whose own instincts were sharper than his ambitions were bold.

The spring of 1922 would seem an unlikely time to holiday among the Austrians. Unemployment was worsening by the hour, hyperinflation made food unaffordable, and the chancellor's cabinet would resign in May. Yet none of these factors deterred Kahn, who headed off for a week-long Austrian "music spree" in the company of composer Richard Strauss and "several other artistic lights," including his presumed lover, Maria Jeritza. Watching Kahn leap into the world of music and art at this moment struck Max Warburg for its contrast to the "misery" and "decay" everywhere, but Warburg as well as the Kuhn, Loeb partners knew well enough to step back and let Kahn go "Richard Straussing." While Kahn wanted "nothing to do with business" during his vacation, it was unlikely that he could expect to seek only pleasure in the midst of such crisis. Hyperinflation left no hideaways anyway. The panicked reality invaded all corners of the world, even the most opulent Leopoldskron, Max Reinhardt's Baroque Salzburg castle, which seemed strangely unromantic when lit by candlelight because the cost of electricity was so dear. Conceivably trying to lighten everyone's spirits, Kahn joked: "What's the trouble? Short circuit at the Reinhardts?" Of greater consequence, he reassured the dramatist that plans to underwrite his upcoming visit to America were secure.

Kahn also wound up paying some business calls in Vienna. He had come to Austria aware that Kuhn, Loeb would take no new financial stake in the country and its depreciating currency "as long as things are what and as they are." He left Austria with a renewed commitment to European rehabilitation. Feeling "the whole world is pining for strong and wise leadership," he vowed, "what little I can do to help . . . I shall be only too happy to do." Swinging next through Paris, Kahn addressed a meeting of French senators (convened by the Group for Foreign Relations) and found them "greatly alive, on the whole, to the seriousness of things in Austria, sympathetic towards the Austrian people, and very desirous that something should be done to straighten things out." As important, French politicians were "most encouraging" to Otto Kahn.[19]

He was on a campaign, and soon enough it became a contest with the Morgans. The Morgan houses had declined proposals for Austrian government loans in November 1921 and May 1922. They still thought "the late enemy" to be "undesirable business" in October 1922, when Grenfell reported, "Mr. Otto Kahn is busy in it . . . the whole thing is in the air and very likely to come of nothing." He added, "The arrangements are being made by people with no practical knowledge of finance," and concluded, "Better leave such things to Kuhn, Loeb." Contrary to Grenfell's impression, in any case, something important did come of the current discussions. The League of Nations presented a reconstruction plan, authorizing a $130 million loan to be tendered internationally and guaranteed by foreign governments. Grenfell was still skeptical, continuing his snickering about how Kahn was "offering his congratulations to everyone at Geneva and elsewhere," but the reconstruction plan, with its strict fiscal and monetary austerity, halted the freefall of the Austrian currency in November 1922.[20] Afterward, the Morgan banks mustered the courage for Austrian financing. In the following spring, they joined the Bank of England in issuing the British share of the lending, while the New York house started organizing U.S. bankers for the American share.

Considerable risks still lingered, of course. Germany, Hungary, Poland, and Russia all were by now likewise suffering hyperinflation. Everyone was racked with fear since, in a dispute over reparations, French and Belgian troops had occupied the Ruhr, the principal center of German steel and iron production. The bankers who gathered to support the American portion of the loan also lacked any guarantees from their government. Kahn later commented that "a good deal of doubt and hesitation" gripped members of the American sponsoring group, and it was not calmed by the way "Jack Morgan presided" over his fellow bankers, or the "exclusive Morgan color" and "one-sided handling" that he hated in his competitor. At one such meeting in late April, Kahn would at first sit quietly, masking his envy while Jack Morgan opened the meeting with "a moving address" on the Austrian bonds. Kahn actually thought it was hypocritical for Morgan to lecture now about the "plain duty of American financial leaders to participate." However, this was not the moment to challenge Morgan's authority or in any way impede the greater good that would come from Austrian recovery. It was hoped that the financing might resolve one of Europe's fundamental traumas and pave the way for subsequent loans. Nevertheless, when the Morgan senior went on to state the terms of the Austrian issue, more than a few of the bankers twitched nervously because the offering, at "around an 8 percent basis," would require a "temporary financial lockup of reasonable proportions," and that contradicted a sacred rule in conservative financing, by putting the underwriters' capital at risk. In Kahn's view, Morgan's haughtiness made it more objectionable. Having announced that J. P. Morgan & Co. "would even be willing" to risk its capital in order to assure American participation, the Morgan senior continued, "If between us we could not place from fifteen to twenty-five millions of intrinsically good bonds around a 8 percent basis, it would be a sad commentary."[21]

Kahn was to speak next. Whether the terms were a surprise or not, he started carefully, with an "eloquent endorsement" of the business, then even more carefully tendered an alternative proposition. "The proper price to bring them out would be an 8½ percent basis, less 5 to 6 points," he said, taking a position that was more to the liking of several other bankers, including Charles Mitchell, president of the National City Company, who seconded Kahn's opinion. The meeting adjourned with the terms unresolved and Kahn only half-pleased to have set in motion a "veiled menace" by contradicting Morgan.[22] Back in the confines of his own office, Kahn more candidly admitted the weakness of his firm in these negotiations. There was little chance of "K.L. & Co. . . . having a position of practical equality with Morgans." The Austrian Loan had become "League of Nations business, or, to be more correct, Bank of England business." Kahn saw "no particular need that the Morgans have of us in this instance, inasmuch as they are close to the seller, i.e., the League of Nations or Bank of England and have with them the various distributing houses for liquidating the business." In other words, Kahn could stir up a little trouble, but the Morgans had the power of the manager. That power brought the right to define the terms of the loan, as well as the parties invited to join the underwriting group, along with the allotments among the participating firms. Kahn resented that such power should reside with the Morgans, but he respected it as he would respect his own.

A double deception followed. Kahn was right and wrong to think the Morgans did not need Kuhn, Loeb. The Austrian Rehabilitation Loan required unity among the leading American bankers, and Kuhn, Loeb was given equal billing in the public offering, with its name appearing side by side with J. P. Morgan when the American portion of the loan was issued on June 11, 1923. Co-management gave an impression of the firms acting equally, but nothing could be further from the truth, and later events reveal that Kahn was more dissatisfied with the arrangement than Mortimer Schiff, who felt the Morgans had treated Kuhn, Loeb decently.

This all had great significance as well as grave consequences. New York's German-Jewish investment houses had flourished since the Civil War in large part because their access to capital intertwined with ethnic and familial ties in Europe. Firms like Kuhn, Loeb dominated American dealings with the German-speaking cultures. Even after the German houses of America failed to support the German-speaking nations in wartime financing needs, it was presumed they would return to leadership after the war. That expectation was founded upon another experience. The custom historically was "one good deal deserves another." As a rule, once a large investment house satisfactorily sold a security issue, there was a permanent connection between the issuing government or corporation and the banker. Considering that the Austrian Loan of 1912 originated with M. M. Warburg and Kuhn, Loeb, under normal circumstances, the American share of the Austrian rehabilitation loan should have been principally Kuhn, Loeb's business.

American financing for the Japanese government speaks to the same point. Jacob Schiff twice financed Japan during the Russo-Japanese War, and Japan ranked high among his achievements in international finance. Yet no one at Kuhn, Loeb seemed to suspect anything when Morgan partner Thomas Lamont made a tour of Japan in 1920 and began befriending top figures in Japanese economic life, through whom he would quietly lure the Japanese government into the family of Morgan clients. After the Tokyo-Yokohama earthquake of September 1, 1923, at any rate, Kahn cabled Mortimer Schiff from Paris with news of Japan's rumored interest in a major foreign loan. Kuhn, Loeb's partners presumed the loan would be made under their own leadership, and in this instance, Kahn did not push for immediate action; he felt "rather bearish" about "how the American market will regard a Japanese loan," perhaps still thinking, as he said less than three years earlier, that the American "Man in the Street" was worried about Japan's "aggressive designs" among "strategically important islands in the Pacific." For some time now, though, Kahn's private lack of interest in Asian affairs evidenced the limits in his internationalism. He once told a correspondent, "I do not know what to make of those impenetrable Japs. I have met many of them and have often tried to read them, but in vain."[23]

With Kuhn, Loeb waiting for the right moment and terms, Lamont quietly made his own moves, persuading the Japanese to go with the Morgan house, which he indicated was stronger in New York and London than Kuhn, Loeb. He said as well that the Morgans offered better cooperation from "the entire American investment public," possibly implying that Kuhn, Loeb was limited to a German-Jewish niche. At any rate, news of the switch was delivered to Kuhn, Loeb by a delegate from the Japanese Ministry of Finance, whom the Morgan partners had coached in the etiquette of how a client broke from its traditional banking house in America. In Lamont's words, the Japanese "expected their friends Kuhn, Loeb & Co. to tell them this course was a wise one." Kuhn, Loeb yielded as gentlemen should, but it was a humiliation that put Kahn in additional supporting roles, and when he discussed the Japanese loan with Morgan partners on at least three occasions during January 1924, it appears that he was acting under the authority of Mortimer Schiff to find face-saving compromises. The resulting arrangements allowed Kuhn, Loeb and the National City Company to share equally in the purchase group apportionment, with Kuhn, Loeb getting the public appearance of a slightly better role in published announcements of the offering. This time the firm's name appeared beneath J. P. Morgan & Co. but above the National City Company in the advertisements for the issue.[24]

Kahn did not take these blows lightly. He had gone into something of a frenzy about the Morgans after the Austrian loan, warning his partners during the autumn of 1923, "Morgans are very busy everywhere in Europe and one comes across their tracks constantly." At the time, he pleaded for Mortimer Schiff to maintain Kuhn, Loeb's stake in Creditanstalt, reminding him, "If we want to be a financial factor in European affairs . . . we have got to keep up certain points d'appui [of support]." In competition with the Morgans elsewhere, Kahn was trying "to push us ahead of them in Italy," boosting Mussolini's regime with favorable remarks to the press and pulling out all of his best social, financial, and artistic connections at once — only to see the Morgans ultimately get the business that Kahn sought.[25] After the Japanese business added to his indignation, all sense of entitlement or earned respect seemed to evaporate, and a most vexed Otto Kahn nearly exploded as the London Reparations Conference convened in the summer of 1924.

To begin with, Kuhn, Loeb partners held no position at the conference that was to finalize the Dawes Plan and set the terms for an international loan to Germany. There was also much dissension within and among the various national delegations. And the French were grumbling about Lamont, who, in alliance with the Bank of England, seemed too readily interested in the political advantage of the British when demanding that the Transfer Committee rather than governments must determine whether Germany was guilty of "flagrant default." During the second week of the conference, Etienne Clémentel of the French delegation threw up a disturbing if not strong threat, intimating that a competitive financial group could be organized by the Banque de Paris et des Pays Bas and Kuhn, Loeb to "underwrite the loan on easier terms than [the Morgans] as to security, although perhaps at a higher rate." The rumor found its way into published reports, and one French newspaper specifically lamented the "absence of Mr. Otto Kahn who is so alive to the needs of France." The most recent French criticism found Grenfell and Lamont half-heartedly admitting that "this would be a happy solution to the situation." They were cautious even as they discredited the likelihood of competition from Kuhn, Loeb.[26]

If Otto Kahn did not dirty his hands in planting the threat, he was willing to cultivate it. Passing through London in late June, he arranged to "talk about the European situation" with U.S. Ambassador Frank Kellogg. He next went off to the continent for two weeks, returned to England, and then headed to Scotland. While observing the conference from a distance, he was also getting insiders' reports on the negotiations from Paul Cravath. Kahn, alarmed by one such report that said Kellogg was proceeding as though Lamont could act on behalf of Kuhn, Loeb, instantly fired off a cable to his partners in New York. "If this understanding should not be correct," he proposed to "take whatever steps seem to you advisable." He was, in fact, itching for permission to "meet some of the big guns in London," and when his partners' reply arrived, Kahn welcomed what he took to be marching orders. "Too late now to get a position in the conference," he answered. "However shall see Lamont Tuesday and define our position as stated by you." By Tuesday, all the same, a correction arrived from New York that "warned" him to cool down. Kuhn, Loeb had "given Lamont no authority to speak for us," Kahn was reminded, "but in view of our general relations with them and their jockeying in Austrian loan and Japanese loan we do not think we should take steps at this time." Kahn was now authorized to act only "if an opportunity offers to solidify our own position in eventual loan." This pretty much sealed it. Kuhn, Loeb would accept a role "at least as good as in [the] Japanese loan," expecting the Morgans would give them something better in return for its "special German relations" and good name. His partners instructed

Kahn: "We should do utmost to be placed even more on equality with [Morgans] . . . and superior to National City Bank and others."[27]

Interpreting the message as liberally as possible, Kahn shifted between obedience and insubordination. He made a brief, busy stop in London, stirring trouble along the way. There had been "a pleasant and indulgent telephone chat" with Lamont, in which, Kahn said, he had canceled their scheduled meeting without saying why he had asked to convene. But Lamont did not interpret their discussion similarly. A few weeks later he complained to Schiff about Kahn's behavior. Kahn defended himself to Schiff:

> I never said to Lamont or anyone else that "anyone who would block the German Loan undertook a great responsibility." . . . Nor did I "talk very bullishly on the possibilities of American placing" or minimize the difficulties. . . . The fact is that I was in Scotland all the time the Conference was in session. . . . I spoke to no one [in London] on this subject, except [Kellogg's secretary, James A.] Logan and Clémentel, in neither of which interviews the questions of the attitudes of the bankers was discussed (apart from a few cursory references), inasmuch as a day or two earlier the Loan formula had been definitely agreed upon. I did say to both of them, as you did to [Owen D.] Young and Logan, that I believed it was essential for the success of the Loan that it should not be given the color in any country of being any one banker's specific domain. . . . Maybe Lamont heard something about that; maybe he felt sour generally, realizing that the handling of the situation by him and his fellow-bankers at the Conference had exposed him and Morgans to considerable criticism. . . . Maybe it was reported to him that Clémentel had said certain things . . . favorable to me and not so favorable to him; maybe he attached credence to reports in the press to the effect that K.L. & Co. were inclined to handle the loan with the Banque de Paris. . . . Whatever the explanation, he is mistaken as to his facts.

What actually got communicated was probably mutual duplicity. Kahn did use his swing through London to assert influence on the weak points in the Morgans' negotiations. When Kahn met with Logan, he knew Kellogg's subordinate was "not totally in sympathy and accord" with Morgan and the Bank of England, but appeared "to have the liking and full confidence of the French." Logan made a good target for Kahn's self-described "Machiavellian finesse." No matter how it appeared, though, Otto Kahn was not looking to steal the business outright. He and Kuhn, Loeb disliked the idea of an independent group emerging "irrespective of Morgan's attitude." Nor was Kahn in the position to strike a major upset. But in saying, "There would of course have to be leaders who would primarily direct the matter," he had suggested to Logan and Clémentel that American leadership "would most appropriately be exercised by Morgans and ourselves, perhaps with the addition of another leading bank." That was sufficient meddling to upset the Morgan partners.[28]

Such efforts stood on an uneasy foundation. Privately Kahn admitted defeat: "I do not believe that we shall be able to obtain a real equality with Morgans, they are too firmly entrenched, and several leaps ahead." Publicly, he masked any hint of backsliding. Instead, he acted secure in the top ranks of financial leadership, and he was able to do so partially because his convictions still told him that he was qualified to participate. As if playing a bridge match or poker game, Kahn kept the face of an able equal, holding fast to the opinion that "most businesses of the first rank are corralled by K.L. & Co., J.P.M. & Co., City Bank, etc." — until the next round or deal. At one point, Kahn expressed a clear preference to win, then backed away from it: "I should love to call [Lamont's] bluff and have K.L. & Co. go ahead and become the leaders of this business. Money is so easy, the loan is intrinsically so sound . . . the sentiment towards foreign loans so much improved, that at the proper moment and under the right conditions, it ought to be possible . . . to handle . . . from $75,000,000 to $100,000,000. . . . However, I am sure we shall not assume that position, nor would Morgans let us, and I am inclined to doubt whether it would be wise policy for us to do so even if they would let us." Kahn knew "the prominence which Morgans had in the Conference negotiations" was decisive.[29]

As a result of the London conference, the German External Loan of 1924 facilitated Germany's payment of reparations under the Dawes Plan, a definite turning point in the twisted postbellum return to stability. It also came with a slyly cutting penalty for Kuhn, Loeb when the syndicate manager of the American group, J. P. Morgan & Co., wrote the rules and assigned shares among the purchasing group. The Morgan house in New York initially figured Kuhn, Loeb should have the same percentage as First National Bank and National City Bank in the original purchase. On all printed forms and notices, J. P. Morgan & Co.

would "appear on a line by itself," above the rest, and some freedom to negotiate the order of names in the second tier could be left for City Bank and Kuhn, Loeb to "settle between them," but the New York partners expressly did not want to repeat "the method employed in the Japanese loan."[30] Further changes were forthcoming after Jack Morgan and Thomas Lamont received the proposal in London. Within twenty-four hours they revised the shares of the respective purchasing houses, increasing the percentages taken by J. P. Morgan, First National, and City Bank, while reducing all other participants' shares. They also tellingly cast aside one of their New York partners' suggested courtesies — that the draft should be presented for the approval of Mortimer Schiff and Charles Mitchell, who were also in London — saying, "It is hardly necessary to go as far in gaining Mortimer L. Schiff's cooperation as you suggest." "While Schiff may make nominal complaint," they concluded, "he will be satisfied with any such proportion" (Table 4.1).[31]

The private war between America's leading international financiers, it seems, had finally come to decisive victory, through terms abstracted within the Dawes Loan. Whatever the ultimate distribution, the advertisement announcing the German External Loan finally ran with Kuhn, Loeb, First National, and City Bank on the same line, all beneath J. P. Morgan & Co. But the illusion of even near parity ultimately took a sardonic turn. When the Dawes Plan was denounced by the Nazis, Kuhn, Loeb's share of the blame was disproportionate to either its role in constructing the plan or its participation in the issue.

Why did Kahn and his partners go along? Because any promise for the stabilization of Germany had to be supported. Even if the scheme, as Kahn said, "does not in itself constitute a highroad, smoothly paved, broad, straight, and free from obstructions," the Dawes Plan was "a bridge," and he publicly pardoned its builders for choosing the "somewhat incomplete equipment and inadequate material at their disposal." Kahn threw his support in favor of a fragile and incomplete structure, hoping it would lead "to prosperity and to neighborly relationships among the nations." Trusting that "recovery will still require time, patience, skill, care and forbearance," if the end of conflict was finally nearer, and it ended in reconciliation, good business would follow.[32] Besides, if Kahn needed to tease more cheer from the immediate situation, he could emphasize Kuhn, Loeb's enduring roles rather than its curtailed stature. Indeed Kuhn, Loeb was the only American house of German descent in the original group. Impossible as it was for Kahn

TABLE 4.1. *The German External Loan of 1924: Percentage Allocations of the American Group*

Original Purchase Group as of October 2, 1924		Original Purchase Group as of October 3, 1924	
J. P. Morgan & Co.	25.00	J. P. Morgan & Co.	30.00
Kuhn, Loeb & Co.	12.50	First National Bank	15.00
First National Bank	12.50	National City Bank	15.00
National City Bank	12.50	Kuhn, Loeb & Co.	10.00
Guaranty Co. of N.Y.	6.25	Guaranty Co. of N.Y.	5.00
Bankers Trust Co.	6.25	Bankers Trust Co.	5.00
Kidder, Peabody	6.25	Kidder, Peabody	5.00
Lee, Higginson	6.25	Lee, Higginson	5.00
Harris, Forbes	6.25	Harris, Forbes	5.00
Dillon, Read & Co.	6.25	Dillon, Read & Co.	5.00

Source: Charles Steele, W. H. Porter, Dwight Morrow, Thomas Cochran, R. C. Leffingwell, George Whitney to Morgan, Grenfell, Oct. 2, 1924, 177/21, and J. P. Morgan and Thomas Lamont to J. P. Morgan & Co., Oct. 3, 1924, 177/22, TWL/H-B.

to think of issuing a German Loan without the Morgans, it was similarly unlikely for Kuhn, Loeb to be excluded from the offering group. In direct contrast, the Speyer house was expendable and omitted — with Jack Morgan deciding conclusively, "Appearing with Speyers degrades us."[33]

However much war and generational succession changed their relationship, the Morgans still needed to work with Kuhn, Loeb, but the Morgans also exemplified the standard to which Kahn and his partners compared themselves. Mutual misgivings and ill-feelings did not alter the fact that Kuhn, Loeb partners thought of the Morgans as they thought of themselves — a house of first rank. If, for instance, Thomas Lamont seemed to take a superior tone when commenting about "OHK and Clarence Dillon both hurrying [to] Rome in hope of some business," the associates of Kuhn, Loeb sounded similarly arrogant when in one or another assessment of European financial opportunities they concluded "the main difficulty is the competition of second-rate people who are prepared to take bigger chances and do things more cheaply." The disdained competition in this instance included Blair & Co., Inc., where future Kuhn, Loeb partner Elisha Walker happened to be president. Also mentioned was J. Henry Schroeder & Co., merchant bankers since 1815, and the London representative of Dillon, Read & Co., whose unstoppable emergence in foreign financing was a challenge to Kuhn, Loeb and the Morgans alike.[34]

When it came to choosing between speculative and conservative business, Kuhn, Loeb remained restrained. The house was more like J. P. Morgan in this regard than the upstarts of New York. Kahn, himself never a maverick banker, stayed deeply invested in the balance of dynastic and traditionalist principles. These preserved Kuhn, Loeb over the generations, and in the short run Kahn meant to protect a place in the firm for his own future progeny, as his son Gilbert would soon gain admission to the partnership. Yet at least once in August 1924, Kahn remarked that one of the "really trying things" in New York's financial life was to watch Dillon, Read "successfully bringing out an issue of one kind or another almost every day," while, by comparison, Kuhn, Loeb's offices seemed much too quiet. Soon enough Dillon, Read proved far more daring in Germany than any other American house, especially after it hired a European-based partner with the authority to pursue business aggressively. Ironically, that partner was Ferdinand Eberstadt, Kahn's younger American-born cousin, a graduate of Princeton University and Columbia Law School, whose first year with Dillon, Read brought the firm's underwriting of German business to increase threefold (from $39 million in 1925 to $117 million in 1926).[35] Kahn could hardly say as much on behalf of Kuhn, Loeb. The only consolation came later when Kuhn, Loeb would ride the crash of 1929 better than more speculative houses.

. . . .

COMPLEMENTARY BROKERAGES

Whatever the successes or failures Kahn experienced in the banking world, he always looked upon the world of art as a realm where he could find fulfillment, respect, and appreciation. Art brought him nearer to realizing an internationalist vision that Kahn articulated in 1916, when he warned of art's vulnerabilities in the postbellum era if it were forced to compete with the vast material concerns of reconstruction. Granting that he had not expected the vacuum in postwar leadership, he had identified a "privilege and duty" for America — and himself — "to become a militant force in the cause and service of art, to be foremost in helping to create and spread that which beautifies and enriches life."[36] The weight of his convictions increased each year after the war. Seeing the world's financial center shift indecisively between London and New York, and New York's German houses lose authority over the international financial decisions affecting the German-speaking peoples of Europe, Kahn held tightly to the goal of being "a business man who has tried not to degenerate into a mere business machine," and faithfully sought "to preserve that degree of 'all around *Bildung*'" that he brought with him when he first arrived in America thirty years earlier.[37]

Art was "the truest League of Nations," Kahn also liked to say. It could at once "rearrange the details of modern life, so to reflect it, that it might satisfy the spirit," while at the same time reconstruct the good in humankind, in this "sadly out of gear" world. Kahn looked for art to accomplish what statesmen could not—to correct the "aberration of the human spirit" that lingered from the war.[38] When all was said and done, his idealism about art and patronage gave Otto Kahn a specific ongoing role of international importance. Neither a dollar-a-year man during the war, nor an industrial statesman after, he became the preeminent, cosmopolitan patron of an aesthetic crowd with indisputable force, flash, and wit, if not entirely new ideas, setting the values of café society.

As Otto Kahn gravitated toward the arts that were complex and collaborative, capturing the momentum of modernity, he drew himself nearer to those who were constantly on the cusp and who self-consciously created statements and agitations that once asserted and transcended the American character. *Chauve Souris*, a showy cabaret revue that appeared in New York during the early 1920s, captured this congregation most cleverly, when a painted curtain dropped between acts, and instead of brocade or velvet, the audience saw themselves caricatured by artist Ralph Barton. Titled "A Typical First Night Audience" when reprinted in a slightly different version for *Vanity Fair*, the caricature was captioned, "Ingredients in the Mixed Grill of Metropolitan Life; A Social Panorama." In each depiction, the celebrated banker-patron, Otto Kahn, sat conspicuously among more than one hundred select luminaries. There was Condé Nast and Frank Crowninshield, arbitrators of the stylish, *Vanity Fair*; the choreographer Michel Folkine and violinist Jascha Heifetz (Russian transplants both); and Elizabeth Marbury, the American decorator with Parisian sensibilities. A handful of theatrical managers dotted the crowd, including two Shubert brothers, Morris Gest, and Flo Ziegfeld. A few chic heiresses from the Vanderbilt, Whitney, and other millionaire clans were on hand, too, and

FIFTEEN CENTS

TIME

The Weekly News-Magazine

OTTO H. KAHN
Cosmopolite, Metropolite
(See Page 19)

VOL. VI, No. 18

NOVEMBER 2, 1925

Otto H. Kahn, "Cosmopolite, Metropolite," 1925. (TimePix)

the occasional celebrity from civic and political life cropped up in the likenesses of Herbert Hoover and Louis Untermeyer, but the most legendary of America's opera world were by far better represented. These included an alignment that set Maria Jeritza on one side of the Met's general manager, Giulio Gatti-Casazza, with Geraldine Farrar and Mary Garden on the other, in a sly comment on the succession of

Seniority without Authority

popular divas: Jeritza was then taking New York by storm, and Farrar was entering retirement. Elsewhere the Gish sisters, stars of stage and screen, flanked D. W. Griffith, the motion picture director. There was also America's best-known cinema artist, the British-born Charlie Chaplin; playwrights George Kaufman and Marc Connelly; the powerhouse of Famous Players Lasky (Paramount), Adolph Zukor and Jesse Lasky; and the Austrian-born stage designer and architect Joseph Urban. America's own stage-design genius, Robert Edmond Jones, was there, as was Kenneth Macgowan, author of *The Continental Stage* and editor of *Theatre Arts*, who with Jones and Eugene O'Neill (another caricature on the curtain) were to be the Provincetown Players' new "Triumvirate."[39]

For the most advanced students of society here was a chance to read every caricature's relation to another. It is not without significance that Otto Kahn was in some way connected to a near majority of everyone in this scene. He was also the only international financier among these stars and celebrities, but more interesting was what this crowd meant to postwar modernity: they constituted a new internationalist elite. By comparison, the emissaries at Europe's financial commissions were ineffectual, predictably plain and dull, lacking the wit, fashion, or excitement of the art world. For that among several reasons, *Chauve Souris* may best illustrate the verve of Kahn's patronage.

The Algonquin crowd staged a droll parody of the revue, calling it *No Siree!*, which is probably better remembered, and inasmuch as a few wildly successful runs of *Chauve Souris* in New York were commercially profitable, it stood against the notion that Kahn's patronage cared nothing about monetary return. But *Chauve Souris* was nonetheless suggestively typical of the unbounded cosmopolitanism of Otto Kahn and much of the Euro-American modernism to catch his interest. *Chauve Souris* was "the talk of New York." The show came originally from Moscow via Paris, the creation of a Russian Francophile, Nikita Balieff, and it opened in New York on February 3, 1922, to radiant reviews. The critic Oliver Sayler counted it among New York's most important stage productions in fifteen years: it was different, new, and important, the only production of its kind in America. It was also precisely the kind of artistic venture that Otto Kahn wanted for an enlarged theatrical experience. Whether the art or intellect was made in America or Europe, what interested Kahn was its combining force and originality. Kahn was interested in pushing forth art's frontiers. In this case, one innovation was to dissolve the fourth wall and make the audience part of the show, disrupting restrained postures of audience etiquette, and melting the icicles that producer-dramatist Arthur Hopkins said Americans carried in their pockets to art theater. As the revue returned the clown to theater's "artistic calendar," that sign of the reverence for *commedia dell'arte* in neoclassical modernism connected well with the potential artistic merits of America's light theater, vaudeville, and variety stages.[40] Gilbert Seldes noticed the same point when praising *Chauve Souris* in his popular 1924 book, *The Seven Lively Arts*, which happened to carry a frontispiece by Ralph Barton, in the style of his curtain for the revue. Seldes joined the chorus of acclamation: "Here was something certainly vaudeville . . . appealing to every grade of intelligence . . . good music, exciting scenery, and good fun." And he concluded with an observation that echoed the envy of many American artistic ambitions: "Now if our native product were only like that."[41]

Kahn's way of saying the same was through actions—taking tickets for opening night at the Shubert's *Gaieties of 1919*, or losing money on a John Murray Anderson musical, then investing in another. He would back vehicles for Gershwin and the musical team of Richard Rodgers and Lorenz Hart, while at the same time showering affection upon the Theatre Guild founders and wanting to put similarly high-brow artistic goals before a wider public. As early as 1922, he and Met board members also began investigating the possibility of making live radio broadcasts of Metropolitan Opera productions. An idea pushed by RCA and Clarence Mackay, it stalled mainly because no one yet realized how to compensate the company for its performance. Kahn, meanwhile, took to the bully pulpit, encouraging municipal sponsorship for the arts, more frequent open-air concerts, and the cultivation of music in the public schools. His appreciation of music and public endorsements also grew to include America's own hot new music, "generically known as jazz." At the time, when jazz was widely discussed, and occasionally performed on Broadway, the always-influential Kahn wrote, "Instead of 'turning up our noses' at jazz, in superior musical virtue, we ought to take the attitude of spurring it on with friendly interest." During that same year Kahn's younger son, Roger, had put together a band that played the Hippodrome, with his father in attendance for opening night, underwriting the expenses. Soon after, Roger recorded for the Victor label with his orchestra and did a few motion picture shorts for Vitaphone, on his way to becoming a well-known white jazz dance bandleader, remembered today for co-writing the brisk tune to "Crazy Rhythm." Its lyrics, written by Irving Caesar, a Gershwin collaborator, includes an ironic passage, in light of the present discussion: "Here is where we have a show-down, I'm too high-hat, you're too low-down."[42]

Otto Kahn was certifiably one of the "Opera Hat Brigade," in *New Yorker* parlance, and never "too low-down." Even so, good taste would not preclude good times or risk-taking when it came to backing the promise of emerging artistic movements. Kahn's aesthetic opinion and patronage would accommodate — indeed advocate — a popular following for both the serious and the playful, as long as production standards were high. The arts could be somber, fun, popular, bourgeois, and intellectual. Be it opera, cinema, poetry, jazz, or comedy, all art had cultural value and spiritual purposes. Kahn positioned quality art as a civilizing agency. That much had not been changed by the war. The course of Kahn's postwar patronage was different, though, for it mapped a path for the modern arts as they moved hurriedly past the "new" of Kahn's *fin de siècle* to the configuration of "young" and "new" in the artistic life of the 1920s.

It would be hard to overstate Kahn's influence upon that eclectic modernism, with its undertones of newness, neoclassicism, and romanticism, but a connective tissue between the older Kahn and his own youth found its form therein, as the 1920s reinvigorated a Paterian-inspired urgency for Kahn. In an address on "The Value of Art to the People," he recited the famous quote from Walter Pater's *The Renaissance*: "We have an interval, and then our place knows us no more. . . . Our one chance lies in expanding that interval, in getting as many pulsations as possible into a given time."[43] That theme would guide him equally in the concerns of art and money. It spelled out why he would not settle for an eighteen-hour day on Wall Street, and explained why Otto Kahn would not slow down, even when his doctors counseled rest.

The very idea of rest and isolation spelled boredom — a curse whether he was well or ill. During the 1920s when Kahn's cardiac condition required more prescribed rest, these periods were spent in the fashionable spas of Europe and his new winter cottage in Palm Beach, Florida. Kahn went through the motions of relaxing while planning for the next cycle of social, financial, and artistic appointments, or, whenever feasible, enticing some friend or acquaintance to drop by and break up the monotony. He was always cheering himself and the public with reports of a good prognosis, as he insisted that the doctors had "laid me low" to recover from an "attack of the gout," the "strenuous winters" in New York, or some other minor ailment. Wit did once betray his battle, when he admitted, "My health stupidly and irritatingly has chosen . . . to remind me of the fact that I am no longer twenty-five years old."[44]

In the mid-1920s an uncharacteristic melancholy swept over Kahn. His younger daughter later said that she noticed he was slowing down, and at least one other person glimpsed a strange sullenness about Kahn: soprano Grace Moore, the musical comedy star whom Kahn helped to launch a career in grand opera and whom he possibly took as a lover along the way. In the summer of 1924, shortly before the London conference would convene without him, Kahn and Moore spent a holiday together in Venice. During an afternoon visit to the Galleria dell'Accademia, Kahn gazed long and hard at Giorgione's *The Tempest*, then after fifteen minutes said, "This is one of the very few things in life that I am unable to buy. Everything has its price but this." Whether he meant the painting as a possession, or the emotional impact of art, the statement accented a sense of incompleteness. It appeared again not long after, with Kahn moodily reflective about the future: "We were all living on the vitality of our forefathers and leaving very little to give the coming generation." Moore teased him, trying to lift his spirits, but Kahn rejoined "wistfully" — "I only regret I'm not fifteen years younger and you ten years older." She eventually concluded Kahn was depressed "because he liked living so much and age was the beginning of the end."[45] He was fifty-eight and she, just under twenty-three, was younger than some of his children.

In her memoir, published after Kahn's death, Moore kept the details of their affections secret, ignoring gossip and innuendo and avoiding proof or confession. In doing so she flirted with ambiguities, which was not only part of the fun but also a measure of the discreet commitment necessary in an affair with Otto Kahn. That pattern had been established earlier between Kahn and Maria Jeritza. Only twenty years younger than Kahn and herself married, Jeritza was a star of the Vienna State Opera for nearly a decade before making her New York debut in 1921, allegedly beginning an affair with Kahn when she arrived at the Metropolitan Opera. In contrast, Grace Moore was single (until 1931) and had not yet debuted in grand opera when her affair with Kahn ignited. Yet the two women were similar because neither sought to marry Kahn nor expose him. Such boundaries kept Kahn's liaisons in balance with the demands of his marriage. It appears his affairs were accepted by his wife, who apparently knew but never questioned them deeply. If Addie did ask, Kahn could give a serviceable if improbable denial, not unlike the one he gave to Grace Moore at their first meeting, when she inquired "whether he ever fell in love with the Opera's prima donnas." He responded that his passion was for the opera, not the singers.[46]

As women with whom Kahn had more than a chance encounter, Moore and Jeritza answered Kahn's needs in ways that transcended purely carnal motives. Perhaps in an equal sense, their appeal went beyond beauty, talent, youth, and discretion. These talented women were bound up with Kahn's more complex wishes for a cosmopolitan world. Jeritza, the transplant from Europe to America, represented long-awaited gratification for Kahn, in that she was among the artists whose debut in America was delayed by the Great War. When Jeritza finally arrived in New York, Kahn eased her loneliness in that she knew neither "a single, solitary soul in the United States" nor the language. He also helped her through the trauma of her Met debut, in Puccini's *Tosca*, during which she had to overcome resistance from the fans of Geraldine Farrar, America's most beloved native-born soprano who had long ago claimed preeminence in the title role. The Met had signed Jeritza explicitly to sing Tosca, and her powerful interpretation was actually hastening the popular Farrar's retirement. The difficulty this caused Jeritza made Kahn's soothing hand especially comforting, but in the end Kahn's satisfaction was stroked by Jeritza's success. She became the Met's new blonde *prima donna*, a star of "volcanic energy" who reigned there for twelve years. And when she sang Wagner in German, the renaissance of the Met's internationalism was surely at hand. The corollaries for Kahn were evidenced in Vienna in June 1922, when Strauss himself conducted Jeritza in *Salome*—in honor of both Kahn and Gatti-Casazza.[47]

Jeritza was Kahn's diva from Austria's imperial court. Grace Moore was his discovery out of American stock. As savvy around millionaires as she was flirtatious, Moore arrived on the scene at the right time and with enough ambition to think herself a worthy successor to Geraldine Farrar. It helped that the Met's management knew an American presence was needed to satisfy nationalists, and that Kahn had twice arranged for her to audition for Gatti-Casazza. The first, conducted in the

Seniority without Authority

presence of Kahn, came up short but not without hope, as the general manager encouraged her to train further and return within a year. The second, a complete bomb, occurred in Kahn's absence. Moore was told to stick with the career she was in, which was not altogether bad advice. Already a celebrity-star, she had quite recently introduced Irving Berlin's smash hit "What'll I Do" in John Murray Anderson's *Music Box Revue* (1924), sharing the bill with Fanny Brice. Her success regularly brought her to the star-studded circuit of glamorous parties, mixing well within the ranks of George Gershwin, Alma Gluck, and Elsa Maxwell, as well as with nearly everyone in the Algonquin crowd. As Moore recalled it, the disastrous second audition at the Met led her to stumble around the streets of New York that day, at first feeling pummeled, then angry, then adamant about not giving up her operatic ambitions. She decided to train harder and try again, and so went home and phoned Otto Kahn in Florida. Knowing he would not overrule a verdict of the Met's management, she nevertheless counted on his ongoing encouragement and wagered that her debut at the Met would come within two years. Kahn took the bet, one he hoped to lose. Moore then went to Europe, where she studied and trained until her voice improved sufficiently for Kahn to recommend one more audition at the Met. After this third try, she was signed, and Kahn lost the bet.[48]

All of Kahn's extramarital transgressions preserved the appearance of propriety, and his closer friends were protective to the point of ignorance, if the remarks of Lady Pat Russell are any indication. She lived rent-free with her husband, Henry, at Kahn's house in Antibes, and at times prearranged parties for Kahn that included Moore. Their rumored affections once led Russell to sketch a cartoon in which Kahn and Moore arrive at Cherbourg, with the famous financier stunned by her pretense of purity. At another time, Russell talked of Moore in pursuit of Kahn, indicating she would not give her Kahn's address without his permission. All of Kahn's trysts were similar games of prudent prurience, which he played with superb sensibilities, steering clear of scandalmongers. He apparently remarked to Russell on one occasion that he preferred to distance himself from the "air of abandon" for which the fast set of writers, artists, and millionaires who summered at Antibes were famous. Russell jokingly advised him that "the community . . . are far too exhausted by their swimming, tennis playing and cocktail drinking to do anything more immoral than — sleep!" Beyond all of his levelheaded choices, however, any explanation for Kahn's faculty for holding gossip in check must also point to his charm. If Lord Beaverbrook had "no finesse" when he preyed on showgirls, as actress Louise Brooks once said, no similar condemnation from a woman has yet been found about Otto Kahn. It does seem as though Kahn desired the romance, the tenderhearted amorous exchange, not merely as sexual service, and this endeared him to women. Yet in one platonic letter to his daughter, he also once spoke most intimately of the deep place for loved ones in his "none too easily accessible heart," suggesting that a finite range of emotional entry points, his detached inner workings, were Otto Kahn's best guards and restraints.[49]

Amidst all the innuendo, one plain fact remained. While Kahn was "a faithful husband and a fastidious connoisseur of beautiful women," women such as Jeritza and Moore were musical talents who also ornamented the social life of Addie Kahn. On the day of Moore's debut at the Met, for instance, the Kahns hosted a luncheon for her parents and several dignitaries, then attended the performance as a group.[50] Kahn and his mistresses might have been hiding in plain sight of Addie, but Addie's tolerance for her husband's wandering affections was no doubt easier as she advanced in years. Having supervised the construction and decoration of their new mansions, Addie had become more independent in her own social life by the early 1920s. She traveled abroad frequently, building not only an art collection but her own circle of friends, which included Bernard Berenson in a relationship whose intimacy was hardly interrogated as closely as her husband's liaisons. With child-rearing well behind her, the presumptions of authority that came with parenthood were also slipping away. When eldest child Maude decided to marry a British military man in June 1920, her parents apparently tried to dissuade her, arguing that it did not seem to be a well-made marriage under the terms that had united Addie and Otto Kahn. Maude, however, was motivated by love rather than status or security, and in the end her parents accepted the fact that, as a friend of the family noted, "we cannot control the heart with millions."[51] That lesson conceivably said much about the boundaries in the long-lasting marriage of Addie and Otto Kahn. Addie still possessed the greater reservoir of untouched capital, and though Kahn's profits paid many of her expenses, she needed her husband's money less than the security of being Mrs. Otto H. Kahn.

Addie had wanted more from the marriage and continued to indicate her disappointment, telling the children and perhaps Kahn di-

Margaret "Nin" Kahn and John Ryan with the bride's parents.
(Photograph by Underwood and Underwood; private collection)

rectly that a distinguished banker should not be running around with
the likes of Harpo Marx. Yet often enough, Kahn's social and artistic tastes lined up with her own. The couples' joint interest in musical patronage was most apparent at the Philharmonic Society, which
counted Addie as a member of the (Women's) Auxiliary Committee
and Otto as a director and vice president. And it was not without some

irony that they appeared together at the Met in February 1922 for a performance of *Salome* staged by the Chicago Opera in a benefit for devastated France. The charity evening was a *cause célèbre* not only because it had been organized by an organization headed by Ann Morgan, whose father had previously banned *Salome* from the stage of the Met, but also because the opera's star, Mary Garden, who had made her debut in 1906, was retiring that season. The Kahns went to the performance with Paul Cravath, who happened to share Addie's emerging interest in the birth control movement.[52] A few months earlier, she had been at Town Hall (without her husband) when the police arrested birth control advocate Margaret Sanger, and for many years after, Addie Kahn was one of Sanger's most dependable benefactors in supporting the reformer's efforts to advance both scientific research and legislative reform for safe, affordable contraception. She not only wrote checks, but also hosted meetings at the Fifth Avenue mansion and visited the birth control clinics in Manhattan.[53] Whether Otto Kahn approved of or merely tolerated Addie's interest is less important than the fact that the couple had settled into a marital routine that accommodated and enhanced each of their lives.

CHAPTER FIVE

Protocol of Patronage

Long after Kahn's chances for nobility, elected office, or economic statesmanship had faded, the insignia of a generous patron remained. The role evoked two distinct ancestries. After the patron of Horace and Virgil, he became known as "Otto H. Kahn — Maecenas," "Manhattan's Maecenas," and "the Maecenas of our Rome." Elsewhere he was compared to the Medicis of Renaissance Italy and dubbed "the greatest patron since Lorenzo the Magnificent," "our Lorenzo the Magnificent," or simply "Otto the Magnificent."[1] Such epithets could be used in reverence or ridicule, but whatever their intent, they modeled Otto Kahn upon the past, finding a precedence for his patronage of new arts. Underlying such declarations as "Otto the Magnificent" or a "Negro Renaissance" in Harlem was the double-coded newness of America and the usable past of Europe. Within that mixed-culture language, a reincarnated Maecenas or Medici stood against the dilemma of artists in the twentieth century. As Charles Jencks points out, artists of the era lacked the "defined social relationship to the patron — the State, Church, or an individual" that characterized early modernity (or the age of the Medici); they were instead tossed about by the "competitive and agnostic" marketplace of the machine age.[2]

Otto Kahn put forth something less absolute. Modernity splintered the economic zones of art. New intermediaries emerged as brokers of cultural production, including publishers and critics, gallery owners and dealers, agents and publicists. Still, private patronage was no more extinct than the church or state. Kahn would administer it as an office of traditions and transitions. In a similar vein, when Ezra Pound looked for patrons "to bring on another Cinquecento," he hit upon part of the role that Kahn perceived for himself. "A renaissance in the arts," Pound claimed, "comes when there are a few patrons who back their own flair and who buy freely from unrecognized men."[3] A better understanding of this process emerges when we ask certain basic questions. When was Kahn inclined to support an artistic endeavor? How did artists gain and sustain his interest and good favor? What was expected of his money? How were changing modes of cultural production understood? Which social interactions coalesced in conventions, and when were the operative ones unexpressed? Such issues are harder to see in a gloss over Kahn's entire patronage. The galaxy of star names is stunning, but a complete catalog allows little room for analyses—leaving Otto Kahn to seem no more than a dilettante, "bobbing up here and there" with cash and aid, as Matthew Josephson once described him.[4]

A close analysis of three of Kahn's beneficiaries is more serviceable. One is Norman Bel Geddes, the pacesetting industrial designer of the "Futurama" exhibit at the 1939 World's Fair, whose professional life began in the American theater arts movement with help from Kahn. The second is actor and singer Paul Robeson, ambassador of the Harlem Renaissance, who came to stardom and commercial prosperity with some assistance from Kahn. The third is Hart Crane, whose poem *The Bridge* was dedicated to Otto Kahn. Each was undiscovered and under thirty years of age when he first applied for Kahn's aid. Kahn, in his fifties when these relationships began, seeded their careers and, as the saying goes, became the genius who discovered genius. Their success was his success, and in this sample of native-born Americans, each would achieve the cosmopolitan success that Kahn envisioned for the American historical trajectory.

These three artists' stories follow the protocol of patronage in its many levels of interaction. Each occasions how young, undiscovered talents approached Otto Kahn, became beneficiaries of his largesse, and developed multiyear relationships with the banker-patron that endured highs and lows, misunderstandings and forgiveness. Each story discloses socially relevant expectations for money and financial security, along with the artists' illusions of independence. In all three cases, Kahn extended the money in the form of a loan, a practice that may be distinctive of his largesse. But the money, in any form, was one of several ways in which he could express support. Other gestures to be extended or withheld included introductions to other cultural brokers and invitations to his home.

Whether one looks for the inner logic in an individual relationship or for its logical extension in broader networks of artistic production, the banker-patron's position was that of the middleman. His transactions were as complex as they were numerous. There was amicus as well as animus in associations that were also personal. Charity could converge with envy; honesty might mix with guile. Money, like art, was a domain of mystification through which the patron and beneficiary drew parallel satisfaction. Whether Kahn's patronage was requested or volunteered, his attention signaled recognition. Younger artists especially took away a sense, as John Murray Anderson phrased it, that "my star was in the ascendent."[5] Of course, the artist was invariably less secure than the patron in these relationships. Kahn could more easily find substitute talent than the artist could find substitute patronage. In addition, while Kahn evidently felt comfortable with the fact that he lacked the talent to be a successful artist, the artists he supported might have been wrestling with the same conflict that Kahn had long ago abandoned, and looking to find the confidence to succeed.

. . . .

BEGINNINGS

In looking at how Kahn and these artists first got together, one is reminded of a point made by Edward Said: "A beginning is already a project underway."[6] The outset of these relationships was determined by Kahn's fame for dispensing aid, along with the artists' imperfect knowledge of the patron's practices. Bel Geddes, Robeson, and Crane all approached Kahn in similar if not identical ways, as did numerous others. If an artist initially tried to reach Kahn by telephone, his staff would usually instruct him to write a letter, which all three produced with strikingly similar vocabulary and content. Each applicant presented credentials concerning previous experience and referred to some mutual acquaintance who could validate the artist's talent; they would also describe some ordeal and suggest how Kahn could help. The evaluative process then began, with Kahn reviewing the petitioner in discernible stages before commencing an act of patronage.

Bel Geddes conveyed the same story about Kahn for many years. In 1917 he was living in Los Angeles and down to his last seven dollars; he read of Kahn's interest in America's best art, then sent off a telegram to the patron, asking for a $200 loan so that he might travel to New York and pursue a theatrical career. The gamble paid off in a few days: Kahn sent the fare, invited him to an interview in New York, and gave Bel Geddes his chance to work with the Metropolitan Opera. More than a career was born as a result. The young talent's chutzpah became a fable of opportunity in America, which was canonized in Dale Carnegie's bible of self-promotion, *How to Win Friends and Influence People.* It was also a streamlined version of events that changed the tale in significant ways.[7]

The famous telegram to Kahn, now lost, was actually preceded by a more formal communication that arrived on Kahn's desk seven months before Bel Geddes came to New York. It was also typed on the letterhead of Aline Barnsdall's Little Theatre in Los Angeles, where Bel Geddes was working. And Bel Geddes pleaded not for funding but sponsorship. He asked Kahn to "become interested in my work . . . [and] make it possible for it to reach the market," a request for more than what Kahn was prepared to offer. The patron instead suggested "an advance . . . sufficient to cover" a round trip to New York, but Bel Geddes then declined the offer because, before Kahn's reply arrived, the designer had secured a $10,000 contract for one year's work with the Universal Film Company, eliminating his immediate need of money or a trip to New York. However, in a wise hedge, he asked Kahn to remember him should financial assistance again be needed. Kahn agreeably replied, "The offer that I made to you in my last letter holds good in case you should require it at some future time," he wrote.[8]

By year's end Bel Geddes contacted Kahn again, complaining about motion picture makers who were not ready "for what the artist has to offer." He had quit Universal and now wanted $200 to get him to New York, where Kahn and theatrical producers might see "examples of my work" in time for the spring productions. Kahn advanced the money, extended an invitation to meet, but offered nothing more concrete than cordial wishes for "every success in your artistic aspirations and purposes."[9] After an appointment had been delayed at least once due to the banker's other obligations, Bel Geddes toted his designs to 1100 Fifth Avenue for a Sunday morning breakfast meeting. Kahn reportedly darted from the table mid-meal to take "a quick look at some of the sketches" and found the work sufficiently impressive. The two then resumed dining and further conversation, with Kahn trying to probe more fully the designer's experience and prospects. Getting around to mutual acquaintances and interests, they talked of Ziegfeld's productions and Diaghilev's ballet (Bel Geddes had seen the latter on tour).

When the chat touched upon Reinhardt's *Sumurûn*, some five years after Kahn had helped to import it, someone mentioned a veteran of the production, Richard Ordynski, who was currently working at the Met, where composer Charles Wakefield Cadman was set to premiere his opera *Shanewis* in March. Bel Geddes seized the moment to say that both men knew him from California and "would like me to design the new Cadman opera."[10]

By the meeting's end, Kahn had promised an introduction for an interview at the Met. It came with a standard warning that artistic judgment was left to the company's artistic management. "In everything related to productions at the Metropolitan Opera House," Kahn wrote on another occasion, "Gatti-Casazza is 'boss.' " As a rule Kahn would intimate his wishes at the Met, but rarely issue dictates. "I know that many people believe that at the Metropolitan my views and wishes are paramount, but indeed they are not, and they must not be," he explained. "A theatre or opera house must be run on the principle of one man power." That opinion not only reflected his philosophical position on theatrical management (and suited the temperament of Gatti-Casazza); it also limited the expectations of those who approached the patron.[11]

Ten days after his meeting with Kahn, Norman Bel Geddes signed a contract with the Metropolitan Opera. It was less than the most prestigious assignment—he would "do settings and costumes for the second [act]" of *Shanewis*. Kahn's support had opened a door at the Met for Bel Geddes, not overthrown the entrenched establishment. "Altho I can do nothing of a very original nature at The Metropolitan," he wrote Kahn after signing, "I feel sure that you have eased my getting started in New York by putting this in my way." Kahn replied, "I am very glad that you are going to get from the Metropolitan Opera Company the opportunity which you desired. From what I have seen of your sketches, I am quite sure that you will do full justice to the occasion, and I hope it will be the forerunner of much other successful and artistically distinguished work."[12] Bel Geddes's commercial and artistic aspirations were, for the moment, his own responsibility. Otto Kahn thus initially did for Bel Geddes what he would do selectively for many others: introduce the talent to management, then step aside and allow an interplay between artist and marketplace. He might again intervene on a talent's behalf, of course, by talking through problems, helping to find a new project, providing financial assistance, or mediating conflicts of personality and contract. He managed to be always the patron, but rarely the complete protector.

Kahn's patronage of Paul Robeson also came after a false start. When Robeson, the Phi Beta Kappa and All-American from Rutgers College who had recently graduated Columbia University Law School, first approached Kahn in March 1923, he too was seeking not money but the chance to "get before any theatrical managers and playwrights, especially those who may possibly have Negro roles: (Eugene O'Neill)." In a brief testimonial, Robeson highlighted his role in the New York and British productions of May Hoyt Wiborg's *Taboo*. Offering three theatrical references, including Augustin Duncan, who had directed him in *Taboo*, Robeson put forth yet one more connection: "I am approaching you because I know that you are a trustee of Rutgers, and might be interested in me as a Rutgers graduate."[13]

If one wanted an introduction to Eugene O'Neill, Otto Kahn was a good choice. But O'Neill's recently completed work was *Welded*, a play without the "Negro roles" that Robeson sought, and the playwright had not yet begun writing *All God's Chillun Got Wings*, his next work with a racial theme. Furthermore, the original Provincetown company, to which Kahn subscribed and for whom he paid one season's rent (1918–19), was inactive and on the edge of dissolution in 1923; the group had not yet reformed as the Experimental Theatre (commonly known as the Provincetown Playhouse). Consequently Kahn could be honestly unaware of tangible possibilities for Robeson in March 1923. He responded cordially, promising "to bear your wish in mind and to communicate with you if an appropriate opening comes to my attention." He also encouraged Robeson to pay a call "at my office any day during business hours," which was a clear sign of interest, if not a guarantee of support. Robeson did not take up the invitation, but instead found entry into the Provincetown circle, with help from Augustin Duncan. He subsequently made his way to O'Neill and secured the lead in *All God's Chillun*, which opened on May 15, 1924.[14]

Newly reconstituted under the Triumvirate of Kenneth Macgowan, Eugene O'Neill, and Robert Edmond Jones, the Provincetown enterprise soon won Otto Kahn's serious interest and financial backing. Just as important, Kahn stood by the Provincetowners throughout the controversial run of *Chillun*, which faced frenzied, merciless objections to its portrait of interracial marriage, and to Robeson, "a full-blooded

Negro," being kissed on the hand by a white actress. The opening threatened to incite a white race riot, and William Randolph Hearst's *American* reported a rumor, later proven false, that Kahn had "intimated a desire to withdraw his support should the play go on." Instead of withdrawing, Kahn asked to reserve two tickets, "not complimentary," for the opening. Undeterred in supporting the company, two months later he attended its gala dinner to "raise a small endowment fund for the future"—an idea that Kahn had suggested to business manager Eleanor Fitzgerald. On May 6 his latest contribution to the Provincetown Playhouse Fund increased from $3,000 to $5,000.[15]

Chillun had a successful run of 100 performances, alternating with a Provincetown revival of *The Emperor Jones* that also starred Robeson and kept the actor-singer working into October. A chance meeting between the banker-patron and the Provincetown's new star perhaps occurred along the way, but by the time of their first documented meeting, Robeson was an emerging celebrity, about to open in a limited run of *The Emperor Jones* on Broadway. They crossed paths at the midtown apartment of Carl Van Vechten, whose fabulous parties were coupling points between emerging Harlem talents and the standard bearers of café-chic. Van Vechten's relish for the genius of the New Negro Renaissance was almost as great as his conceit for finding and announcing new careers, and his party in mid-January 1925 was one such occasion to show off both. The evening's highlights included Robeson singing, a dance by Adele Astaire, and George Gershwin playing a rendition of his own "Rhapsody in Blue." Kahn, described by Van Vechten as one of the "minor celebrities" in attendance, had recently put out his favorable remarks concerning jazz, including the suggestion that it could answer the longstanding search for an American opera of excellence. At the party, he chatted with James Weldon Johnson and volunteered funding for a "Negro Theatre." At the moment, though, there was no solicitation to support Robeson, and another six months would pass before Kahn directly entered the role of Robeson's patron. In the interim, Robeson gave his breakthrough concert of Negro spirituals with accompanist-arranger Laurence Brown. This "must-see" musical event of the New York season, which Kahn missed because he was in Europe, was staged, free of charge, at the Greenwich Village Theatre, another venue of the Kahn-supported Provincetown company.[16]

Such ongoing linkages and Robeson's rising celebrity made his new appeal to Kahn different in mid-1925 than it had been in 1923. The second approach also bore the imprimatur and guidance of Van Vechten, who took credit for suggesting it. In addition, the banker this time heard not just from the actor-singer, but from Robeson's wife, to whom Robeson deferred much of his personal management. It was Eslanda ("Essie") Goode Robeson who telephoned Kahn's office for an appointment; she was told it would be better to write, since Kahn was "flooded with work" after his recent return from Europe. Her letter was essentially a plea on behalf of "my husband, Paul Robeson," who had been cast in the lead of the London production of *The Emperor Jones* and now stood "at the brink of what we hope will be a very remarkable career." Kahn was encouraged to hear him sing again, now accompanied by Laurence Brown, whose arrangements of traditional Negro spirituals paired beautifully with Robeson's voice and interpretation. The collaboration with Brown had everyone raving, and it also meant that Kahn might expect to hear astonishing improvements since the performance at Van Vechten's party, so between the lines Essie Robeson was catering to Kahn's flawless taste. A clearer difference in Robeson's solicitation of 1925, in any case, hinged on expectations of his commercial success and the couple's creditworthiness, for they were asking to borrow $5,000. Robeson's bookings for stage performances and phonograph recordings — which represented his potential earnings and thus his ability to repay Kahn — were set alongside a budget for spending the loan. A hefty portion ($1,500) would clear old debts before Robeson went to London. An equal amount would be earmarked to copyright and publish the Robeson-Brown repertoire, while also sending Brown on a collecting tour for new material from the South. The remainder would underwrite domestic expenses and voice lessons. "Back him for two years," Essie wrote, requesting an implied date for repayment. If Kahn would do so, the Robesons promised "to make you never regret it any way."[17]

When the letter crossed Kahn's desk, he took up the matter with Van Vechten, who clearly gave an unrestrained endorsement. A few days later a gathering was held at Kahn's Long Island estate, where Robeson performed for a handful of guests before Kahn stepped aside for a personal conversation with the husband and wife. The patron inquired about the prospects for Paul's career, asked whether another backer could be found, and then offered a loan that would be secured by a life insurance policy on Robeson, along with his concert and theatrical contracts. Within twenty-four hours a check went out to Robeson for $2,500. It came with Kahn's promise to provide an additional $2,500 if the couple was unable to find further sponsorship. Beyond that, all Kahn asked was Robeson's acknowledgment of the money's receipt and a schedule of the installment dates proposed for its repayment. Essie Robeson had gotten what she first asked for: "a straight loan." Typical of how his largesse was administered more liberally than his banking, Kahn had released a large sum of money to a young, newly acquainted artist after a short ceremonial interview and a verbal rather than formal agreement. The details of their understanding could be contracted later, but the details would be put into place. Whether or not Kahn would press for repayment was a highly stylized matter, governed by unspoken rules, with the patron's decision based on his evaluation of the borrowers' etiquette and ongoing needs.[18]

In comparison, Kahn's patronage of poet Hart Crane began in a far more compressed frame of time. On the first Wednesday of December 1925, the unemployed poet rang up Kuhn, Loeb "to request an interview" and some "temporary assistance." When advised by a secretary to write, Crane understood that he should be "explaining the exigencies of the situation and the application I wished to make." A long letter followed in which Crane included some personal references along with reviews of his published work. There was also an explanation of "the pressure of my present circumstances" and a project to be proposed. Crane wanted to write an epic poem to "enunciate a new cultural synthesis of values in terms of our America." The idea and intention had been with him for several years, but attempts to write it "between night and morning" while not at his day job were fruitless, he explained, because *The Bridge* would require "a steady application and less interruption."[19]

That Crane should ask for a loan, rather than a grant or commission, does suggest some knowledge about Kahn's practices. A loan might have been suggested by friends in the artistic and literary world or by Kahn's secretaries, considering that the press did not discuss Kahn's patronage as temporary loans. In any case, Crane was fairly sophisticated in formulating the terms. The son of a businessman, he asked for $1,000, "at any rate of interest within six percent," and offered collateral in the form of an inheritance expected upon the death of his grandfather's widow. He also indicated a sense of economy and a work plan whereby he would "live . . . cheaply in the country for at least a year and not only complete this poem, but work on a drama." He closed the appeal with confidence, decorum, and deference: "I honestly feel that my artistic integrity and present circumstances, merit the attention of one like yourself, who is and has been so notably constructive in the contemporary and future art and letters of America."[20]

When one of Kahn's secretaries responded on Saturday, Crane took the earliest appointment offered and arrived at the patron's mansion on the next day. He found Kahn "keenly interested in what Waldo Frank and Eugene O'Neill had said" about him, but there was also much about Crane to uniquely interest Kahn. They each loved music, which, while central to Crane's poetic device, would in Kahn's mind wed the twin Paterian principles that on one hand said, "All art constantly aspires towards the condition of music," and on the other gave perfected "lyrical poetry" a revered place within the hierarchy of artistic forms. The poet's published work offered additional parallels. Kahn could be egotistical enough to think his own cultural activism had cultivated Crane's "To Portapovitch (*du Ballet Russe*)." It might amuse him as well that Crane's poem, "For the Marriage of Faustus and Helen," had put Helen of Troy in the subways, while Kahn's support of Isadora Duncan had ignited the "strange new word, DIONYSION . . . over the roof of the Century Theatre." Beyond such matters, the patron and the poet also seemed of similar minds in wanting an art that transcended the ages and brought hopefulness to the postwar world. All the better if that art should suggest the cultural maturity and leadership of America in the world.[21]

Their backgrounds struck another odd coincidence. Both Kahn and Crane knew something of the struggle to overcome parental interference with aesthetic ambitions. Crane often complained that his father disapproved of his poetic mission and considered it a cause of his indigence. Unlike the young Otto Kahn, however, Hart Crane overruled his father and rejected the financial security of his father's business (the Cleveland chocolate maker had invented Life Savers candy in 1912). Crane suffered through years of family conflict as a result. Having also cast off academic options for his financial security, his livelihood depended on publishers, critics, and literary peers, as well as patrons, who would forever subject his talent to judgments of relative worth.

"Anointment of Our Well Dressed Critic, or Why Waste the Eggs?: Three-Dimensional Vista." A Hart Crane contribution to the Little Review, *Winter 1922.*

This was exactly the hard course of artistic development that Otto Kahn did not choose for himself but was willing to support in others.[22]

In addition, Hart Crane differed from the patron's other applicants because the poet was singularly impatient, or less able to brook delay. He came to Kuhn, Loeb within the week to obtain some money. Receiving $60, probably in cash, he was promised another $940 by check through the mail within a few days. Crane later recalled this as the moment when Kahn bestowed "not only means for fruitful leisure, but a kind of accolade — toward conquests." It left him exhilarated. His body a "nervous tremor," he told the patron that he "felt like a race horse!" Kahn's own pleasure was more subdued. Unlike Crane, Kahn knew better than to think the poet had become instantly rich. Instead Kahn's pleasure revolved around purchasing the poet's relief "from material cares for a while," as he put it. Bestowing a token of confidence answered another of the poet's needs, but when Kahn passed on good wishes for Crane to "prove . . . a master builder in constructing 'The Bridge' of your dreams, thoughts, and emotion," it also drew the patron toward a state of vicarious fulfillment.[23] At such a moment, money made art a collaborative rather than an individual process. While it seemed to insulate the making of art from market forces, it would also refashion those relations.

In these three cases Otto Kahn shared some of money's pleasures and let the artist explore a few of money's secrets. A sizable advance from Otto Kahn injected cash into the artists' spending stream. It freed the talents from financial worries and sometimes carried with it the sweet dream of artistic liberation. Being a guest in Kahn's mansions or seeing and tasting a bit of great wealth made the illusion more elastic, yet overall the loan mechanism was a delicate indication that Kahn was acting not as a patron-client but rather as a banker-patron. The borrowers' note implied a credit and debt relationship different from the contracts that characterized Renaissance and Baroque patronage, because the loaned money did not need to be absorbed by the direct costs of producing art. The money could be used to ease household expenses, pay old debts, underwrite the cost of travel, or fulfill whatever the patron and the artist agreed — in principle — was needed. The spending went without an audit per se, except for affable letters and other messages that in effect told of the artist's income, cash balances, and liabilities. Such letters could also provide information useful in both promoting the patron's ongoing flow of goodwill and in Kahn's assessment of the talent's ongoing need. Thus, the loan mechanism tied the artists' ability to repay to both the protocol of patronage and the exchange value of the art.

From another view, it was ironic that world events and private patronage both should revolve around the ability to pay. In a way, the issues of Allied war debts and German reparations were echoed in Kahn's approach to patronage. Like indebted governments of the day, artists had cause to think the creditor was not (or should not be) seriously committed to debt collection. The lender did not need the money as badly as the borrower might need cancellation of the debt. Indeed, Otto Kahn could forgive a loan as easily as he could accept repayment, and it was sometimes more difficult to demand repayment, if only because the practice of collection might conjure the image of "Uncle Shylock."[24] Why then did Kahn resort to loans rather than grants? One reason was tax relief. It might not have amounted to much, but bad debts were charged as losses against the patron's profits at tax time, and Kahn was always trying to reduce his tax liabilities. When deducting the uncollected debt from his own earnings, Kahn was in effect transferring the functions of private patronage to the tax-paying public. Thus his staff had reason to monitor delinquent loans in order to prove their efforts toward collection and declare a legitimate deduction.

Kahn decided to collect or forgive on an individual basis and, inasmuch as he publicly expressed his belief that good art was a good investment even if it lost money, the artists had legitimate reason to think of the loan as a mere formality. Language undoubtedly contributed to some misunderstandings: Kahn's correspondence with the artists normally used the more ambiguous term "advance" rather than loan to describe the borrowed money. But other perceptions weighed heavily as well. With no serious money to be made in poetry, unless *The Bridge* one day were to become a libretto, neither the patron nor the poet ever expected it to be repaid, and indeed Crane's debt was written off as worthless in 1928 without confrontation. Crane's greater concern was not repaying the debt, but rather getting more money and attention from Kahn. The same was true for Bel Geddes, who made repaying the borrowed money part of his strategy. When he earned $6,750 in 1918 from various jobs outside the Met, Bel Geddes promptly returned $200 to Kahn. The Robesons' story, however, was undeniably different — they were asked to repay the loan, and the question is why.

In the beginning, Essie Robeson seemed to appreciate and observe the rules of a healthy artist-patron relationship. She corresponded regularly for the remainder of 1925, telling Kahn how his money had gone to pay back debts and update their wardrobes. The money was a succor for the couple, making them happy and "secure" to be "at last on a firm financial footing." With the future looking bright, she wrote to Kahn on their transatlantic crossing, promising "very satisfactory artistic and financial reports" from London. She then sent clippings telling of Robeson's acclaimed debut there, along with stories about their lodgings and casual details concerning expenses, right down to buying proper undergarments so "Paul doesn't catch cold."[25] Kahn, in turn, extended "cordial congratulations" for the artist's "veritable triumph" and looked forward to further news of their lives. When news arrived that *The Emperor Jones* would close after a run of only five weeks, Kahn wrote the Robesons words of encouragement: "The main purpose of your European adventure has been fully achieved," given that the play had proven a critical if not a box-office hit and had made Robeson the toast of London. Kahn also approved of plans for the couple to take a rest in southern France (via Paris), where, he was told, Robeson could recover from the "strain of the 'Emperor'" and the English climate before returning to America for his concert tour. Those upcoming concerts, of course, were part of the collateral that secured Kahn's loan, a subject now raised only indirectly, but in this phase of correspondence, Essie's stated concern for economy kept the issue of the loan in play. For instance, when she volunteered that the couple could live in France "for about 30 francs a day . . . including meals," she was clearly hoping that Kahn would think them frugal. Polite and heartening in reply, the patron sounded more like a friend than a banker, saying "a rest in the south of France," one of his own favored venues for repose, "would put your husband in first rate shape for his work in New York next winter."[26]

Such summaries and exchanges could only please Kahn. Having hit every audience with meteoric force, Robeson was breaking into the right social circles, getting great publicity, and, thanks to Essie's letters, keeping Kahn up-to-date. Knowledge of their familial details added to his delight, for if Robeson became the topic of conversation in Kahn's social circles, he held the most current information — an insider's knowledge. Even though the letters said nothing of their encounters with racism, or the discontent within their marriage, Kahn would think himself well acquainted with the Robesons, at least until the end of 1925, when Essie abruptly stopped writing and the couple started forgetting about their financial obligations to the patron. In November they missed the quarterly premium payment ($25.35) due on Robeson's life insurance policy. When told of the policy's impending lapse, Kahn instructed his staff to pay the premium and "collect it from Paul Robeson when he returns." The collection was not pursued.[27]

Over the next three years Kahn heard nothing directly from the couple. Essie's chatty letters ceased and not a single installment was made toward repaying the loan. A few questions persist with regard to what happened and the extent to which the change was noticed by — or revealed to — anyone other than Kahn. The shift began in a layered context. Robeson's concert tour of early 1926 drew smaller crowds than expected, creating a shortfall in revenues. Then, after his concert in Boston was not well received by the critics, Essie may have hoped to avoid discussion of bad notices, in fear that the mention of flaws and strains in her husband's voice would undermine Kahn's interest and support. In addition, when the Robesons faced a string of racist indignities, harsher in the United States than in their recent tour abroad, the resulting dispirited mood gave Essie something else to keep shrouded from Kahn. One last trying issue to avoid was the couple's marital turbulence. They fought over money and even took separate vacations in 1926. Ignoring the loan may have developed as an extension of their troubled relationship. However, it would appear more complicated than merely a wife with planned or unconscious motives aimed at avoiding tension with her spouse, or even creating difficulty for him. Essie's silence seemed as much bound up in her own sense of self, for in previous correspondence with Kahn she mentioned nothing of her own creative talents, or, for instance, that while on the Riviera she was writing a play. In other words, if Essie viewed Kahn as her husband's patron, not her own, and believed Kahn saw her as the wife, manager, and caretaker and no more, then the loan's delinquency was a personal embarrassment, something else she would want to avoid. As likely in the end, though, somewhere Essie simply may have hoped that forgetting the debt would just make it disappear.[28]

Kahn's thinking about the Robesons' financial negligence at this stage is equally unclear, but there is evidence to indicate the behavior he generally expected from borrowers. On at least one occasion, a delinquent borrower, owing one-fifth of what the Robesons had borrowed, received notice that Kahn was "disagreeably surprised that you should have thought it proper to simply default your payments without at least observing the courtesy of advising him that you were unable to pay, and of asking his consent of an extension."[29] Kahn anticipated timely, consistent responsibility from those who took his advances, even if the indebted were incapable of repayment. Margaret Anderson of the *Little Review*, for example, understood this convention. Between September 1920 and October 1921, Kahn loaned Anderson $1,500 and when her notes fell due, she replied promptly, and courteously, with sound reason for delay: "May I extend my note for another six months [?] That was my original request when I wrote you first and, with our developing *Inter-Arts* plans, the payment in October will be a much easier matter than at the moment." After "thanking you again a million time[s]" and seeing the loan extended, repayment might have then receded to the back of her mind for a few more months, but when again Anderson could not pay, she wasted no time, writing in good humor to ask, "Is it this month or next that my horrible note is due."

She then made a request in good faith "to buy your indulgence for a little longer time / —not *very* long I think." Kahn extended the note another three months, and at the year's end wrote it off.[30]

In addition, Kahn treated the commercially successful artist differently than the artist without resources. Among those who seemed only to lack the discipline rather than the resources to repay his loans, Kahn's relationships with screenwriter Herman Mankiewicz and playwright Marc Connelly illustrate the banker-patron's willingness to take a sterner line. This suggests that Kahn's management of Robeson's obligation was consistent with other cases in which Kahn authorized collection on the debt and used a staff member or an attorney as the intermediary, at which time the delinquent borrower paid.[31] Of course, he also had the power to forgive any artist's debt outright, as he frequently did, but collection showed a stronger signature in his value system. Indirectly he was saying that the able borrower should repay the bank that backed the arts, and a successful artist should adjust to the demands of the real world. The latter attitude extended beyond the loan mechanism as well. In 1925, for instance, George Gershwin was looking for a midtown apartment with a monthly rent of $100–$125. He was interested in taking the top floor of a building owned by Kahn at 39 West Fifty-fourth Street, but decided not to rent it because Kahn would not lease the space for less than $2,500 per annum.[32]

The Robesons' years of silence coincided with public acclaim for the actor-singer that would lead Kahn to believe the artist was doing well. A contract dispute with Caroline Dudley Reagan did get Robeson suspended from Actor's Equity in 1928, but otherwise he had given sensational concerts in London, Paris, and New York, and *Variety* reported his ability to take $1,250 in fees for a single performance. The couple attended parties hosted by Kahn's friends, and during 1927 Robeson appeared in New York in *Black Boy*, a short-lived play produced by Horace Liveright, another acquaintance and beneficiary. All along, there was no direct exchange between the patron and the Robesons until his headlining role in the London production of Jerome Kern's *Showboat* again demonstrated Robeson's undisputed stardom and accomplishment. It was then that Kahn contacted the Robesons, reminding them of their delinquent debt and inquiring about their plans to repay it.[33]

Essie Robeson immediately swung into action to court the patron with a new round of letters. Offering excuses, apologies, and promises, she asked Kahn to forgive her (though not the debt) and took sole responsibility for the lapse in letters, saying her husband was unaware it had occurred. She also explained how money intended to repay Kahn had been diverted to legal expenses in the dispute with Caroline Dudley Reagan. In other words, she had neither forgotten nor ignored Kahn's loan. As proof she pledged a cash windfall — a £1,000 advance from the British publishing house Doubleday and Doran for her forthcoming biography of Robeson — calling it "my chance to wipe out our debt to you . . . at one swoop." Another itemized budget was presented, but now for a family that included a son, Paul Robeson, Jr., as well as her mother. Kahn reacted benevolently. He extended the loan for an unspecified time, resumed cordial correspondence, and expressed hopes of seeing them. A flurry of exchanges followed: an offer of seats for Robeson's next concert at Albert Hall, a meeting with Essie and her toddler at Claridge's Hotel, then plans to gather in Berlin during May, which were postponed by Robeson's concert schedule in Prague, Vienna, and Budapest.[34] In May 1929, Essie reported, "I am on the last lap of my book." Overlooking that the book advance had been previously earmarked to pay Kahn's loan, she instead declared that a film contract promised to Robeson would "enable me to clean up our debts in one fell swoop" by July. And indicating that Kahn's loan was not their only debt, she added, "I am looking forward with pleasure to surprising my generous creditors favorably." She promised, "As soon as we arrive in New York, we will send a note to you asking for an appointment. I shall bring along newspaper clippings, and will arrange to settle our debt with you at once."[35]

Nothing could be more right. Since many continental producers known to Kahn were now interested in Robeson, including Max Reinhardt, the resumed contact with the Robesons restored that sense of connection that the patron truly enjoyed when, as he put it, "Echoes of the truly remarkable success of your husband have reached me at various times and places." And when he hoped "to have the pleasure of seeing you both" in New York, it was part of the enjoyment restored; concurrent with his favor, Kahn mentioned nothing of their debt.[36] But July passed, the Robesons came in and out of New York, and no meeting with the patron or a payment occurred. It seems unlikely that Essie tried to contact Kahn while they were in New York; if she had, it would have been with repayment in hand. Her correspondence again lapsed until early October, when Essie wrote from London, "By now you must

*Paul Robeson as Othello and Peggy Ashcroft as Desdemona, from the
1930 London production of Othello. (Rutgers Special Collections
and University Archives)*

think we are completely impossible." In her only indication to Kahn
about the racial barriers hindering Robeson's career, she explained his
motion picture contract was canceled because the producer, Charles
Rogers, "couldn't obtain a suitable vehicle for him in the 'Talkies.' "[37]
(Unlike so many others, the Robesons did not ask Kahn for an introduction to Paramount.) The couple had spent the summer without
remunerative work, with Paul studying music, languages, and the title
role for the following year's production of *Othello* in London, while
Essie revised her book and a play. Since they would be in New York the
following month, Kahn was invited to one of Robeson's Carnegie Hall
concerts in November and promised "a substantial payment on our
debt to you" before they went abroad again.[38]

The payments never mattered to Kahn as much as the courtesy of
contact, and when all of 1930 passed in silence, it was no longer a
matter of trust but principle. With no letters or meetings, no move-

ment on the loan account, and three payments missed on the life insurance policy, the matter was turned over to Kahn's attorneys. They issued a summons for payment, which brought Robeson to a meeting with Kahn's representatives in which he blamed the default on his wife and claimed to have no previous knowledge of the delinquency. He accepted responsibility for repayment nonetheless, and thereafter 50 percent of his concert profits went to the debt until it was paid.[39] At the end of 1931, Essie resumed friendly correspondence with Kahn, inviting him to join her for a home-cooked meal at their flat in London. She sounded anxious to tell her side of the story and Kahn agreed to come around, but a health crisis upon his arrival in London forced him to cancel all appointments and perhaps his hope of seeing the Robesons again.[40]

A common link in the Robeson and Bel Geddes stories was Carl Van Vechten, who offered them various tips for handling Kahn. He advised the Robesons to hire a clipping service, write letters, and stay available for private concerts whenever Kahn wanted them. He also recommended they say nothing of Kahn's support among their friends, lest Kahn's office be "deluged with indigent coloured folk." Earlier, when Bel Geddes was anxious to get more from Kahn than the initial loan, Van Vechten counseled a strategy of patience and continual courtship: "When he finds your stock good," he said of Kahn, "his investments in you will continue with a zero or two added." Angling for the big payoff would take time, and so Bel Geddes heeded the advice while being shrewd in other ways.[41]

Smaller dividends were evident early at the Met, where Bel Geddes sensed what it meant to have Kahn's approval among others who sought it. The designer learned to play his privilege sensibly—for all and not more than it was worth. "Address me care Otto H. Kahn, Kuhn, Loeb," he wrote to producer Morris Gest. That ploy succeeded in getting additional work for Bel Geddes, but it was followed by an even smarter move. When Gest disputed Bel Geddes's fee for work on the Century Roof Garden, the designer did not ask his patron to resolve the matter, although Kahn was in a position to do so. Making another wise, low-key gesture just before the premiere of *Shanewis*, Bel Geddes asked Kahn to underwrite a public exhibition of his best designs, then took the patron's rejection in polite stride and immediately replied,

"[I] half expected the answer as it came. . . . The demands on you at this time must be most overwhelming." He swore to go forward, albeit more slowly without Kahn's help.[42]

However much he sensed it would do no good to put nuisance complaints or petitions before Kahn, when Bel Geddes found his chances for advancement at the Met not to his liking, he decided to play a different card. He accepted an offer from the Chicago Opera Company, with hope that creative opportunities and recognition there would lead to a triumphant return to New York. As he was also keenly aware of inter-institutional rivalries between the companies, he sent an obliging letter to the patron, explaining, "I did not want you to think that I was unfaithful to your organization." Kahn grasped the intended message and responded, "I appreciate the loyalty and delicacy of your attitude toward the Metropolitan Opera Company and myself. . . . We have neither [the] right nor desire to stand in the way." He offered a word of encouragement, concluding with a desire to see the designer's "work next season, when the Chicago Company comes to New York." He was indeed still, "Very Faithfully Yours, Otto H. Kahn," and, judging by the clippings and letters from Chicago that followed, Kahn's earlier estimation of the designer's talent was confirmed. The patron seemed nearly ready to sponsor Bel Geddes's return to the Met when a new obstacle fell in the way, as Bel Geddes became embroiled in disputes that not only led to his premature departure from Chicago, but opened a serious breach between the designer and the opera establishment generally. He had antagonized publisher–copyright manager George Maxwell of Ricordi & Co., which controlled the rights to many of the best-known Italian operas. Gatti-Casazza, who had no great affection for Bel Geddes anyway, steered clear of the designer rather than risk Maxwell's ire, and Kahn, for the moment, stayed away from the fray.[43]

More than ever Bel Geddes needed to make it on his own. He continued to send clippings and occasionally pitched a theatrical plan for Kahn's underwriting, getting cordial encouragement without financial or other support in reply. The pattern would not change through 1921, when at year's end Bel Geddes unsuccessfully sought Kahn's sponsorship for a dramatization of *The Divine Comedy*. His designs for that play subsequently became a huge artistic success, and the following year saw Bel Geddes fast emerging as the next great American-born modernist theatrical designer, a genius in line with Robert Edmond Jones and Lee Simonson — "the Karl Marx[es] of our dramatic revolution," as one critic phrased it. Good newspaper notices, along with favorable exposure in such high-brow periodicals as *Theatre Arts* and *Architectural Record*, were topped with the Provincetown "Triumvirate" including Bel Geddes in the reorganized experimental company. In addition, his designs for *The Divine Comedy* went abroad for exhibitions in London and Amsterdam, where they were seen and admired by Gordon Craig and Max Reinhardt.[44] Then came *The Miracle.*

Max Reinhardt's giant Baroque spectacle, which Kahn had long wanted to bring to America, was finally coming stateside, thanks to Kahn's advance of $400,000–$600,000 to underwrite the technically complicated production. In a controversial decision, Reinhardt passed over the more experienced Joseph Urban, who co-designed the prewar German and Austrian productions, and instead entrusted the scenery and some three thousand costumes to the younger Bel Geddes, a designer of very recent acclaim. Reinhardt, who looked upon America as the great "Dollarika," well appreciated that an American designer on the bill could contribute to the show's promotion and popularity. But Bel Geddes had never been to Europe or seen an authentic cathedral in the early Gothic style required for *The Miracle.* So he spent four intensive weeks living and working with Reinhardt in Austria, coming away with topnotch approval from the master. That was all Kahn needed to finally stand firmly in support of Bel Geddes. No old or new disputes with Gatti-Casazza or Gest would get in the way. In the end, when *The Miracle* found both critical and commercial success, Kahn was so pleased that he underwrote the expenses of a multiyear national tour, crowing, "The Miracle as now presented is a far more beautiful and impressive thing than it was . . . in London" at its 1912 premiere. He singled out Bel Geddes as one of the reasons for its current triumph.[45]

The patron's stock in the designer had finally skyrocketed, and as a result Bel Geddes enjoyed new rewards. Kahn became more receptive to his projects and more involved in promoting his career. In February 1924 he arranged for Bel Geddes "to at least submit sketches for *Pelleas et Melisande*" to the Met, and although that commission went to Joseph Urban, Kahn's recommendation to Jesse Lasky at Paramount, written during the next month, sent Bel Geddes back to Hollywood, where he expected to learn "every phase of the development of a complete motion picture" before himself becoming a director. Assigned to work with Cecil B. DeMille on *Feet of Clay*, he got entangled in another argu-

SECTIONAL VIEW, SHOWING THE MECHANISM
OPERATING "THE MIRACLE"

The Miracle, *set design by Norman Bel Geddes.*
(Scientific American; *from program in author's possession*)

ment because, according to Bel Geddes, DeMille wanted an art director, not a director-in-training. After Bel Geddes vented his side of the story to a columnist, DeMille terminated the designer's contract. Bel Geddes then telegraphed an appeal to Kahn ("situation ridiculous and unjust"), which the patron forwarded to Lasky with a judicious cover note: "I do not mean to act as an advocate of Bel Geddes or to endorse its contents, but I simply want to bring his views to your attention for such consideration as you may think they deserve." In August the designer told Kahn that Lasky had resolved the matter in his favor, giving a "definite go-ahead" for his first picture.[46]

Until 1925, however, the only direct financial assistance from Otto Kahn to Norman Bel Geddes had been the first $200 advance. The turning point came in February 1925. Bel Geddes formed a theatrical partnership with Richard G. Herndon, former business manager on the American tour of the Ballets Russes, and they approached Kahn with the idea "to produce three serious plays next season." With Bel Geddes to "do the staging," and Herndon to handle "all the business details," their plans were firm enough to promise that one play would showcase actress Eva Le Gallienne. (In a separate 1925 enterprise, Bel Geddes would direct and design her *Jeanne D'Arc* in Paris, another project under Kahn's patronage.) Liking the proposition, Kahn signed on as a silent backer and pumped in $65,000, which should have been enough money for two shows.[47] But Kahn's money was all spent on one production, *Arabesque*, a tremendous flop that closed after twenty-eight performances, leaving a debt of more than $15,000. Kahn was furious, but that did not stop Bel Geddes and Herndon from trying to revive his goodwill. In the process, the partners turned against each other, with Herndon, the one personally liable for the debt, condemning Bel Geddes for wildly escalating costs, while Bel Geddes swore the production costs were only $25,000. In the absence of an auditor's report, which Herndon was avoiding, Bel Geddes howled, "I don't know how the money was spent." Both petitioned Kahn for individual loans to tide them over, and Herndon was told, "While regretting the position in which you find yourself, I do not see my way to comply with your request." Bel Geddes received more generous consideration:

My reaction to the lamentable failure of "Arabesque" is akin to yours, but mine appertains not to the judgment and attitude of the public, which, as you know, I predicted unqualifiedly when I saw the dress rehearsal, but to the judgment and attitude of yourself and Herndon in recklessly frittering away a vast amount of money and your own great talent on so utterly worthless a play. Under the circumstances, it seems to me that I ought to be the last man to whom you should turn for further funds. However, in view of my continuing admiration for your gifts within the field which is really yours, and for your artistic purposes, I am willing, though reluctantly, to comply with your request, and accordingly enclose herewith a check for $3,000 as an advance, to be repaid within one year.

Kahn then retreated from providing anything more. In February 1926 Maurice Wertheim, another important theatrical patron in New York, tried to intervene on Bel Geddes's behalf, only to hear from Kahn, "I already aided the gentleman . . . by a personal loan a few months ago. In view of this and the Arabesque episode I do not see my way to comply . . . although I appreciate his talents highly and wish him well."[48]

Less than two months after the *Arabesque* fiasco, Hart Crane had his first interview with "Otto the Magnificent." With no blueprint for dealing with Kahn, a father-son resemblance complicated this patron-poet relationship. The transitions from traditional to modern patronage caused as much confusion and affected the production of art more for Crane than it had for Robeson or Bel Geddes, however, partially because Crane's calculus in promoting the patron's esteem and support became tied up in his unrealistic projections concerning the amount of time and money needed to write *The Bridge*. He went to rural Patterson, New York, sharing a household with Alan and Carolyn Tate, where he expected to compose a work as important as T. S. Eliot's *The Waste Land* in a short period of time, and instead confronted "many unexpected formal difficulties in satisfying my conception."[49] Writing *The Bridge* and making Kahn's money last from one installment to the next proved more formidable and entangled than anyone has realized.

His friends and later critics offered various reasons for Crane's creative struggle, from alcoholism and homosexuality to self-love and self-hate. One commentator blames Kahn's money itself, or at least the circumstances surrounding Crane's expectations for more money in March 1926, as Crane sent Kahn an extraordinary exegesis of the poem's plan and progress; this line of thinking contends that the "intense pressure of commitment had prompted the premature account of the poem to Otto Kahn, and this, in turn, had blocked him." There is another way to look at it. From the start, Crane aimed to stay on the patron's good side, and in January 1926, while still freshly blooming with self-esteem over his recent recognition from Kahn, Crane wrote to his mother, "If my poem when completed seems good enough to [Kahn], it may be, of course, that he will be further interested." He knew it was best to stay in touch without pestering the patron ("he wants to hear 'from time to time' as he puts it—about how my poem is progressing"), but Crane was also already looking over the calendar, figuring that he could get another $1,000 from Kahn as early as May and planning to drop him a note in March. The puzzle pieces did not neatly fit together, however, and Crane was avoiding more than one annoying reality that could make him blanch with fear. He lacked any written pledge of further funds, for example, although from the start Crane had told everyone that Kahn had "given the sum of two thousand dollars." He was also saying that Kahn expected the money to last for a full year, which actuated another fear, because Crane spent money quickly and worried how Kahn would judge him on that account. All together, these factors could have choked Crane's creativity before March rolled around. Nevertheless, when panicked over his hardship, Crane steadied himself to ask Kahn for more support. This established a pattern in Crane's relationship with his patron: he relied on his solicitations for money to force himself into creative productivity.[50]

First, his appeal for fresh funding started in silence on the subject of money. He instead composed a letter than provided the patron with an intricate peek at the poetic process, showing all its attendant pathos, pride, and difficulties. Crane then renewed his promise: " 'The Bridge' will be a dynamic and eloquent document." The sequence worked to reassure the poet's own doubts along with the ones that he projected upon the patron. Crane was putting on his best face in order to shield Kahn from another point of view—namely, this once-in-a-lifetime, fully focused period had left the poet ambivalent about country living, bickering with his house partners, and insecure about his talent. Elsewhere Crane whined that a job in New York might be better, because he at least then could feel "part-time useful" and there "wouldn't be the suspense of weeks going by without a written line." In fact, the process of corresponding with Kahn carried Crane closer to writing those lines. In March 1926 the pattern culminated with an extensive outline of the entire poem, which the poet sent to Kahn with "Atlantis," the finale and only written section of the work-in-progress. Afterward, Crane felt able to ask Kahn for more money.[51]

It is striking how differently the patron and the poet perceived the money. Upon receiving Crane's request for funds in April, Kahn absentmindedly asked his staff, "What did I give him?" He was told, "Loans of $1,000." The patron then replied to Crane, "I am prepared to add $500 to the advance which I made to you last February." These words twisted Crane into a tailspin. He was counting on $1,000 to clear other debts, so not only would he fall short of additional obligations, but the reduced amount could also have indicated that Kahn's commitment to the poet was less certain than Crane had represented. There are no notes in Kahn's files to suggest that he had promised more than the original $1,000, and no further funds were promised when Kahn sent the additional $500. Thus it is impossible to say why Crane continued to expect more. If Kahn had initially offered $2,000 and later forgot, it would not have been the first instance of such absentmindedness. Margaret Anderson, for instance, once thought she had secured a $4,000 pledge for the *Little Review* and could not understand why Kahn declined the call for funds. On the other hand, if Kahn had in fact casually offered Crane as much as $2,000, his commitment was fainter than Crane ever chose to recall. In either scenario, it would increase Crane's anxieties related to money and self-esteem.[52]

An additional reason for Crane to be seized by anxiety lay in the appearance that he spent money too quickly or extravagantly. Bel Geddes and Essie Robeson dealt with this as well, but Crane was especially self-conscious and defensive about it because he was more dependent upon Kahn's money, and because, while he was spending it freely, Crane knew that tales of him "squandering money" were circulating "about town." He had to be concerned about them reaching Kahn's ears. When Crane used the second advance to change venues (moving to the Isles of Pines in Cuba), he was sure to tell the patron, "Summer months are not exactly the most propitious time to live in the tropics. . . . I shall have few expenses, no rent, etc."[53] Kahn voiced no doubts or ultimatums, but Crane's fears of seeming profligate, and the consequences of failure, were tied to Kahn all the same.

Crane wrote in April, "If I can't somehow succeed in taking advantage of this one opportunity given me by Mr. Kahn, I don't know how I'll feel about life or any future efforts to live." He was nowhere nearer completion and nearly out of funds once more by mid-June, at which point Crane half-lamented the help from "our friend, the banker," imagining again that he would have been better off "with my nose to the grindstone" at some job, where he could "fancy that freedom would yield me a more sustained vision: now I know that much has been lacking all along." One more time, though, as soon as Crane's self-confidence failed him, his sense of duty ("to discharge my debt to Kahn's kindness") and the prospect of another cash installment pushed him toward a focus. His tone and output changed once he decided that "the final 500 from Kahn can't be solicited until August or later — if at all, for I shan't ask for it unless I am writing again by that time." And within three weeks, he fired up another spell of serious writing. By July's end he could send Kahn the poetic equivalent of cash, letting the "Dedication" and "Columbus" section of *The Bridge* stand as installments or proof of the poet's creditworthiness. In September he reported that the poem was three-quarters done and asked for another advance. In November Kahn sent $500, which the poet presumed to be the last installment of the pledged $2,000.[54] A mad dash to finish the poem before the year's end followed, but Crane came up short. He sent nothing to Kahn until September 1927, when a five-page single-spaced typed letter arrived along with a nearly finished manuscript of *The Bridge*.[55]

Crane's September letter offered another remarkable guide to the poem's intentions and method, it made a plea for further support, and it closed with a request for Kahn's impressions of *The Bridge*. Once in Kahn's hands, the banker-patron left a few telling reactions in the form of marginalia — on the letter rather than the poem. He marked the paragraph where Crane shifted from the poem's exegesis to his request for help in finding a job and another "800 or 1,000 dollars" to finish *The Bridge*. He left no marked reaction to Crane's potentially offensive assertion that "a great poem may well be worth at least the expenditure necessary for merely the scenery and costumes of many a flashy and ephemeral play, or the cost of an ordinary motor car." Instead the Maecenas scratched "X"s at the block in which Crane compared himself to Virgil, put "the historic and cultural scope of *The Bridge*" on par with *The Aeneid*, and declared his own work to be a "symphony with an epic theme."[56]

The poem itself went home with Kahn over the weekend of September 18–19, where he "perused" it, or so he said. If he read it, and read it straight through, this is how the poet all along had said it should be read. If he only skimmed it lightly, or not at all, between other engagements and entertainments, Kahn's sentiments about the poem were already preformed nonetheless. In addition to his earlier looks at Crane's drafts, large portions of *The Bridge* had already appeared in *The Dial* and *The American Caravan*.[57] On Monday the patron tendered a reply:

> Owing to the overwhelming demands to which my time is subject, I must ask you to excuse me from stating in writing my "impression of the poem as it now stands," except to the extent of saying that I am confirmed in my opinion of your great and singular talent. It is too bad that your efforts to find employment have been unsuccessful thus far. I shall be glad to speak about you to Mr. Guard, head of the Publicity Department of the Metropolitan Opera Company. . . . And I shall look around among my friends and acquaintances to ascertain whether any other appropriate opening can be found for you. Meanwhile, I am willing to advance you another $500. When your way takes you to New York, any day *after this week*, you can adjust the formalities with my secretary, Mr. Dartt, and you and I can have a talk about "The Bridge."
>
> Believe me, with best wishes, Faithfully yours,
> Otto H. Kahn[58]

These details are important because, when comparing Kahn's brevity to Crane's intensity, Kahn's remarks have been labeled "comical" and "distant," leading some to the conclusion that Kahn was unable to comprehend the poem. The origin of that viewpoint was Crane himself. On one of those occasions when neither effusive nor boastful about Kahn's enthusiasm for him, the poet told Matthew Josephson that Kahn neither understood the work nor cared much about it.[59] A more generous appraisal of the patron might have resulted, of course, if Kahn had come up with another $1,000 year after year, or if harsher first readers than Kahn had not found *The Bridge* famously incoherent. Crane's sour take on the patron, in other words, not only came amid a mixed critical reception for his epic poem, it was also evidence of his disappointment when *The Bridge* found a place in Kahn's pantheon of art but brought no big cash payout. More generally, it reflected a problem in the transitions to modern patronage.

On one hand, Kahn's expectations for masterful art at once reflected his own good taste and the stature of talent who received his recognition. On the other hand, the patron did not make explicit demands upon either the artist or the content of subsidized work. The latter aspect of his patronage gestured respect for the freedom of the individual artist; but the subvention came at a price, or it implied certain boundaries. Kahn resisted complete economic dependence upon his singular patronage. While he invited creative persons into his house, he did not invite them to join his household, or host them permanently. Under the best of these circumstances, face time with the patron was something to desire, not only for the chance to pitch an idea and receive funding. In their initial meeting, for instance, Kahn offered Crane more than money alone. An interesting conversationalist who loved to be the perfect host, Kahn enjoyed a developed though not scholarly grasp of the arts, which could leave an artist feeling incredibly flattered and self-important. However, the scarceness of his time could subsequently also leave any artist feeling critical of Kahn's aloofness and shortchanged. Crane usually understood that Kahn was not being insensitive: "There are so many others whom he is always helping that his time is largely taken up anyway. What with two personal secretaries and a whole corps of personal office help — *besides* his huge financial machine . . . he must be a busy man."[60]

Indeed, every day on Kahn's calendar was fully appointed and efficiently executed. The demands of his correspondence alone were staggering. Over the course of three months he could accumulate 3,769 letters in "57 varieties of jobs and engagements."[61] Managing that mountain of paper once led Kahn to admit, "Letter writing, except for definite purposes, is for the very busy person an invention of Satan, and becomes largely a matter of form."[62] His correspondence style typically reflected it. A reply might begin as marginalia on the incoming letter, or Kahn might dictate a response with the incoming correspondence in hand. His staff then handled the final preparations, often inserting Kahn's formulaic comments or providing excuses related to the overwhelming demands on his time or money. At bottom, Crane was the "man of letters" who slaved over finding just the right words, but Otto Kahn handled a greater volume of correspondence in any given year. Compared with the many thousands of letters contemporary to the Kahn-Crane correspondence, the poet's share of Kahn's time and interest actually ranks quite high. His replies were polite, precisely on point, and better humanized than his business communications.[63]

The real oddity, in any case, was not brevity but the reversal of responsibility when Crane is compared to the Robesons. In Crane's case it was Kahn who did not fulfill all the expected roles of the patron-banker-critic, rather than the artist who did not assume the proper behavior of the beneficiary. In any event, Kahn and Crane each had a time management problem of a different kind and degree, though neither realized it to be a potential point of conflict. Kahn may have heard or understood that Crane could not cope with complete freedom to write. Some people do better with less time. On Crane's side, the initial conversation offered a taste of Kahn's good humor, charm, and intelligence — which the poet thought was now open to him. Thereafter, Crane was likely to hear how Kahn was "overwhelmed with accumulated work and engagements"; or could grant an interview "unfortunately . . . only . . . of limited duration."[64]

The manners and strategies for arranging meetings also became twisted up with Crane's disappointment concerning Kahn's reaction to *The Bridge*. When Kahn first invited him to "have a talk" about the poem, Crane responded compliantly, agreeing to wait until the next week for an appointment. Then his anticipation moved into full drive, and, rather than waiting as the patron had asked, he instead rushed to Kahn's office for money on September 23, 1927. He received his funds, and, at that moment, the money was more important to Crane than a meeting with Kahn. When the two finally saw each other on October 11, it was a hurried conference, arranged again to better serve the schedule of the poet than the patron, but annoying to Crane nonetheless. By that time, Kahn's applause for *The Bridge* was muffled by the absence of a great cash windfall. Adding to his bitterness, the poet had to ask his father for money on the same day. By the third year of the patron-artist relationship, when Crane recounted yet another "interview with 'Papa Kahn,' " his festering transference of filial anger to the patron was better evident.[65]

Aside from Crane's unique paternal issues, the artistic competition for Kahn's patronage more generally produced the equivalent of sibling rivalries with all the attending resentments and deceptions. There was always someone angling for Kahn's support, or wanting to influence his opinion in favor of one talent over another, and one such person was Waldo Frank, whose own pursuit of self-interest must be read alongside that of Crane. Around the time that Kahn's payments to Crane tapered off, Frank, the poet's sober Yale-educated friend, was becoming one of Kahn's favorite dinner, theater, and weekend companions. Whether that occurred at Crane's expense is anybody's guess, but at the end of 1927 Frank began receiving $4,000 annually in loans from the patron for a period of four years. It is unlikely that the poet knew that his friend was getting exactly what Crane himself wanted from Kahn. Frank said nothing of the money in his autobiography.[66]

Whether or not Kahn understood *The Bridge* is another matter. Kahn was neither stupid nor blind, and at the very least could grasp Crane's promotion of the industrial and commercial commonplace to an artistic reflection of American modernity. The poem invokes visions of cinemas and subways (both objects of Kahn's financial dealings), and it offers many images of Wall Street and lower Manhattan (Kahn's daytime domicile). Could Kahn not see himself in Crane's use of the "Chan" pun? George Jean Nathan had illuminated the satiric intent of the Kaan in *Marco Millions* for readers of the *American Mercury* in 1927. Kahn also probably understood that Crane's elision of "Thomas a Ediford" was better than clever — if he was not studied enough to independently appreciate its Joycean qualities, then because, like Edison and Ford, Otto Kahn always made B. C. Forbes's list of *Men Who Are Making America*.[67] At any rate, no single image of *The Bridge* would speak more directly to Kahn's experience than the railroads. It was mainly from the railroads that Kahn saw modern America, as he put it, "this vast country, with its unprecedented mixture of races . . . traditions, climate, surroundings and life." In his own celebration of the attendant myths and consciousness, Kahn wrote, "underneath what the surface shows of newness, of strident jangle, of 'jazziness' and 'Mainstreetness,' there lies all the raw material of a great cultural and artistic development." Even E. H. Harriman, a man hardly known for aesthetic interests, was part of this artistic development. Kahn agreed with a European colleague who once said of Harriman, "That supposedly 'hardboiled-man' is a great poet; only he rhymes in rails."[68] Overall, *The Bridge* etched an optimism that was consistent with what Kahn needed to find in his adopted country and the postwar world. The very idea of bridging was a powerful analogue for Kahn. He bridged the New and Old World, Wall Street and Bohemia, Jews and Gentiles, along with the divisions of art and war. He had called the Dawes Plan a bridge.

Finally, Otto Kahn never shrugged off Hart Crane; an artist in whom Kahn was truly interested rarely was. That included Bel Geddes, who eventually made his way back into the patron's favor, obtaining a letter of introduction to the Pennsylvania Railroad that helped get his earliest commissions in industrial design. Herndon and Kahn would socialize again as well. As for Crane, after the money petered out, Kahn extended other forms of patronage, including an introduction to Jesse Lasky at Paramount and a letter of recommendation for a fellowship from the Guggenheim Foundation.[69] But there were cases in which Kahn soundly rejected an artist after a long history of support. His treatment of the Irish-born author Frank Harris, for instance, reached an impasse in 1925 over Harris's sexually explicit autobiography. "Leaving aside the morals," Kahn opined, "it comes down to a question of taste. . . . There are certain truths which need not be discussed in a detailed way coram publico." When the autobiography, already banned in England and America, was also censored in France, Kahn declined to join the protest on behalf of Harris's treatment by the French courts.[70] The disputed boundaries of proper bourgeois modernity forever put a wedge between them.

A rejection from Otto Kahn could confuse and frustrate a career as much as his approval or support could excite it. The greater mystery was how, given the limited access to his time and millions, Kahn still managed to gain a generally favorable reputation. On the positive side, the talent in his orbit escaped the controlling, suffocating horrors and favoritism that were better evident, for example, between Langston Hughes, Zora Neale Hurston, and their patron Charlotte Mason. But any orbit was bound to bring complaints from creative talents. Some might have despised every dependence on Kahn, the careful stroking of his ego, and the very process of asking for money, or the continual need "to beg from these tin-horned bastards, Catholic or Jew, for my plays," as Eugene O'Neill once put it, before concluding that commercial managers were "not less insulting to one's self-respect . . . [than] Kahn" and his "sincere" patronage of "the best in theatre, whatever that is."[71] The protocol on the artists' side more or less repressed the urge to offend Kahn directly with such remarks. It was simply too risky, and plainly stupid, when there were safer ways to vent and keep the money flowing. From sneaking a sneer behind his back to flashing a glimpse of his flaws in some smart satire, the process of compromising was a measured contest — gauging and guessing how good-natured the patron could be. With some other artist or publisher or producer always angling to secure his support, Kahn's patronage was itself a site of cultural competition.

Creative talent, meanwhile, became Kahn's court and cohort, a way to requite the obscenity of great wealth. It compensated for Kahn's lack of talent and courage if he could not himself make great art, for he could at least collaborate in its making while enjoying the process. But Kahn thought the *mécène* served a higher purpose than merely self-gratification. The whole of Kahn's patronage ran contrary to the notion that New York, the hub of cultural America, emancipated itself from Europe after the war.[72] Instead, everything came back to continual cosmopolitanism. Crane self-consciously blended Old World classics with Joycean modernism and American imagery; Robeson was a sensation from Harlem precisely because he was a great success in Europe; and Bel Geddes's biggest break as a stage designer, *The Miracle*, asked him to emulate the theatrical modernism of Europe. Relevant to this argument was a debate that regularly erupted in *Theatre Arts*, where Waldo Frank, who was hardly hostile to European theater, wrote, "Do we want great art? Easy: just import it." Most of Frank's assault landed upon theatrical enterprises that Kahn happened to sponsor, including Max Reinhardt, the Moscow Art Theatre, and *Chauve Souris*: "America's continued prostration before whatever comes here from abroad, clad in prestige and the pathos of distance is disheartening. . . . We gobble up everything and digest so little. Money buys so readily all the substitutes."[73]

Kahn could argue with Frank's point of view and accept legitimate criticism, then fund a solution. Turning conflict into cooperation helped forge their friendship. Both wanted more from America and agreed, in Kahn's words, that "while genuine art is national in its roots . . . [the arts] . . . of the world have at all times reacted upon, and stimulated and influenced, one another."[74] If such interdependencies could look like invasions, it was no less for New York's nationalists than Europeans who clamored about American cultural inroads and the surge of direct investment by American corporations in the 1920s. Kahn perhaps could see the issues from more sides than most. In the end, though, it was quite impossible to separate the American from the European in Otto Kahn. He was seeking neither Europe in America nor Americanized Europe, but rather a wholeness in European and American culture, and economics that acknowledged aesthetic practice.

CHAPTER SIX

Tears and Bears

On October 29, 1929, after the bull market for American common stocks came to a mighty crash, Fox Movietone telephoned Otto Kahn. They wanted a few words that could help "in steadying the situation." It would have been a perfect opportunity for Kahn to play the pundit and predict the future, but on this occasion he decided not to speak. How could he ask the staff at Kuhn, Loeb to manage a media circus in addition to the one emanating from the stock exchange? Besides, it would do no harm to reserve his words for a later moment. The market would survive without his comment. For much of the year, Kahn had been expecting the business cycle to dip toward a short-run "interval of comparative inactivity."[1] This gave him another reason to stay quiet. To sound like a bear, and suggest that stocks were overvalued, could worsen the tear. A veteran of four decades in high finance, Kahn could stand poised, expecting events to grow predictably from an experienced, coherent past, and have no clue that the closing bell on October 29 began another conjunction in world time — throwing his modern, North Atlantic fusion into final crisis.

The next fours years felt like twelve, a perilously kaleidoscopic shift bringing social time into total calamity. Kahn soon enough found himself confronting the joint failures of capitalist and humanist development, all within a single context that curtailed the promise of the Enlightenment. But if only a fraction of these issues are evident in an account of Kahn on the day of the crash, the point is to see how naturally Kahn's experiences could steady his expectations, thoughts, and actions. At the end of 1929, Otto Kahn could attempt reasonable predictions. Future events grew from a known past, and the cycles of business, politics, and life had always had coherence for Kahn—at least until the business cycle remained impervious to revival and a reign of painful suspense toppled the projected outcomes. The events after the crash conformed to a clear architectonic sequence only in hindsight, yet, to be living in Kahn's time, the language of theater and political economy could be coupled into a functional interpretive construct. Performance was more clearly fundamental to evaluation, as when the anticipated worth of stocks crashed or when debtors defaulted on bonds, when fresh loans ran dry, and when paper money stopped being an expression of gold. Performance was no less crucial when governments and individuals sought contrivances to restore the form of a well-made play.

· · · ·

THE EARLY PROGNOSIS

Otto Kahn made money in stock market speculation during the 1920s, but he did not get rich quickly. He was already rich and always a conservative financier, so Kahn could be a dyed-in-the-wool optimist, yet stand apart from what John Kenneth Galbraith has labeled the "seminal lunacy" of the 1920s market boom and the "Wall Streeters who helped to foster this insanity."[2] Instead, Kahn's optimism was characteristically as cautious as it was unshakable throughout the twenties. He frowned upon the "extremes and the excess" of bull and bear pools alike. Calling each a "gullible crowd of get-rich-quick devotees" who let "unreflecting desire for gain . . . or unreflecting fear" rush them to frenzies of buying and selling, respectively, Kahn noted that the alternative, "correct and profitable judgment of intrinsic values," was a more considered formulation, whereby value should be based on present earnings, past results, anticipations for the immediate future, and reasonable expectations for the longer future. Kahn's more statesmanlike approach both to investments and social psychology steered clear of gloom or euphoria, and instead emphasized steadiness within generalized instability. By 1926 this applied to conditions in Britain, France, Germany, and Italy, but less to Eastern Europe. As for America, Kahn always believed it would make a continuous "forward march" toward economic growth, and he figured an "orderly pulling back, not a panicky rout" of overpriced stocks by itself had little relevance for the overall economy. Recessions, which were also natural, required the combination of specific, adverse circumstances—such as "grave foreign complications," "persistent overproduction or overtrading," and "major credit disturbances or acute monetary stringency." He did not think these lay ahead.[3]

During 1928 Kahn shifted his emphasis within this general approach. He seemed to be waiting for the day when bull and bear mentalities came to equilibrium. The longer it took, the more dangerous it became. Looking back, Kahn reflected, "the handwriting was on the wall" for "perfect mania" because "money was far too easy" and the diversion of capital into U.S. stock speculation was dangerous for Europe's dependence on short-term loans. Kuhn, Loeb began bracing for the inevitable burst. While the general trend among America's leading financial and industrial companies would increase loans to brokers (call loans backed by securities as collateral), Kuhn, Loeb reduced the call loans on its books by 24 percent. "Some of us reached the conclusion . . . that things could not go on," Kahn later recalled.[4] A few had the courage to predict a certain break, including his former partner, Paul Warburg, whose reward for honesty was a tar-and-feather retribution from many in the financial community. But if Warburg felt duty-bound to warn of the danger at its fullest, Kahn was constitutionally obliged to project composure. In an unpublished interview in early spring 1929, he told Paul Einzig of London's *Financial Times* that speculation had been overdone, but there was "nothing in trade conditions in the United States to justify any fears of depression." Kahn was in part articulating his hope and belief, as well as playing it safe with mass psychology, always a factor in market and social behavior.[5]

Then the summer of 1929 brought the stock market to new heights. With the Dow Jones Industrial Index rising from 300 in January to 380 by the end of August, the investing public seemed "determined to speculate," and "a runaway feeling throughout the country" forced Kahn to rethink his position once again. "Persuaded by the course of events that the thing could go on and did go on," he later compared his own and similar opinions to that of the dissenting "twelfth juryman" who inevitably thought himself wrong "when everybody else says, 'This thing is going on for a few years longer.' " Doubters like Kahn came to think, "We do not want to assume that our judgment is right as against everybody else's."[6] But such uncertainty lasted only until October. After three erratic weeks for stock prices, "Black Thursday" (October 24) and "Tragic Tuesday" (October 29) unleashed three weeks of unprecedented mayhem. Average stock values were halved.

Tears and Bears

His associates immediately assumed Kahn was financially solid and Kahn himself had good reasons to feel secure. For one, the experiences of 1893 and 1907 as well as 1919 and 1924 prepared him for cyclical downswings. The financial world was full of shocks and breaks. In a sense, October 1929 was no more chaotic than the sinking of the *Lusitania*, as each event produced a similar "very unpleasant experience" and "some sleepless nights." In both cases, Kuhn, Loeb had large issues in the offering—but "made good," "stood in the breach," and demonstrated that a first-rate banking house knew how to limit risk exposure. It could roll with unforeseen calamities. As for his management of personal wealth, in November 1929 Kahn assured Lady Diana Cooper, who had an account under his direction, "Neither you nor I have been busted by the recent debacle in the New York Stock Market." He reminded her, "Your funds, having been invested in non-speculative securities, did not participate in the dizzy rise of the defunct boom, but neither did they come down to earth with a sickening thud."[7]

When its books closed for 1929, Kuhn, Loeb registered $120 million in assets, a substantial increase over the previous year, and the firm remained solvent, if at times profitless, through the worst of the Great Depression. It also appeared faultless with regard to a number of ethical questions. For once, being excluded by the Morgans was beneficial. Because the Morgan-led "Bankers' Pool" that failed to stem the panic of October 24 did not include Kuhn, Loeb, Kahn and his partners were not immediately tarnished as Wall Street leaders who failed to prevent the crash. Nor would a Kuhn, Loeb partner be directly humiliated, as Albert Wiggin of the Chase National Bank would be, for seeming to use the bankers' pool for personal gain. In addition, since as a rule Kahn and his partners declined corporate directorships if they could not allocate sufficient attention to the appointment, Kuhn, Loeb avoided the kind of disgrace that later fell upon the old Boston firm of Lee, Higginson. That firm's representative on the board of Kreuger & Toll never attended a meeting of the worldwide empire of holding companies and finance agencies, which collapsed in 1932 after years of shockingly fraudulent practices. Other safeguards for Kuhn, Loeb lay in the fact that it mostly refrained from the rage for investment trusts during the 1920s—it sponsored only one, the Pennroad Corporation, while more than 700 investment trusts were formed during the period 1927–30. In the end, Kuhn, Loeb's record in financing U.S. railroads and foreign issues was also better than the industry average.

With all these practical and psychological underpinnings, Otto Kahn was cautiously confident after the crash. He took "a very modest flyer or two," buying stocks "when the picking seemed good during the recent wreckage." He genuinely believed that "purchases, at the existing level of prices, are bound to turn out profitably in the long run," yet he "would not venture upon an opinion whether or not we shall see lower prices before the upward reach sets." If he believed there was truth in the more catastrophic predictions of Paul Warburg, Kahn kept such thoughts very private and guarded. Instead he emphasized other aspects of reality—those that favored the impression of normalcy and equilibrium.[8]

Kahn waited several months before issuing a public statement specifically on economic conditions. In the interim, a feature on America's artistic future for the *New York Times* captured his financial composure. Calling him a picture "of quiet self-possession, of deliberate refusal to let men, circumstances of events rush him off his feet," the journalist implied that neither the crash nor any day of "storm or stress" could shake this man, the Wall Street he represented, or his office, which, "in its subdued light, seemed a sequestered library far from the city's life." The banker in his *mise-en-scène* was something akin to Titian's *Portrait of Jacobo Strada* (1569)—which Erwin Panofsky has noted reflects the many facets of the subject's personality (scholar, counselor, collector) and places him in an "air-tight" compartment. Making Kahn a subject of the twentieth century rather than the early modern era was the absence of gold coins from the picture. Instead, "tickers in the adjoining room clicked off quotations." The banker, meanwhile, "went on."[9]

Apparently one thing had not changed for Kahn since the crash. He still wished that art and intellect could be spared from hardships that originated in a market of political folly. Some of Kahn's private letters from November 1929 enlarge this impression. One series involved S. N. Melamed, editor of the *Reflex*, a periodical for American Jewry, which had previously run a flattering feature, "Otto H. Kahn—Maecenas." Now in arrears on a $2,000 loan from the banker-patron, Melamed's subscribers "lost all they had" in the crash, and the editor was unable to pay the loan. Kahn empathized, "It is too bad that the repercussions of the Stock Exchange crash have invaded even the sanctum of the publisher of 'The Reflex.' . . . I hope for your sake, sundry others' sake, and the country's sake that things settle down to reasonably normal conditions in the early future." With the mark of a fully functional Maecenas, Kahn postponed Melamed's debt until the *Reflex* was back in the black.[10]

After October 1929, the consistencies in Kahn's patronage were mainly overshadowed by the attributed effects of the crash. In this respect, his refusal to save the Provincetown Playhouse in December 1929 was notable and controversial. The Provincetown had chronic financial shortfalls and considerable artistic triumphs before the crash. Paul Green's *In Abraham's Bosom* and e. e. cummings's *him*, for example, both had sold-out runs but lost money. Kahn, who was the Provincetown's most stalwart supporter, concluded earlier in 1929 that the company needed greater capacity. The company took his advice, left the Macdougal Street theater in favor of a larger midtown house, and pursued an expansion that required greater membership subscriptions and a $300,000 production fund. By September 1929, however, less than $50,000 in cash was raised — $18,000 of it Kahn's contribution, by far the largest single donation. This paid the first two months rent at the Garrick Theatre, along with the production expenses for the season's first offering, Mike Gold's *Fiesta*, which lost money. The next production broke even, the third never came off, and a gala benefit on November 17, 1929, failed to cover the cost of the benefit itself. With the company facing $25,000 in current obligations and unable to find new donors, Otto Kahn closed his purse.

Provincetown thus suspended operation in December for lack of funds, leaving two unanswered questions: was Kahn responsible for its demise, and did the stock market crash cause his withdrawal? The single answer to both echoes the Pirandello play, *Cosi è se vi Pare:* "It is so if you think so," or "Right you are if you think you are." The crash made it hard to raise funds generally, but Kahn was also exercising his principle that artistic efforts "should not expect me to do that which, in the long run can, and should, only be done by group action or by the patronage of theatre-goers." Some board directors and advisers complained that "he got them to a certain extent in the pickle" by pushing the expansion and then not pulling out all the stops to see that it succeed. In Kahn's view, fourteen years of his generous contributions made it time for "so rich a community as New York" to provide more funds. In private, he said flatly, "If New York does not care to do so, I know of no way to make it care." In contrast, during the same December, Kahn gave $5,000 to the Philharmonic Society, which was facing a $200,000 deficit and did not close. In other words, Otto Kahn would not be there first, last, and always — unless others joined in sufficient number. His responsibility was limited within wider market networks.[11]

A different but equally important perception of Kahn's responsibility became the issue elsewhere in his correspondence from late 1929. With uncanny coincidence, two German Americans tried to entice Kahn into telling his life story immediately after the crash. One was Melamed, and the other was poet-publisher turned "big name interviewer" George Sylvester Viereck, a long-time acquaintance of Kahn. The crash, in part, motivated both solicitations, as each author hoped Kahn's vanity and compassion would lead to a commissioned biography or contract to ghostwrite his autobiography, or simply some money when Melamed and Viereck needed it. The situation with Viereck, though, revealed other twists in expectations for Kahn's support and generosity. Having speculated heavily during the 1920s, Viereck's circumstances more closely approximated the Wall Street calamity. He had become rich quickly and, according to one biographer, thought himself "independently rich, or at least well-to-do." However, his portfolio was built with brokers' loans, and his stock purchases were collateralized by securities. When the value of his investments plummeted, his debt did not. "The gyrations of the [stock] ticker" pushed him to the brink of bankruptcy, Viereck explained, and he asked Kahn to rescue him.[12]

Kahn was in an awkward position. He wanted both to limit his associable responsibility and to offer help. He also sought to control what he could never control — the context, interpretation, and impact of his presence and remarks. In the best of times, of course, an association with Kahn or underwriting by Kuhn, Loeb might be parlayed into success for cultural or commercial enterprises. In tough times this association became even more important. When Kahn retired from the chairmanship and presidency of the Metropolitan Opera Company in 1931, for instance, his successor was acutely aware that Kahn's continuing presence on the new board of directors was needed for ongoing confidence. In other instances, however, association with Kahn led to comical confusion. For example, at the beginning of 1930, writer Mike Gold found that nobody believed he was broke, since he was a friend of Otto Kahn.[13] Those who wanted Kahn to be their investment angel were a special class. Many had sought Kahn's investment advice over

Tears and Bears

the years. The few who received his closest attention, such as Anna Pavlova and Diana Cooper, opened accounts at Kuhn, Loeb and left him to manage their funds with a free hand. A greater number thought Kahn could at least give inside information on trading stock, pointing them toward good picks, wise buys, and smart sales. As a rule, Kahn told them stock speculation was not his forte and rebuffed such requests, giving his views on the market generally, much the same as he would to the press. But he also bent his rules and occasionally slipped a tip or two to his friends. Louise Brooks, for instance, tied trysts to tips during the twenties, recalling later how, "as a pussy cat, I sat under many a king's chair . . . and absorbed many a business deal" from Kahn, among others. Long after the profits evaporated, Brooks better realized how her own extravagance contributed to her bankruptcy. By comparison, when explaining how he managed to become one of the rare losers in Wall Street speculation while everyone else was getting rich from the bull market, Horace Liveright blamed his washouts on Kahn's advice.[14] If such grumbles were typical, like all grumbles about Kahn, they were generally made behind his back.

Viereck more boldly complained directly to Kahn. He pleaded for the patron to "take my little fortune under your protecting wings" and expected Kahn to cover the losses as he might forgive a loan. Instead, the details of Viereck's predicament must have left the banker-patron shaking his head. Viereck had a $125,000 loan, due at the Equitable Trust Company within five days, which was inadequately collateralized by slumping bank stocks. Reading this, Kahn immediately scribbled an idiom that more generally applied to the market crisis of the moment: "*ist guter Rat teuer*" (or "what a mess" and "what are we to do"). In his formal reply, Kahn wrote, "I wish you had asked me earlier. . . . I should have advised you, as I did others long ago, to get out of carrying stocks on margin, or, at least to lighten your load. But now, at this late date, after the collapse has come, *'ist guter Rat teuer.'*" He declined to take over Viereck's loan. Even so, he did offer to ask the creditor for consideration on Viereck's behalf, which was a significant gesture, since Kahn was a director of the Equitable Trust. At the bottom line, however, he offered nothing more concrete than his earnest hopes that "you are more frightened than hurt."[15]

The next day brought another round of letters. Viereck persisted, called for Kahn to do more, and explained why he thought Kahn was so obligated. Several years earlier, he recalled, when Viereck asked Kahn "whether I should sell some of my bank stocks," Kahn handed him the stock adage, "Fear and greed were the worst counselors in investments," so Viereck promptly sold one half. Shortly afterward, bank stocks began to rise, and Viereck claimed Kahn's "suggestion, however sound from the point of view of banking, involved me in a loss of fifty to seventy-five thousand dollars." Then, not long after the 1929 crash, Kahn repeated the slogan while the two discussed the market over lunch. So Viereck "refrained from selling," assuming "in the stormy financial weather [Kahn] would be the most reliable pilot." This time he lost $100,000 within a day or two.[16]

The logic backfired with Kahn, who turned around abruptly and summarily tossed aside the two matters under discussion. Regarding Viereck's proposition for the biography, he wrote, "That is up to my family, after I shall have departed from this valley of tears and bears. I hope they will resist the temptation." On the other matter, Kahn continued with admonishment. "Inasmuch as you have convinced yourself that, acting upon your interpretation of general views I expressed (you will recall that I never gave specific advice as to what you should, or should not, do in respect of purchases or sales of stocks) you have incurred considerable losses, I must ask you to excuse me from offering any views on such matters now or henceforth. Nor can I see my way to take over a portion of the loan which you now have from the Equitable Trust Company."[17]

Stated together, there was a poetic intensity in Kahn's double refusal. Using the phrase "tears and bears," Kahn played the clever man of letters and finance. If meant to rhyme, "tears" evoked a wrenching rip or wound, like recent stock market conditions, while "bears" were the Wall Streeters who sold stocks anticipating further drops in value and had recently wreaked havoc upon the market. At the same time, Kahn toyed with the sense divisions of English words. "Tears" could be read as weeping (especially within the context of "valley of tears") and "bears" also can suggest suffering. This added sorrow and pain to the rhyme, and also placed Kahn in the house of mourning rather than the house of mirth: he had been wise while another had played the fool. Finally, Kahn linked his everyday life and wordplay with the play world of traditional theater. He seemed to be showing off familiarity with the hero of Shakespeare's play *Pericles, Prince of Tyre*, who, having been wrongfully told of his daughter's death (act 4, scene 4), is described thus: "He bears / A tempest, which his mortal vessel tears, / And yet he rides it out." With its theme of endurance in the face of adversity, *Pericles* could counsel the besieged Viereck. As important, the sea storms that toss Pericles from one fantastically bad fortune to another would separate him from country, property, family, and general composure; but in the end they subside, justice restores all to the good, and the gods' "kindness makes my past miseries sports." The denouement Kahn desired was pure *theatrum mundi*.

All this proved too smug and sermonizing for Viereck, who erupted in an attack on Kahn that struck the heart of discord between the banker-patron and the writer. Using a slight knowledge of Kahn's life history as leverage, Viereck, an adherent of Freud's psychoanalytic theories, served up a bitter analysis of Kahn's subconscious: "You once told me that as a boy you wrote a play in verse and that it was your ambition to be a poet. . . . Evidently you preferred money to art or you would not be a great banker. I, in spite of excursions into the stock market, prefer literature to finance or I would not be what I am. I wonder if there is not some subconscious jealousy of yourself which subsists in me and whether you do not at times envy the poet."[18] It was an amateurish, simplistic view of modern free development, but it hit its mark. After reconsideration, or perhaps now mindful that Viereck could publish such negative reflections, Kahn apparently realized that some of his financial advice over the years had been more direct and specific than he initially recalled. In the end, Kahn took over one half of Viereck's loan.[19]

To fully understand the effect of Viereck's remarks, it must be understood that Otto Kahn thought of himself as good. Fostering art and literature had accrued personal honor for Kahn. As he offset the materialism, monotony, and strain of modern life, Kahn toppled the image of a soulless, parasitic capitalist, or so he believed. Kahn needed no autobiography, biography, or monument to garner esteem or defend himself. Having served both god (art) and mammon (money), he believed he was reckless in neither his underwriting nor his advice. And because he was neither careless nor cruel with his wealth, Kahn would think himself well protected from the fate of Wall Street sinners after the crash. But Viereck's accusations, however ill-tempered, says something of what Kahn might have feared: he was not an artist, or an authentic hero, but merely a banker, a lover of money, who, as in Mat-

thew 6:24, was forced to "hate the one, and love the other." Stripping
Kahn of his artistic impulse could lead to the one impression that Kahn
had worked his entire life to avoid—that of merely a money-loving Jew.

If not yet a turning point, Jews of German origin were unlikely to
think their fate was irrevocably sealed in 1929. Rather, by the late 1920s,
those aspects of cosmopolitan identity most important to Kahn might
have seemed on the verge of recovery as easily as on the brink of collapse. Politically, by 1926, Kahn was more hopeful for Franco-German
relations, "now that the ignorant and arrogant Junker element is no
longer in control of Germany." A visit to Germany during 1927 left him
"very much and very favorably" impressed, as he found "the things
which used to jar one in former years are vanishing, or have vanished to
the background." Kahn declared, "Put me down as a booster for Germany." The following years also brought favorable new prospects for
business. As Kuhn, Loeb took fresh initiatives in the flow of capital from
America to Germany, it originated and managed the State of Hamburg
$10 Million 20-year 6% Bonds (1926) and the North German Lloyd
$20 Million 20-year 6% Sinking Fund Gold Bonds (1927), and also
brought out 175,000 American common shares for North German
Lloyd (1928). Longstanding alliances stood in place, of course, with
M. M. Warburg (still the most important private bank in Germany)
and with Paul Warburg's International Acceptance Bank (a pioneer in
American short-term credits to Germany). But much of Kuhn, Loeb's
recent activity was additionally animated by a new connection. Jakob
Goldschmidt of Darmstaeder & Nationalbank in Berlin, one of Germany's four largest banks, was steering Kuhn, Loeb toward fresh contacts in Germany and encouraging the firm to take some of Dillon,
Read's business for itself. Meanwhile, Kahn's own family provided
improved business connections in Germany in 1922–28, while Felix
Deutsch served at the helm of AEG, although following the death of his
brother-in-law in 1928, Kahn felt that AEG was "not favorably inclined
towards K.L." Not long after, his cousin Ferdinand Eberstadt heard
from Kahn: "As one gets on in life family ties are apt to assume enhanced significance." No longer a partner of Dillon, Read, Eberstadt
was then serving the American delegation negotiating the Young Plan,
which promised to revitalize Germany's credit and reparations' payments. He had also built a mansion for himself in the same township as
Kahn on Long Island.[20]

The spring of 1929 found Kahn as pleased with his own political footing in Germany as he was with the momentum building for his firm's business. Vilified by the German press during the war, Kahn now received an invitation to address the Reichstag. He accepted it in anticipation of his next trip. At the same time, he was pursuing deals with the German electrical giant, Siemens & Halske, as well as the Krupp munitions group. If Kuhn, Loeb succeeded in getting these two interests on an exclusive basis, their financial ally Goldschmidt boasted, "We shall have the very finest [business] there is in Germany, which will make great impression and place us on top of heap." Other proposi-tions in the offing included financing for the cities of Bremen and Ber-lin and new business with the Reichsbahn. In addition, there was jockey-ing for Kuhn, Loeb to organize a holding company to acquire the Triergon patents for sound-on-film technology. For a number of rea-sons, however, most of these proceedings stalled. The sound film situa-tion needed several more months to resolve itself, while the other busi-ness went slowly in part because the partners at Kuhn, Loeb thought the timing was wrong. Market conditions in the United States were consid-ered "very unfavorable" for the Siemens business, or "any issues with-out speculative attractions," and the Reichsbahn deal worried the New York partners expressly because if it seemed too aggressive, it might queer the firm's share of the reparations loan then being negotiated at the Paris Reparations Conference. Kahn's partners told him, "We must avoid possible conflict with German Government Loan."[21]

By now Kuhn, Loeb generally accepted its subservience to Morgan leadership in such matters. Although Kahn was in Paris during the reparations conference in June, neither he nor other Kuhn, Loeb part-ners were among the official delegates. Nor would he try to seek in-clusion or replay the agitated episode of interference that character-ized the London conference of 1924. This time Kahn knew his place was "behind the scenes," and he indicated as much in congratulatory notes to Owen Young of General Electric and Thomas Lamont of J. P. Morgan. (Lamont shared the limelight in negotiating this settlement, which bore Young's name and superseded the Dawes Plan.) Between the best of all worlds and a better world, the Young Plan offered, in Kahn's view, "a promise of vast benefit." Indeed, as recently as April, he and many of his German contacts had expected the conference to fail. With his hopes now refreshed, more than a decade after Versailles, there was finally "an instrument which should prove potent for the peace and welfare of nations."[22] A newly established schedule for reparations, and lately created Bank for International Settlements, might smooth the way toward a stable political and economic future. Resolving the economics would push politics into order and allow the German cultural traditions that Kahn valued to prosper.

If anxious about the right wing in Germany, Kahn was using a counter-rationale to hold fast against cultural pessimism and doing his best to reconstruct cultural cosmopolitanism. Likewise, by the late 1920s, it was possible to sense a poised recovery in international respect for German civilization. Its spas and festivals, cabarets and cafes drew streams of international tourists and artists; its cinema and theater regained and reinvented the cutting edge of serious art forms; and German architecture and opera both stepped up the notion of the new. Perhaps the best sign of recovery came in 1929, when Thomas Mann won the Nobel Prize for literature. All together, Weimar Germany flashed an uncommon montage of modernity. With new talents emerging and established ones continuing, an inventive fusion of middle-European, Soviet, and American influences seemed in the making.[23] Apart from his own annual trips to Germany, and Kahn's ongoing subsidies to the Bernhard Kahn Lesehalle (a reading room in Mannheim that honored his father), the banker-patron's commitment to Germany and its postwar reconstruction meant bolstering its appropriately central status within international networks for both money and culture. That was further evidenced in Kahn's America, where he aided in importing Reinhardt's productions, in staging Ernst Křenek's jazz opera *Jonny spielt auf* at the Met, and in sheltering Josef von Sternberg from the Hollywood film machine that would have shelved *The Last Command*. All were elements of the larger syntax or synthesis that Kahn sought. While his personal command of the German language had grown rusty and he preferred to correspond in English, memories of the liberal, humanist Germany and nostalgia for "the land of Goethe" trickled into Kahn's discourse through aphorisms. At other times such nostalgia overwhelmed him with typical teary rapture; for instance, he urged Mike Gold "to experience the spell of Bamberg, Nürnberg, Dinkelsbuhl, etc." Kahn would be the last to downplay this as his "silly emotionalist" side, yet it would be wrong to interpret Kahn's sentimentality as totally naive and maudlin.[24]

In looking for the culture of his youth and prewar years, in looking for a romantic and progressive modernism, Kahn's German idealism sought the unlikely combination of cosmopolitan *Geistgemeinschaft*

Tears and Bears

(community of spirit), individual wholeness, and liberal internationalism. Cosmopolitanism perhaps sheltered Kahn from a more authentic sense of the German experience and he ultimately underestimated the force of German authoritarianism, yet a German idealism always resonated in Kahn's hopes and thoughts. He had struggled with such hopes since the Great War, when Kahn tried to mend the Anglo-German synthesis, believing the humanism of Goethe, Schiller, and Kant would triumph, but also that the Allies could "rescue" it. Then, as Kahn adjusted to the disappointment of Versailles, he clearly, if not foolishly, trusted that a resurgence of liberalism would come to postwar Germany once the politics of peace, war debts, and reparations were settled. In this sense, Kahn was struggling with the unfinished business of 1848 as much as the aftermath of 1914—and was on the losing side. The forces that obstructed liberal internationalism, aesthetic cosmopolitanism, and progressive modernism were overwhelming.[25]

It is not possible to pinpoint the moments or friends of greatest influence upon his changing consciousness. Nor are we likely to forget that Kahn's sensibilities about anti-Semitism were well established. However, Kahn's awareness of the obstacles made him wrestle differently with Jewish identity during the 1920s. What matters more than whether Kahn was affected by the wit, wisdom, and welcome found among Jews in his social and artistic circles, or by the 1922 assassination of Germany's Jewish foreign minister, Walther Rathenau, or by the anti-Semitic diatribes of Henry Ford's *Dearborn Independent*, is this: when Kahn recognized the changing face of anti-Semitism after the war, he came to identify himself more clearly as a Jew. The specter of Nazism and depression-era anti-Semitism did speak to the mature Otto Kahn with a clarity that had not penetrated his youthful consciousness. If Kahn might have been slow to admit the extent of economic tragedy unfolding after 1929, it took less time for him to identify the terror taking hold in Germany. What became clear in 1930 was that Otto Kahn could stay in character and remain guardedly optimistic about economic matters and artistic enterprises much longer than he could about the future of Germany and its Jews.

· · · ·

MAKING STATEMENTS, 1930–1931

Almost everyone in the financial world failed to perceive the lurch toward unprecedented crisis at the start of the new decade. On the contrary, the stock market "smiled" during the spring of 1930. The Dow Industrial Index rebounded to nearly 300, and during that season Kahn noticed that new housing starts were up, at least among the wealthy in Palm Beach, Florida. Also, among the financial houses, it was widely known that Kuhn, Loeb had fared better than some other firms during the early shakeout. Upon sending Kahn a set of his lithographs inspired by the crash, gallery owner and artist James N. Rosenberg added a cheerful comment: "The firm of which you are a member was rather unique in that it didn't join in the magnificent process of lemon distribution."[26]

The wave of distress among artistic enterprises did not necessarily foretell disaster either. February 1930 saw the Metropolitan Opera post its first official losses in two decades, but the company's paid-in capital was still strong. More serious by comparison were the net losses at the Little Cinema Theatres, Inc. ("Little Carnegie Playhouse"), where Kahn could still reasonably think that a change in management would resolve the problem. Additional signs of stress fit within a normal range of market tendencies or managerial troubles. For example, less than 10 percent of the Actors' Equity Association worked in the winter of 1929–30, but actors were always woefully underemployed. Furthermore, Kahn still charmed the hearts and energized the productivity of struggling talent, so that a few dollars from Kahn would lift the spirits of playwright Em Jo Basshe, allowing him to take in a "little season of theatre going" with his wife when they could no longer afford it. Cheery meetings with the patron proved important as well to Basshe, who started penning "thousands of notes, scribbled on all sorts of paper" after Kahn made a visit to his Greenwich Village apartment.[27]

By mid-1930, then, neither the always underfunded arts nor any stress upon his own financial position worried Kahn as seriously as the overall course of politics, social psychology, and their effects on the economy. His key concern was the Smoot-Hawley Tariff, enacted by the U.S. Senate on June 17, 1930, significantly raising duties, which, he said, "tended, at least psychologically, to intensify depression." As the Dow dipped toward 212 in late June, Kahn decided to issue a pamphlet containing his views on the depression. Public relations counsel Ivy Lee, whom Kahn had earlier brought on the Met's board of directors, worked over the draft and managed its distribution, as he had done for Kahn in many previous instances; the product was consistent with Kahn's earlier positions. While he tried to restrict his remarks to the

Oct. 29 Dies Irae, *depicting the crash, by James N. Rosenberg, who sent the drawing to Kahn. (Courtesy of Anne Geismar)*

American situation, at nearly every turn Kahn asserted "the main phenomena with which we are dealing are world-wide." He looked back to the war, citing *The Economic Consequences of the Peace*, John Maynard Keynes's "remarkable book": "Those chickens were bound to come home to roost." When he singled out an efficient cause of the current malaise, he pointed to the "narrowly nationalistic economic policy" of America's new protectionism, arguing it was contrary to what the world's creditor nation should do.[28] But giving into failure and not seeking solutions, he believed, was also a cause of contemporary problems. Looking on the bright side had benefits — "The sooner we stop talking one another into a blue funk . . . the sooner we shall pass out of the shadow of the present emergency." Alongside that proverb, Kahn flashed an incipient Keynesianism. In his conservative liberalism, Kahn steered clear of wanting a "sunshine movement" or "whistling to keep up our courage," and he expressly rejected a wait-and-see approach while the crisis ran its course, instead conveying that "ways must be found to deal . . . with the general subject of unemployment."[29]

If no single day or year was going to turn Kahn into a pessimist, there appears to be one that cracked the mold. On September 14, 1930, Kahn was resting at a resort in Montecatini, expecting to visit Berlin in October, when the suspense concerning German liberalism took a turn toward the end. As soon as the news arrived about the Reichstag elections of that day, in which 18 percent of the popular vote and 107 seats in the Reichstag went to Hitler's Nationalsozialistische Deutsche Arbeiterpartei (NSDAP), making it the second-largest party in Germany, a shocked and depressed Kahn canceled the German leg of his tour then and there. One friend in Berlin, trying to change Kahn's mind, hastily sent a cable: "Outcome elections utterly ineffective and irrelevant. Hysterical Jews are slightly perturbed, wise ones remained indifferent. . . . Right and left extremists are much safer inside Parliament than outside. . . . Coalition means compromise, compromise means steadiness and continuity there will be. More noise that's all." Kahn was not buying it. The election results were "so replete with troublous potentialities" and "so offensive," he had decided, the "time [is] inopportune for me to visit Berlin." A cable from Kahn to Mortimer Schiff and his partners in New York clarified matters: "In view recent election any business seems out of the question for some time nor is there any other inducement to visit Berlin. . . . Outlook uncertain and atmosphere tense." He deemed a "visit at this time might be misinterpreted" as support for the current turn in politics.[30]

Like so many others, Kahn's remaining hopes were pinned to an economic upturn, or at least an economic plateau, which during early 1931 did lead some experts to think the bottom surely had been reached. When that interval turned out to be only a pause in the downward spiral, those who thought they were in a garden-variety recession, as Joseph Schumpeter later said, "felt the ground under their feet was giving way."[31] Whether they called it anomaly or mystery, almost no one fully understood what was happening, why it happened, what it meant, or where it would lead. As in any good suspense, tension mounted toward getting answers, and although there were many complex questions, some were as simple as "Who did it?" Even Kahn could no longer speak publicly of the present experience as anything less than a "grave depression." Though his efforts to maintain good humor and outward confidence effectively concealed his more desperate feelings from public view, his own money was getting tighter, as neither he nor his firm made a profit in 1930. Finding himself "Swamped with S.O.S. calls" from charitable and artistic organizations, but unable to make contributions in accordance with the increasing needs, Kahn confessed, "[I] must cut my coat according to my cloth, which, like everybody else's, has shrunk." Elsewhere, his rhetoric made a subtle turn toward metaphors of illness and recovery. In the coming years, when he spoke more readily of the need to find remedies for the depression, he was at the same time encountering personal physicians who were at a loss to prescribe anything better than rest for his own cure. Otto Kahn would not live long enough to see "Dr. New Deal" become "Dr. Win-the-War."[32]

The spring and summer of 1931 turned into a complete debacle. Late April found Kahn in London, taking meetings with the Rothschilds that included discussion of how Kuhn, Loeb might replace Dillon, Read in a new American group for Brazilian finance. Back home, the stock markets were in bearish rage, bringing numerous American brokerages to failure. Baffled by "where all that furious selling comes from, what it will lead to, and how it will end," he conceded that "in all of my forty odd years in business, I have seen nothing like the present situation. . . . The world has fallen upon evil and gloomy days."[33] It only got worse. The word out of Austria on May 11 was catastrophic. More than half the capital of the Creditanstalt was lost. Under Austrian law, the bank had failed. The effect brought an immediate run on all the Central European currencies. When Kahn cabled New York saying "situation from this distance looks pretty serious," it is unclear whether he meant Europe or the United States. His partner's reply stayed focused on America's own weaknesses. Too many banks were carrying "substantial lockups," which put their capital at risk. Gossip and real fear circled the prospect that, if depositors "should get panicky, a serious [liquidity] situation might arise." And with bad corporate earnings everywhere, Mortimer Schiff reported, "The bears are having things their own way," bringing "what looks like very real liquidation" and leaving everyone completely dispirited. Overall, money was "practically unlendable," yet these partners in the money lending business struggled to maintain some sense of proportion, hoping that each round of bad news would be the last stop before recovery. That applied to the "Central European mix-up," where the firm could still hope for negotiations between Creditanstalt and the Bank for International Settlements to salvage something.[34]

Soon enough, Kahn would come to see the Creditanstalt crisis as the latest stroke in which statecraft worsened conditions more than necessary. In the end, France, to its own and everyone's injury, objected to a loan from the Bank for International Settlements unless the Austro-German Customs Union was dissolved. Austria's refusal brought the downfall of its government. Then Germany announced that it could no longer pay reparations, which led Kahn to comment, "The Germans have proved once more their incapacity, astonishing in a nation so intelligent, for understanding the psychology of other nations."[35] The result was a heightened run on Germany's foreign exchange. In June, the United States tried to stop it, but unwittingly weakened the benefits of its own proposal for a one-year suspension of war debts and reparations when it announced the Hoover moratorium without first notifying the French. Consequently, the inevitable parley over the moratorium's legitimacy created a situation that financial historian Charles P. Kindleberger likens to "discussing who really owns a house and who should call the fire department when the building is going up in smoke." Germany's financial upheaval went unabated. The Reichsbank's gold and foreign exchange reserves ran down to legal limits and in mid-July the Landesbank of Rhine Province and the Darmstaedt and Nationalbank both failed. The latter carried nearly $40 million in deposits from London banks. Another serious run on the German banks ensued; then a two-day bank holiday was declared, during which time the illiquidity of Dresdner Bank was announced. In these darkest times for international finance that Kahn's generation had ever known, M. M. Warburg & Co. was for all practical purposes bankrupt, although a massive infusion of personal funds from the Warburg brothers in America kept the firm afloat. On the world stage, with Germany issuing emergency decrees, erecting foreign exchange controls, and freezing short-term, foreign-owned assets, it was, as Kindleberger says, "the end of the line for the Reichmark and the beginning of the end for the pound sterling."[36]

By the end of July, Kahn was back in New York, coping with unfamiliar responsibilities and grief. Mortimer Schiff had died at the end of June. When the news reached Kahn in Royat, France, he hastened to London, making calls of reassurance at the prominent financial houses. Before returning to New York, he wrote of Schiff, "I cannot get used to the idea that I shall be at 52 William Street and not see him again." Now feeling increasingly pressured to spend more time with the firm, Kahn was in his office practically "uninterruptedly every business day" through the year's end.[37] Perhaps even more than his partner's death, the lengthened work schedule and the increased stress at the office wore on Kahn both emotionally and physically. With only one stock market rally since February (during the enthusiasm for Hoover's moratorium in June), trading on the exchange was slow for most of the year and very few new stocks and bonds were issued. Between February and early September, the Dow registered a 17 percent decline for industrials and a modest 7 percent downswing for utilities, but railroads, the core of Kuhn, Loeb's business, were off by an incredible 31 percent.[38] None of this closed or lightened Kahn's mind and heart to the affairs of Europe. With his thoughts wrestling over "the catastrophe reigning in Germany," he wrote to his sister in Berlin, "I do what I can behind the window blinds," watching and worrying, "neither young enough" nor "qualified under existing circumstances" to assist substantially.[39]

Recent events in the industrial countries brought capitalism itself into doubt and criticism. A stream of foreign bond defaults in the United States also helped to heighten invectives against business leaders, who "failed to produce leadership in the present emergency." Kahn addressed these attacks with a new public statement in September 1931, which rephrased familiar themes in light of recent events and tried to deflect criticism from business to politicians. Critical, but glossing lightly over the errors of judgment and "gravely censurable" acts committed by some businessmen "during the mad days of 1929," Kahn contended it was political mismanagement over the longer term that made the collapse inevitable. "The derangements which the peace treaties have created" now included "the apprehensions engendered by the growth of Hitlerism and similar movements of extreme and aggressive nationalism." Still and all, a solution was possible, Kahn held, if governments stopped playing "the ostrich act." What was needed were immediate multilateral actions to ease indebtedness and reparations, and to move toward more mutually advantageous, "give and take" liberalized trade and foreign credits. The last was no easy point to sell, since some Chilean bonds originated by Kuhn, Loeb had recently gone bad. "In times of extreme crisis and worldwide upset . . . some losses . . . are in the nature of fair business risks," the senior spokesman of Kuhn, Loeb explained. Finally, when Kahn focused on existing problems in the United States, he put forth a litany of longstanding policy recommendations — relax antitrust laws, repeal prohibition, aid the farmers, promote efficient government, reduce income taxes, and modify the Federal Reserve Act, but maintain voluntary regulation of banking. He also added a slight note in favor of public relief spending.[40]

Equally important as the inventory of Kahn's opinions and analyses was how and why he masked his mounting hopelessness and contradictions. In private correspondence, Kahn expressed the opinion, quite contrary to his public statement, that financiers had indeed "failed in effective leadership." The contradiction between his public and private face suggested a larger convention holding through the crises. The point is perhaps best drawn by comparing Kahn's published statement with a confidential report from Ivy Lee in mid-September, which confirmed what Kahn actually knew and feared to be the consensus among political and economic experts. "Competent European opinion," said Lee, was looking toward the coming winter "with little short of terror," in anticipation that "time is running very short" for the gold standard and Germany. All but the French seemed to know that if Germany was "pressed too hard," it might be thrown into "political upheaval . . . [that] will result in . . . some fascist or communist government." Likewise "the capitalist system may come to be regarded as having proved so ineffective in meeting the current emergency" that the "growing criticism of banks being muttered in all European countries" could restrict the "freedom of world banking" and "place another obstacle in the way of prompt world recovery." What Lee said about public disclosure also mirrored the strategy that Kahn was employing in public remarks. Lee, the public relations expert, advised, "The situation is too delicate indeed for frank treatment by the newspapers of many disquieting facts. Confidence has been too badly shaken; it is highly important not to 'rock the boat.' "[41]

As sound and sane realists pitched toward unprecedented despair and radical doubts, the remystification of confidence was a lubricant for their own and popular hopelessness. It provided a means for holding the market and political elements of the social theater at the center while the cosmos blew apart. Here in microcosms were clues to more general accommodations. A conscious effort toward impression management, which would not deny crises, could drape explicit reference to some of the more terrifying anticipations.

September 1931 brought an undeniable convergence of emergencies. The Sterling Crisis hit Wall Street hard and fast, making September the toughest month of the year as well as the beginning of a heart-stopping, four-month decline. Trading was heavy and the Dow indices lost half their value.[42] Setting aside many of the serious indicators of crises — from the soured market for stocks, bonds, and money, to Kuhn, Loeb's shrinking balance sheet, and the swelling ranks of unemployed — Kahn's relations with members of his German-born family perhaps best illustrate the seeds of impending pathos.

Beginning in late September Kahn received a series of upsetting letters concerning his widowed sister, Lili Deutsch of Berlin, who wrote for help in fear and embarrassment: "The greatest part of our fortune is lost. . . . What is left and whatever still can be saved must be secure." The details of her distress were as interesting as they were ominous. She had a relatively large pension from AEG, but complained that as much as half went to taxes. Meanwhile, the salary of one son (Franz) had been halved, and the husband of her daughter, Gertrude, was expecting his salary to be reduced by anywhere from 30 to 40 percent. Unable to meet the expenses of her "big house in Berlin," and altogether terrified by the implications of Germany's "foreign exchange decree as well as the other emergency decrees appearing also daily," it was thought best that Lili Deutsch should leave for Switzerland or France. The Deutsch family was thus trying to transfer their remaining cash to safety. One reserve was a blocked account with AEG. The other consisted of "a number of securities and a credit" in Holland ("which now, according to the emergency decree, had to be turned over to the Reichsbank in Berlin"). It would be illegal to transfer funds, Lili Deutsch admitted ("we must be extremely careful"), yet the Deutsch family wanted to do it anyhow, and while they seemed sure that the risk rested with them rather than Kahn, they also felt the risk was worth it.

"Things look very threatening here," said Lili Deutsch. "The great strength of the country, the power of labor cannot be employed, everything is too late. I often think of what Walther Rathenau told me: 'We shall go through a time like the one following the thirty years' war, complete impoverishment.' "[43]

An anguished Kahn replied to his nephew, George Deutsch: "I am very sorry to say that I know of nothing my firm or I can do as long as the account in Germany is not free for transfer abroad. Nor can I think of any other way to enable your mother to live out of Germany. Please tell her how distressed I am to hear about her worries and how gladly I would help her if I could." Otto Kahn lived long enough to regret this. Lili Deutsch, as well as his brother Robert and other siblings, were stripped of their German citizenship under the Nazi decrees of July 14, 1933. But Otto Kahn did not live long enough to realize the full consequences for Germany's Jews: Lili Deutsch eventually fled Germany with her daughter, Gertrude, and son-in-law, Gustav Brecher. Last seen in Ostende during 1940, they vanished en route to the south of France — possibly having committed suicide.[44]

There are several ways to explain Kahn's action — or lack of it. One consequence of the Dow's decline was that Kahn, who administered the inheritances of his father's heirs, reduced the allowances for his surviving siblings in Europe. However unpleasant the reduction, Kahn might have reasonably thought the deflationary spiral made less worth more. (Kahn's attitude, by the way, reflected what has since been identified as a serious complication of the deflationary period — reduced investment yields lead directly to reduced purchasing power.)[45] But Kahn's response to Lili Deutsch did contrast sharply with his actions toward his younger brother, Felix. A long-time resident of America and Otto's closest sibling, Felix had earlier been the agent for Kahn's interest in the Mutual Film Corporation, and, since 1920, represented Kuhn, Loeb on Paramount's board of directors (as later did William Wiseman and Kahn's son Gilbert, as partners of Kuhn, Loeb). Felix Kahn was also a stock market speculator in trouble. As early as the spring of 1931, his brother Otto helped by covering his margin on 3,500 shares of Paramount stock. On that occasion, Kahn wrote to his panicked sibling, "Of course I am the feller to turn to. Don't worry about your position. It will be protected." Kahn then deposited the necessary securities in his brother's collateral accounts.[46]

By late September, when Lili Deutsch was desperate for Otto's help,

Felix Kahn was again struggling with the latest stock market crisis. Through the remainder of the year Otto Kahn kept rescuing his brother's repeated margin calls by loaning him securities or cash as needed. The question must be raised: if he was capable of assisting Felix Kahn, why did Kahn decline Lili Deutsch and other family members? The illegalities of Deutsch's request probably inhibited him, but this does not explain Kahn's reluctance to set up an account for her in France, where he could have made deposits against the Deutschs' holdings in Berlin until the ban on foreign exchange was lifted.[47] It seems plausible that his brother's concerns appeared more urgent, since they were closer to Kahn's business life and Kuhn, Loeb was the sponsoring house for Paramount's public financing. In addition, Kahn likely thought the Deutschs' proposal imperiled his own liquidity more. On one hand, Felix Kahn's needs could be satisfied by stock collateral, while Lili Deutsch wanted cash. On the other hand, his brother's requests came in increments, while his sister petitioned for a large, lump sum, which was harder for Kahn to manage. Finally, Deutsch's request implied nearly complete financial dependency upon Kahn until her German funds were again accessible.

Whether ill-prepared or unable to comply, Kahn perhaps thought it unnecessary or unwise to assume the complete dependency of his siblings, their children, and his many European cousins — all of whom felt the impact of the financial crises. To this extent, his extended family was treated like artists-in-need — he shunned complete reliance. But Kahn was also constrained by forecasts and understanding (and hardly alone in this). Scrambling to protect his own assets, with no end to the crisis in sight, and with so much good money being thrown after bad (the American Warburgs, for example, had rushed $9 million into the tumbling M. M. Warburg), Kahn could convince himself that the difficult but correct decision for the long run was to protect his portion of the extended family's resources. Indeed, by February 1933 Kahn came to admonish Felix Kahn's escalating need for money ("Inexcusable that after many years in well paid position and all I have already done for you [to] ask me for funds," read his telegram). Kahn then set a limit to his aid at $3,000 in annual loans.[48]

Along the way, he failed to remember that experience can be another name for mistakes. While correct in his fears that the future might yet grow worse, Kahn neither expected a complete collapse of cosmopolitan civilization nor did he realize that the opportunities to help his loved ones would be shorter than the obligations implied by their dependency.

On October 26, 1931, Kahn made another difficult decision regarding dependency. Like so many times in the previous twenty-three years, Kahn convened a meeting of the Metropolitan Opera Company's directors in his Kuhn, Loeb office. On this day, however, he surprised his fellow directors by resigning his dual post of president and chairman. He agreed to stay on the board of directors, but stepped down from its leadership, explaining that the demands upon his time and health since the death of Mortimer Schiff required him to "divest myself of outside activities."[49] He had recently resigned from the boards of the Chase National Bank and the Equitable Trust Company, giving the same reasons, and before long he would rotate off the board of the Philharmonic Society as well. But the sudden closure of Kahn's leadership at the Met also reflected immediate financial trouble there, and multiple, long-term failures of a very sensitive nature.

The bottom line was hemorrhaging at the Met, reversing the financial fortunes the company had enjoyed during Kahn's tenure. Until recently this had been a matter of pride as well as power for him. Back in 1903, when Kahn joined the Met board, the performing company had always lost money. His mentor, E. H. Harriman, had advised him to run it like a business, and under Kahn's leadership the performing company turned a profit every season until 1929–30. Even though door receipts were always insufficient sources of income, the company's books were balanced by other sources of revenue, including program and restaurant concessions, artists' fees from outside engagements, and income from phonograph recordings. Lately, revenues from radio broadcasts had begun to trickle into the stream as well. All along, the performing company had sufficient financial reserves for normal shortfalls — until the 1929–30 season significantly depleted the reserve. Thereafter, financial catastrophes seemed to feed on themselves, and even the normal practice of investing the Met's cash for income soured. Under Kahn's authority during 1930, for example, $40,000 was put into the stock market, but the investment lost $8,000 and had to be withdrawn. Market forces might have been blamed, but if it seemed Kahn had lost his touch, that perception could only have intensified during the 1930–31 season, for production costs stayed high while subscriptions dropped, and the deficit ballooned to $322,231. As

Tears and Bears

though the Met had been a railroad, the bottom line told the financier that it was time for reorganization.[50]

The barb pained Kahn, because he had seen the need for financial restructuring during the 1920s, when he failed in a well-known attempt to build a "bigger, better and more democratic" new opera house. For as long as Kahn had been chairman, he considered the house at Thirty-ninth Street and Broadway to be antiquated and inadequate. One-sixth of the seats had no view of the stage and, as Peter Conrad notes, "The design of the auditorium contrived to snub anyone not in a box."[51] But the opera house owners were long reluctant to discuss a new theater, and Kahn never pressed too hard until the mid-1920s, when he forced the issue. Spending approximately $2.5 million of his own money to purchase land between West Fifty-sixth and Fifty-seventh Streets, Kahn offered to donate it as the site for a new house, where MORECO would no longer have proprietary rights. This was already a risky proposition, but Kahn made it harder to sell when he included stronger language in his proposal at the suggestion of board members Roger Winthrop and Paul Cravath. They found Kahn's initial draft went "too far in placing your plan in the hands of the distinguished elderly gentlemen who constitute the Board of Directors of the Metropolitan Real Estate Company." Hence Kahn's official missive, which opened with perfunctory gratitude for all past "wisdom and public spirit" of MORECO and pledged an ongoing interest in cooperation, shortly after launched an undisguised if impractical threat of independence: the performing company could finance the new building alone, although it would prefer MORECO stockholders to take the lead, "either through their present organization or in their individual capacities."[52]

The rest of Kahn's lengthy proposal affiliated financial imperatives with a pragmatist's populism. Offering a plan to service artistic and public interest alike, he laid out the existing problems first. As a matter of pride: "A new building has become an urgent necessity if the Metropolitan is to do its duty by the opera-loving public of New York and is to maintain its rank as the foremost operatic institution in the world." As a matter of fairness: "The accommodation for those patrons of the opera who cannot afford to buy the more expensive seats, i.e. the masses of the music loving public, is inadequate as to quantity and wholly unsatisfactory as to quality. Indeed, a considerable number of lower priced seats are so bad that it is really an act of unfairness to take money for them." As a matter of function: "Everything behind the curtain is antiquated. . . . The wings are far too narrow, the stage lacks depth, the facilities for scenery, wardrobe and stage effects . . . the dressing rooms and . . . ventilation of the House [are] sadly inadequate." And conclusively, as a matter of money: "The cost of giving opera in the style befitting the Metropolitan and called for by its audiences is steadily mounting. . . . The limit of income . . . within the capacity of the current House has been reached. . . . The limit of artistic effects which can be produced on the present inadequate stage has been reached." Then came the solutions:

> The ideas of my colleagues and myself . . . are as follows: a) Its auditorium ought not be any larger than the present one, but it ought to be — and easily can be — so planned that . . . the sight lines [are] uniformly good. b) There ought to be only one tier of boxes. The number ought to be reduced from . . . 35 to say 30 . . . to make the box circle shallower and . . . the upper tiers to be brought forward correspondingly nearer the stage. c) The present system of boxes being *owned* and then rented out or given away . . . has proven . . . inconvenient, troublesome and expensive to the owners, and detrimental to the value of the boxes. . . . Therefore, it is suggested that in a new opera house there should be no box *owners*, but only box lessees. . . . The cost of thus renting a box for one evening or matinee each week would be approximately . . . at the rate of about $145 for each performance. d) It is not contemplated that the new Metropolitan need be a monumental and ornamental building, rivaling European Opera in appearance. Our conception is that it should be plain and dignified, on good but simple lines, seeking its distinction in being perfectly adapted to its purpose, both on the stage and in the accommodation to the public, rather than in outward impressiveness. e) Whether the new Metropolitan building should have, as the present one has . . . apartments, and studios is a debatable question. There should seem to be little doubt that such accommodation would prove a profitable investment inasmuch as many music teachers and artists would assuredly desire, and find it to their advantage, to be located in the Metropolitan Opera Building.[53]

All his points played well with the press, and that was Kahn's best weapon. Since his operating company was not fully committed to mounting the new house independently, Kahn was gambling on several

fronts—that publicity would make MORECO amenable to modernizing both the architectural symbol and institutional workings of the
Met; that MORECO would rather remain affiliated with the performing company than see it take up residency separately at a new site; and
that friendlier MORECO directors would prevail over resistance and win
the day.

The MORECO trustees immediately stymied the proposal, however. In
January 1926 "it was decided that the Company would not undertake
the erection of a new building. . . . It has no intention of continuing to
produce opera if a new building . . . should be provided for that purpose." If Kahn wanted to go forward, he was "at liberty to approach the
stockholders [individually]." For his part, Kahn appeared ready to negotiate. Having heard or surmised that MORECO was concerned first
with the loss of its investment in the old building, he began introducing
prospective buyers, including one willing to offer as much as $9.5 mil-
lion for the property. Also, using Ivy Lee as an intermediary, he released excerpts of the two boards' correspondence to the press. That
began a public relations volley, forcing MORECO at least to consider and
discuss the plan, if not accept it.[54]

Kahn kept bargaining. Trying to make it work over the next two
years, he adhered to the pretensions of cooperation, while many among
New York's social citadel utterly opposed and resisted him. Some box
owners considered the current house adequate. Others wanted a new
house at a different location. And added into the mix were those who
seemed ill-disposed toward the modern architectural aesthetic that
Kahn proposed. These several lines of contention drew out an underlying power struggle, which soon found Kahn's financial scheme weakened by revisions, because MORECO rejected such "commercial fea-
tures" as the income-producing shops, apartments, and studios. Since
eliminating them undermined some means for a self-sufficient operatic
enterprise, another method was needed to compensate for the lost revenues. MORECO proposed that substitute revenues should come from
restored box ownership rights. Consequently, the estimated cost to
stockholders in the new facility was to climb from $145,000 to $245,000
annually. The stockholders then began balking at the increase, or using
the revised financial plan as the outlet for simmering resentment of
Kahn, and finally MORECO rejected his proposed house. Kahn tried to
stay open-minded and negotiate in good faith, yet every alternative

Unrealized French Art Deco design for the Metropolitan Opera House by architect Benjamin W. Morris, 1928. (Metropolitan Opera Archives)

seemed in some crucial way less inspired than his original proposal. By April 1928 he wrote, "Pulling teeth is a delectable diversion as compared to getting anything out of these people."[55]

If, as rumored, the Old Guard families of Gilded Age New York had torpedoed his plan in open secrecy, Otto Kahn kept quiet about it. Instead of blaming MORECO for the ballooning estimates, for instance, he discreetly said the original proposal "was considerably more costly than we had been led to believe on the basis of informal estimates." In turn, he shouldered unfair criticism of his financial skills, including a *New York Tribune* remark to the effect that "the entire arrangement was upset by a factor least expected to be faulty in the operations of a banker — the financial figures."[56] Kahn, who since his first days as a junior partner at Kuhn, Loeb had fought the impression that he was an impostor within the ranks of first-class financiers, suffered this humiliation without comment.

All together, his campaign for a new opera house unintentionally awakened the sleeping giant of MORECO. In effect, Kahn broke the working consensus, precipitating a rally for control not seen since his earliest days at the Met. Plainly, MORECO did not want to hear what

Tears and Bears

Kahn was saying. The more his plan for a new opera house approximated a reasonable, enlightened vision, the more it baited opposition. Instead of constructive dialogue, Kahn faced an effort to discredit and defeat him at every turn. Checked and checked again, Kahn seemed to give up, selling his land at West Fifty-sixth and Fifty-seventh Streets. The newspapers announced "polite warfare ended," but the stress continued to mount behind the scenes while discussions about an alternative site took up the possibility of Rockefeller Center. Meanwhile, the financial outlook for the performing company grew dimmer. Then in early 1930, as the opera company faced its first deficit in twenty years, MORECO dusted off and brandished its ultimate weapon: the contract to lease the existing house, due to expire on May 1, 1933.

Kahn was being pushed back to where he had started. Haggling endlessly over old issues left him increasingly irritated. Perhaps the greatest insult was that after all these years anyone in the negotiations could presume they knew better than Otto Kahn what the Met needed. The next greatest affront was MORECO's desire to put added financial responsibilities upon him, which Kahn roundly resisted. In April 1931 he warned that if a suitable contract could not be arranged, the Metropolitan Opera Company "would be glad to do what it can to facilitate the task of whoever may be its successor" in the house. By now the Metropolitan Opera Company was in even deeper financial trouble, and needlessly so, Kahn must have thought, since he had tried to reform its financial structure before the Great Depression threw it into crisis.

Once more Kahn tried to pitch a strategy for the Met's solvency. This time his personal role was more clearly emerging as the underlying contention. "In every city where Grand Opera has a permanent home, it is subsidized by the State or Municipality" or the underwriting of a private syndicate, he argued in April 1931, referring to himself in the third person.

The only exception is New York. The Metropolitan Opera Company has never asked for outside help. The fact is, however, that there are only three stock owners in the Metropolitan Opera Company, apart from a few merely nominal holdings, namely Mr. Kahn, Mr. Clarence H. Mackay, and the Estate of Harry Payne Whitney. Mr. Kahn owns 83% of the total stock. That is, manifestly, an undesirable situation. An organization like the Metropolitan Opera Company ought not to depend to any such extent upon one individual. . . . It is respectfully suggested and urged, if contractual relationship is to continue between the Real Estate Company and the Metropolitan Opera Company . . . that it be sought by joint action to create an underwriting syndicate aggregating, say, $250,000 annually, . . . the direction of the organization to be in the hands of the underwriters.[57]

What role Kahn intended to play in the underwriting syndicate was unclear, yet he seemed to be drawing a line that he would not cross. Perhaps the MORECO directors did not take the warning seriously or believe Kahn would relinquish control—he had bluffed before, and blinked. On the other hand, they quite possibly wanted him to leave. However, if in the spring of 1931 they thought Kahn was insincere in his threat, it would explain why—after Creditanstalt and the Sterling Crisis brought Kahn to realize that his own wealth could not (and should not) sustain the performing company—his resignation came as a surprise.

Resigning did not merely protect Kahn's own purse. He sacrificed himself to make a point: it forced both boards to face some ugly facts in a financial emergency that could not be denied. In a meaningful sense, he was just being Otto Kahn, acting out of the same principles that risked the demise of the Provincetowners. The Met, of course, gradually rebounded and survived, but it never achieved the ideal of pluralism that Kahn sought, even though, as Kahn predicted, it needed at least a renewed commitment and guarantee from New Yorkers (and eventually the municipality) to ensure the continuation of grand opera.

A few days after his resignation, Kahn offered a more complete interpretation of what was going on and how it all affected the art of opera. In remarks to Olin Downes, music critic of the *New York Times*, a disappointed Kahn reflected upon his many years and negotiations with the Met boards: "They were content to have [me] take much of the responsibility for the practical organization of the company . . . as long as it gave them no trouble or additional burdens." He conceded that they had always maintained a "coolness" to him, understanding it was because he "was a Jew, and that they were not wholly favorable to having a Jew as chairman of their board of directors." Kahn was isolated, working "almost entirely alone, with very little cooperation from any but one or two of the members," and it inhibited him: if he "had had cooperation and been given a greater amount of support," he "would have experimented more boldly than the Metropolitan had experimented, with repertory and in various aspects of stage representation."[58] This said a lot. Kahn had walked a tightrope, censoring his own artistic impulse, while believing that if he was not too pushy (read: too Jewish), he could make some progress. But there had been substantial trade-offs, not only with *Salome* or the wartime banning of German opera. Every year, like a toned chord, when Kahn weighed the likelihood of offering Prokofiev or other contemporary composers, he usually deferred to the more conservative judgment of his hand-picked general manager, Giulio Gatti-Casazza, who screened out some of Kahn's more insurgent tastes. The arrangement kept stable Kahn's relations with the boards of directors and box owners.

Kahn ultimately realized how much his balancing act had compromised the artistic project of the Metropolitan. He was clearly distinguishing between the quality of the Met's performers, in which he felt completely confident, and the preponderance of old chestnuts, which blunted the artistic edge of the repertory. In hindsight, even the loosely experimental works mounted at the Metropolitan Opera during his tenure, such Janáček's *Jenůfa* and Křenek's *Jonny spielt auf* or John Alden Carpenter's ballet *Skyscrapers*, seemed insufficient in number to make the Met a legitimate venue for the modernist impulse toward newness. The Met lacked a modernist commitment to improvement in its formal structures, whether they were architectural, financial, artistic, or social. In his disappointment, Kahn found evidence of ongoing, increasingly universalized contradictions within the bourgeois codes upon which he had built his life's aspirations.

Obviously, Kahn's mistakes began years earlier. If he had committed his financial resources to Oscar Hammerstein's Manhattan Opera House rather than New York's high society, for instance, the aesthetic outcome might have been more experimental, the financial structure more flexible, and the cultural dissemination of the opera more diffuse. Kahn, in other words, might have found the satisfaction that he indicated was missing. However, to have backed Hammerstein in the beginning would have denied the striving Otto Kahn a place at the pinnacle of society, where he thought his wealth, his aesthetic convictions, and his cosmopolitan synthesis would be victorious. Kahn thus staked himself to a contract and role that made him the exceptional Jew among non-Jews—who fundamentally despised him and resisted his arrival. If Otto Kahn once felt himself so heroic or confident that aesthetic production and social reality might grow more experimental and inclusive, by the 1920s he believed that a new house and economy for the Met were both the answer and the accelerator. He also thought it possible to modernize the management, theater, audience, and repertory by prodding the existing institutional codes and currents. Rather than spark a popular uprising or split the performing company from the real estate company—and he had the chance to do both in the 1920s and with his resignation in 1931—Kahn restrained himself from full-blown war or conduct inappropriate for his social position.

This at once suggests an unwillingness to admit the failing contradictions in his social contract, as well as an extraordinary control of his anger when incompatible roles and ideals collided. He was not, after all, E. H. Harriman, but Otto Kahn. Although, like Harriman, he enjoyed the action and the winning, Kahn was more tightly bound to the ceremonies of deference and demeanor. By late 1931, furthermore, Otto Kahn was clearly disillusioned. He seemed to sense that his career at the Met was a masque. What had been at the beginning was still fixed at the end—he was just a Jew. All the wealth and social talent in the world could not unlock certain doors. In earlier years, Kahn might have turned the other cheek if not a deaf ear against the anti-Semitism. But it was one thing to feel maligned, unappreciated, and undermined when Kahn was younger, healthier, wealthier, and feeling more confident about the greater arc of human progress. It was quite another matter, and one that Kahn would not accept, when he felt himself being fully robbed of his dignity. Being "that Jew" at the Met was an old story; what Kahn could not yet accept, or any longer accept, was being made to feel he was a nobody pretending to be a somebody, and especially being made to feel this way by America's equivalent of empty-headed burghers who had learned nothing new about the meaning of aesthetic culture. In vacating the presidency and chair, Kahn seemed to be acknowledging the end of a plot's development as well as his own role. His remark to Downes ensured that all the relevant facts were somewhere revealed.

One last action made Kahn's resignation from the Met's leadership more than a face-saving gesture. The gamesmanship of the Met boards was as antiquated as the house itself. Yet rather than leaving an empty chair or maximizing the breach at the Met, Kahn tempered his disgust and cooperated with his successor. He could believe that later acts or the next cycle might actualize some of his thwarted reforms and ideals. In other words, Kahn clung to optimism. In the worst of times even more than the best of times, when tragedy threatened to overwhelm the community of belief, there was optimism, a stalwart of bourgeois behavior, and, incidentally, an important component that Keynes's theory later expressed in different terms. Without optimism things would stay depressed indefinitely. Kahn drew upon this sentiment in his public statements on the Great Depression as well as when Lili Deutsch was in trouble. He could not discredit the future of the Metropolitan Opera any more than the future of capitalism, though privately he was plagued by many doubts.

CHAPTER SEVEN

The Third Act

December 1931 found Kahn in a reflective mood, quoting Hans Sachs in Wagner's *Die Meistersinger von Nürnberg*, "Wahn Wahn, überall Wahn!" (Illusion! Illusion! Everywhere illusion!).[1] Nothing appeared immune. The leading economic indicators in most countries were unprecedentedly grave. After Germany and Britain departed from the gold standard, the pressure shifted to the U.S. dollar, with the Federal Reserve raising discount rates in defense of its currency, precipitating the worst shakeout in the history of American banking until that time: more than two thousand banks suspended payments; banking losses from loans and securities amounted to more than $550 million. Liquidation was out of control. Tight money discouraged corporate expansion. Unemployment worsened. And while the U.S. market for new stocks and bonds stood dead in shallow water, investment trusts and American-held foreign securities were rocked by rampant defaults. All this not only eroded the profit base of the investment banking business, it destroyed the reputations of investment bankers. What greater devastation would yet come? The financial editor of the *New York Times* outlined the prospects: "It was now no longer a question of what shocks must be endured before recovery should come, but a question of universal bankruptcy."[2] Something was wrong with capitalism. No ordinary view of life was stable, except that perhaps of the collective, tragic despair.

It became all the more essential for Kahn to maintain his mask of cheer. By presenting a public face of order and calm, Kahn hoped to radiate a quiet optimism that suggested the world situation would stabilize. Portions of the news media helped to sustain such impressions. The early issues of *Fortune*, for instance, emphasized steadiness at Kuhn, Loeb, where Kahn was still the best-known partner, still an international banker of the first order, and still the "most perfect example of the modern patron of the arts." In other words, Kahn's public identity was as secure as the firm, and the firm was stable despite its losses, "thanks to their high equity capital and their carefully selected and therefore more crisis-proof assets," as one historian put it. In addition, a new crop of partners emerging at Kuhn, Loeb, with one son each from the Warburg, Schiff, and Kahn lines (*cursus honorum*, said *Fortune*), signaled other strengths among its ongoing traditions.[3] Never mind that each assurance had a contradictory counterpart. The next generation of Schiff and Warburg partners cared little for either the senior or younger Kahn, who were still minority participants in the firm's capital, and a new era of interfamilial rivalries was emerging. Kahn's activities as a Maecenas were winding down as well. If the creative talents in Kahn's orbit were gradually realizing that "even Otto Kahn cannot support EVERYONE all of the time,"[4] the specific circumstances of December 1931–May 1932 would eventually lead many more to surmise that even Otto the Magnificent could be swept into the maelstrom of hard times. Not that he went down easily, but Otto Kahn himself would feel vulnerable in every role — the Maecenas, the Wall Street millionaire, the German-born Jew, and the cosmopolitan aesthete.

. . . .

SIDESHOWS

In June, Republican isolationists and Democratic partisans in Congress stirred heated opposition to the Hoover moratorium. Some assailed the moratorium as a plot by international bankers, and in one lone tirade, the renegade Republican Louis T. McFadden of Pennsylvania alleged the president was an "agent" of Germany, the Warburgs, and Kuhn, Loeb. Most of the legislators steered clear of such shameless slashing, but themes of devilry, conspiracy, and treason were widely present in fears that the moratorium would underwrite European militarism and the merchants of death. The greatest cohesion among moratorium critics, however, was the fear of burdening American taxpayers with the Allied debt while the U.S. federal deficit mounted. This tipped Republican conservatives into the same camp as Democratic critics, who more clearly labeled the moratorium as "financial buccaneering," a way to help international financiers "collect their private loans from abroad" — a "dole to these international bankers" when none was available for the unemployed.[5]

By December, most of the foreign securities issued in America had defaulted, and Washington summoned Wall Street leaders for a probe into the broader foreign securities debacle. Not the first, last, or grandest of financial investigations, the censure of financiers and the regulation of securities were nonetheless looming as the corrective. The procedure was familiar to Kahn, who had acted in such ceremonies many times before. The summoners asked questions, the summoned gave answers, and nested therein was a conflict of doctrinal content perhaps as old as medieval dramas of repentance. The financiers, Kahn knew, could be pitched toward one of two extreme character types, the perfect savior or the double-dyed sinner, and lately the latter held sway. More than anything, it was these ambiguous issues of character, performance, and punishment that made the Finance Committee's hearings meaningful and, from Otto Kahn's point of view, purposeful for him and the country. Kahn could hope his testimony would help clear the air of suspicions, revive a good image for bankers, and hold back what he feared was a rising tide of new statutory regulations.

The historical scope and the national spotlight excited him, too. After all, this was a part he was happy to play. The libretto in his mind drew its substance from his many public speeches and pamphlets, which over the years addressed the same broad field of themes and questions that the legislators would revisit.[6] Relaxed, affable, and clear-headed, Kahn believed that policy and recovery could be swayed by personal impressions. His best-stated points were tutorial and pacifying. It proved an effective way to ease his audience's distress over the soundness and propriety of private banking and internationalism. Questions about international debts, reparations, and the gold standard nonetheless required a skillful tack. Kahn had to candidly admit that Kuhn, Loeb would not presently underwrite another loan to Germany, although he predicted that "unless she is driven to . . . helplessness," Germany would eventually repay its private debts. Reparations and Allied debts to America were separate though related matters and, wisely, Kahn would neither be drawn into their detailed discussion nor predict whether these would, could, or should ever be paid. Short of advocating cancellation, he appealed to universal frustration: "If it were possible to find a way by which all these reparations and war debts which hang around the neck of the world like a millstone could be taken out in the ocean and sunk, I should welcome it. . . . Insomuch as there is no such way . . . the best thing is very calmly and with great self-control and great self-restraint, and with a little swearing and cussing beneath our breath . . . [to] try to evolve something which will come as near to being a helpful solution. . . . Nearly everybody's nerves are on edge and some are nearly frazzled."[7]

Turning next to the innuendos that Kuhn, Loeb and the Warburgs were puppet masters in the Hoover moratorium, Kahn defended his firm: "Any allegation which connects us with the negotiations or proceedings of the moratorium, or with President Hoover whatsoever in the matter is utterly and outrageously unfounded." That assertion was important, and Kahn's ability to insert it suggested how he played the scene. Since no senator prompted Kahn directly on the subject, he was pushing the boundaries of prescribed conduct. This was the legislators' show, yet here the witness rather than the interrogators initiated dialogue. Kahn did so again when asked how France's debt to America should be handled. "It is beyond the province of a banker to answer categorically so many elements which are not of a financial nature," he replied. Then, recasting the matter as jointly financial and political, Kahn rephrased the question and implied the answer he should like to hear from the legislators: "It is purely a question of . . . what is expedient for us to do. . . . How can the world, including America, best get out of the mess that we are now in?"[8]

One specific factor weighing in favor of Kahn (and the Morgans as well) was a conservative banking record. When asked how many defaults his firm experienced in the last twenty years, Kahn could reply, "The number of defaults in our case is very limited." This helped because Kahn wanted to modify what he felt were wildly exaggerated reports of bankers' profits, and counter the impression that bankers either intentionally or carelessly issued and distributed bad bonds. His own firm had made only a modest average gross profit of $260,000 per annum from the sale of foreign bonds since the war, and it had not engaged in high-pressured salesmanship. "For every bond that we issued we declined six others, or nine or ten others," he explained, "because we always wanted to be sure that what we offer is intrinsically sound." So Kahn could gracefully agree that greater restraint was desirable among the more reckless members of the financial community, while at the same time he could argue statutory regulation of securities was unwise and unnecessary. From Kuhn, Loeb's perspective the banker's best assets — his liquidity and public confidence in his judgment — were still functional, and from Kahn's perspective this checked against the sale of overvalued securities.

Kuhn, Loeb's conservative banking principles gave him a defensible record, but Otto Kahn played the scene well because he was able to match the balance sheet of the firm with a positive image of the banker. When nothing about his financial theories or recovery programs was original, Kahn was still a creative personality, serving up a character who was neither a dry ledger man nor a rogue. The politicians wanted a "horned beast spitting fire," said a *Times* editorial, but instead they got Otto Kahn — eloquent, good-humored, candid, and accessible, a gentleman whose personal behavior could extend into the realm of public responsibility. It "left his . . . assailants more than a little dazed, and with nothing to do except to sheath their daggers of criticism."[9]

Kahn made his interrogators momentarily abandon disbelief. He could not completely dispel all enmity toward bankers, but he could at least develop images and answers that all could agree were good. If this banker was not a thieving creature, then perhaps the financial world of the banker was not evil personified.

He also played the scene well because the congressional hearings were not unlike the modern dramaturgy that Kahn knew better than any banker. Congress's practice was to stun and stimulate its political audience with revelations, then stage its version of reforms. Modern theater had a similar mission. Although the Washington spectacle seemed stiff and studied by comparison, one could ask whether America's theatrical modernists were any more provocative, explosive, or effective than their political counterparts. Indeed, serious theater was raising its own questions about the economic malaise. In the same December as these Senate hearings, Kahn happened to see *1931–*, one of the first dramatic treatments of unemployment and the Great Depression. He found the play impressive, but, more significant, Kahn's interest in a political subject on stage indicated how he attuned politics and theater in resolving social conflict.

It is worth a moment to consider why Kahn would be impressed with *1931–*. Most of all, there was a tradition of newness, or a defiant continuation of newness. *1931–* was produced by the fledgling Group Theatre, and when director Lee Strasberg embraced Stanislavsky's method, it extended the impact of Kahn's earlier support for a run of

The Third Act

the Moscow Theatre in New York. The play itself was authored by Paul and Claire Sifton, veterans of the class-conscious New Playwrights Theater (founded and sustained in 1927–29 with Kahn's money). Even its failure to win praise from the critics held relevance for Kahn. Although most critics hated *1931–*, and one wryly expected the year would be remembered longer than the play, the performance was memorable for its electrifying impact upon theatergoers, especially upon those in the cheaper seats, who cheered for its working-class lovers, no longer degraded by unemployment and indigence. It was a story that could appeal to Otto Kahn's sympathies because it gave the common man an uplifting victory. True, the protagonists found serenity in joining with communists, but that would matter less to Kahn than a story in which economic privation ended without hope or harmony. He would be impressed by the escape from despair and tragedy, not the literal solution of communism. To him, the humanism was more powerful than the revolutionary idealism of American Marxian melodrama.[10]

The point speaks to a dense pack of issues, including Kahn's underlying confidence in capitalism and his feeling that theater should explore social dilemmas. Kahn undoubtedly felt it was better for revolt to occur in the theater than in the streets. He was certainly liberal enough to say that "neither Wall Street men nor Socialists have claws or hoofs," preferring to find common ground, "to seek and emphasize . . . that which unites us instead of searching out and . . . exaggerating that which separates us."[11] Such flexibility let him condemn Bolshevism yet stand between American red-baiters and the Moscow Art Theater, then later put $12,000 toward Max Eastman's documentary film of the Russian Revolution (*Tzar to Lenin*). He also converted socialist writer Upton Sinclair from a hostile critic into a zealous fan, perhaps during the battle for a new opera house; but in any case, Sinclair, who earlier had admonished the opera's patrons in *Metropolis* and abused Kahn in *Mammonart*, later became the producer of Sergei Eisenstein's *Que Viva Mexico!*, in which Kahn invested $10,000. When the project lost money, the patron forgave the debt.[12]

There was surely more to all this than championing the legacy of Ibsen, or believing that "art for art's sake" included political themes. Kahn's aesthetic cosmopolitanism always had some corollaries in the interdependence of nations and economies. It was further evident in Kahn's continuing association with the American-Russian Chamber of Commerce, which reorganized in 1926 (without Morgan dominance) and shifted to a pro-trade position regarding the Soviet Union.[13] Other evidence makes Kahn's cultural, economic, and political positions clearer. When reproached for his benefactions to the author of *Jews without Money* ("To help Michael Gold is practically to help the Communist Party"), Kahn took a position indicative of his general thinking: "I hold that there is a sharp and distinct line of demarcation between a man's artistic capacities and activities, and his political views or endeavors. . . . [Gold is] an unusually gifted and interesting writer. . . . I believe him to be essentially a dreamer, a poet and an idealist. He is very poor. I can see no reason why I should not extend financial aid to him once in a while." Commenting further, he called *Jews without Money* a "meritorious literary work, having not the remotest connection with Communism or similar preposterous and objectionable political notions, which, maybe, in [Gold's] case, will vanish in the course of time." Young artists and intellectuals, he surmised, were passing through a romantic phase and Kahn was unperturbed by it.[14] Apparently Kahn also sensed greater value in giving support rather than scorn. Through his acceptance, radicals became more conforming, and for them the millionaire-capitalist seemed a touch less evil. A bundle of negatives could be compensated by a few positive traits. Obviously, money for freely developing art and intellectual expression helped to foster a fair and respectful exchange between Kahn and left-leaning artists and intellectuals — each saw something good and unthreatening in the other. "You are a bloody capitalist," Mike Gold later joked, "yet as a person I have always found you generous spiritually, a friend of the young and new."[15] Kahn tried to establish a similar kinship with Washington and wider audiences watching Wall Street.

After his Senate testimony, friends and associates quickly congratulated Kahn on "a good job well done." One friend cabled immediately to applaud "a witness who knows his business and knows how to handle himself on the stand." Another called Kahn's testimony "illuminating . . . unique in the sense that to most people (not a few Senators included) it was a genuine revelation." A third predicted it would help to "restore confidence in New York." Then Henry A. Vernet, a director of Robert Benson & Co., Ltd., hit upon an additional aspect of Kahn's performance that should not be overlooked — "You seem to have thoroughly enjoyed yourself," said Vernet. Kahn confessed it was true.[16] In a world gone berserk, this theater of interrogation gave Kahn an arena where he could hope to make a difference. It gave him a bounce when everything seemed to be sinking. It was the kind of bounce that Kahn believed everyone needed.

Though perhaps lacking complete confidence, he also had good reasons to hope that a strong leap would soon occur in the U.S. economy — not because the natural forces of capitalism had run their course, nor because he had done his personal part to support the integrity of banking. Rather, Kahn's expectations for recovery took shape from two further perceptions: the federal government appeared to enact measures that Kahn considered effective moves toward recovery, and Kahn seemed to read this moment as though the crisis had entered not only its third year, but its third act, and all would soon come out well. Entering this most critical phase, from Kahn's perspective the last best hopes for the revival of business activity were both possible and essential. He told the Associated Press that America would "come back" from the slump in the next few months. Indeed, the newly established Reconstruction Finance Corporation (RFC) and more aggressive open market operations by the Federal Reserve Bank gave 1932 a promising start. Bank suspensions halted and the stock market jumped 19.5 percent over two days in mid-February, hovering near the high for a few weeks.[17]

. . . .

REVERSAL OF FORTUNES

In the balance of recent years, good news too often tended to be erased by bad omens and further catastrophes. Kahn's correspondence with his European colleagues was still rife with such warnings, when, almost as an aside, oil magnate Calouste S. Gulbenkian alerted him to the "trashy" articles that were lately being written and circulated by François Coty, the world-renowned innovator of stylishly mass-marketed perfumes, and the proprietor of *Le Figaro* and *l'Ami du Peuple*. Coty was using the latter newspaper to advance his anti-Semitic views of international money-lending conspiracies, and he had singled out Kuhn, Loeb with unambiguous vehemence. His articles could be piled on a mounting heap of demagoguery that fueled the notion of Jewish financiers controlling the world. Kahn knew this to be both irrational and dangerous, yet he typically fashioned a reply in his best English upper-class style, in this instance calling the slander "so utterly crude and idiotic that it does not even irritate me." He continued, "I suppose we could force a retraction but, manifestly, it is not worthwhile to dignify that rubbish by taking public notice of it."[18]

Thinking as though these were reasonable times, Kahn might have discounted the danger based on the fact that, rather than controlling the world, financiers were helplessly ineffectual. "We are living in a state of uncertainty and marking time" was how Gulbenkian put it, seeing "no justification at present for a revival" and admitting that "we are groping in the midst of fogs, not knowing which way to navigate." All other things being equal and rational, such realities made Coty's railings simply absurd. Nevertheless, if that line of reasoning did not defeat the demagogues, Kahn believed that the worst anti-Semitism would be left behind when the economy pulled ahead, and his sanguinity was bolstered by events in the United States, where, he noted, "Just at present, sentiment is distinctly improved and a breeze of hopefulness, timid as yet but still noticeable, is beginning to make headway." He attributed it to "constructive measures which President Hoover inaugurated, and which Congress has enacted with unusual promptness."[19]

Knowing these signs to be small when measured against the fears that prevailed everywhere, Kahn's optimism was actually anxiety. His take on the situation in the United States could be likened to the perspective of another colleague from abroad, who wrote of the "extraordinarily rapid recovery" in England, then next served up warnings with regard to Creditanstalt and Central-Eastern Europe, which were again "approaching chaos." Finally, with the presidential contest between Hindenburg and Hitler approaching in Germany, it made it all the more timely and imperative that the winter's tale of 1931–32 should shift toward recovery—lest tragedy undermine everything.[20]

At his most diplomatic, Kahn said getting out of the mess was more important than determining what caused it. (During the Great War, he had suggested essentially the same to Felix Deutsch regarding the question of war guilt.) Time would be better spent looking for solutions than fault. With some prescience Kahn thought that when historians solved the question of blame for the Great Depression, they would need to splice, measure, and match the complicity of "governments, banks, industrialists, and the public at large . . . as well as the war and peace treaties." Meanwhile, if the most vocal and frightening blame was being thrust upon capitalism, international financiers, and Jews, Kahn himself was handily laying responsibility for the world's disarray upon politicians. Indeed, as the spring of 1932 began, he was sure that politicians had worsened the American economic situation.

The Third Act

When the bounce of a few weeks turned into nothing more than a bitterly brief intermission, Kahn wrote on March 23, "We are still trudging along the weary road of gloom and depression, all the more aggravating because largely unnecessary. . . . Within the last few days, a combination of wild and reckless men has suddenly taken hold of things in the lower house of Congress, turned against the leaders of both Parties . . . and set out on a course of utter mischief." There was little hope for "sober, second-thought" to assert itself in the Senate. A few days later, he remarked, "In the contest which has been going on among the nations for making a mess of things, I think the U.S.A. takes the cake."[21]

Why was the American government eliciting such censure from Otto Kahn? Its palsied leadership in world affairs was only part of the problem. From a career-long perspective, Otto Kahn had emerged in an early-twentieth-century America that quite passionately "discovered how business interests were corrupting politics in quest of special privileges."[22] In subsequent decades of administrative and regulatory realignment, Kahn neither completely opposed reform and regulation, nor did he hold businessmen above disrepute. Rather, he long ago conceded that "black sheep are to be found in every walk of life," and asserted that, in the interest of good society, "it does become necessary to insist upon reform in prevailing practices," because "ethical conceptions change." Yet since the days when E. H. Harriman personified business power, Kahn thought an excessively harsh light was cast upon business practices. Good men looked bad and "innocent transactions" took on "sinister meaning" in the heat of inquiry. Now, in the early thirties, anti-business sentiment worried Kahn because statutory regulation of financial markets would be conceived amid revelations of immorality and offered up as a solution. Furthermore, if, as many believed, the railroads provided the best precedent of regulation, Kahn considered the results to be "a patchwork makeshift . . . of conflicting legislation." It had long been Kahn's position that supervising the industry "down to the minutest detail" strangled the railroads. As the Great Depression deepened he gave fuller voice to that warning.[23]

In the throes of capitalism's worst world crisis, then, Kahn sensed politics had not only corrupted business, but also its recovery. In March 1932, his concerns centered on three specific legislative activities and their market impact. First, to persons of great wealth the House of Representatives had become like Milton's *Pandemonium* — the capital of hell. The "wild and reckless" congressional rebellion to which Kahn referred was threatening to raise the maximum surtax rate on incomes over $100,000 to 65 percent. Second, criticism was emerging with regard to the RFC, and finally, Kahn and the Wall Street chorus who had performed so well in the recent foreign bond hearings found their burnished image was completely ephemeral. A new, more hostile round of Senate investigations of Wall Street began, and it eventually recalled Kahn for deeply probing testimony in the pursuit of landmark reforms.

What mattered more than the order of emergence was the coalescence and consequences of these three concerns, but problems with the RFC became evident first. On February 3 the *Wall Street Journal* reproached the RFC for making banks "sell-out collateral before seeking a loan." The policy was decaying morale in the financial community. Next, the RFC railroad loan program turned into a political explosion, and one flashpoint came with its $12.8 million loan to the Missouri Pacific Railroad ($5.85 million of which was earmarked for payments on the railroad's loans with J. P. Morgan, Kuhn, Loeb, and the Guaranty Trust Corporation). The ICC resisted the Missouri Pacific bailout, and in Congress, liberal Democrats and progressive Republicans attacked the RFC as a "dole for millionaires." By early April, presidential hopeful Franklin D. Roosevelt famously juxtaposed the "forgotten man at the bottom of the pyramid" with the "two billion dollar fund which President Hoover and the Congress have put at the disposal of big banks, the railroads, and the corporations."[24]

Debate over income taxation strategies in the Revenue Act of 1932 echoed these same themes, entangling Kahn further in the contradictions of appropriate policy and the privileges of wealth. Kahn's position on federal income taxes was a textbook example of what became the supply-side argument, for he was a pioneer of its lobby, having assailed the punishing, "unduly narrowed and concentrated" regime of America's individual and corporate taxes since the war. "Surtaxes imposed at a reasonable rate," he had said during the 1920s, "would produce a larger revenue than do the excessive rates." Having won tax reductions in that decade, Kahn revived his argument in 1931. Saying that " 'Take it from the rich!' has its obvious limitations in economics and practical feasibility," Kahn stuck with the drive for a more widely shared tax burden, advocating a "fair trial" for federal sales taxes.[25]

These issues raced toward a climax in early 1932. When Hoover asked Congress for a one-third increase in revenues to balance the federal budget, Democratic insider Bernard Baruch and the newly appointed Republican secretary of the treasury, Ogden Mills, both suggested a general sales tax. On March 7, by a 24–1 vote, the House Ways and Means Committee brought out a Revenue bill that derived half its income from a new 2¼ percent sales tax. It might have offended Kahn's tax philosophy that the other half of revenue would come from increases in income, estate, and corporate taxes, but he could live with the compromise. Indeed, over the long run, Kahn wanted exactly what the sales tax opponents feared — a shift away from reliance upon the wealthiest individuals and corporations. For the time being, however, the proposed sales levies promised to increase Kahn's immediate tax burden, because his losses during 1930 and 1931 left him with no profits, and he paid no federal income taxes in those years. Events in the short run, though, rendered such speculations moot, as unexpectedly embittered, bipartisan opposition to the sales tax coalesced in the House. High-powered lobbying by sales tax advocates, including Kahn, could not turn back the tide.[26]

A compromise bill did carry assorted new sales taxes to be levied on gasoline, tires, and passenger cars, along with electricity, telephone use, luxury goods, and stock sales. But the Revenue Act of 1932 also imposed the highest income surtax rates yet known in peacetime history. From a total maximum rate of 25 percent under the 1928 law, the rate on incomes over $1 million increased to 55 percent. It not only affronted Kahn's tax school, it slammed the door on Wall Street's recovery in the current year. The Dow responded with a violent decline of profit-taking (or loss-salvaging): a sell-off before the taxes on stock sales took effect. And the market's sharp breaks came at a time when the stock loan market was tight, leaving short sellers imperiled, and making April a month of "business autopsies," as one commentator put it. All told, the Dow lost 50 percent of its value over eleven weeks. Sinking to its lowest point in more than thirty years, the Dow dwindled to little more than one-tenth of its 1929 worth, and Kahn painted Wall Street as a scene of "gloom, frustration and helplessness."[27]

Adding to the shock was the assembly of what seemed to be legislative hanging parties. In January the Senate Committee on Banking and Currency authorized a cycle of financial investigations, because Hoover believed Wall Street Democrats were plotting bear raids to destroy public confidence in his presidency. The committee was empowered to probe all the buying, selling, loaning, and borrowing practices of securities exchange. The investigation would continue until 1934, yet the "Senate Bear Hunt," as it was called, at first uncovered no conspiracy, illegalities, or anything of partisan political value. The financial press guessed a deep exposé was on its way, but the committee seemingly stalled out of fear that "hurling bricks at Wall Street" would do more harm than good. Its hearings were suspended in June and did not resume in earnest until 1933. The first round nonetheless turned up a few "serious sins" of two related classes. One concerned the use of publicity agents, newspapermen, and radio announcers, who boosted stock offerings without disclosing they had received payments for their endorsements. That appeared to abuse the principle of *caveat emptor*. The other focused upon particular investment houses. Here, bad judgment and poor performance appeared to abuse public trust. Goldman Sachs was prominently embarrassed by the handsome profits made from trading and dealing securities that ended up nearly worthless.[28] No wrongdoing was pegged to Kuhn, Loeb, except the moral code that Kahn espoused was being discredited by the conduct of others.

"If there is one group which has come through this depression with the greatest unpopularity of all," Edward House told Ivy Lee in 1932, "it is certainly 'the bankers.'" Withering stock values and the steady dumping of securities kept eroding the bankers' position. Then came the late-breaking discoveries of massive fraud on the books of the Kreuger-Toll Company and its subsidiaries, including the International Match Corporation in America. Here was a smoking gun, "a public scandal of grave magnitude," providing legitimate grounds for questioning the competence of bankers. It intensified fears more rampantly than the collapse of any single financial empire, and increasingly left people thinking there was no way to know how many companies broke down not because of bad luck or bad conditions, but rather from dishonesty and incompetence. A wild wolf was at the door and its escort — the bankers — could not be trusted to tame it. Kuhn, Loeb sat far from the center of the Kreuger-Toll fray, having abstained from its financing, but Otto Kahn was concerned. To him, the scandal further undermined any chance of confidence among business interests and the public alike.[29]

All told, the spring of 1932 was harder than the autumn of 1929. The later slump seemed an avoidable, unnecessary, political calamity —

a surprise and hence more of a shock as well as a low point. Moreover, as Washington and the public grew more hostile toward Wall Street, the rich and well-to-do also felt down and out. For Kahn, the crash of 1932 differed from 1929 as well because it more clearly broke his competence as a Maecenas.

· · · ·

UNMASKING

The pitch and movement of Kahn's crisis are best introduced by Kahn's exchanges with poet Ezra Pound, who was always seeking money for his own as often as other artists' projects. His relationship with Kahn, dating back to the *Little Review* and *Ulysses* in America, stayed current over the years as the patron respected Pound's discussion of numerous issues. They would thrash out trends among writers, composers, and publishers, yet also discuss practically every edifice of contemporary civilization. They shared a pronounced admiration for Mussolini along with mutual dislike for the League of Nations. In addition, by the late twenties, Kahn was being cultivated as a patron for Pound's opera in progress, *Le Testament of François Villon*. But more than all these together, Otto Kahn and Ezra Pound were each obsessed with what the latter called "Maecenism." They connected as kindred Paterians, cosmopolites who wanted a Renaissance for modernity and felt, in Pound's words, "the American millionaire is not serious in this matter of the arts." Of the two, Pound more scornfully denounced "millionaire illiterates." The poet usually stayed reserved enough to keep from stinging Kahn straight out, with remarks about "dumb and speechless tribes of unconscious pawnbrokers," which he made to others, but Pound was vaguely condescending to the banker-patron in criticizing the capricious dilettantism ("muddle, blah, sentimentality") that Kahn could also symbolize.[30]

Where Pound's *Cantos* introduces the originator of paper money, he once calls Kubla "the Kahn." Far less delicate language flew behind the scenes. American journalist William Bird, as Pound's agent for the Villon opera in 1927, played the masquerade with spirited pride, acting decently toward Kahn at a dinner party in Paris, then, in the privacy of correspondence with Pound, engaging in the burlesque of "the Otto Kahn, or Aga Khan," who "spoke French . . . with a strong boch [German] accent" and "took a keen interest in me wife's subsequent singing"—"the old *cochone*" (i.e., pig). A few weeks later, Bird was still courting Kahn and his "Opera minions," when he quipped, "If the [Villon] Opera doesn't go over, try to sell [Kahn] stock in some company, doesn't matter much what company. They say he falls for anything." All one had to do was promise the patron of post-Duchampian moderns "a good chance of getting the Grand Cordon of the Porcelain Throne." More dream than plan, Bird had a ready-made idea for a vast international celebration of the Villon half-millenary in 1931: he would "boldly tackle M. Otto Kahn" for as much as $20,000 to underwrite a subscription edition of Villon and a week-long festival in France, which would draw to its close with "the Opera of M. Ezra Pound" and an announcement that Kahn would "make up the deficit."[31]

Nothing as majestic or as potentially satirical occurred. Although when Pound and Kahn met in Paris during the spring of 1931, they undoubtedly spoke of Pound's opera,[32] what preoccupied Pound as much at this moment was money, the capitalist system, and the economic persecution of art. These issues became the focus of a gathering storm for Pound, whose letters to Kahn began to thunder about "banks breaking around the country," the tyranny of the Federal Reserve, and the evils of short selling. There was a flash of conflict in December when Pound wrote, "Capital is doomed so far as civilization is concerned if it insists on getting its art from fresh-water profs and the subeditors of licherary [literary] weeklies. During the past 20 years I have known a fair number of the best creators in Europe. . . . No 'ploot' [plutocrat] has ever been in touch with any of them."[33] Writing again in March 1932, Pound revisited his point. This correspondence was more clearly in rivalry over who should wear the crown of cultural brokerage. He challenged the banker-patron to assess the "scoreboard" of capital. Could Kahn offer anything as convincing about the value of capitalists as the poet had presented for his own work and productivity? Self-assured that the banker-patron could not, Pound was ready to call Kahn's bluff. He raised the "open and increasingly acute question whether a man of letters can honestly support an economic system which does no better than this." Sounding as though he had won a hand playing cards, Pound hinted of the winnings he deserved, and it was more than coins to cover his expenses. Pound wanted to be compensated for past abuse. When he reminded Kahn, "The endowed foundations, as I told you in Paris, AVOID the best as if it [were] bubonic plague," the underlying tension related directly to the disparity of influence exercised by Kahn and Pound at the Guggenheim Foundation.

The foundation had ignored Pound's nominees for fellowships until Kahn intervened on behalf of one, George Antheil, whose fellowship took him to Germany in mid-1932 — well after the composer's best years, Pound thought.[34]

In another comment to Kahn, Pound declared the need for a " 'liaison' officer between the 'governing classes' and 'the best that is known and thought.' " Kahn mistakenly interpreted this as a plea for the banker-patron to resume his traditional role. But Pound was saying something else. In raising himself above Kahn, the money-master, Pound was claiming to be the better intermediary between art and money than any of the "governing class," including Otto Kahn — and he wanted that acknowledged. Kahn's still secure sense of self-importance led him to reply differently. Unable to deny "that capital has not shown up very well during the past year," and incapable of explaining why, he deflected the blame toward government, "the principal culprit for the mess." But his refusal to recant went further. Casting himself as a victim of adversity, Kahn continued to claim the role of cultural prophet for himself: "I agree with you that someone should 'act as a liaison officer' . . . (assuming there are governing classes, which I doubt). If I were a little younger and . . . if my situation were not so characterized . . . by curtailed income, undiminished 'overhead,' doubled taxation, and numberless commitments and demands, I should apply for the job myself." The patron-banker then offered nothing to relieve Pound's present financial needs, only his trust for "a 100% recovery in the not too distant future."[35] Nor did he address the issue of foundation sponsorship, although Kahn's faith in the foundations among related institutions of modern artistic patronage was being tested by other events.

A few days later, directors of the Metropolitan Opera Company met with reporters and announced that what had once been a $550,000 reserve (most of it Kahn's stock) was wiped out. "A crisis of paramount importance" made future seasons at the Met uncertain. Yet if any good was to come of it, hopes could be pinned on a new non-profit membership corporation called the Metropolitan Opera Association, which promised to take over the performing company, and, as the newspapers expounded the objective, "permit a departure from aristocratic traditions of support . . . as well as the eventual departure . . . to a new opera house at Rockefeller Center . . . where the electrical industry behind radio broadcasting is eager to make opera popular in America." Accordingly, all the directors "seemed pleased." Kahn, "who proposed a new opera house in ... 1927 ... and who always has argued that opera should be produced for a widespread public, seemed especially pleased," wrote the *New York Times*.[36]

His public smile and confidence were surely inflated. If there was any real pleasure in this moment, it was simply a matter of sticking it to MORECO, which had continued its demand for the performing company to pay its own way. The Rockefeller interests incidentally made the same insistence, and, to this end, additional revenues were sought not only from the National Broadcasting Company (NBC), but also from the Juilliard Musical Foundation. The latter had not previously assisted the Met, because Kahn's support made it unnecessary, and because Juilliard's president, John Erskine, despised the Met's musical and social traditions. In fact, after one of Erskine's many attacks upon the Metropolitan was published in October 1930 by the *Nation*, he was invited to lunch with Otto Kahn, who "though gracious as always, had a touch of grimness about him," Erskine recalled, since the remarks were making it "more difficult than usual to get promises of aid for the Met for the new season." In spite of everything, Erskine reserved a fair amount of respect for Otto Kahn's vision for the Met and sympathized with his troubles there. They were additionally aligned in assisting George Antheil, who happened to be Erskine's collaborator on the opera *Helen Retires*. In other words, Kahn and Erskine could be allies, while the Juilliard Foundation's efforts to rescue the Met would give Kahn greater hope that artistic as well as architectural reforms were again around the corner.[37]

Things did not work out nearly as he had hoped. Neither NBC nor Juilliard offered sufficient resources. The Met ran deficits for years to come and the new regime never brought the company to Rockefeller Center. Austerity was the only expectation fulfilled on the spot. After a nominal economy was derived from its new nonprofit status, which eliminated a sales tax on tickets, the company's formula for survival included lower prices to fill more seats and an abridged season to reduce overhead. The main reduction in operating costs came with salary cuts for the talent. The artists, who had volunteered a 10 percent reduction in their pay during the 1931–32 season, found their loyalties repaid by a new "democratic" Metropolitan demanding a deeper, contractual pruning of their salaries. It was the perfect time "to start making very sizable cuts in the compensation of all artists," reasoned Henry R. Winthrop, Kahn's successor as the chair of the executive committee. The Chicago Opera was bankrupt, South American cities were no longer competing for the performers, and theatrical as well as concert tours were doing poor business. "The artists would be glad to sign any reasonable contract," Winthrop conjectured, for "if they are not employed at the Metropolitan, there is nowhere else for them to go."[38] In the meantime, a few of the opera stars resigned in protest, music critics began tossing mud at the Met's patrons, and some of the mess was landing in Kahn's lap.

In the days ahead, the unshakable optimist, the conservative financier, and the Olympian patron plunged toward an unimaginable bottom, as Otto Kahn wondered whether capitalism was indeed doomed. A European correspondent, reflecting upon "frozen moneys as lost moneys," concluded that "the whole world will go to the dogs and we will go with it." Kahn was unlikely to disagree. The discussion by May 20 buckled over "the total collapse of American securities," with Otto Schiff, a banker in London, commenting, "It is almost inconceivable, particularly that your [American] railroads, which were supposed always to be very conservative in the distribution of dividends, should find themselves almost next door to bankruptcy. If some of the prices of bonds represent their real worth, then surely a very large number of the Common Stocks must be valueless." Kahn echoed this trepidation; his platitudes seemed as worthless as his experience or his portfolio; and there was new meaning in his stock phrase, "Whether we shall sink to any still lower depth before we rise, I cannot attempt to foretell." Kahn admitted that prices so low offered "utterly unthinkable" bargains, "provided one can afford to bide one's time" and wait for recovery. But buying cheap stocks was not currently an option that Otto Kahn could afford, and that too was once unthinkable.

If this banker's bench was not yet broken, Kahn heard splintering. Losing more money now than in 1929, his thinner reserves after 1931 made the blows harder to absorb. In addition, Kuhn, Loeb's reputation as a solid house of issue was called into question with the fate of its railroad financings. But the keywords of the changed situation, such as "inconceivable" and "utterly unthinkable," had Kahn admitting the possibility of total breakdown. The springtime skid on Wall Street left him frantic and wondering if all his received beliefs had truly collapsed. Was everything in the stock market totally worthless? The banker-patron was facing a single break in all his conventions—a despair that he could no longer disguise completely. It forced him to vacate his seat as the central banker of the arts. This much was evident when the Group Theatre came calling for his support.

The Group Theatre had all the right credentials, intentions, and endorsements to entice Otto Kahn. They began as a laboratory of the Theatre Guild, boasting ideals of collective theater, artistic honesty, and a unified acting style. A young, intelligent, and messianic bunch, they were determined to produce socially relevant plays and lead America's next wave in dramatic innovation. Their artistic manifesto, while bold, also notably lacked respect for the older innovators at the Theatre Guild, which stirred board member Phillip Moeller to say, "What's so new about that?" The seasoned playwright, director, and producer made a valid point. After all, the Theatre Guild had tried to institutionalize actor training with Stanislavsky's cooperation while the master was in New York, and after that plan did not materialize, the Guild formed its own Acting Company, which trained the Group Theatre's founders. The Guild also put socially relevant dramas on the boards (including Howard Lawson's *Processional*, directed by Moeller). As important, Moeller and other powers at the Guild were veterans of the Washington Square Players, for whom the manifesto of "experiment and initiative" was still quite alive, despite the many critics who accused them of its abandonment. They thought themselves to be no less inspired than the Group Theatre's leaders who thought the Guild to be stodgily out of date.[39] A classic generational conflict ended in a schism, with the Group Theatre breaking off on its own, looking for sponsors. In other words, the Group Theatre met another perquisite for Kahn's patronage—they were hungry.

By now the word must have gotten around that Kahn was more likely to provide kindness than cash. A few months earlier Kahn declined to give a loan to Zora Neale Hurston for her Caribbean carnival-concert, *The Great Day*, though he was "greatly impressed" by a rehearsal. Kahn also lately turned down an appeal to help conductor Antonio Brico, who was then "in Berlin quite without resources." Meanwhile, Kahn's string of loans (as yet unforgiven notes) to Waldo Frank had come to an end. His patronage continued in other forms, as the two played night owls together at dinners and clubs, talking on many subjects, including violence in America and the beating inflicted upon Frank during the coal miners' strike in Harlan County, Kentucky. When Frank turned their discussions to the subject of the Group Theatre, which he endorsed, Kahn likely expressed how lately he was compelled "to abstain from supporting things which . . . are not of immediate necessity." The men nonetheless hit upon an idea for the banker-patron to be involved without committing money to the Group Theatre — they could use Kahn's retreat of 2,000 acres on Shelter Island for the summer's rehearsal period.[40]

An appointment was promptly arranged for Kahn to meet Group Theatre co-founders Harold Clurman and Cheryl Crawford on April 15 at the offices of Kuhn, Loeb. As Clurman later remembered, Otto Kahn began the meeting in keeping with the role of the famous Maecenas. His greeting warm and full of praise, Kahn spoke highly of their productions, ideals, and abilities, then asked what the Group Theatre wanted from him. Primed to answer, "Not money," Clurman sprang to life, running down the list of plans and problems, while Kahn listened attentively if not altogether patiently, until he abruptly interjected, "But you are talking of nothing but money!" Crawford took over the pitch, and Clurman observed a very strange Otto Kahn: "dejected, vague, uncertain. We did not know how hard hit he had been by the crash. We could not conceive of his millionaire's worries. . . . He spoke of 'those damn-fool congressmen.' . . . He murmured something about the capitalist system not working well, 'but what else is there?' Finally . . . he spoke, as if in soliloquy, of a total abandonment of effort. . . . He was tired, at a loss."[41]

No headlines proclaimed, "Maecenas Blabbers Senselessly," and Kahn never talked like this on the record. Nor would the Group Theatre immediately collapse under the weight of Kahn's crash. As Frank later explained to Kahn, within a year the company would "put on plays they could raise money on, rather than plays they wanted to produce." Ironically, the Theatre Guild was forced to make the same compromise during the allegedly prosperous twenties.[42] What Clurman witnessed in the meeting with Kahn was nonetheless a complex response to cumulative circumstances. For the first time since the crash of 1929, Kahn's judgment of past years' performance and expectations for the future added up to unmitigated despair. Maybe the crisis culminated for Kahn when he could no longer guide cultural development or count upon capitalist expansiveness. Much had changed since only two months earlier when, in this same office, Kahn had written with some aplomb to Pound and held a conversation with George Antheil that the composer called "a very sincere pleasure and inspiration." The decorum of the office had not changed, and Kahn still dressed with the same suave style, but the self-enclosed system of signs did not produce the same ceremonial outcome.[43]

Perhaps Pound was right after all. Otto Kahn had finally failed in the crucial test of artistic patronage—bringing along the newest of the best. It happened, furthermore, at the same moment when the most sacred principles of conservative finance also gave way. Nothing, it seemed, was depression-proof. The mask slipped, exposing something of Otto Kahn that neither he nor his guests were prepared or wanted to see. "What is interesting about people in good society," ran a Wildean principle, "is the mask that each of them wears, not the reality that lies behind the mask."[44] Neither the artist nor the patron desired this shared sense of devastation or common fate. It was not a glaring sense of impending tragedy that they wanted, but a softer, easier light.

Hart Crane's death before the end of April 1932 points up other relevant conclusions related to the patronage system and beyond. In the aftermath of Kahn's subsidies, Crane fumbled two alternative sources of support. First he failed in his attempts to write commercially, for Hollywood and *Fortune*; then, on a Guggenheim Fellowship in Mexico, he again could not produce a poem on schedule. His time in Mexico, however, did grant Crane an escape from the breadlines of New York and the harsh realities of America—the nation and culture that, he said in 1931, "seems a long way off from the destiny I fancied" when writing *The Bridge*. Rather than return to "wail around the grave of capitalism" after his fellowship term expired on March 31, 1932, Crane planned to stay in Mexico, except that a lawsuit against the estate of his father threatened the modest inheritance he expected. With nothing to live on, the poet headed back to his hometown of Cleveland. On April 22, the day before sailing from Vera Cruz to New York, he wrote ambivalently about the prospects of his "middle western exile." Three days into his voyage, Hart Crane climbed over the ship's rail and fell into the sea, drowning, probably a suicide—though no one knows for sure why.[45]

When Crane slipped into the Caribbean, a couplet in the artist-patron relationship closed. A symbol of Kahn's hope for the artist in a market economy was lost, along with the ideal good of individual or foundation patronage. And death hovered about as a motif. The destiny of poet and patron intersected on this theme, or threat, as Kahn and Crane were both unsettled by life's meaning and logic, its purpose and direction, and one's place in America. It was all the more bewildering because each had so many accumulated hopes for a cultured and transnational world, finding its spiritual discovery both in and from America. Indeed, the quandary had parallels in Kahn's scene with the Group Theatre, or at least that portion of the Group Theatre's promise in which Waldo Frank saw wholeness, a "vision of the Cosmic" that was analogous to the mission of *Seven Arts* magazine in earlier years, and his more recent treatise, *The Rediscovery of America: An Introduction to a Philosophy of American Life* (1929). On the stump for the Group Theatre's fund-raising drive, Frank had said, "I believe in the Group Theatre because . . . I am primarily interested in a new society, a new humanity in the moral and spiritual as well as in the economic sense." Kahn believed as much, but the banker-patron was frozen out of place, especially when Frank proposed breaking "the alliance of the intellectuals with the money class," and forging instead "an alliance of the men of mind of vision, the artists, with the People."[46] The Maecenas model, as Pound so frequently complained, was always imperfect. In the spring of 1932, it seemed insurmountably alienated.

. . . .

A POLITICAL CODA

On May 3, 1932, Kahn wrote to Helen Ingersoll of the Neighborhood Playhouse, a long-time beneficiary of his support: "I regret to say that I must be excused from making a financial commitment to your organization this year." With uncanny equity, Kahn on the same day declined to make any contributions to the New York State Republican Committee. The second decision marked another clear change, though it is uncertain where Kahn's divisions with the Republicans began or where it led him, other than to vote for Roosevelt in the next presidential election. A dependable Republican voter and party contributor for many years, Kahn was not a blind Republican loyalist, a Wall Street reactionary, or an unqualified supporter of Hoover. During the 1928 campaign he backed Hoover, but, wanting to repeal Prohibition, Kahn felt more in accord with Al Smith's views on the Volstead Act. In addition, he had said, "A Democratic Administration will be just as desirous to promote the country's prosperity as a Republican Administration." Perhaps that is why the Republican Party snubbed him in 1929. Named as treasurer of the National Senate Committee in October, his appointment was hotly protested as soon as it was announced. The newspapers attributed the opposition to Republican insurgents and White House advisers; however, anti-Hoover Republican progressives in the Senate were hardly averse to Otto Kahn, one of the Wall Street liberals, who supported farm relief as well as western development. Idaho senator William E. Borah privately assured him the resistance came not from progressive Republicans, but rather an unnamed "coterie of gentleman who are perfectly certain that they own the Republican Party" — presumably the Eastern elites. Kahn did not know who to believe. Whether rejected by a White House that owed him support or blue-blood Republicans, he shrugged off the incident with a face-saving remark: "Whatever motives actuated those concerned, they have done me just grounds for withdrawing from . . . a difficult and thankless job."[47]

Kahn's defection thereafter evolved slowly and erratically. In May 1930 he told Bernard Baruch, "You have repeatedly expressed your conviction that I shall never vote the Democratic ticket. You may be in for a surprise before long." Baruch was not convinced. Indeed, Kahn stayed with the Republicans during the 1930 elections, and on the surface, nothing seemed odd in early 1931, when the New York State Republican Committee sought multiyear pledges from its contributors, and Kahn sent a check ($1,000) for the current year only. Kahn was still a party stalwart. He served on the advisory committee for Republican Associates of the State of New York and in mid-year he contributed an additional $500 toward interest on the deficit of the State Committee. Considering the prevailing gloom of 1931, then, it may have been common sense rather than a sure sign of retreat when Kahn looked at the upcoming presidential election and wagered that a Democrat would next take the White House. Nor was there anything new in his political loyalties when, finding common ground with Democratic senator Robert F. Wagner of New York, Kahn declared, "I fully share your opinion as to the value of a state operated, Federally coordinated national system of unemployment offices." Kahn also favored a reform program to include old-age pensions. Not even on May 3, 1932, when called for a contribution to the state Republicans, did his hesitancy signal defection from the party as much as an inching away. With the national convention approaching, Kahn said, he would not contribute to the party, even at the state level, until the national party "defined its attitude towards Prohibition."[48] For various reasons, he had little to say publicly concerning the 1932 presidential campaign.

CHAPTER EIGHT

Endings on the Horizon

In late May 1932 Kahn sailed for London, muttering that his health could be worse and his spirit could be better. He was still keeping his own battered ego well hidden from public view, when a reporter caught him lunching at a London grille and concluded, "Kahn was apparently unscarred by the depression." The reporter congratulated the banker "on looking so well when he had just come from the front line of the American financial war." Kahn responded, "Why wear gloom like a suit?" A few days later, he suffered what may have been a stroke, a heart attack, or extreme angina. Under doctors' orders, Kahn cleared his schedule of everything from his regular round of business meetings to an "Irish adventure" with friends from the Abbey Theatre, then went packing off "to start my Royat cure with as little delay as possible."[1]

The prescription was complete rest—a punishing regime for Otto Kahn. When imposed on previous occasions the always hyperactive banker-patron seemed at best to compromise by doing less, rather than nothing at all. This time Kahn came nearer to a halt, except he could not resist making a few private comments about the most recent turns in world affairs. The Lausanne conference, which brought an end to reparations, elicited his praise, even as Kahn took care in perceiving "the antics of those Nazi Kaffirs and their Nationalist associates bid fair to upset what gave promise of being . . . a reasonably auspicious adjustment of things." The ongoing paralysis in American politics also had him burning. "Now it's America's turn!?" wrote Kahn, longing for heroics that seemed unlikely from Hoover's administration. In July he was thrilled to read reports of the Democratic National Convention. He telegraphed a colleague, "Roosevelts flying visit to convention was gallant, picturesque, and appealing," and Roosevelt quietly became Kahn's candidate in the presidential election of 1932. He made his pick without public endorsement or attracting attention to the political divisions on Wall Street, where even the Kuhn, Loeb partners were divided between Hoover and Roosevelt camps, and judiciously bet on both horses. However, when after the election Kahn congratulated Roosevelt supporters, explaining, "Circumstances made it impossible for me to join in the fray" of the campaign, he was more likely referring to his doctor-prescribed seclusion from public affairs than to his tactful silence.[2]

Royat had cured nothing. Upon returning to New York, in September, his doctors newly discovered a lesion in Kahn's left lung which was probably tubercular. It put him "out of commission" for another six months, and the first leg of his convalescence had him sequestered at 1100 Fifth Avenue, where he was "permitted to sit up in an easy chair and do a little walking around the house." When allowed to communicate with the outside world, he complained about confinement, "the tyranny of my doctors," and missing the New York season of the Abbey Theatre. At any rate, for the first time in Otto Kahn's life, the public took fuller notice of his failing health because, when his medical condition excused Kahn from a court appearance, his infirmities became a matter of public record. Newspapers in America and Europe quickly spread the word of his diagnosis, "high blood pressure and angina pectoris with complicating pulmonitis." The news came as a shock for the banker-patron, and it benumbed those who knew him. For Kahn's side, such publicity was exceptional and unseemly. Always vain, Kahn never so much as allowed a photograph of himself wearing reading glasses, and in recent years, it was rare to even get a photographed glimpse of his profile, for it might betray the plumper neck and wider waistline of his advancing years. On a more practical level, his good health was better for Kuhn, Loeb. The firm would not want Kahn's condition to panic clients, or give competitors a sense of weakness, and threaten business that Kuhn, Loeb could ill afford to lose. An optimistic prognosis helped to control the damage. Kahn's health problems, all were assured, had been caught early and were "positively curable."[3]

Addie Kahn became "the most devoted and efficient garde-malade," as she worked in concert with the staff to keep Kahn isolated from stress and solicitations. When Norman Bel Geddes wanted Kahn to endorse a new book on industrial design, he was told, "On the doctors' orders, no letters, the answering of which would call for any kind of mental effort, are being brought to Mr. Otto H. Kahn's attention for the time being." Not withheld from Kahn, however, were Bel Geddes's next messages, which came with an inscribed copy of his book *Horizons*.[4] In general, admiring wishes for Kahn's quick recovery were allowed through. These typically extolled and appreciated Kahn's good works. One, calling Kahn "the best friend the modern theatre has ever had in this country," blessed him for "so many memorable hours which we otherwise would have missed." Another labeled him "the only human and natural millionaire I know and one of the very few men of his type who really does care for music and those things which cannot be bought (though they can be sold!)."[5] Elsewhere, a tangible fear invariably leaked through the gratitude and respect. As admiring dependents struggled with the fear of losing Otto Kahn, their personal and financial lots were intertwined with his fate. Who would cover their mortgages, pay their rent, forgive their debts? Good manners held back any explicit statement of such fears, but people were wondering what other patron would support them.[6]

As for Kahn, fatality crept forward as part of a great, general battle with hopelessness, where death mixed with destiny in a struggle more perplexing than Kahn could expect. Years earlier, the death of Abraham Wolff had signaled Kahn's final transition to adulthood. Then the deaths of E. H. Harriman and Jacob Schiff figured prominently in Kahn's arrival at seniority. In the latest cycle, the men with whom Kahn had been young were dying. The last stage of seniority had arrived — only what prevailed of one's life's work? With the collective signs of economic internationalism hastening toward collapse, a death could mean many things — an answer, a punishment, a symptom of general conditions, or a clue to the riddle of ruin. Death could rob a hero of his aspirations. As Paul M. Warburg lay dying in late January 1932, he apparently recanted all his renowned expertise for finance and economics, while global events left him saying, "I have come to the conclusion that I know nothing whatever." Struggling similarly, Hart Crane found no bridge for the mental gulf between past optimism and present despair. One's goals and values, no less than economic systems, could course toward an anxious, disorientated conclusion. The point came home to Kahn with the death of Edward Steinam, his retired private secretary and a cousin of Addie Kahn. Having gotten into "serious trouble" during the 1932 crash, Steinam seemed steadfast and cheerful until the end—"one of the last men capable of such an act of despondency," Kahn thought, after Steinam committed suicide. With some parity, Kahn also remarked privately in mid-1932, "It is not thinkable that the distressed nations of Europe will commit economic suicide."[7] Self-inflicted or not, death was a denouement. Not just an ending, but a sturdy generic climax for tragedy; to punish before re-demption was a way to avenge the dismay. Death was a metaphoric monster.[8]

Alone with his fears, the ongoing needs of admirers and dependents could give Kahn reasons to live, or, if the condolences sounded like eulogies, their words could depress and discourage him. That left Kahn particularly refreshed by "the tone, spirit and affection" of Mike Gold. With good humor and "real affection," Gold said in Yiddish, "*Zei gezunt*" (be well): "The country might be going to hell for some, but my dear Mr. Kahn, a great new life will come out of this chaos and suffering." And, Gold promised, "In a revolution we would have to make you go to work running the opera house or the movie industry." It was reassuring as well as refreshing. Gold was among the fifty-two artists and intellectuals (many of them former beneficiaries of Kahn's largesse) who recently issued an open call for committed, political action by intellectuals and rejected "the lunacy spawned by grabbers, advertisers, traders, speculators, salesmen." Gold anchored the left wing of those who proclaimed, "We shall not permit business men to teach us our business." But Otto Kahn was an ordained exception, the banker-patron beyond the scorch and sizzle, because Kahn had a soul. He would have a place in the new order. Indeed, he could be trusted to teach aspiring revolutionaries how to run the culture industries. Kahn chuckled in reply, "The prospect of being placed in charge of the movie industry almost makes me welcome a revolution."[9]

He was not completely joking. Financial and managerial affairs at Paramount were collapsing in ugly chaos and Kahn was partly responsi-ble. In November 1931, at the time when Kahn's brother Felix, a mem-ber of the Paramount board of directors, was scrambling to cover mar-gin calls on his shares of tumbling Paramount stock, Kuhn, Loeb was also struggling to keep the company out of receivership. Otto Kahn had prompted the appointment of John D. Hertz, a founder of the Yellow Cab Company (1915) and the Hertz Drive-Ur-Self Corporation (1924), as chair of the Paramount finance committee. His results at Paramount were disastrous. Hertz alienated everyone with salary cuts,

In Hollywood during better days (left to right): Douglas Fairbanks, Kahn, and Charlie Chaplin. (Private collection)

expense reductions, and extensive audits. Key officers resigned, including Jesse L. Lasky, one of Hollywood's pioneers. By December 1932 Hertz and Paramount chief Adolph Zukor were at each other's throats. "Kahn, ill at home," recalled his lawyers, "believed both men invaluable and vainly sought to reconcile the controversy." There was no truce. Hertz left and Paramount, having lost $21 million in 1932, con-

Endings on the Horizon

sented to the appointment of receivers in January 1933. In March the company filed for bankruptcy. Thereafter, a "campaign uninhibited in vituperation of Kuhn, Loeb," said the firm's lawyers, broke loose in hostile litigation. The controversy centered on stock repurchase agreements, which financed Paramount's aggressive acquisition of theater properties during the twenties. Repurchase agreements or buybacks, incidentally, are used extensively in the open market operations of the Federal Reserve; in other words, they are not financial novelties. As it turned out, however, the Paramount buybacks, which guaranteed repurchases at $80 per share on a fixed date of maturity, fell due at the worst possible moment for the company: the stock was trading below fifty, theater attendance was off by as much as 50 percent, and, without a surplus, the obligations drained Paramount's cash reserve. Because Kuhn, Loeb partners had invested in the repurchases and two partners were Paramount directors (William Wiseman and Kahn's son Gilbert), it looked as though the firm's partners were winning while other investors were losing. Some of the losers thought the game was rigged.[10]

Paramount was not the only serious reversal to invade what should have been Kahn's protected sanctum. Another was the Pennroad Corporation, the only investment trust sponsored by Kuhn, Loeb. Launched in April 1929, and thought to be more solid and conservative than speculative, Pennroad was also a matter of great pride for Kuhn, Loeb. The firm had successfully underwritten and managed its $45 million offering in October 1929, even as the crash hit midway through the selling period. Early in the Great Depression, this investment trust stood solidly while weaker ones collapsed. Yet year after year afterward, as the stock market and economy slumped, Pennroad's investments helplessly fell to a fraction of their purchase price: the $133 million raised in 1929 was eventually worth less than $33 million, and shares in the company, which traded at nearly $30 in July 1932, tumbled to a low of under $4. Its sorry performance reflected the industry average for railroads, along with the soiled story of investment trusts, but it also marred the prestige of Kuhn, Loeb as a house of sound advice and reputation. In hindsight, a cable from Kahn to his partner Felix Warburg conceded privately, "Fear cannot say honestly that am persuaded wisdom our having joined investing corporation."[11]

Wisdom had shifted to folly. The financial and personal competence of money managers was on everyone's mind, and the Metropolitan Opera was no exception. In the spring of 1932, Met directors hastened to raise $150,000 for the company's next season, and over the year public controversies kept mounting about the institution's crisis. Among those taking positions that would disturb Kahn was composer-critic Deems Taylor, whose first operas had been commissioned by the Met, but who now turned disloyal to the company's directors. Complaining of their tightfisted short-sightedness, he said they had "carried no burden for twenty-four years" and were "accepting far more credit than due them." Kahn and Paul Cravath, his successor as the Met's president and chairman, each took turns in rebuttal, declaring "the Metropolitan Opera house has probably been more liberally supplied with money than any other opera house in the world." Otto Kahn's individual contribution was estimated as $1 million, and Taylor eventually conceded that his criticism did not apply to Kahn.[12]

In addition, all year long, Juilliard Foundation president John Erskine was bothered by another accusation and hunting for its source. *New York Times* critic Olin Downes contended that the foundation had put "funds... intended for the Metropolitan" into the "bricks and mortar" of Juilliard's own music school and theater. Erskine confronted Downes and asked "on what he based his charge." The information, he was told, came from Otto Kahn, a claim the banker-patron subsequently denied with a skillful admission. He recalled "having mentioned this subject in casual conversation with Mr. Downes," but Kahn also knew, and did not tell Erskine, that when Met directors were casting about for sources of aid earlier in 1932, funding from the Juilliard Foundation was considered unlikely, inasmuch as Paul Cravath had said, "No, they have no money because they have put all available money into the building of the theatre." Nor did Kahn reveal that he personally thought the foundation should have maintained a reserve fund to support the Metropolitan. Instead Kahn said, "I never questioned, and do not now question, that the [Juilliard] Trustees, in whatever they did, faithfully and to the best of their judgment, [intended] to carry out what they understood to be [the late Augustus] Juilliard's wishes." His diplomacy was meant to secure explicit as much as general ends. In working to ensure no further breach between the Metropolitan and the foundation, Kahn was protecting his own reputation as well. Erskine could embarrass him because Kahn had earlier declined the foundation's support during flush times at the Met.[13]

By February 1933, as America slid perilously into its latest, all-time worst banking emergency, the Met's deficit mounted toward $340,000. Even fewer patrons were responsive to the crisis than during the 1932 drive, when Kahn's $10,000 was the only five-figure donation from a board member. With the lease on the house about to expire, the performing company was ready to quit, and MORECO was bracing to announce "no effort would be made to give opera another year." Then the impasse ended, deus ex machina, in a new show of unity and re-alignment. A "Committee to Save Opera at the Metropolitan Opera House" was formed. In its break with the past, the group brought representatives of the Met's two governing boards together with members of the artistic roster, and appealed directly to the general public "as a last resort" to protect 700 jobs and keep opera running at the Met. It petitioned the Carnegie and Juilliard Foundations, sought donations from wealthy patrons, and launched a crusade for new public contributions ("from a dollar up") through radio and newsprint campaigns. Fund-raising and cost-cutting being two sides of the same coin, the Met reduced the length of the next season and halved the artistic payroll without reducing staff.[14]

By now Otto Kahn was geographically if not emotionally removed from the daily action. Too ill to attend the season's opening night in November, he headed to the French Alpes Maritime in December, where he was still in recuperation when the latest crisis broke. "You are fortunate in being away from New York," Cravath wrote in February. Spelling out the Met's grim details and last chances, he half-hoped that Kahn would send money above and beyond his contribution from the previous year, only to be stunned when Kahn cabled back, "Very sorry but for reasons which shall explain verbally cannot decide now as to subscription." A flurry of telegrams followed, with Kahn sticking to his position: "find it impossible to modify my attitude" and "extremely reluctant to disappoint you in matter of contribution."[15] Eventually Kahn contributed to the subscription drive, but granted only $5,000, half the amount of the previous year.

Whether too strapped for cash or having decided it was time to let the rest of New York prove its commitment, Kahn otherwise grew skeptical and rancorous about the direction of the Met. His pride bruised easily in these days, perhaps too easily. He felt neglected, for instance, because the board of the performing company forgot even the courtesy of sending him a copy of its official resolution regarding his resignation from the presidency and chairmanship; but Otto Kahn was also coming to believe that no one in New York's opera world was sufficiently respectful of him. In a heightened state of pique and self-defense, his estimates of past financial contributions grew taller as his current contributions declined, and he instructed Cravath, "Would like committee and perhaps suitable others to know that my connection with the Metropolitan cost me three millions," adding, "Gatti[-Casazza] was never stinted but always received without question everything he asked for."[16] Evidently, Kahn also disliked the newly found prominence of Cornelius (Neil) Bliss, a Yankee scion of the box-owning families, who had been active with the MORECO committee that opposed Kahn's plan for a new house during the 1920s. Out of "anxiety to interest [Bliss] and the people with whom he is associated," however, Cravath was now putting Bliss on the fast track to power, calling him "a tower of strength" and encouraging him "to take the center stage" with the Committee to Save the Opera. Cravath saw to it that Bliss was named a director of the new Metropolitan Opera Association in May 1933 and became chairman of the executive committee before the year's end. Along the way Bliss asked for and was granted the authority to stock the board and executive committee with any new member he wished. Eventually, the boardroom of the Metropolitan Opera at Lincoln Center was named in his honor.[17]

Aside from old reasons for Kahn to feel repudiated by the succession of Bliss, a new one arose before the end of 1933. Bliss irritated Kahn by putting him out to pasture without a second thought, when he decided independently, "in view of [Kahn's] desire to avoid responsibility," that the banker-patron "would not care to be on the Executive Committee." Given not even the courtesy of an invitation, Kahn had had enough. On November 17, 1933, he resigned from the board of directors. In no time Cravath intervened, wanting Kahn back in the fold before the press grabbed the story and used it to amplify growing apprehensions over the Met's stability, but also before Kahn's displeasure with Bliss had a chance to sour John Erskine, whose goodwill toward the Met, said Cravath, was "much influenced" by "his friendship and admiration" for Kahn. Keen on an alliance with Erskine and the Juilliard Foundation, Cravath added, "We need him and his money very much." In the final tally, Cravath also made it clear that Otto Kahn's role with the Met was still one that only Otto Kahn could play. Having explained away the innocence in Bliss's blunder, he promised Kahn would be "promptly appointed and welcomed" to the executive committee. Offering other words that Kahn needed to hear, Cravath called Kahn "the guiding genius of the Metropolitan Opera House for so many years," concluding, "It is hard to think of the Metropolitan Opera Company without your name associated with it." Once his significance was thus acknowledged, Kahn withdrew his resignation in short speed. Official announcement of the new executive committee mentioned nothing of the tussle.[18]

Kahn took his place on the executive committee, but not his past leadership. Finding little fulfillment in the direction provided by other New Yorkers on the board, two possible futures were at odds, as contemporary no less than later critics would be quick to note. In one, the Met's crisis afforded opportunities to cross traditional boundaries of artistic content and audience composition. Indeed, most of the traditional overseers were now exposed for their lack of economic clout and, by pumping $50,000 into the guarantee fund for 1933–34, Erskine was trying to use the Juilliard's money to leverage more modern, American, and educational opera. Live radio broadcasts, in addition, brought the Metropolitan Opera to a national audience, and reduced ticket prices brought new faces into the hall. Sounding much like Waldo Frank on the subject of the Group Theatre, conductor Artur Bodanzky hinted that the opera could be taken away from "the 'wealthy few' and put it into the hands of the 'appreciative public.' "[19] Yet the transition to broader public support was nonetheless preserving what observers of the Metropolitan would point to, long after box owners sold out: the opera house remained an artistically timid "hideout for the grand manner and the high style."[20] The gala benefit provides a vivid illustration. At the costume ball held for the 1933 fund-raising drive, one-time actress and soon-to-be member of the Metropolitan board Eleanor Robson Belmont paraded her version of the *grand dame*-turned-philanthropist-and-democratizer while dressed in "the role of the Empress." Set in the Parisian court of circa 1860, the gala returned to the style that Kahn encountered earlier in the century, during Mrs. Astor's reign, except now the millionaires pleaded for public subsidies while preserving their courtly ways.[21]

The Met's continued conservatism was evident in the artistic repertory as well. Consider one of the Met's few homages to modernism, the
world premiere of Louis Gruenberg's *Emperor Jones* in January 1933.
The operatic version of O'Neill's play premiered in New York instead of
Berlin, according to Irving Kolodin, because conductor Erich Kleiber
decided "a music drama with an American Negro as the central figure
would not flourish in the current political climate" of Germany. It
would not exactly blossom at the Met, either. The cultural lag in New
York continued with *The Emperor Jones* as it had with *Jonny spielt auf*—a
white singer played the lead in blackface, as the Met had no African
American singers on its roster.[22] Was the time not ripe for African
Americans to perform at the Metropolitan Opera? Marian Anderson
was then making a sensational concert tour of Scandinavia, and the
always popular George Gershwin was composing his first attempt at the
operatic form with *Porgy and Bess*, which Kahn hoped could premiere at
the Met. As it turned out, though, Anderson, the first African American
to sing at the Met, did not make it to the stage there until 1955, sixteen
years after her famous concert at the Lincoln Memorial. *Porgy and Bess*,
one of many works in which race, music drama, and grand opera might
have collaborated, instead opened in a commercial house in Boston in
1935 — and did not arrive on the stage of the Met until 1985.

Kahn's ego would not allow him to see that his own many compromises left him partially at fault for the Met's incapacity to pioneer new
cultural sensibilities. A natural contradiction — his blame for lingering
acceptance of blacked-up opera singers, for instance — could be offset
by his pains taken in earlier years, when Kahn endorsed jazz as an
operatic form, or showed interest in financing an all Negro-revue, then
backed up his commitment with an $12,500 loan to the Walton Pro-
ducing Company. The company was supposed "to establish a Negro
theatre in New York," but at least helped bring Frank Wilson's *Meek
Mose* to Broadway. Kahn attended opening night and wrote off the loan
afterward, though he did not like the play. He also later discussed its
lack of merits, along with questions of racial authenticity, in correspondence with Jasper Deeter, founder of the Hedgerow Theatre, who
had appeared in the first New York production of *The Emperor Jones*, and
was sharply critical of star vehicles that "circused Paul Robeson and
Porgy into longevity and dollars." Finally, because Kahn's office was so
often the destination of hopeful if not fully realized African American
talent, and not all went away disappointed, he could believe he had

Lawrence Tibbett in Louis Gruenberg's opera The Emperor Jones, *Metropolitan Opera, 1933. (Metropolitan Opera Archives)*

done his share of advocacy and not be entirely wrong if, in 1933, he concluded that the Met's cultural progress would be obstructed by the "Old Guard."[23]

Perhaps nothing was better illustrative of the stagnancy than the fanfare that accompanied the announcement that *Salome* would be included in the 1933–34 season. Intended at best to boost ticket sales, it created a sensation quite different from either the 1907 scandal or what might be accomplished by a new opera, such as *Four Saints in Three Acts*, which premiered in Hartford less than a month after *Salome*'s return to the Met. The latter work, a collaboration of Gertrude Stein (libretto), Virgil Thomson (music), Florine Stettheimer (sets), and an all-black cast of performers, did not come to the Met until 1973. On the other hand, reinstalling *Salome* quickly established a strange and stalwart myth, as reflected in a centennial history of the Metropolitan Opera (1983): "The process of public fund-raising emancipated the new Association from Morgan and the pruderies of the box-holders,"[24] thus making possible a new production of *Salome*. Kahn knew differently. As early as 1915, MORECO had indicated that a conservative staging of *Salome* would create no further disturbance among its power brokers. It allowed the 1922 benefit performance by the visiting Chicago company to come and go without protest; afterward, since Maria Jeritza wished to play the part herself with the Met and the company had acquired the production rights, MORECO once again assented to *Salome*. That it was not presented for so many years after Pierpont Morgan's death was more likely due to Gatti-Casazza, who was none too keen on the opera and always had some excuse to avoid it. In 1920 Kahn, looking with envy upon the artistic and financial success that the Chicago Opera enjoyed with *Salome*, wanted Geraldine Farrar to perform it at the Met. Gatti, however, drew a contrary conclusion, explaining that Richard Strauss was demanding excessive compensation for "an opera fifteen years old" that was a staple of the Chicago company and "can always be given, when it is convenient to do so."[25] Long before 1933, in any case, Kahn knew *Salome* was hardly a sign of artistic revolt. The idea of its liberation — however false — made good publicity in 1933; no less daring than positioning Bliss with power, it merely served convenience rather than reform of the Met's old flaws.

A few remaining issues make the complexity of Kahn's opera stories clearer. His battles with the Met boards ebbed as he dropped back from active leadership and authority, but Kahn would neither abandon the Met nor allow himself to be discredited or rendered invisible by his detractors and enemies. Nor were his experiences with the Met isolated from what was occurring on a wider historical map for Kahn. By some stroke of coincidence, *Salome* had premiered in New York when Washington so badly wanted Harriman's head and Kahn had made his debut in the public role of banker-patron; the promise to revive *Salome*, "the bygone scandal of another generation,"[26] happened to reprise more than old memories. Otto Kahn's last battles for dignity within the Met were being waged simultaneously with his more public and time-consuming struggles to secure the integrity of private banking culture within the New Deal. And, more painful than ironic, *Salome* would return to the Met while its composer was helping to legitimize official Nazi culture as president of the *Reichsmusikkammer*.

The Met always tested Kahn's cosmopolitanism and Jewishness, but it was the rise of Hitlerism that brought Kahn's identity as a German-born Jew into sharp focus. It furnished the larger context for his shortened tolerance with regard to slights and oversights, and it also diverted his remaining philanthropic resources. Exactly at that moment in early 1933, when Kahn at first withheld his contribution to the Met's guarantee fund, he was elsewhere reflecting upon the recent Nazi assumption of power. In a timely exchange, written on February 20, the day before his sixty-sixth birthday, Kahn turned back a suggestion to consult a medical specialist in Berlin: "I cannot avail myself of his professional skill as I do not feel it compatible with my self-respect as a Jew to visit Germany now, much as I always like to be there." He proceeded in a somber mood, homesick and heartbroken, torn between love and hate, "thinking of the Germany of my youth and of its spirit, at least in South and Middle Germany." No less significant than Kahn's point of view was the recipient of his remarks: George Sylvester Viereck, who thought that Hitler offered hope for Germany and that the Nazi's anti-Semitism was a disagreeable, temporary phase — exaggerated by "the enemies of revision."[27] Viereck was on his way toward becoming a paid propagandist for the Third Reich, while Kahn was counting himself among the exiled and coming to final terms with what it meant to be a German Jew.

Otto Kahn quit New York's Deutscher Press Club in March 1933 as a protest against "the insults and attacks to which my co-religionists . . . are subjected." His censure of Germany no longer distinguished between the German people and the German government, as it had during the war. Now the source of evil was the nation's sins — waged "with the knowledge and tolerance, if not the direct approval of the present German government, representing the majority of the German people."[28] In his search for direction, he drew another specific conclusion when asked, early on, whether it would not be better to emphasize the broader issues of humanity and freedom than to focus on the persecution of German Jews — since "so many German Gentiles no less than Jews have been put upon the rack." Kahn agreed in part, saying, yes, "the world's protest should be based not merely on the issue of the . . . Jews." But he made an important distinction. The "dismissal of men of liberal convictions from their offices or occupations," Kahn reasoned, "is an incident, however deplorable and sickening, of a reactionary revolution." He found "a still more revolting degree of infamy in having the mass of German Gentiles turn hate, cruelty and ruthless oppression upon 600,000 German Jews merely because of the accident of their being born Jews." He called it "unadulterated and cowardly barbarism," and never swayed from this position.[29]

If Kahn assumed that upper- and middle-class Jews in Germany were slightly safer than the rest, that optimism was diminished by the mounting propaganda, boycotts, and violence directed against all Jews. After April 7, when German legal machinery barred Jews in civil service positions from their livelihood, Kahn had to entertain the possibility that Nazism meant "the Jews are finished in Germany." During the spring of 1933, he turned to his Kuhn, Loeb partner Felix Warburg for guidance and solidarity. The honorary chairman of the American Jewish Joint Distribution Committee, Warburg was to Jewish philanthropies what Kahn was to the arts, *Fortune* magazine once said. He was better known, informed, and influential in Jewish communities than Kahn ever wanted to be, or thought he needed to be, before Hitler's seizure of power brought Kahn to realize how much now, as a matter of conscience, he had to be.[30]

In a scramble to help the disenfranchised, Kahn was solicited by E. R. A. Seligman, who appealed on behalf of his former student, Alvin Johnson, in the drive to find fifteen donors, "at $4,000 each," to raise $60,000 annually for The University in Exile at the New School. Considering the financial uncertainties everywhere, Seligman admitted, "It would scarcely have been possible to choose a more unfavorable time" for an appeal of any kind, and indeed when Kahn pledged $500 a year for two years, he apologized to Seligman, writing, "I cannot see my way to make a contribution more adequately expressive of my sympathy." The $5,000 recently given by Kahn to the Metropolitan might have seemed more precious, if not regrettable, under the current circumstances, as it likely did again in June when Addie and Otto Kahn donated only $2,500 to the German Relief Campaign of the American Jewish Joint Distribution Committee.[31]

Throughout 1933, Kahn was redefining himself, a process to be measured only partly by his purse. For most of his life, Otto Kahn idealized bourgeois enlightenment, embraced its liberalism, and practiced its credo of *Bildung*. Modernity offered cosmopolitan progress, and assimilation without renunciation of his Jewish identity was as much a matter of conviction for Otto Kahn as it was, in the words of Peter Gay, "characteristic for German Jews of the Wilhelmine generations."[32] Such ideals had long strung knotty compromises while eluding clarity. But, no matter how irreligious, Otto Kahn was always a Jew. He neither converted to Christianity nor developed any "pretension or competency to be counted among the leaders of the Jewish race," as Kahn put it. He seemed at once to be a Jewish outsider and to be standing outside his Jewishness. For every occasion when openly anti-Semitic journalism led Kahn to pen a protest, there were many more instances in which Kahn thought it impolitic and undignified to publicly express his "contempt and disgust." Kahn similarly lacked an "active interest in specifically Jewish affairs and problems." His patronage more generally attended secular or ecumenical concerns, and his donations to Jewish philanthropies were slim by comparison. He also doubted whether Palestine "or any other country, should become, or is destined to become the 'real national ground' for the Jewish race," and, with regard to "the wisdom and desirability of the fundamental conceptions of Zionism," Kahn vacillated between ambivalent, "open minded," and "not yet persuaded."[33]

Over the years, though, assimilation and evasion had also combined to create the mistaken popular impression that Kahn had converted to Christianity. Out of this came a joke about Kahn strolling down Fifth Avenue with Marshall P. Wilder, the humorist and performer, who happened to be hunchbacked. It was also Wilder who likely originated the repartee in which Kahn says, "You know, I used to be Jewish," with Wilder replying, "You know, I used to be a hunchback."[34] But Otto Kahn's Jewishness was never something that Kahn could or would deny. This was no less true when Kahn denied that he had stopped being a Jew than when the Metropolitan directors saw him always as the Jew. When, for example, he corrected misunderstandings with regard to his conversion, Kahn explained, "My parents were not practicing Jews and did not bring me up to be a practicing Jew. But I never left Judaism and have no idea of doing so." More succinctly, he declared, "I was born, and shall remain a Jew."[35]

Allegiances to his Jewishness took a long route — escorted by adversity, and mapped in part by the illiberality of anti-Semitism in Europe and America. It brought Kahn's resolve to the interesting if not unique conviction that his Jewishness rather than *Bildung* was the taproot of his humanism. It still remained important that he not be denied his role as a guardian of high culture, especially after he was no longer good for the money and no longer found much dignity in being the exceptional Jew among genteel Gentiles. True enough, the anti-Semites in Kahn's American arena differed from those in Germany, in part because they lacked a state to institutionalize the most extreme expressions of their enmity, but the difference also motivated Kahn to prove himself too strong for Americans to dismiss him as easily as the Nazis might.[36]

Subtle shifts occurred in his patronage. There would be no triumphs on the order of what Kahn had done to rescue transatlantic cosmopolitanism during the war. Nor did he establish a refuge for German Jews comparable to what he had done with St. Dunstan's in aid of blinded British veterans during the war. More than money was missing — resolve and foresight were absent as well — but money was a factor in Kahn's comparative paralysis, for at least there were profits during the war. After three years of economic depression, the "heavy shrinkage in our personal possessions and our income" brought the financial tally of the current era to a different and dismal conclusion. Two unprecedented classes of disturbance became the priorities for Kahn's reduced philanthropic capacity: "relieving the misery caused by the persecution of Jews in Germany, some of whom have special claims on me," and "relieving want, need, and suffering in my own country, where unemployment is still distressingly large."[37] The arts still had a special hold on Kahn, at any rate, though he admitted lacking the means "to attempt Maecenas' functions again" when declining an appeal from Waldo Frank, who had written, "I don't see anyone to take your place."[38] "Backers have been swamped by the 'crise,'" echoed an American composer living in France, and Otto Kahn, upon whom so many depended as the backer of last resort, had become a missing link, which some still tried to restore.[39]

As the deciding questions in Kahn's philanthropy were reformed in double time — to measure the world's money crises and the horrors at Germany's epicenter — the protocols of patronage were rewritten to reflect the new terms. Artists, on the demand side, adjusted their projects and pitch accordingly. George Antheil provides one illustrative case. When Kahn turned down his request for assistance during July 1933, the banker-patron issued his now standard regrets and a litany of excuses: "Ordinarily I should have been glad to aid you towards meeting the emergency which confronts you, but under the existing circumstances, I find myself simply swamped with responsibilities, commitments and demands (to which the Nazi persecution of the Jews, which has made many of my co-religionists, including artists, writers, teachers and scientists penniless, has added very urgent claims)." Reminiscent of the old protocol, Antheil waited two months. Then he appealed again, swearing, "I have honestly tried to help myself, for I understood perfectly the great good work you were doing in Europe." He demonstrated knowledge that the German situation "threatens to throw the whole world into darkness," courting Kahn's sympathies further, but Antheil's main aim was to jockey himself through the thick crowd of those seeking Kahn's largesse. He appealed to the patron hero-to-hero, characterizing himself as one who had "given all, and suffered courageously . . . these last ten years . . . for American art in Europe." Weighing everything, Antheil believed it incredibly unjust to face starvation at the very moment that he expected artistic triumph in his homeland. Adding, "Of course there are many people who have suffered this last year," he asked Kahn to think of how the Antheils "have suffered for many years . . . and not to sustain life, as most of the unfortunates are now doing, but for a great and idealist purpose." Kahn, the banker-patron and hero of better times, declined again: "Circumstances have [changed] . . . and with them, alas, my ability, for the time being, to aid artistic causes and individuals in the way and to the extent I should like."[40]

No one easily surrendered even the slimmest hope of financial underwriting from Otto Kahn, and Antheil was not alone in contriving a way to satisfy Kahn's preoccupation with Germany. When Waldo Frank arranged for Charles R. Walker of the Theater Union to meet with Kahn, Frank promised the patron that "he is not going to ask you for money." Even so, Walker came away from the meeting with a better sense of how to next approach Kahn in search of funds. Four days later he sent a written appeal, asking the patron for "anything you choose or can afford to give from $5.00 to $1,000." Adding a specific bait for Kahn, Walker explained, "Since our talk we received the scenario and several scenes of a play by Frederick Wolf, author of 'The Sailors of Cattaro.' . . . He is a German-Jewish doctor, and playwright. The new play is based on his own experience — there is both humor and tragedy in it." Although the Theater Union had found artistic work that should have lured Kahn, he did not write a check.[41] In at least one instance in 1933, however, the ploy of linking an appeal for Kahn's patronage to the theme of Germany succeeded. That case was a solicitation from Em Jo Basshe, who had recently returned from Hollywood, where working on Paramount's version of *The Island of Dr. Moreau* turned out to be an experience "just too terrible for words," and left him feeling ill-prepared for the business of self-promotion that was obviously necessary in the movie industry. Basshe came back East and found "little prospect for work" in New York City, so he retreated to High View, New York, and was now "working on a Nazi play" that promised to be partly Kahn's legacy. It not only drew upon their mutual sympathies, it was also the direct result of Basshe's term as a Guggenheim Fellow in Germany, a fellowship that Kahn had helped him to get.[42]

Better illustrative, though, was the swelling number of pleas that did not need to dream up a connection with Germany, yet exposed Kahn's inability to provide effective aid or agency. Otto Kahn, famous for his own art collections, could think of no one to buy art and other valued possessions from a cousin in Germany who hoped to abandon his home on Adolf Hitler Strasse in Auerbach and who sought cash to book passage to Palestine. Nor would Kahn's modest donation of 100 marks relieve much of the trouble facing the "last remaining Jewish theatre director in Mannheim, at present inactive," who was himself "approached by a great many former Jewish actors for help." Kahn was stymied again when a friend wrote of the many disconsolate, exiled, Jewish intellectuals in Switzerland, and the terrors confronting Jewish publishers and journalists in Germany.[43] It would seem no tale of Nazi persecution was too distant to leave Kahn feeling personally unaffected. He could think of his deceased, jurist brother, for instance, when an appeal arrived from Friedrich H. Maier, for whom the Nazis made it impossible to practice or teach law in Germany. And Kahn could more clearly picture himself in the place of German Jewry when Max Warburg was dismissed from the Hamburg American Line (HAPAG) during the spring. Grieved by that particular stroke of Nazification, Felix Warburg wrote, "The steamship line which a brave Jew, Albert Ballin, built up with all his patriotism and energy, now flies the Nazi swastika on the yardarm." Ironically, Kuhn, Loeb was invited to sit on the board of North German Lloyd in 1929; Kahn would have been their appointed director, and would have been dismissed in 1933 had the firm not adhered to its policy of declining directorships if the partners could not also regularly attend board meetings.[44]

Meanwhile, a heroic effort to find a home abroad for the *Kulturewissenschaftliche Bibliothek Warburg* proceeded in secret negotiations, ultimately bringing this premier center of art and intellectual history to London as the Warburg Institute. No such counterpart was to outwit Nazification in June 1933, when, having transformed the *Volkhochschule Mannheim* into a German school, the Nazi regime dismissed Paul Eppstein, honorary supervisor of the affiliated Bernhard Kahn Reading Room, and rejected any further subsidy from Otto Kahn. The Jewish Telegraphic Agency asked whether Kahn wanted to issue a statement, and he replied, "I have no information." Asked later to help Eppstein find an opportunity in America or elsewhere outside of Germany, Kahn brought the matter to Stephen P. Duggan of the Emergency Committee in Aid of Displaced German Scholars, who promised "personal sympathetic consideration," if not much hope. Reporting back to Eppstein, Kahn's secretary cautioned, "That organization is in receipt of a great many applications similar to yours and the opportunities for complying with such requests are necessarily limited." Then, at the year's end, a reminder to make his annual donation to the Reading Room emerged from Kahn's tickler file, and the patron wrote, "Nothing to be done."[45] No amount of money could have saved the Bernhard Kahn Reading Room, or the liberal principles previously presumed in Kahn's German-Jewish genealogy; but where money and influence or better prescience could at least help, Kahn regularly lacked enough of any and all.

Finally, the circumstances confronting Kahn's surviving older brother, Robert, most profoundly suggests the context in which Kahn was working when he took offense with the Metropolitan board during 1933. Robert Kahn, who labeled himself religiously unaffiliated, had not yet been expelled from the Prussian Academy of Arts (he would be ousted in February 1934). As Nazification of musical life meanwhile removed his modernist Jewish colleagues from the academy more rapidly (Arnold Schoenberg and Franz Schreker lost their posts in May

1933), Robert Kahn and his wife left Berlin for Feldberg, retreating to Obdach, their summer home, which was named for one of his romanticist songs, *"Ein Obdach gegen Sturm"* (A refuge from the storm).[46] As though in counterpoint to the running chaos, Robert Kahn then wrote a memoir about his hero, Johannes Brahms, which he forwarded to Otto in New York. It began in 1886, recounting Robert's embarrassment when introduced to the composer (he spilled champagne on Brahms's trousers), and it recalled their conversations and outings in Vienna during the next year. The memoir, by itself of interest to musicologists, makes an esoteric point about its author, Kahn's family, their heroes, and their expectations, for in broaching this past, Robert Kahn was looking as much for guidance as validation. And if, as one noted scholar argues, considerable distance lay between the easy romanticism claimed by Brahms in the twentieth century and the reception of Brahms (as "a conservative difficult modern classicist") during the nineteenth century,[47] then the Kahns of Mannheim should have shared a similar transition — moving from difficult to easy acceptance, and thereby fulfilling the promise of assimilated emancipation as moderns. But this is not where the arc of assimilation had taken them. With the liberal past outweighed by atrocities and deception in the present, Robert Kahn was confounded. Had the arc moved into irreversible declension or might it again ascend?[48]

Throughout 1933 many friends urged Robert to leave Germany, and by year's end he seemed ready to depart, but he did not. He waited until 1939 before finally emigrating to England; in the interim, Robert weighed the prospects of expatriation, watched the exodus of friends to foreign lands, and, from within the sanctuary of Obdach, he followed a course that one eminent historian of Germany describes as "'inner emigration' . . . an attempt to live in a state of ambiguity and contradiction."[49] His letters to Otto Kahn expressed how Germanness was fixed in his identity and pride. When telling his American brother the story of a medical doctor who, after searching for a long time, found a place for himself and his family in Ankara, Robert began to reveal his own torture about cultural uprooting. He could not yet imagine himself in such foreign surroundings, or that the quality of life could be better in Turkey than in Germany unless one had no other choice for survival. Nor could he imagine the total debasement of every possible good in Germany. Had his homeland grown so foreign to him? He waited, with diminishing degrees of security, hoping some agree-

Endings on the Horizon

able outcome would make these into "interesting times" in history books of the future.[50]

In 1933 modernity meant madness. At a loss for words and much more, Otto Kahn's direct reply to Robert on November 15 leaned on Hans Sachs's "Wahn Wahn, überall Wahn" once again. Two days later Kahn moved at least to set himself right with the Metropolitan crowd. In that small battle of resignation and restoration, the cosmopolitan of assimilation helped to reassure himself that the liberal future would look better in America than in Germany. But the rungs on the ladder of emancipation were being snapped. Dockside, upon returning from a European trip in late September 1933, for example, New York reporters had rushed him for a comment on anti-Semitism in Germany; Kahn said, "As a German Jew, you can imagine how I feel." Such a remark from Kahn would have been unthinkable only a few years earlier, but then the question would have been, too.[51]

Coming so late in life, Kahn's words lacked some of the context and intensity needed to be convincing. Paul Cravath, for instance, had not yet caught on to Kahn's heightening self-identification as a Jew. That much was clear in his negotiations on behalf of the Met, but it was present in another casual oversight, in early December, when Cravath tried to tempt Kahn into buying some fine Rhine and Moselle wines— forgetting, overlooking, or unaware of the American Jewish boycott of German goods. Kahn, in declining, politely educated him: "My predilection for those excellent and salubrious wines is in conflict with my loyalty to the race from which I sprang. . . . My self-respect as a Jew forbids me to place orders for German wines."[52]

As 1933 drew to a close, the future of Germany's Jewry darkened, and Kahn relinquished much of the sanctuary that ambiguity and evasion had afforded. Becoming more articulate in his commitment, more centered in self-identification, he proclaimed himself in a few sentences while serving with David Sarnoff as co-chair at a dinner of the Federation for the Support of Jewish Philanthropic Societies. "This is not the time or the occasion for the Jew to blow his own horn and to point to the immortal achievements of his race and to the outstanding services which it has rendered in every field thrown open to its genius," he began. "The enemies of our race are doing that by the very infamy and atrocity of their warfare." "But this *is* the time for us all to take increased devotion to the Jewish race from the very sorrows which have now befallen it, one of its most tragic chapters in its long history of sorrows (a chapter unbelievable in our day and generation, but alas! hideously true.) In the face of bitter and ruthless provocation, this *is* the time, indeed, for every one of us to heed the call . . . and proudly to stand up and be counted." It was, he concluded, the "occasion . . . for conspicuous and resounding . . . Jewish cohesion and charity."[53]

CHAPTER NINE

Style and Substance

The New Germany and the New Deal arrived in world history with remarkable simultaneity. Each presented different if not always separate issues for Otto Kahn, who neither loathed the new president nor lived long enough for the New Deal to significantly disappoint him. In March 1933, Kahn was happy to be rid of Hoover and impressed with Roosevelt's management of the banking crisis, which quite conservatively stabilized much of America's banking system within days of his inauguration. Kahn began to think the new president could keep the American people from becoming "semi-hysterical" and that perhaps the latest banking crisis was a blessing in disguise. Although he was still "altogether off prophesying," Kahn would freshly hope for "the long expected, frequently foretold, and ever so often deferred turn of the tide" to better times.[1]

As important, Kahn could improvise in accord with the new president, who laid down a familiar melodic line at his inauguration by saying, "The money changers have fled from their high seats in the temple of our civilization. We may now restore that temple to the ancient truths." In Kahn's variation, the conservative investment bankers were still capable of the values that could guide the restoration. So when an investor panicked over Charles Mitchell's expulsion from the presidency of the National City Bank, Kahn counseled him to keep his account with that bank. "The principal reckless people are out," and City Bank's new president, he said, was "a thoroughly sane, calm, conscientious and conservative fellow, who is sure to steer an absolutely safe course."[2] Overall, the correction of monied power was merely unfinished business of the Progressive Era, with FDR offering a middle course of reform, promising the recovery of prosperity and sound financial practices. Kahn agreed in principle, though he understood getting there would not be easy.

If the abounding errors of recent Wall Street history were to be fixed in the new mixed economy, Washington would first want to probe and parade all the wrongdoing. And by early 1933, the federal forums for such investigation seemed limited only by the number of committees that could be humanly staffed and scheduled by the Senate and the House. The one most relevant for Wall Street, however, was the investigation of stock exchange practices by the Senate Committee on Banking and Currency, which began hissing steam in January 1933 after appointing Ferdinand Pecora as its new chief counsel. A Bull Moose Republican turned Wilsonian Democrat, the former chief assistant district attorney from New York City had previously exposed and prosecuted financial abuses and misdeeds in that jurisdiction. Pecora came to Washington expecting to wrap up the committee's business and write its report, yet quickly enough proved there was more to investigate. After running a probe of Samuel Insull's collapsed empire of public utilities, in February he exposed the scandals of City Bank and its investment affiliates, forcing Charles Mitchell to resign. Soon, rather than ending the committee's work, the Senate decided it should be extended, in an across-the-board investigation of all stock exchange practices, with a view toward writing far-reaching, corrective legislation. This turned a searchlight upon private bankers in an unprecedented examination.[3]

Otto Kahn would sit as the lead witness for Kuhn, Loeb. Though he might have stayed abroad or otherwise retreated under cover of poor health, Kahn never seemed to entertain the thought of hiding from this examination. By desire and instinct, Kahn not only wanted to participate, he came to the interrogation intrinsically more trusting of his safety in America than in Germany. He believed that, yes, America was soured by anger, mired in cynicism, and perhaps desperate to find and expel a scapegoat, but it was not Germany. All liberal connectives were not expiring here. Otto Kahn remained welcome in America. FDR's regime would not strip his character of all dignity. On the contrary, it more likely would support Kahn's belief that America would succeed within its inherited liberal traditions.

If such investment in the American destiny gave Kahn a sense of refuge and confidence, there were yet precarious, vulnerable sides to

Kahn's situation within the New Deal. One illustration developed during the spring of 1933 when Lili Deutsch, his sister in Berlin, drew upon what may have been her last American assets. Closing her account at Kuhn, Loeb, she ordered the balance of $35,067 transferred to Paris in care of her son, Frank. Kahn sent the deposit, aware that Deutsch needed ready cash, which make the final details puzzling and meaningful. The money was converted from dollars to francs, a decision Deutsch made with some hesitation, and only after asking Kahn which currency was better. It is puzzling because Roosevelt took America off the gold standard on April 19, and the buzz, if not divine wisdom, in Washington and Wall Street spoke of "imminent inflation," without knowing how it would unfold or its full impact. Yet on April 27 Kahn advised Deutsch, "Have no definite views concerning dollars or francs." The consequences of his indecision were unambiguous. The deposit arrived just as exchange rates felt the effects of the Thomas Amendment, an inflationary measure passed by the Senate that allowed Roosevelt to cheapen the dollar. Dollars declined heavily against francs, reducing Deutsch's yield in the currency exchange by nearly 9 percent.[4] Whether Kahn was careless or unlucky in attending to his sister's needs, he interpreted this situation within a particular frame. Trading in foreign currency had proceeded cautiously during the week of April 19–26, awaiting Washington's next word about the dollar's future value, but the dollar was gaining abroad when Kahn cabled his indifference about the conversion to francs. On the same day, Senator Carter Glass of Virginia spoke out in pained opposition to the White House, urging allegiance to a sound currency. Kahn likely constructed a future in which this logic would prevail. Instead he was dealt another lesson in how appearances could deceive.[5]

An anguished explanation and apology followed. "The dollar deposit turned out so badly," Kahn wrote on May 8, because "it was impossible to judge before hand with any degree of definiteness. Our government's decision to let the dollar find its own international level and, furthermore, take to itself power of inflation, came overnight. Until it did come, the prevailing opinion in most responsible quarters here, as far as I could ascertain it, was that a deposit in dollars would turn out quite as favorably as in francs. The Democratic Party platform had pronounced itself emphatically for the maintenance of sound money and President Roosevelt, only a few months ago, had reiterated his adherence to that policy." Kahn continued toward the conclusion: "It is a crazy world, struggling confusedly with unprecedented problems and facing unprecedented events. Heaven only knows what will ultimately turn out to be the best course of protection to pursue in one's affairs."[6]

Otto Kahn thought himself to be an innocent amid misfortune. Like a protagonist in liberal tragedy, accidental adversity had transformed the hero into a victim. As a modern perched between the romantic and existential, the flaws that tormented Kahn were alterable social conditions, beyond his will or making, and seemingly indifferent to his best intentions. The one course left to save his honor was a renewed attempt to affect the social conditions surrounding him. To "refuse the role of victim and become a new kind of hero," as a founder of cultural studies articulates it, was a consistent trait of the modern dramatic formula that Kahn knew well: "The heroism was not in the nobility of suffering," but rather in "self-fulfillment," for "any such process was a liberation."[7] It was against this private background of struggling confidence and aspirations that Otto Kahn gave a suave, precise, almost faultless performance before the Senate Committee on Banking and Finance.

He walked into the hearing room seeking *succès d'estime* under the most difficult circumstances. The odds stood against any investment banker. Kahn was trying to revive the composed, collected, respected character of old, at a moment when there was no better example of how precariously fragile social perceptions could be than the public's construction of financial morality. Beyond the typecasting of good and evil was the absence of effectual dialogue between Washington and Wall Street, a component clear to Kahn after he contacted Roosevelt in May with regard to the pending Securities Act (House Resolution 5480). The president had replied on May 12: "The difficulty about the opposition to the Securities Bill is that no one seems to be in the least specific in regard to what section or sections will hurt legitimate business. I know you will not mind me being frank with you." Kahn then responded, "I purposely refrained . . . from putting before you specific criticisms . . . inasmuch as I did not feel that I was justified in infringing upon your attention to that extent." He therefore forwarded a "memorandum covering specific points," and reminded the president that lawyers for the Investment Bankers Association had made "a very detailed and complete statement on that bill" in "a full day's session with Chairman Rayburn and some of his associates . . . going over the bill paragraph by paragraph, line by line." Such eleventh-hour lobbying went nowhere at present. The securities bill became law on May 27.[8]

The Pecora Hearings offered an alternative forum, one in which Kahn could distinguish himself from other Wall Streeters. He was an older, more prestigious financier, distinctly different from rapid risers and former salesmen, such as Clarence Dillon, co-founder of Dillon, Read, whose company's default rates climbed well above the average. And unlike "Sunshine Charly" Mitchell of the City Bank, whom Edmund Wilson said looked "cheap in court," Otto Kahn was so appropriate and stylish, one might think he had come from the "Big White Set" of a Fred Astaire movie.[9] The idea is fantasy, but not wholly foolish. As a famous anecdote from the 1920s reminds us, when Kahn attended the premiere of Eugene O'Neill's marathon play *Strange Interlude*, he went directly from his office to the midtown theater for its four o'clock curtain. He later disappeared during the dinner-hour intermission and returned on time for the next curtain, having changed from his office attire to evening wear. Reckoning that Kahn had raced across town and up to his mansion at Ninety-first Street, then back, theater pundit Alexander Woolcott noticed that the financier's earlier companion was missing and presumed she had been left hanging in Kahn's closet.[10] The point of remembering the story is the consistency of Otto Kahn. As fresh as the tea rose that often adorned his lapel, Kahn had a calculated way of injecting new energy into a situation. Thus, under the heat of inquiry through four days of testimony in late June, with a blazing sun beating down on the Capitol and his physician sitting in attendance, Otto Kahn "always appeared immaculately groomed."[11] A "Paradox of Art Lover, Banker and Liberal," he was so uniquely able to move with ease between different houses of illusion that a *Newsweek* journalist only half-imagined him one day in the tiny Greenwich Village playhouse, wearing his perfect tuxedo, seated amid "the cheers of the New York Communists and allied intelligentsia," and adding his own "politely enthusiastic applause" when laborers turned victorious on stage — knowing well that any day soon he would be "playing a star role himself on the Washington stage."[12]

Not surprisingly, when Kahn shared the boards in Washington, one other financier once again topped him on the bill: Jack Morgan. Granted, in terms of banking prestige and investment practices, Kahn was more similar to Morgan than other Wall Streeters. Kuhn, Loeb and

J. P. Morgan stood apart, both from the high-rolling, risk-taking new-comers, as well as from a few other old-line firms that either succumbed to mania or in other ways exercised embarrassingly poor judgment during the 1920s. Kuhn, Loeb and J. P. Morgan came off as twins of respectability, even if Otto Kahn and Jack Morgan were far from identical witnesses. But in the whole universe of banking houses, J. P. Morgan was exceptional—it was the bankers' bank, an unchanging symbol of financial command and control. No firm came close except Kuhn, Loeb, for in railroad financing the two firms were practically on even terms. City Bank originated more new securities in 1929 than Morgan and Kuhn, Loeb combined, but, in Pecora's words, the impression held fast that "J. P. Morgan was, and still is, far and away the most important single factor in the field."[13]

Jack Morgan's appearance also engendered an "almost hysterically intense" atmosphere. Practically everyone in America knew his name; hardly anyone knew his face. Over the years, out of "extreme aversion to photographers and interviewers," Morgan had delegated public relations to other partners, who proved more adept, debonair, and relaxed when standing before the press and its cameras. In this manner he was completely different from Otto Kahn, whose many scrapbooks of press clippings evidenced how frequently studio and roving photographers were given access to him. Catching him on the golf links, backstage at the Met, in his study at home, and in his office at Kuhn, Loeb, there were newsprint photographs of Kahn standing beside Enrico Caruso, clasping the hand of actress Mary Astor, and watching Jo Davidson sculpt Mussolini. The celebrated banker-patron occasionally flickered from the silver screen as well. Appearing as himself in *Glorifying the American Girl* (1929), a feature produced by Florenz Ziegfeld, Kahn is shown arriving for an opening night at the theater, having been announced with an enthusiastic welcome for "a really big shot."[14]

Morgan, who lacked anything approaching Kahn's experience with the public gaze, encountered a bizarre moment of embarrassment in his congressional appearance. At a tense moment during Morgan's testimony, conservative Democrat Carter Glass vented his annoyance with chief counsel Pecora's seemingly endless, aimless questioning, saying, "We are having a circus, and the only things lacking now are the peanuts and colored lemonade." A few weeks earlier, during the House debate over the Securities Act, Representative Sam Rayburn had also quoted P. T. Barnum's remark "that the American people pay to be

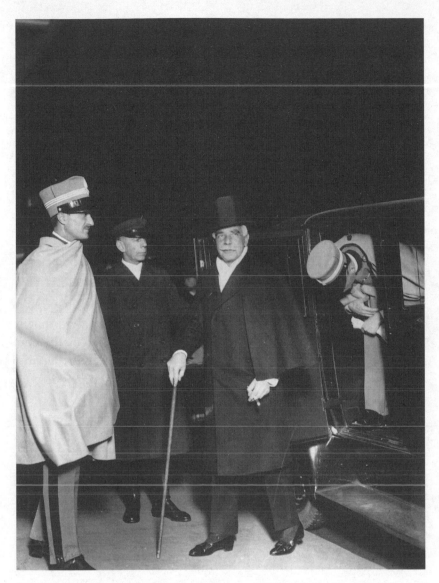

The familiar Otto Kahn arriving for opening night. (Robert Tuggle Collection)

gulled," then continued, "Millions of citizens have been swindled into exchanging their savings into worthless stocks." With one comment following the other, Ringling Brothers and Barnum & Bailey Circus smelled the chance for publicity. A press agent brought one of the circus's midgets to the hearings, and on the morning of June 1, while awaiting the resumption of the proceedings, a newsman escorted the tiny woman into the Senate Caucus Room, where within minutes she was seated on Morgan's lap: flashbulbs popped, shutters snapped, and the result was one of the more unusual portraits ever made of a Morgan. Some contended that the picture humanized the banker, but the photo mishap appalled Morgan, his partners, and others, including the Senate committee's chairman, Duncan Fletcher of Florida, who issued a reprimand: "I understand that some photographers had a sort of performance here when a certain picture was taken of Mr. Morgan with some midget on his lap. . . . I consider that wholly undignified, wholly unwarranted. . . . I think it was taking advantage of him. . . . I am asking the newspapers not to publish that picture or those pictures. . . . In fact, I think we shall do away entirely with the taking of pictures from now on." In any case, the visual pun of the titan and the midget proved too irresistible for news editors, and the picture when published brought laughter nationwide. It could only have been worse if a tommy gun had been slipped under the arm of the money lord to illustrate the popular elision of banker and gangster—the bankster. Riotous giggles probably broke loose at Kuhn, Loeb, where Kahn was preparing to be the committee's next witness, and Frederick Warburg (son of Felix) flippantly said Kuhn, Loeb's testimony would "be like the Morgan investigation, except that we're going to bring our own midgets."[15]

On the sober side, warning the photographers helped Kuhn, Loeb. This was still the legislators' show and they did not want *commedia dell'arte*. To avoid expulsion from the caucus room, the photographers practiced greater decorum with later witnesses, and the more restrained environment gave Kahn a custom-built setting for the cameras to capture his most handsome, tutorial poses. One of particular note displayed Kahn in conversation, "half reclining on the conference table." With his body resting on the right hip and elbow, and his left palm stretched flat for balance, he leans toward Pecora—eyes fixed on the inquisitor—while a dozen listeners surround the table, hanging on every word. Kahn, a cigarette burning in hand, is relaxed, and Pecora—better known for unrelenting belligerency—breaks a congenial smile.[16] The picture means more when viewed alongside the testimony of Kahn among other Wall Streeters. With moneylenders condemned in the court of public opinion, these hearings were intended not to distinguish between good and bad moneylenders, but to agitate and condemn them all. Bankers frequently resisted, without

Style and Substance

much success, except for Otto Kahn, who substituted diligence for negligence and prudence for recklessness.

His testimony began at ten o'clock on the morning of Tuesday, June 27, 1933. Escorted to the hearing by three attorneys from the firm headed by Paul Cravath, and by a few Kuhn, Loeb associates to coach him, for the better part of four days Otto Kahn was the firm's only sworn witness. Ferdinand Pecora, counsel to the committee, presided over a panel of seven senators. The two legislators best versed in financial matters were absent: James Couzens, Republican of Michigan, was attending the London Economic Conference, and Carter Glass had gone home for the summer. Both had been present and vocal during Morgan's testimony. Whether that meant Kahn was considered a second-tier witness is unclear, but their absences certainly made it easier for him. The presence of Kahn's personal physician likely helped him more. Both Pecora and the committee knew of the banker's illnesses, and consideration for his health may well have dulled the cutting edge in their questioning. Nonetheless, while another man in his seat and physical condition might have been admonished in a modern version of death and the miser, what made Kahn's circumstances more conducive to empathy was more than merely his costume, condition, popularity, or ethics added together. Kahn's command of rhetoric, purely if not simply, enticed his audience not only toward congeniality, but also toward his desired conceptual framework. That much was evident almost immediately.[17]

Within the first half-hour of testimony Kahn began to unsettle his examiners' preconceptions. Offering the idea of "reciprocal fairness" as a substitute for avarice, he set out the similarities between investment banking and the services of the lawyer, plumber, or tailor, and, to prove himself and his point, Kahn stressed the ethical congruities of consumer choice, bringing high finance into a middle line of vision. Using the parallel most effectively when he compared the investment banker to the physician who neither advertises nor chases clients, he explained that a banker builds a practice by his reputation, integrity, good work, and results. Perhaps public knowledge of Kahn's own frequent consultations with medical experts made this analogy folksy and sensible, yet Kahn built it into a sophisticated, efficient rhetorical convention: "Clients feel that if they have a problem of a financial nature,

Dr. Kuhn, Loeb & Co. is a pretty good doctor to go to. . . . Our only attractiveness is our good name and our reputation for sound [advice] and integrity. If that is gone, our business is gone. . . . Every leading banker holds his position, solely by reason of the confidence of the community in his skill. . . . If I am known to be a pretty good doctor I am likely to keep my patients. If I am not . . . the patient will quit me, he will quit me cold." There was no mistaking his rhetorical intent. Otto Kahn gave his audience something for which their cynicism was unprepared—the plausible truth of honest virtue surviving on Wall Street. That set up common ground on the contentious field.

In an instant, his inquisitors paraphrased Kahn's metaphor in questions more specific to the investment banker's practice, asking him how, after the relationship has been established and advice dispensed, the rate of compensation for services was decided. In principle, it was an easy question that Kahn could answer with approximate truth, but that was not the same as being persuasive. Bankers' compensation was hotly contested in the current context, where everything about securities exchange held potential for federal regulation. Like margin loans and short-selling pools, the "spread," or the difference between the proceeds received by a corporation and the price paid by the public for an issue, was, at the moment, serving the idea that securities' exchange milked the public while prioritizing the profits of bankers and brokers. Kahn's response elaborated the reciprocal fairness of a "reasonable spread"—stabilized over time "between 2¼ and 2½ percent" to compensate the originator for risks taken. Pecora then directed Kahn to explain the "rule or custom among bankers to keep hands off the client" of another banker. Kahn sought further common ground. "I should think that rule is very much in the spirit of the kind of code proposed by the National Industrial Recovery Act," he said, trying to share some of the favorable light that currently shined upon the New Deal.[18]

The rhythm of his speech accelerated spontaneously. Kahn next gave an unsolicited example to clarify the virtues of fair competition over cutthroat competition. He spoke of the years 1926–28, "when to my knowledge 15 American bankers sat in Belgrade, Yugoslavia, making bids, and a dozen American bankers sat in half a dozen South and Central American States, or in Balkan States . . . outbidding the other foolishly, recklessly, to the detriment of the public, compelling him to force bonds upon the public at a price which is not determined by the value of that security so much as by his eagerness to get it." When he finished, Senator Edward P. Costigan, Democrat of Colorado, asked him to "describe in greater detail the competition of bankers in Europe to which you made reference." Kahn answered, "I'm not certain what reference I did make." He had stepped into trouble by going off-script, and for a few moments thereafter Costigan pressed to know who the bankers were, and if they were leading bankers. Kahn would neither "graduate them" to the ranks of leadership nor name names. He merely intended to emphasize that Kuhn, Loeb stood above the mad competition and would not stoop to it.[19] Tougher terrain came with the following question: "Would not the corporation seeking financing obtain better terms if there were more competition among bankers for these financial operations?" A known opponent of competitive bidding, Kahn had long fought its implementation by the ICC, and his ideas directly challenged the sentiments of Pecora and the more liberal senators on the committee. Kahn figured the committee would attack his views as slavish self-interest, so he made a preemptive move. "I am too old to have axes to grind," he replied. "I am trying to answer according to my best judgment and through long experience." In an extraordinary public reference to his own life expectancy, he volunteered that his opinion about competitive bidding had nothing to do with how it "affects my pocket for the next few years that I still have, but not for very, very long."[20]

This first round of his examination thus revealed Kahn's basic heuristic procedure. Everything said previously mattered in both exploring the problem and supporting his conclusions. Everything ultimately came down to character. In other words, Kahn had established a series of repeatable units that could be used in various contexts to make his audience more receptive to his own point of view. Almost always, Kahn's position was supported by his forty years of experience, but also his ability to map postulates of similarity rather than contrariety. It followed that competitive bidding was "bidding at the expense of the public . . . gambling with the back of the public," and the consequence for the corporation and the public, he concluded, would be the loss of "year-round," long-term, learned service of the best bankers, who would likely abstain from bidding "a price which is unduly high."[21] The warning was fully consistent with a position taken in one of his pamphlets from 1922. "If I had to write it again," he said upon introducing it into the current record, "I would write it exactly the same way."

Indeed, his colloquial version of the argument presently differed only in the efficient comparison between investment bankers and other service providers, which Kahn used to drive home one point—a client's loyalty to the banker was a matter of rational choice rather than coercion or extortion. A railroad could turn to another banker just as easily as a person could choose another plumber. ("If he overcharges me I go to somebody else. If he tries anything crooked on me I go to somebody else.") It was much like choosing a tailor, said Kahn: do you want a cheap suit of clothes to keep you warm for awhile, or you are looking for quality and lasting value?[22]

Through most of the morning session, then, Kahn had some control of the committee—not enough to overcome all of the differences of interpretation, but enough to reduce them. During the next phase of discussion, the focus fell upon the general workings of the Kuhn, Loeb partnership and its affiliates. Other witnesses from the firm spoke occasionally and Kahn more frequently consulted his associates for answers. As the questions grew more varied, his answers grew shorter and the intensity subsided. But before the luncheon recess, Kahn advanced a few additional impressions of a favorable kind. In one, he made it clear that depositors' funds were always protected by ample reserves. In another, he described the firm as "a family affair," with partners who "sit close together all day" and "know pretty well what goes on." They did not take official meetings together, Kahn said, because whenever the partners convened a meeting, "Everyone wants to 'shoot off his face.' " Time was wasted on just "too much talk" (and probably more than a few squabbles, he neglected to say). What he did reveal, however, served two purposes. Mainly, Kahn supplied a reasonable explanation for why there were no minutes from partners' meetings for the committee to examine, and without minutes, Kahn took an easy route toward another important impression—his firm had nothing to hide. As a private bank Kuhn, Loeb was not legally subject to public audit, but Kahn said, "I personally see no reason why we should not be examined. . . . Knowing my slant of mind . . . it probably has always been my attitude." His advocacy of disclosure was in direct opposition to the Morgans' position on the question. Not without interest to Kahn was the committee counsel's thorny history in prying information from the house of Morgan, which legally challenged Pecora's right to examine its statements of profits and losses.[23]

If by now Kahn had won Pecora's respect, the committee's counsel was not ready to reveal it. Instead, after the luncheon recess, Pecora grilled Kahn once more on competitive bidding. This time he focused specifically on the ICC's requirement of competitive bidding for railroad equipment trusts. The effect was choragic. Numerous senators joined in challenging some of Kahn's core propositions, and Kahn's explanations grew more eloquent as the questions grew more redundant. When the chairman tempted Kahn into a criticism of the ICC, his response was so judicious that Kentucky Democrat Alben Barkley drew a round of laughter by injecting, "Are there any vacancies in the diplomatic service?" Kahn was really on his game now. Never missing a beat, he kept rolling toward his point, so neither Kahn nor anyone else weighed the twisted irony—the idea of putting this rhetorical talent into diplomatic service was nearly twenty years too late.[24]

Next, Kahn told of the mania years from his vantage point. Since Kuhn, Loeb "did not join in the general scramble" of creating securities corporations, he could use the best possible light to do so. At some length, he recalled the "on and off" signs of mania in the late 1920s, when the public was convinced "that every piece of paper would be worth tomorrow twice what it was worth today," and "the whole banking community together" had neither the power to create nor prevent this mood. When "bankers tried to pull in their horns" (i.e., curtail their bullishness), outsiders and industrial corporations came in, sensing the chance to loan money, and said, " 'If the banks will not loan enough, we are going to loan, ourselves,' " according to Kahn. He disliked the unprecedented level of brokers' loans and explained that "the Federal Reserve might have stemmed the mania" before "anything but a catastrophe could have stopped it." Kahn was taking a softly monetarist position, except in his vision of what America really lacked: a moral influence, which no legislation could provide. But it might be found, Kahn emphasized, if the Federal Reserve was a right-minded force, like the governor of the Bank of England, possessing the "power to control and restrain and be listened to and heeded, utterly and impartially and disinterestedly except for the good of the country."[25]

Upon Kahn's powerful conclusion, Pecora promptly changed the subject, introducing a matter more likely to embarrass Kahn's wisdom as well as his morality. This is how it unfolded:

Mr. Pecora: I want to ask you about an issue of $20 million guaranteed sinking fund 6½ percent gold bonds, which was made by your firm in conjunction with the Guarantee Co., on about June 25, 1925, on behalf of the Mortgage Guarantee Bank of Chile. Are you familiar with the transaction?

Mr. Kahn: You have touched a sore point.

Mr. Pecora: I did not know how sore it was.

Mr. Kahn: It is the only issue which my firm has made since the war, the only foreign issue which is in default. We made it after what we believed to be a very careful and thorough examination. We had before us the record of a country which for over 70 years had never been in default. We had before us the record of a country whose constitutional history was almost free from revolutions and which for many, many years had a favorable balance of trade then. We had before us the history of a concern whose business was the making of first mortgages, which was guaranteed by the Government of Chile and which was vouched for by the [U.S.] Department of Commerce in the records that we found. . . . Everything that we could find out seemed to prove that this was a bond that we were completely justified in sponsoring.[26]

Kahn sounded rehearsed as he made his next move, which was evasive. The late Mortimer Schiff had been the partner in charge of the issue, and Kahn was in Europe when the negotiations occurred. This allowed Kahn to deflect responsibility from himself and leave it to his partner, Benjamin Buttenweiser, to untangle the five separate issues ($90 million in bonds) that Kuhn, Loeb had issued for the Chilean National Mortgage Bank between 1925 and 1929. But before leaving the lead witness role, Kahn tasted a little of what Buttenweiser would get. If Kahn assumed that he or Kuhn, Loeb could guide the morality of the American investment public, Pecora was out to discredit that impression. The Chilean issues made Kuhn, Loeb part of the general scramble for foreign loans, and Pecora had previously embarrassed the National City Bank with a similar line of questioning.

The committee's counsel would also raise doubts related to Kuhn, Loeb's competence in assessing relevant political risks and economic forecasts. The former was introduced with this question: "What kind of government existed in Chile" at the time of the original issue? Kahn answered, "They had a new deal, and a new government came in . . .

with a moderate degree of violence." Senator Barkley chimed in, "It might have been called a raw deal," and Pecora rhymed, "It was cold steel." Indeed, there had been two military juntas between September 1924 and January 1925, three heads of state in 1925, and persistent crackdowns on organized labor throughout that year. Kahn replied, "But we were advised by counsel that the acts of that government were absolutely valid in law and in every other way." Pouring more salt on the wound, Pecora asked, "Do you know what the present market quotations are for those bonds?" Kahn answered, "Unfortunately I do know, yes." They were quoted at about 13; they had been issued at 97 or more. Later Pecora contended that Kuhn, Loeb had ignored published warnings of the U.S. Department of Commerce, which in early 1927 considered the overproduction of nitrates and the Chilean financial situation to be "very serious" and "adverse."[27]

Questions of this nature were pursued through the remainder of the first day and nearly the whole of the next, with Buttenweiser giving the answers and Kahn getting some time to rest. Kahn sat by attentively and occasionally asked if he could "butt in." At mid-morning on Wednesday, he tried to clarify the practice by which originators support the selling price of a bond, and made two minor rhetorical errors in the process. First, he tried to compare the buyer of a bond with the shopper at a department store, saying neither could return merchandise for a refund. Pecora interposed, "Isn't that a rather unfortunate analogy, considering the growing practice of the department stores to make refunds?" Kahn answered, "As far as I know that practice does not prevail. It has never prevailed in my instance." Pecora rejoined, "Then you do not shop in the same stores as Mrs. Pecora does," getting laughter with the reply.[28] Of course, Otto Kahn was unlikely to buy clothing, bric-a-brac, or anything else at Macy's or Marshall Fields. In overstating the universalizing quality of his analogy, Kahn had inadvertently constructed the image of himself as an elite who knew little about the everyday, common experience of the "forgotten man." Kahn quickly moved away from the digression and toward the special circumstances affecting bonds if the distribution takes longer than initially expected. Bonds are less speculative than stocks, Kahn explained. "A bond is not like a stock that shoots up like weeds. A bond is a tender plant. It has got to be nursed" and "has to be watered." Laughter broke in again and Kahn realized what he had done. "I do not mean 'watered' in the sense of stock . . . [or] 'stock watering,' " the slang for overvaluing stock.[29]

Minor in the context of the Chilean discussion, Kahn's interjections had consequences for the next phase of the hearings. He had called attention to the millionaire's lifestyle, and intimated the banker's extraordinary power to protect against losses. These threads were soon entangled in the most harrowing hours of the inquiry for Kahn, which began as the second day of testimony and discussion of Chile drew to a close. Pecora now began questioning Kahn about his personal income taxes. The subject was anticipated, and the basic facts were clear. Like the Morgan partners and Charles Mitchell, who earlier went through less intense interrogation on this matter, Otto Kahn had paid no federal income taxes for the years 1930, 1931, and 1932. Pecora's probing led the bankers nearer to the trap with which the government had caught Al Capone, but the income tax stories were also guaranteed to grab the next morning's headlines, which is what Pecora needed after a long, boring day of unrevealing testimony on Chile. In a related agenda item, Pecora was providing "the backdrop for the 1934 Revenue Act" by exposing loopholes in the current tax statutes, including a few that Kahn regularly exploited. Among these, the most prominently discussed was the year-end practice of selling securities at a loss to a relative, then buying them back at a later date.[30]

What sounded logical in rehearsals worked against Kahn under oath. He came ready to portray himself as a busy man with many interests, who let others prepare his taxes and who gave little attention to such matters himself. He intended to claim a legitimate lack of knowledge, memory, or recall, then show he knew more than expected—except that he fumbled, partly because he was fatigued from the length and heat of the day, but mostly because he came prepared to discuss the tax years 1931 and 1932. Instead Pecora asked him about 1930. It left Kahn shuffling, sounding evasive, and in missing his mark of effective persuasion, one statement would haunt him with particular regret: "My ignorance of income-tax affairs is abysmal, and always has been, and I am afraid always will be. . . . I cannot tell you anything about it which would be any more than the merest guesswork." In hindsight, Kahn thought it sounded stupid coming from a man who made so many speeches about federal tax policy.[31] As the hearings adjourned for the day, Pecora warned, "I would suggest, then, Mr. Kahn, that between now and the session tomorrow morning you seek to refresh your recollection, either by consulting records or by consulting the recollection of any of your counsel." A humbled Otto Kahn replied, "I will diligently

Style and Substance

do so. I will try my best to do so, Mr. Pecora, and I hope to be able to be a more competent witness tomorrow than I am just now."[32]

Kahn spent the evening talking on the telephone with accountants and tax attorneys in New York, scribbling notes, then cramming to fill his mind with details. Sleep came hard that night. Between the heat, his wrestling with the doubts raised about his character, and his promise to perform more competently, an old memory of E. H. Harriman likely helped Kahn to regain his balance and determination. Years earlier Kahn had told the world that his first vivid impression of Harriman had occurred on "a hot summer afternoon" in 1897, when, "looking pale, weary and tired out," the railroad magnate pitched an idea for new business at the offices of Kuhn, Loeb: "We did not particularly care for it, and told him that we preferred not to join in the transaction. He argued to convince us of its merits, and, finally, not having made any headway, he desisted. I thought he had accepted our refusal. He got up to go, but turned around at the door and said: 'I am dead tired this afternoon, and no good any more. . . . I will tackle you again to-morrow, when I am fresh. I'm bound to convince you and to get you to come along.' He did . . . and we yielded to the sheer persistency of the man, and to the lucidity of his arguments." The anecdote could now inspire the protégé who had since become a senior. Coincidentally, he was staying at the home of his mentor's widow, Mary Averill Harriman, while in Washington. In any case, Kahn would return more confident and better informed about the data in question.[33]

. . . .

RESURGENT

When the hearings resumed, Kahn read a statement, "jotted down in a rough way," that reflected his overnight conversations with counsel and relevant facts with regard to the securities from 1930. An additional attorney, familiar with Kahn's tax returns, had arrived from New York, ready to offer further information, documents, and supportive testimony. Kahn proceeded in better form. His recollection sounded less elusive when balanced by fewer lapses of memory, and Kahn regained trust in the process, for there was a previous ruling in Kahn's favor by the Tax Appeals Board of the Internal Revenue Service on the same stocks in question. But his best opportunity to again snatch the momentum and direction of the hearings began with his explanation of motive. Pecora wanted to know whether Kahn sold stocks to his daughter in anticipation of further decline in their market value, and whether such sales were his "annual custom." To the former question, Kahn responded, "That would be a very mean element, and I hope I was not guilty of it." The answer to the latter question was a simple yes, so Pecora pursued it further:

> Mr. Pecora: Was there any reason why you picked out at that particular time in each year for the making of sales of substantial blocks?
>
> Mr. Kahn: I suppose . . . to determine how much I owed the Government.
>
> Mr. Pecora: Just what do you mean by that?
>
> Mr. Kahn: To determine what was my loss as compared to my income.
>
> Mr. Pecora: Well do you mean that they were made in order to enable you to take what is known as a tax loss?
>
> Mr. Kahn: Tax loss is an ugly term and is an ugly connotation. I suppose it will be abolished forever after you finish with it here.

His last remark intrigued Pecora. But in asking Kahn to explain it, the chief counsel let Kahn turn from the minutia of individual stock transactions toward generalized, philosophical subjects. The senators on the committee, judging by their silence through nearly the whole of the tax questions, shook off their boredom and came to life with greater interest.[34]

Kahn moved from the petty toward a colloquy, making a direct statement of his opinion about the capital gains penalty. "However just in itself it may have been intended," Kahn considered it bad law, "apt to irritate public sentiment and cause resentment." Asked by Senator Frederick Steiwer of Oregon to elaborate on his objections, Kahn added, "The Government speculates on people making money or losing money. In my humble opinion, that is not the business of the Government. The Government ought to be assured of a steady revenue in good or bad times." Steiwer then gave Kahn another gift, when, switching to other effects, he wondered whether the capital gains tax "was a factor in the great [stock] inflation of 1928 and 1929" because it discouraged profit taking. Next, Senator Barkley volunteered the inverse scenario, that selling at a loss for tax purposes "may depress the value of stocks." Kahn was in a position to exploit the paradox. He agreed with them both, adding another evil to the list of effects: "It encourages bear cliques who throw themselves on the market and say . . . 'Let us depress the market for a while.'" Heads turned in stunned recognition:

Style and Substance

Steiwer noted that Otto Kahn was "the first witness connected with the New York banking fraternity" to admit that "bears are able to depress the market." Previously, representatives from the New York Stock Exchange had roundly denied or minimized the negative impact of bear pools. Kahn, in contrast, said, "I haven't any doubt about it. . . . Bull pools or bear pools are . . . a social evil. . . . They ought to be looked into. . . . Whatever your committee can do to regulate and correct the damaging effect . . . ought to be done."[35]

Suddenly, Kahn was more than neither adversarial nor malevolent. He was philosophically aligned with the investigators — an expert whose opinion acknowledged much of the emerging consensus. For instance, Kahn said, short selling was legitimate, but bear raids were "a socially damaging thing" ("You get a gang of people together and they say, 'Now, we will raid the market. Now we will spread rumors. Now we will create fear. Now we will scare people out of their stocks' "). Speculation, he continued, was just and necessary "in every line of business." Its difference from gambling was the distinction between reasonableness and rashness. Speculation became gambling, said Kahn, when it was "not in proportion to a man's available means," and when it put one's ability to meet future obligations at precarious risk. The distinction was "a matter of moderation." Then, he made a moderate concession to the need for regulation, saying if more supervision would curtail the harmful effects of wild speculation, it would serve the public interest. Kahn was now at the crossroads of past, present, and future trends in the federal supervision of securities exchange. Neither the position nor Kahn's intention was unique. Many from Wall Street agreed in principle with the recent securities legislation, while they also opposed specific aspects of the law and sought its amendment. In a private moment during the hearings, Kahn also told Pecora the "housecleaning" was good: "Wall Street's leaders, Kahn said, had been aware of the abuses and evils," but were "reluctant to expose friends and business associates" or "disturb the great stock market boom."[36]

At Pecora's prompting, Kahn offered a further critique of what went wrong in the 1920s. He began another narrative, choosing to picture the "megalomania" of America and its ironies: "We thought we were bigger than we actually are as yet" and "thought we could swing the whole world," yet could not reconcile contradictory desires — "You cannot be a great exporting nation without being . . . either an importing nation or a great loaning nation." There was as well a lapse in courage and judgment—"We thought we would like to be a great loaning nation," but as soon as there were losses, Kahn said, America turned off the tap. At the same time, everyone in America was saying "a new era had come . . . an opportunity the like of which the world has never seen and which would not end for years to come." All sorts of experts lent a hand in creating this atmosphere: bankers, brokers, salesmen, journalists, professors, and politicians. As to which was the most responsible, Kahn said, "It is difficult to allocate the leading share to anyone." At any rate, the result was clear. Most people stopped discriminating between good and bad stocks or bonds. There were havens of conservatism, and of course Kuhn, Loeb was one of them, yet with "hardly a sane person in America," he said, "we were all swept away by the belief . . . that everything was going to be good."[37]

Otto Kahn was clearly back on his game and enjoying himself. Pecora had to cut him off before Kahn completely dominated the tournament, so he returned to the more tedious discussion of banker's taxes. The senators' voices fell silent again, and the remaining hour before lunch mainly repeated much of what had been said before Kahn began his rally. Then the afternoon questioning turned to old chestnuts among potential headline grabbers, and milked the theme of a money trust, its syndicates, deficiencies of competition, and implements of control. It would seem at first to revisit all the suspicions of interlocking interests and financial oligarchy that had famously occupied the House Banking and Currency Committee in 1912, with strident counsel from Samuel Untermyer, in its investigation of the concentration of money and credit, except now Otto Kahn immediately gave it all a contemporary twist. He compared the courtesy, friendly competition, and mutual goodwill of the bankers' gentlemanly code to both the National Industrial Recovery Act and the securities bill. Proclaiming himself "in sympathy with the purpose" of both, he blew Pecora off course.[38] The committee counsel did no better with his next tack. Attempting to break Kahn's impression of "enlightened self-interest," he returned to Kahn's analogy of the banker and the doctor or lawyer, stressing the win-at-all-cost kind of service given by the lawyer to his client, to imply a banker's loyalty to a railroad would outweigh the importance of the public. "If he were a stupid banker, yes," Kahn replied; the smart banker would think "the interests of the public are just as important as the interests of the railroad," and these, he continued, were "identical" with the interests of the banker.[39]

Style and Substance

With Kahn holding firm, Pecora chose another weapon. The remainder of the day and all the next morning was devoted to the Pennroad Corporation, the investment trust owned by the Pennsylvania Railroad, and a complex topic. Pecora would interrogate the motives and form of the company's organization, but also the bank's fees, compensations, and profits from financing it. While the senators said nothing, their counsel pushed into a long round of questions, dividing the whole into pieces like pie, trying to show that each slice was flavored to Kuhn, Loeb's liking. He highlighted those occasions when the firm acquired Pennroad stock "at one price and sold it at a higher price," tallying up better than $5 million earned by the firm during eight months. Pecora alleged that the bankers were buying and selling at prices that guaranteed their immediate profit.[40] Kahn's responses kept looking at the whole pie, as if to say the bankers could never know the taste or texture until they actually took a bite. When Pecora reduced it all to dollars and cents, Kahn elaborated contingencies; when Pecora suggested a sure thing, Kahn underscored risks; and, when Pecora likened fees and compensation to profit, Kahn asserted the difference. The parley reached its peak when Pecora spoke of "fees paid to you for managing underwriting syndicates":

Mr. Kahn: Not only managing but being responsible.

Mr. Pecora: Assuming a responsibility?

Mr. Kahn: Assuming a complete obligation for six weeks, during which six weeks the panic of October 25 [1929] occurred, and during that panic we stood responsible for $45,000,000.

Mr. Pecora: That responsibility was assumed by you and discharged by you in a fashion that returned a profit to you didn't it?

Mr. Kahn: It might have returned a very heavy loss.

Mr. Pecora: I know, but I am speaking of what happened, not of what might have happened.

Mr. Kahn: Well, by the grace of God we got a profit when we stood the risk of a heavy loss.

Later, Kahn added that his firm never sold any of the stock it acquired on option until other members of the selling group had cleared their accounts.[41]

Finally, Pecora introduced a draft of the Pennroad's stock-listing application to the Philadelphia exchange, including a letter from Henry H. Lee, president of the Pennroad, which plainly suggested

Kuhn, Loeb should conceal the bankers' options. Kahn was asked why the application had been so drafted. The question was irrelevant, since "in two conspicuous places" the final application had revealed the bankers' option, but Pecora stalked Kahn, wanting to know Lee's original intent. Kahn resplendently answered, "What motive, or what imp of mischief guided Mr. Lee's pen when he drafted or dictated this letter, I could not possibly imagine. I only know that the moment it came to our attention we said: Of course it must contain a full disclosure of that option. And it does." His sense of timing could not have been better. A few minutes later the committee would break for lunch, and the chairman had earlier expressed "hopes of finishing today." Kahn thus knew his part in the play was drawing to a close. He positioned himself for a strong finale by showing the checks and balances in the practice of a reputable banker.[42]

After lunch Kahn's testimony moved through further particulars about Pennroad, to the context of 1929, and what he felt went wrong or right more generally before and since the crash. On the side of wrong were excessive greed and fear, people who took advantage of the public's gullibility, and people who stimulated the market by pooling, short selling, or short raiding. Asked what could compel propriety in securities exchange, Kahn gave a fairly representative sample of his most idealistic thoughts. Public opinion was the best guardian. "If . . . condemned as something no decent person ought to do," he said, "ultimately no decent person will do it." The watchfulness of the stock exchange came next and, if the stock exchange could not control improprieties itself, it was up to government "to apply severer measures." But mostly Kahn believed Wall Street had been sufficiently educated in recent years. The same mistakes "will not in our generation occur again," he asserted. Finally, the recent securities' legislation would go a long way toward that end. Demanding full disclosure, and putting a "policeman around the corner," it created "a watchdog," Kahn said, "who not only can bark, but can also bite," if Wall Street should "indulge again in practice that are socially, economically . . . undesirable."[43] The problems were mostly solved already, thought Kahn, in contrast to the federal legislators. As Kahn approached his exit, he made one last substantive soliloquy to this effect.[44]

What little remained on Pecora's agenda for Kahn consisted of subpoenaed information that needed to be introduced into the record, concerning the partners' directorships, their loans to directors and officers of banking institutions and other corporations, and a reporting of stocks and bonds offered by Kuhn, Loeb during the period from 1927 to 1931. With previous and later witnesses, Pecora used such information more aggressively than he did with Kahn. Probably because Kahn had been the most courteous and philosophically agreeable witness to face the committee, Pecora did no more than to place the evidence in the record without comment. He then prepared to excuse Otto Kahn. As he had done with previous witnesses, Pecora invited Kahn to offer a final statement. When given the same opportunity, Jack Morgan introduced an essay of some two thousand words that elaborated "certain points we believe are not yet fully clear."[45] Kahn's exit instead evoked one of the fundamental adages of good theater: know when to get off. He simply wished "every possible success to the labors of your committee." Senator Fletcher returned the goodwill ("You have been very kind and generous in your cooperation, and we are indebted to you"). And Pecora insisted the record show a public expression of "our thanks to the witness and his firm for the cooperation they have uniformly accorded us from the beginning of our investigation into their activities."[46] It was the closest this committee ever came to applause and ovation, and Kahn's testimony was the crowning performance of his financial lifetime.

The reviews generally agreed that it was a tour de force. Colleagues in Chicago marveled over Kahn's "German exactness and French wit." One friend from abroad "flushed with pride" over the "sympathetic and appreciative" coverage given to Kahn by British and French journalists, adding, "It was not thus with the Morgan enquiry." Winthrop Aldrich of the Chase National Bank in New York appreciated Kahn's "very well conceived and brilliantly expressed" testimony for other reasons. Aldrich would face the committee as a reform-friendly witness in December. He thought Kahn's appearance had been "extremely helpful in improving the attitude of the Senate Committee and public toward investment banking in general."[47] At first, Kahn was himself nearly "smugly complacent" about his performance, that is, until he began replaying the scenes in his mind. While crossing the Atlantic immediately after the hearings, he became obsessed with his mistakes and misstatements, especially with regard to tax dodging. The soliloquy brought him to composing rejoinders that might "elucidate matters for the plain people and the politicians." His attorneys counseled him to "let sleeping dogs lie, at least for the time being."[48] Kahn obliged for a while. He grew agitated again in August, when a printed copy of the record arrived at Biarritz, where he was supposed to rest and recuperate. Feeling his days were numbered, the testimony evidently was an important element of closure for Kahn, although when he began reading it more closely and critically than anyone else, it was also a way to break the boredom of another long rest-cure. He cringed nonetheless. Spotting a "great many stenographers' errors" and "some unskillfully worded expressions of mine," he complained that his "answers are utterly garbled" and cabled approximately two hundred changes to New York, asking that a substitute record be printed, if necessary at Kuhn, Loeb's expense. His partners and attorneys insisted that the "printed copy reads fairly well" and persuaded him to "do nothing now but let matter await your return in Fall."[49]

Thereafter, Kahn saved his prose for ongoing debate over the next Securities Act. If not written by committee, all his subsequent remarks on economic affairs were scrutinized by his partners before going into circulation. They wanted to catch mistakes, prevent embarrassment, and assure a unified voice for the firm, while at once advancing the investment banking community's principal complaints with the securities legislation. Typical of that community, Kahn conceded "*a* Securities Act was due and overdue," but the "catch-as-catch-can" law of the previous May was flawed. Like most Wall Street leaders, Kahn admonished its civil liability clause, which held individual underwriters responsible for the entire offering, regardless of one's share in the original participation. The law seemed as misguided as Prohibition, Kahn liked to say, except in this instance Kahn wanted liberal-minded reformers to make good use of revision. He was not seeking repeal.[50] Amid what Sam Rayburn called "the most powerful lobby ever organized against any bill," Congress did relax the liability provision in the Securities Exchange Act of 1934 — making underwriters liable for only their share of the offering. But Kahn was absent from the frontlines in the fight. Like the Banking Act of 1934, the Fletcher-Rayburn bill was passed a little more than one month after Kahn's death, making the story of his personal lobbying inconclusive with regard to the law, known as the Securities Exchange Act of 1934. Where this revised federal legislation loosened the civil liability of underwriters, Kahn's side had won. When they set up the Securities and Exchange Commission, Kahn's point of view was half-served. While he favored full disclosure and wanted an end to abusive practices, he would have hated the detailed reporting procedures. By 1941, however, when the SEC made competitive bidding compulsory, Kahn's original position had lost.

The only truly suggestive indicator of Kahn's persuasiveness with regard to subsequent banking and securities regulations was Kahn's effect on Ferdinand Pecora, whose investigation and staff were directly responsible for the far-reaching statutory reform in 1934. Frosty feelings had led Jack Morgan to say, "Pecora has the manners of a prosecuting attorney trying to convict a horse thief." Kahn and Pecora, however, used each other differently. To Kahn's advantage, the Wall Street banker was not a Morgan partner or detectably snobbish, and, like Pecora, he was also foreign-born. Politically, there was also something for Pecora to gain from showing his interests and abilities in promoting a better dialogue between Washington and Wall Street, which happened to be easier for him with Kahn than with Morgan.[51] Pecora would eventually conclude that Morgan and Kahn both possessed ideal ethics for investment bankers — and exemplified the ethics from which most banking houses deviated. However, his memoir of the investigation immortalized Kahn with superlative respect, saying, "No suaver, more fluent, and more diplomatic advocate could be conceived. If anyone could succeed in presenting the customs and functions of the private bankers in a favorable and prepossessing light, it was he."[52]

Of course, no one from Wall Street was better in the public theater than Otto Kahn, either. This was the greatest performance of his financial career. It made Otto Kahn an unforgettable headliner in financial history. Yet even his best performance had shortcomings. When Kahn testified that stock traders had learned to exercise self-discipline, for instance, pools were underway to manipulate stock prices. Instead of representing Wall Street, Kahn was representing himself, and, if honest virtue survived, it appeared the rule only among a small community of conservative investors who, as in the twenties, could not control the rest. However, to call Kahn's performance a tour de force implies an even larger context. Being America's unsurpassed patron of art played significantly in his public reception at a crucial moment in Wall Street's relations with Washington. His famed largesse placed Kahn far away from the philistine. A life-long involvement with the performing arts had perfected Kahn's showmanship. It framed his stylization of character, his sense of audiences, and when Kahn made a rich man good and likable, the urbanity that was Otto Kahn picked through the deadlocked condemnation of Wall Street. One might think of Kahn's performance in Washington as a waltz in swingtime, and more so because Kahn had once loaned money to Con Conrad, composer of "The Continental," which won the first Oscar for best song in 1934, having been the big number in *The Gay Divorcee*, starring Fred Astaire and Ginger Rogers. Elegance was still desired and welcomed in public life.[53]

Finally, when it came to the ultimate public crisis, Otto Kahn's eclectic familiarity with the theater made a unique point about evolving discursive forms of political economy. He could (and we should) understand these spectacles of public life as though they were an Ibsenian drama, a theater in which life's issues were starkly presented, where evil or illness lurking in the dark could be exposed, expelled, and cured. Not open-ended, the scenes and actions of Washington politics were rather discernible spaces, settings, and time. Financial disclosure and incandescent lighting had evolved contemporaneously, suggesting similar forms for controlling the appearance of a character or evidence. In the stage and financial arts alike, the actors and scenic mass were isolated, illuminated, sometimes humiliated and punished. By the 1930s, the courts, the hearing rooms, and Wall Street constituted a stage as multidimensional as any the new theater could design. And who but Otto Kahn could better understand the role and site lines in the hearing room as theater? If he did not enter the Senate hearings carrying a promptbook for Pirandello or training from Stanislavsky, then, from Aristotle or Pater, Kahn knew a hero was both good and bad, but decidedly more good. He would direct his performing energy toward creating a favorable character and come out looking fine when others from Wall Street looked like rogues.

To top it all, Kahn's testimony pressed against crushing fatalism, characteristic not only of the times, but also of him as a Jew at this time in history. If Pecora's grilling seemed like hell on earth to Charles Mitchell and Jack Morgan, it restored a plausible optimism for Otto Kahn, for whatever mischief the New Deal might pursue in purifying America's financial marketplace, Kahn could trust it by comparison with the policies of the New Germany. Indeed, whenever reactionaries in the United States railed against finance capitalists, imagining bankers at the center of a conspiracy allegedly to blame for the war, deflation, and "detestable internationalism" (in the phrase of the anti-Semitic radio priest, Charles E. Coughlin), a special venom was reserved for Jews; but official Washington was not exactly seeking to persecute

Wall Street's Jews. There was a meaningful difference between America and Germany, and Kahn drew confidence and strength in knowing it. Nothing akin to that confidence was available to his cohorts in Germany. What Otto Kahn did in Washington in 1933 was a tour de force in self-fulfillment.

CHAPTER TEN

Missing Otto Kahn

On the first day of 1934, Kahn went to the cinema to see the MGM feature *Queen Christina*, thought "Garbo magnificent," and cabled congratulations the next day to studio chief Walter Wanger. Immediately after the holiday, Kahn also sought to lobby the powers in Washington with regard to the upcoming securities legislation. He tried to schedule a conference with Ferdinand Pecora, who was in the thick of drafting new securities legislation. It seems their schedules prevented a meeting. Kahn would leave New York shortly for a medically supervised rest in Florida, the home state of Senator Fletcher, with whom Kahn was also apparently unable to schedule a meeting. This may have been because the legislator was occupied in Washington, where, as co-sponsor of the Fletcher-Rayburn Bill, he was shepherding its passage into the Securities Exchange Act of 1934.[1]

Generally, on various matters of long concern, Kahn was acting upbeat. His finances and health had sunk as low as they would go and both seemed on the mend, if not reinvigorated. His schedule, still light for Kahn, was picking up, getting him out and about again. His retreat from New York in February looked more like a regular winter vacation than medical necessity. As he spent his sixty-seventh birthday in Florida, he golfed, attended the horse races, entertained moderately, and otherwise relaxed in the sun. It left him "feeling very fit and well physically," though still "somewhat disturbed and confused by the way this foolish, troublesome, fascinating planet of ours is wagging its unmanageable tail nowadays."[2]

Hardly a day seemed to pass, however, without another reminder of the German assault on Jewry. On January 2 there was an appeal to erase the deficit of the Jewish Telegraphic Agency, "the only Jewish source of information from Germany." On January 5, an appeal arrived seeking help for pianist and composer Ernest Toch ("Being a Jew, he has been exiled from Berlin, the German market for his works has been destroyed, and he is now stranded in London, practically starving"). On January 21, Kahn met with the jobless author of a thesis on the judicial structure of the Reichsbank, Dr. Friedrich Weil, who had told him, "The German revolution has robbed me of a future in Germany as a lawyer or businessman, and I came to the U.S.A. in order to find the chance for a career undisturbed by racial prejudice." Another job seeker wrote from Mannheim, "Within a few weeks I shall be without work here, and as chances of getting a post in Germany are really very rare for Jewish people, I am more or less compelled to go abroad."[3] In nearly all cases, Kahn tendered sympathy only. His contributions to refugee assistance leaned toward institutional donations that afforded economies of scale and impressions of cohesion.

Being Otto Kahn, he found other well-established routines to occupy him as well. Kahn stayed involved with business matters close at hand, including the reorganization of Paramount. He likewise stayed personally involved in his own publicity and weighed which "erroneous statements involving me personally" were worthy of his response. In mid-March, he disavowed a "mischievous and foolish remark" that was attributed to him by a Miami reporter and circulated by Gilbert Seldes in the *New York Evening Journal.* Misquoted as saying, "There is a potential grand opera star in almost every home in America," Kahn asked Seldes to set the story right: "What I did say was: 'I believe that a potential music lover may be found in almost every home in America,' or words to that effect. I may add that my conception of the term 'music lover' is a very broad one." He also still cringed whenever the print media alluded to his "tax dodging" days. An article in the March issue of *Current History*, for example, moved Kahn to compose a four-page response defending his past practices and current thoughts on tax policies — a letter that was typed, then laid aside and filed unsent.[4]

Rounding out Kahn's activities were tickets for *Four Saints in Three Acts* on March 6 and hopes "to invade Hollywood next June or July." He was again taking lunches at the Bankers Club with creative friends, and at one with theatrical producer Richard Herndon, Kahn quipped that perfect health made one "as rich as Croesus." He made commitments to a few public dinners as well. The Council on Foreign Relations expected him to preside at its dinner on April 6, where Sir George Paish would talk on "the progress of recovery in Great Britain and the measures necessary for a continuance of world recovery." The entertainer Eddie Cantor had secured a promise of Kahn's presence on April 8, at the Hotel Astor for the Jewish Theatrical Guild's testimonial dinner to jointly fête tunesmith George M. Cohan and producer Sam H. Harris. There were also discussions if not solid plans for a tour of America by the Shakespeare troupe from Stratford-on-Avon, and Kahn vowed to gather "inside information" on its behalf regarding "new [restrictive] regulations concerning the admission of European actors," while trying as well to negotiate the goodwill of Frank Gillmore, president of Actors Equity.[5]

In these days, Kahn's cash donations remained few and dear. Those that he made were more outstanding for their commentary than their amount. With his check for $700, "in payment of the balance of the amount of my underwriting," Kahn asked the Father Duffy Memorial Committee "whether, in view of the limited amount at the Committee's disposal, it might not be worthy of consideration, instead of erecting a statue, to erect a marble or granite block, on the front of which would be a bronze bas-relief of Father Duffy; and on the sides suitable inscriptions and ornaments. That would, of course, be much less expensive than a statue and could be made, I think, no less impressive, dignified and artistic."[6] The point was lost on the committee, which put up a traditional, representational statue of its hero on a traffic island in New York's theater district. In these days, Otto Kahn felt money was better spent on the living than the dead. He remained loyal to a few individuals of past dependence, especially if a small donation made a large difference in sustaining creativity. A loan of $100 supplied only one-fifth of the budget that playwright Em Jo Basshe had calculated as his need, but the patron's attention still managed to spark small embers in his dramatic muse. The funds mattered in the context of Kahn's letter, for it contained "not a word to make us feel that we are 'no where's to go' people," Basshe replied on March 27. "I'll have to make good now when men like you keep on believing in me."[7]

The next day, Otto Kahn prepared a letter endorsing the newly organized School of the American Ballet. Then only three months old, the company was destined to make New York a center for modern ballet. Edward M. M. Warburg, its co-founder and president, had made a presentation to Kahn about it on the previous Saturday, and Kahn found himself "greatly and sympathetically interested" in the whole project, not least of all because the artistic director, George Balanchine, was Diaghilev's last protégé, and determined to build a "ballet company in cooperation with the best American painters, musicians and poets." If Kahn presently was not ready to write a check, he at least was able to pen words of suitable praise, as Warburg asked, knowing Kahn's name and endorsement were still valued in such promotions and could help in the fund-raising. Kahn supplied a letter attesting to the vision and qualifications of the founding team, and its "very auspicious undertaking" in the cultural synthesis of America. He also reasserted his belief in dance as an art.[8] In a moment, it would seem the torch had passed to a new generation, and Kahn could be proud of his own leg in the relay that moved New York to cultural prominence. But Kahn was not yet putting himself out of this game. Instead, reinvigorated by the progress, he felt himself moving forward rather than left behind. He planned to attend a rehearsal of the new dance company that was rightly his legacy.

The following morning was a typical one. Kahn went to his office at 52 William Street. Attending to his correspondence, and dictating some replies to a secretary before lunch, he left a pair to be typed and ready for his signature upon returning from the partners' dining room. In one letter, he acknowledged the receipt of a report concerning the suitability of South-West Africa for Jewish colonization, which he promised to peruse with interest. In the other letter, he offered an appointment to the aspiring producer of *Ounanga*, a music-drama from African American composer Clarence Cameron White. It had been previously played for Kahn in Paris, at the studio of composer Raoul Laparra, and the patron seemed receptive to further involvement with its development, although bounded by the new conventions of protocol, the producer had approached him with the promise that "I am not asking you for financial help in this matter." Kahn obliged guardedly, saying, "I regret to say that I know of no useful advice which I am in a position to offer you. If, nevertheless, you desire to speak to me, I shall be at your disposal."[9] These were to be among Otto Kahn's last words. At the end of his midday meal, while sipping coffee at around 1:45 P.M., Otto Kahn slumped forward on the table, stricken suddenly by a heart attack. As Benjamin Buttenweiser tried to revive him, others raced to the telephones—calling a nearby hospital, Kahn's personal physician, and his family at the Fifth Avenue mansion. In a moment of hope, his limousine was summoned to take him home, but Otto Kahn was dead.[10]

The final ceremonies began. An official public statement was delayed, as customary, until the Stock Exchange closed. Then Buttenweiser announced, "Otto H. Kahn died suddenly today of a heart attack while at lunch at his office," adding, "I hope I never have to give out such sad news again." The draperies were drawn on the partners' floor of 52 William Street. A flag over the portal was lowered to half-mast. Reporters and curious onlookers gathered outside the banking house, and shortly after 4 P.M. a contingent of seniors from J. P. Morgan arrived to pay their respects. Thirty minutes later, with photographers now on the scene, the Morgan partners reemerged from the building and were rushed for comment by reporters. None was made officially by the partners from 23 Wall Street, but according to one report, a dazed Jack Morgan stammered, "Comment? Comment from me? It means nothing." Thomas Lamont interjected, "You know Mr. Morgan never comments. He just came here to express his sympathy." Not long after, Kahn's remains were carried out in a casket, placed in a hearse, and driven home, where they lay in state for several days awaiting burial. Kuhn, Loeb, meanwhile, closed for a period of mourning.[11]

As word of Kahn's death spread, so did reactions and tributes. Broadway, said Douglas Gilbert, "mourned its First Angel." The "players whom he had befriended, producers he had 'angeled,' gathered in groups through the Times Square district, saddened at the loss of their Maecenas." Grief stricken, producer Morris Gest kept repeating, "He was a great man! He was a great man! I cannot talk about him; not now anyway." The arts critics turned to their typewriters and tried to capture the depth, extent, and catalog of Kahn's cultural impact. Most genuinely found it "difficult to detail the many ways in which his participation assisted." Their prose in several instances dressed Kahn as the "first nighter" for a final viewing of his trademark silky grey mustache, his ebony cane, the high hat, and satin-lined opera cape, so often caricatured over the years, that were the stylish signature of this banker-patron, a star in the audience, one of the "most ornamental figures of the theatre." Beloved at once for his wallet, his wit, and his "rebellious playfulness," Kahn was noted for possessing a "scholar's taste for good drama, [and] patiently smiling contempt for bad." He wore his purse close to his heart and "wanted something new," said Gilbert Gabriel, in an insightful column for the *American* that came closer than most in explaining Kahn's flair. Gabriel wrote, "Almost anybody with an exciting new idea in any of the seven arts could have a half-hour of his kindly ear and, more usually than not, leave his office with a semi-anonymous check in his pocket. It was part of the fun. And, for Mr. Kahn himself, almost any theatre was all fun. Nobody enjoyed it more generously."[12]

Aside from the fun of it all, Kahn's fundamental precept — "Our greatest asset is our good name" — was secure in the end. The tributes from all quarters paid the final dividends. A gossip column in the *Evening Journal* predicted "a decided gap in New York's social as well as business world. . . . He possessed, to a remarkable degree, that abstract character which we called 'culture.' " An editorial in the *Herald Tribune* forecast, "A sharp loss to the cause of American culture is the passing of Otto Hermann Kahn." And the *Christian Science Monitor* remembered him as "a modern counterpart of the medieval patrons like the Medicis, whose gold made possible so much of the art of the Renaissance." In the whole montage, it was generally agreed that Otto Kahn, with his old-world cultural breeding, did "more than almost any other man of his time" to enlarge the public's appreciation of art. The *World-Telegram*, which said "Broadway's slang phrase 'angel' might have been coined just for Otto H. Kahn," suggested that New York "is used to rich men who make gifts in the name of religion, education, science and social welfare, but it may look a long time for another such philanthropist who gave so lavishly in the name of art."[13]

A first-nighter was an anomaly among Wall Streeters, whose eulogies nonetheless extolled the "outstanding character" and "high business morality" of Kahn. While railroad executives acknowledged his "sage counsel and support," Winthrop Aldrich of Chase National Bank said that Kahn was "a man of genuine personal charm," one of the "ablest and most influential bankers of his time," and Thomas Lamont, having composed a more polished statement overnight, commented upon Kahn's "long and honorable career in banking and in railway development," adding, "his mind and methods were always constructive." Lamont, like others from the business world, was additionally moved to recognize Kahn's "extraordinarily varied" activities and influence in the arts, but none proclaimed themselves converted to Kahn's humanitarian capitalism or pledged to follow his lessons in art.[14]

Financial editors and journalists remembered the gentlemanly banker from the "old school." Assuring all that snake oil never found its way into Otto Kahn's satchel, they immortalized his prophecies about the "debacle of 1929," and they humanized his mistaken belief, when the market rallied around the Hoover moratorium, that a slow recovery had begun and inflation might possibly follow. They also finally divulged the open secret that "Mr. Kahn was reported a heavy seller of stocks" during October 1931, and that afterward, "his own security holdings were being substantially depressed by constant depreciation of market values."[15] In his syndicated column, Arthur Brisbane commented, "Undoubtedly the 'depression' killed him, with its losses, worries and appeals of friends." He estimated that Kahn "probably found his fortune diminished by forty or fifty millions" since 1929, then noted that the banker-patron "still had many millions left, but what you lose, not what you have left, is what counts."[16]

Both the estimated losses and Kahn's final net worth were beyond verification. Technically, the net value of Kahn's estate was later revealed to be a shockingly small $3,970,860 — a figure belying his true worth because it excluded cash, real estate, art works, and other assets that Kahn previously sheltered from inheritance taxes in private corporations held by his wife and children.[17] Nonetheless, the impression of a cash-poor Otto Kahn at death is a valid one. It was corroborated by his widow's hurried sale of 1100 Fifth Avenue and her search to find a buyer for the Long Island estate. In each transaction, she was compensated with a fraction of the original cost. Yet before the public learned what he left, or to whom he left it, the wider sense of grief concerned not what Kahn had lost, but what was lost with Otto Kahn.

It happened to be the last week of the current opera season at the Metropolitan. Funds for the next season were yet uncertain, when, on the day after Kahn's death, Mayor Fiorello La Guardia spoke from the stage of the Met before the third act of *Parsifal*. To his planned appeal for contributions, the mayor brought the house to silence in tribute to Otto H. Kahn, "a great New Yorker whose name is linked with this institution and who has done so much to make grand opera in New York possible." Previously, in Paul Cravath's absence, Cornelius Bliss had issued an official statement of tribute on behalf of the Met's directors. While it adequately summarized Kahn's finest points, it seemed stuffy and lacking anything iridescent, quite unlike prose that newspaper editorialists and staff writers had offered. It was also potentially contentious, for the press had more freely revisited the struggles between Kahn and the box owners in the Met's Diamond Horseshoe, remembering that the "Old Guard" had denied his vision of a new, more democratic house. Within this context, La Guardia's further comments were conciliatory. The mayor touted the progress at the opera house of late, which had opened the orchestra to patrons who once could only sit in the gallery. Echoing Kahn's statement from a few years earlier, he said, "We cannot depend any longer upon the benefactions of a few individuals. Opera must be maintained by the music lovers in New York."[18]

Among the individual music lovers to subsequently do so were the women of the Metropolitan Opera Guild, organized in 1936 by the charismatic Eleanor Robson (Mrs. August) Belmont, who found a loyal supporter in Addie Kahn. Addie added a directorship at the Metropolitan Opera to her roster of musical patronage, which in addition to the Philharmonic embraced the Manhattan School of Music, the Rachmaninoff Memorial Fund, and the Town Hall Endowment Fund. Moments before her own sudden death from a heart attack in London on March 15, 1949, she was conferring with Eleanor Belmont on the selection of Rudolf Bing as the next general manager of the Met.[19] Not without some irony, Addie Kahn's death came soon after the death of Cornelius Bliss, and thereafter the Bliss and Kahn dynasties were carried on at the Met. Anthony Bliss, son of Cornelius, joined the board, then the executive board, and served as president from 1956 to 1967. During his presidency, Bliss was a determined champion of the Met's eventual move to Lincoln Center. Meanwhile, Margaret "Nin" Ryan, the youngest child of Addie and Otto Kahn, became a major donor and sturdy fund-raiser in the dowager tradition. Women of the Rockefeller, Lasker, and Wallace clans overshadowed her wealth and visibility, but Nin Ryan was a notable benefactress. She sold a Rembrandt in 1950 to underwrite a new production of Verdi's *Don Carlo*, which launched the first of Bing's twenty-two seasons at the Met.[20]

How substitutes for Otto Kahn fared in supporting opera is ultimately another story, but once Kahn's seat was permanently vacated, his legacy extended beyond dynastic successions. In several ways, Kahn's vision was vindicated. One can savor the conversion of a Bliss in the crusade for an architecturally modern house, or cackle because opera patrons came to beg Robert Moses, a Jew, for deliverance from the dilapidated performance space of the Gilded Age.[21] In the perennial sport of evaluating Lincoln Center, we could also add that the new, modern house is situated very much within the vicinity that Kahn had chosen. All these points sharpen the edge of the otherwise sentimental remark of Nin Ryan when the Met opened at Lincoln Center in 1966: "I feel just like a little girl who has realized her father's dream."[22] It is nonetheless important to frame Kahn's legacy as other than deliciously triumphant or decidedly progressive. The historical lore of the Met generally appropriates Kahn's memory either to glorify the greatness or malign the mistakes of the past. There is another view. Met lore also uses Kahn to convey discontinuity within ongoing traditions. Giving us the sense something and someone are missing from the narrative will leave the narrative itself in suspense and on the brink of something new, thereby supporting a notion of modernity that need not be the same as progress. When, for instance, Anthony Bliss went about trying to solve the financial problems of the Met and wanted to explain how "the times are different," he would say, "We have no Otto Kahn today."[23] Not only did this dodge the arguments made by Kahn in the twenties and thirties, but for many years after his death, the absence of Otto Kahn signaled a past that was remembered but unexamined, finished and possibly irrelevant.

Missing Otto Kahn was missing the world that passed with him. The grief combined with a sense of misfortune most immediately and profoundly for the refugees. Without Otto Kahn, his consummate cosmopolitan patron-guarantor in America, Max Reinhardt, for example, encountered unexpected difficulties when starting his career in exile from Nazism. Everything added up differently now. His first job in the United States reunited Reinhardt with Norman Bel Geddes for a production at Oscar Hammerstein's old Manhattan Opera House, in haunted irony; but the promised land of "Dollarika" that Reinhardt imagined in the twenties, along with Kahn's promises to establish an art theater for him in America, were both long past. Without Kahn to erase the red ink, Reinhardt was a marked loser, and in due time he stumbled around Hollywood, a financial failure, missing the "old risktakers," as Eisenstein called the class of studio influences that included Kahn and Jesse Lasky.[24] Some among the next generation of theatrical activists more generally saw Kahn's death as a gap in time. John Houseman, for example, when recalling the mid-thirties, and how "the Mercury [Theatre] came into being," said it was "too late for individual millionaires' capricious benefactions (like those of the late Otto Kahn), too early for the calculated munificence of the foundations." In the breach, claimed Houseman, "We were left to sink or swim in the rough seas of the profit system."[25] Alternatively, in 1936, the deceased Otto Kahn made an easy fall guy for the then worthless bonds of the Theatre Guild, which Kahn had promoted as a "safe investment" in 1923–24. Actually, few would malign Kahn's help in launching the Guild. Most of them probably wished he were around for their rescue and refinancing—and some possibly imagined Kahn had become a different kind of angel, who granted one more favor, when Paramount Pictures subsidized the Guild in exchange for options on its productions.[26] The financier ahead of his time in organizing networks within the culture industries (for profit and not), Otto Kahn was the archaeology uniting Hollywood and New York as well as Europe—a timeless presence in Faustian and other compromises endemic to the cultural marketplace.

Kahn would linger as rare spirit, as money, the memory of past promises for capitalism with a soul. Those "who knew him well" stayed "under the spell,"[27] while the generation that endlessly memorialized its war dead also swept Kahn into a current of afterlife fantasies no different, it seems, than *Miracle at Verdun* (*Wunder um Verdum*), a play from the Theatre Guild's 1930–31 season, in which dead soldiers revisit the postwar world. One of Kahn's appearances in the memoirs of Sergei Eisenstein speaks to the point. Writing in 1946, after another global war and when his own life was ebbing, Eisenstein commented, "Today even the mysterious, all powerful Otto H. has departed *ins Jenseits* [to the other world]."[28] Shortly thereafter, Upton Sinclair drew upon Kahn's memory most unusually. In the seventh of his immensely popular series of eleven Lanny Budd novels, Kahn emerges as the "subconscious friend" of Laurel Creston, a novelist who dislikes the Nazis and to whom, having "discovered herself to be a medium," Kahn appears in psychic trances. One day in the autumn of 1940, Lanny and Laurel take a motor tour through "the farming country of Long Island." Talking of Nazi murders and night raids on London, they periodically stop to look at mansions of American millionaires. These playgrounds, which Lanny once counted among his own party circuits, had slipped from the possessions of their builders, indeed into another world of concave memories, where the imaginations of Sinclair and Eisenstein no less than the Xanadu of *Citizen Kane* were one. When Lanny and Laurel arrive at Kahn's mansion, Lanny says, "The place is said to have cost three millions, and to have been sold for about a fourth of that amount." Laurel replies, "It must have broken his heart . . . assuming that he knows about it!" and Lanny jests, "We'll try a seance, and tell him!" Laurel continues: "What a curious thing to think about, Lanny! Suppose he really does exist and that he knows what we are saying about him!" "We must be careful," Lanny answers, "for he was a distinguished person, and accustomed to be[ing] treated with deference. He had charming and gracious manners, but he never forgot that he was a prince of the blood — or the blood money, should I say?"

At a later time, Kahn does appear in a seance, to convey a warning from another spirit: " 'Tell Lanny to postpone that trip. A calamity confronts him.' He repeated three times: 'Danger! Danger! Danger!' — and then faded away." Budd, who leads a double life as an international playboy and Roosevelt's secret agent in Germany, subsequently embarks upon his latest mission of espionage and goes down in an air crash. He survives, but, in remembering his near-death experience, thinks, "When you were dead you were dead. You didn't find yourself transported to glory, no angel handed you a golden harp . . . you didn't meet the spirits of your ancestors . . . no Otto Kahn, making sophisticated fun of himself." Thereafter, when puzzled, Budd wonders, "What would Otto Kahn have to say about the matter?"[29]

The same question arises in as many instances as one can find the lingering presence of Otto Kahn. What would Kahn say, for instance, about federal funding of the arts by the New Deal and Great Society? Would he be satisfied to nurture the Americanist strain of the cultural synthesis or prefer a more cosmopolitan policy? How might Kahn have commented on the controversies concerning federal Comstockery or defunding of the arts? None of these can be answered, of course, but what can be said about Otto Kahn as a modern life is more manageable. The mission of securing patronage for aesthetic modernity was left unfinished. No comparable millionaire-patron-critic emerged in his wake.

Criticisms of his patronage or his business practices were also part of Kahn's life and legacy. When he seemed whimsical or unpatterned in his patronage, he was labeled a dilettante. When persistent in his aesthetic and other goals, he was a pushy Jew. If some thought his largesse compensated for his own lack of talent or drive or social acceptance, fulfilling his ambition made Otto Kahn important, and evermore so once it was clear that he would never be an ennobled politician in England, or the partner who cut the really big deals at Kuhn, Loeb. Meanwhile, favoring one needy artist over another not only engendered a certain amount of jealousy among the artists, it also fostered some of the animus directed toward Kahn and fixed the idea that his patronage subconsciously compensated for the trauma of his own childhood. All his patronage, however, never cleansed Kahn of money's stigma. In addition, when his power to request the repayment of a loan did not create the impression of meanness, the protocol of stroking the patron carried strains of supplication. His strategy of seeding for the short term, in turn, could also seem superficial, and his final will, leaving no charitable donations, might suggest that he was either destroyed by the Great Depression in the end, or moved primarily by his own pleasure all along. Perhaps the patronage was really about Kahn's happiness in life, and not at all about the permanent advancement of art. Nonetheless, he did write a general clause in his last will that relieved the artists with outstanding debts to him from collection by his estate.[30]

In another mode, Otto Kahn incorporated all the above contradictions. The stock dichotomies became angles of multiple truths. To understand his as a modern life is to locate Otto Kahn in his many worlds and identities, to find him in between the many moderns of money and art — the outsider inside, central and marginal, betting with and against the odds, reaching unmatched heights but coming up short, and always most engrossing when the many elements are considered in the whole. Missing Otto Kahn served a different purpose for those among the next generation of "patron saints," who — as young, wealthy, and well-educated benefactors, like Lincoln Kirstein — could forget Otto Kahn as they turned the mantle of banker-patron into one of patron-critic, embraced the new, and started fresh again.[31] This occurrence, helped along by individual and collective egos in the next generation, was also facilitated by the absence of an heir to Kahn in style and magnitude. During the best years of Kahn's economic life, no one quite matched his patronage. His exceptionalism was noted by a co-editor of the *Little Review*, who appealed for funds from Kahn in 1926, pleading, "I have searched this haystack of stone for that needle: another rich men [*sic*] who will support the arts. You see where I am again?"[32] His uniqueness was a weakness, however, and later, when "death remove[d] a bright figure from the city's color, an exotic in the crowding of Wall Street," no one seemed to take the place of Otto Kahn.[33] That removal perhaps left a more icy strain of modernism to prevail where Kahn had tried to induce something more romantic. Later corporate sponsorships of the arts were missing both the personal touch of the Maecenas as well as many of the imaginative leaps implied by Kahn's sentiments and striving for cosmopolitan totality.

Finally, during his last months of life, Kahn found a firmness in his own sentiments toward modernity, which centered on his Jewishness, without excluding other aspects of his self. Kahn had lately told interviewers, "I was born a Jew, I am a Jew and I shall die a Jew." His affirmation resonated in his funeral services, which, from the moment of Kahn's death, were managed by Temple Emanu-El. The arrangement was likely made by Kuhn, Loeb, but the ritual itself transcended more strictly constructed laws: although Kahn had died on a Thursday, instead of laying the body to rest before the next sundown, his remains stayed at 1100 Fifth Avenue until the following Monday, reportedly because Addie Kahn needed time to recover from the shock. In the meantime, at a concert given by Arturo Toscanini and the Philharmonic Society at Carnegie Hall on Sunday, the funeral march of Beethoven's *Eroica* Symphony was offered in tribute to Otto Kahn.[34] On the next day, a cortege of four or five cars followed the hearse, carrying Kahn's remains to the Long Island house, where a brief service was conducted in the music room of the mansion. The family, servants, and 100 additional mourners were permitted to attend—Jack Morgan among them. A detail of local police tried to keep strangers away from the mansion and the nearby, nonsectarian cemetery where Kahn was buried.

The *Daily News* reported that a crowd of 200 nonetheless crashed through police lines and "converged upon the Kahn plot" at the cemetery. The public's curiosity was undoubtedly keen. An airplane carrying a photographer from the *Daily News* passed overhead that afternoon, gathering scenes of the burial rites, including a photograph of the workmen filling Kahn's grave. The photographs appeared in the next day's paper as if to conclude Kahn's exit in the style of a modern celebrity.[35]

One of the most important idioms of Kahn's modern life went unnoticed. Kahn's attitude toward living was inspired by an expressly Paterian urgency, recalled in his 1924 address, "The Value of Art to the People," in which Kahn quoted from *The Renaissance*: "We have an interval, and then our place knows us no more. . . . Our one chance lies in expanding that interval, in getting as many pulsations as possible into a given time."[36] As an individual patron, Otto Kahn stayed close to the art and its making, experiencing the moment. He would "pass most swiftly from point to point, and be always present at the focus where the greatest number of forces unite in their purest energy," as Pater urged.[37] Nearly always the best of his deeds involved him personally in the experience, or the ecstasy. The doing preserved authenticity. Such perspective better resolves the question of why Kahn left no bequest to the arts in his will ("Having given largely during my lifetime . . . I refrain . . ."). To think solely in terms of Kahn's concern for his family, their needs amid the Great Depression, or their ability to be patrons in the future would miss the point that "Otto the Magnificent" was not "the conventional millionaire," as a journalist explained in 1928, for if he had been, "he would have put aside a certain sum toward . . . a foundation bearing his name, and on the shoulders of the board of directors . . . he would have laid the responsibility of apportioning sums to individuals and groups. . . . An impulse would have hardened into an institution."[38]

Kahn's attitude toward his own biography gives another view of the same theme. When George S. Viereck said, "A person who occupies your unique position in America and in international life should leave a monument to himself," he urged Kahn, "You owe it to yourself and to the World Spirit from which you have received your extraordinary endowments, to write in some way the story of your life." Kahn, though vain in many ways, was unconvinced. He responded, "The idea does not appeal to me at all."[39] To celebrate one's own deeds streaked with too much arrogance, and Kahn seemed at once to reject this self-serving side of burgher and Victorian culture, while also protecting his interior space from public view (the latter less from shyness than from the desire to reserve self-examination as his private privilege). Deeds made the public impression for Kahn. The signature appending a document, his name engraved on a letterhead, like his presence on opening nights or his sworn testimony and scripted speeches, mirrored his impulse and self-image. Biography was less preferred than presence as a medium of social representation.

If a reason can be offered as to why Otto Kahn became such a cursorily drawn character of modernity, it is because Otto Kahn himself had a hand in writing a life that flashed so fast. A life spent burning intensively "with this hard, gemlike flame," as Pater would have it, when finished should vanish away.[40]

Notes

Abbreviations

AJA
   American Jewish Archives, Cincinnati, Ohio
American
   American (New York)
Beaverbrook
   Beaverbrook Papers, House of Lords, London, England
Bonar Law
   Bonar Law Papers, House of Lords, London, England
CMOC
   Conried Metropolitan Opera Company
CSM
   Christian Science Monitor
CUOH
   Oral History Research Office, Columbia University, New York, New York
CVV/NYPL
   Carl Van Vechten Papers, New York Public Library, New York, New York
DN
   Daily News (New York)
EJ
   Evening Journal (New York)
EMH/S-YU
   Edward M. House Papers, Sterling Library, Yale University, New Haven, Connecticut
EP
   Evening Post (New York)
EW
   Evening World (New York)
Ewing/B-YU
   Max Ewing Papers, Beinecke Library, Yale University, New Haven, Connecticut
FAV/CU
   Frank A. Vanderlip Papers, Columbia University, New York, New York
FSP
   F. S. Pearson and Sons Archive, Science Museum, London, England
HCP
   Hart Crane Papers, New Haven, Connecticut

HT
  Herald Tribune (New York)
JHH/NYPL
  James Hazen Hyde Papers, New York Public Library, New York, New York
JHS/AJA
  Jacob H. Schiff Papers, American Jewish Archives, Cincinnati, Ohio
JPMJr/PML
  J. P. Morgan Jr. Papers, Pierpont Morgan Library, New York, New York
Lighthouse
  Lighthouse, Inc., Archive, New York, New York
MG-GH
  Morgan Grenfell Papers, Guildhall
MOA
  Metropolitan Opera Archives, New York, New York
MORECO
  Metropolitan Opera Real Estate Company
MS/LC
  Margaret Sanger Papers, Library of Congress
NYT
  New York Times
OHK
  Otto H. Kahn Papers, Princeton, New Jersey
Pound/B-YU
  Ezra Pound Papers, Beinecke Library, Yale University, New Haven,
  Connecticut
Robins/Fales
  Elizabeth Robins Papers, Fales Library, New York, New York
TAE/ENHS
  Thomas A. Edison Papers, Edison National Historical Site, West Orange, New
  Jersey
TWL/H-B
  Thomas W. Lamont Papers, Harvard Business School, Cambridge,
  Massachusetts
VPC/PML
  Victor P. Carosso Collection, Pierpont Morgan Library, New York, New York
WSJ
  Wall Street Journal
WT
  World-Telegram (New York)

Introduction

1. Gershwin, *Lyrics on Several Occasions*, 4–5; Kahn, *Of Many Things*, 74; Anderson, *My Thirty Years War*, 111, Matz, *Many Lives of Otto Kahn*; Kolodin, *Metropolitan Opera*; Garafola, *Diaghilev's Ballets Russes*.

2. Lewis, *When Harlem Was in Vogue*; 99–100; O'Neill, *Unknown O'Neill*, 191–

92, 200–201; Giles, *Hart Crane*, 32; Pound, *The Cantos (1–95)*, 80; *NYT*, Mar. 30, 1934; West, *Complete Works*, 408.

3. Carringer, *Making of Citizen Kane*, 16–26, 50–59, 94–97; *NYT*, Feb. 2, 1989.

4. Meryman, *Mank*, 84–86; Kael et al., *Citizen Kane Book*, 13–29, 449–56; Herman Mankiewicz to H. S. Meinhardt, Dec. 7, 1926; Meinhardt to Kahn, Feb. 10, 1927; Kahn to Meinhardt, Feb. 10, 1927 and Nov. 11, 1927; Meinhardt to Cravath, Henderson & deGersdorff, Nov. 23, 1927; John Peabody Phillips to Meinhardt, Dec. 1927, and Mankiewicz to Otto Kahn, Mar. 26, 1928, OHK.

5. Josephson, *Robber Barons*, 333. The passage is curious, since Kahn's Long Island estate was built well after 1901. Josephson's own source for the story may have been Van Rensselaer, *Social Ladder*, 295.

6. Kael et al., *Citizen Kane Book*, 91.

7. Bordwell, Staiger, and Thompson, *Classical Hollywood*, 162.

8. Goldberg, "Are There More than One Otto Kahn."

9. See Kimball, *Complete Lyrics of Cole Porter*, 134, which contains the first verse of "Opera Star," from the Yale University Drama Association's *Out O' Luck* (1925 and 1926):

> If the critics have dominion
> Over popular opinion
> I'm the opera's most sensational soprano.
> It's because I have a fashion
> Of my own for putting passion
> In the roles that I portray for Otto Kahn-o.

10. On the Brice song (lyrics by Billy Rose and Ballard Macdonald), see Dizikes, *Opera in America*, 427; Grossman, *Funny Woman*, 170, 175, and Kahn to Victor Talking Machine, Dec. 24, 1927, OHK.

11. Goldstein, *George Kaufman*, 157–59, and transcript from cinema version of *Animal Crackers*, screenplay by Morrie Ryskind, based on the stage musical by George S. Kaufman and Morrie Ryskind.

12. Caro, *Power Broker*, 164–65, 184–85, 277–78, and "Annals of Biography: The City Shaper," 52–53; see also Kahn to Delano & Aldrich, June 5, 1916, Sept. 27, 1915, Oct. 20, 1916, and Aug. 17, 1916, David E. Bennett to Kahn, Nov. 1 and 9, 1927, OHK.

13. Hecht, *Charlie*, 215–16, and *Child of the Century*, 378–79; Duberman, *Robeson*, 84, 596; Kahn to Alexander Woolcott, Aug. 10, 1925, and Sept. 11, 1924, OHK.

14. Author's interview with Margaret Ryan, Sept. 1985.

15. Sergei Eisenstein to Kahn, July [1?], 1930, and Kahn to Eisenstein, July 14, 1930, OHK; Eisenstein, *Immoral Memories*, 141–43.

16. Mann, *Turning Point*, 136.

17. Eisenstein, *Immoral Memories*, 141.

18. Jane Heap to Otto Kahn, May 28, 1926, OHK; Josephson, "Letter to My Friends"; Mayer, *Outsiders*, 311.

19. *Fortune*, Sept. 1932, 36.

20. Ascher, "Reminiscences," 1979, CUOH; author's interviews with Margaret Ryan and John Barry Ryan III, 1985–86; Kobler, *Otto the Magnificent*, 161–67; Paris, *Louise Brooks*, 71; Deutsch and Hanau, *Provincetown*, 173.

21. Barrès is quoted in Seigel, *Bohemian Paris*, 285.

22. Poggioli, *Theory of the Avant-Garde*, and Herf, *Reactionary Modernism*.

23. Stimpson, "Introduction," 3.

24. *Time*, Nov. 2, 1925; *Fortune*, Sept. 1932, 32–36; Strauss, *Men and Decisions*, 84.

25. Langner, *Magic Curtain*, 120; *Time*, Apr. 9, 1934.

26. Fitzgerald, "Rich Boy," 152.

27. *CSM*, Mar. 31, 1934.

28. Allen, *Lords of Creation*, 366–67; *Literary Digest*, July 8, 1933, 7; Chernow, *House of Morgan*, 169.

29. Kahn, *Reflections*, 221, 225, 226. In Jacob Schiff to Takahashi, Nov. 15, 1916, JHS/AJA, Schiff writes, "If . . . we want to spared the horrors of social revolution, we must, through successive measures," pursue "social justice."

30. References to geographic models are drawn from Knox and Agnew, *Geography of the World Economy*, 58–62, and Christaller, *Central Places in Southern Germany*, 59, 255.

31. *Jerseyman*, Nov. 17, 1899, Dec. 7, 1900, Mar. 29, 1901, Dec. 19, 1902, May 1, 1903, Nov. 5, 1915, and Jan. 14, 1915; Rae and Rae, *Morristown's Forgotten Past*, 112.

32. Saunders, *Regent's Park Villas*, 31–35, 134; Samuel, *Villas in Regent's Park*, 23–24; Dark, *Life of Sir Arthur Pearson*; *Architect and Building News, Suppl.*, Feb. 7, 1936.

33. Ruhling, "Castle on the Hill."

34. Landmarks Preservation Commission, Feb. 19, 1974, Number 7 LP-0675.

35. Supple, "Business Elite."

36. U.S. Senate Committee on Banking and Currency, *Stock Exchange Practices: Hearings*, 983.

37. Harvey, *Condition of Postmodernity*, 115; Galambos and Pratt, *Rise of the Corporate Commonwealth*, 6, 7, 11.

38. Mayer, *Persistence of the Old Regime*, 210–15; Levine, *Highbrow/Lowbrow*, 83–168; Tambling, *Opera, Ideology and Film*, 14–15; Conrad, *Song of Love and Death*, 236.

39. Harris and Thane, "British and European Bankers," 228. See also Augustine-Perez, "Very Wealthy Businessmen in Imperial Germany"; Lisle-Williams, "Beyond the Market" and "Merchant Banking Dynasties in the English Class Structure"; Chapman, "Aristocracy and Meritocracy in Merchant Banking"; Cassis, "Merchant Bankers and City Aristocracy"; Cassis, *Finance and Financiers in European History*; Augustine, *Patricians & Parvenues*; Blackbourn and Evans, *German Bourgeoisie*.

40. Bryer, *"The Theatre We Worked For,"* 59, 110.

41. Ortolani, *Pirandello's Love Letters to Marta Abba*, 77.

42. Gulbenkian, *Portrait in Oil*, 62.

43. E. Lara to Kahn, Nov. 18, 1921, OHK; Boyer, *Purity in Print*, 84–85; Ellman, *James Joyce*, 634; U.S. Senate Committee on Banking and Currency, *Stock Exchange Practices: Hearings*, 1210.

44. Berman, *Preface to Modernism*, vii–viii, 3; Habermas, "Modernity—An Incomplete Project"; Seigel, *Bohemian Paris*, 155.

Chapter One

1. Forbes, *Men Who Are Making America*, vi–vii, 214; Cruikshank, "The Great Kahn," 26.

2. Mosse, "Jewish Emancipation Between *Bildung* and Respectability"; Schmidt, "Concrete Totality and Lukács' Concept of Proletarian *Bildung*."

3. Kahn to Milton W. Baer, Dec. 17, 1915, OHK; Fahl, *Tradition der Natürlichkeit*, 5–6; Gay, *Jews of Germany*, 74.

4. Blackbourn, *Long Nineteenth Century*, 106–37.

5. Rostow, *Stages of Economic Growth*, 11; Landes, "Bleichröders and Rothschilds," 95.

6. Blastenbrei, *Mannheim in der Revolution 1848/49*, 37–130; Blackbourn, *Long Nineteenth Century*; Kahn to Don M. Pardee, Jan. 2, 1919, OHK; Eberstadt, "Die Familie Eberstadt"; DFG-Projektteam, *Die Revolution von 1848/49 in Baden* (in which Bernhard Kahn is spelled "Bernhard Kohn").

7. Nadel, *Little Germany*.

8. *150 Jahre Mannheimer Bettfedernfabrik, Kaufmann GMBH & Co.*

9. Kaplan, *Making of the Jewish Middle Class*, chap. 3; Laugwitz, "Robert Kahn and Brahms," 595–611; Watzinger, *Geschichte der Juden in Mannheim*, 103; Eberstadt, "Die Familie Eberstadt."

10. Blastenbrei, *Mannheim in der Revolution 1848/49*, 37–130.

11. Kobler, *Otto the Magnificent*, 9; Matz, *Many Lives of Otto Kahn*, 7–9; Kahn, *Of Many Things*, 73; Eberstadt, "Die Familie Eberstadt"; *NYT*, Dec. 11, 1921.

12. *Wisconsin Jewish Chronicle*, Jan. 6, 1928; Katz, "German Culture and the Jews," 90, 93; Gay, *Freud, Jews and other Germans*, 105.

13. Mosse, *German Jews*, 3; Watzinger, *Geschichte der Juden in Mannheim*, 103.

14. Salpeter, "Otto the Magnificent," 327–28; *Grand Rapids Herald*, May 17, 1925; Matz, *Many Lives of Otto Kahn*, 9–10.

15. Laugwitz, "Robert Kahn and Brahms," 597–98, 601; Fahl, *Tradition der Natürlichkeit*, 7. "Die Familie Eberstadt" registers the birth of an unnamed female on July 21, 1865, the same day as Robert Kahn, and her death in the same year. Franz Michael Kahn's dissertation was published in 1884 as *Zur Geschichte des römischen Frauen-Erbrechts: eine von der Juristen-Facultät Leipzig gekrönte Preisschrift*, and he was posthumously credited as the co-author of *Abhandlungen zum internationalen privatrecht. Zur Geschichte des römischen Frauen-Erbrechts: eine von der Juristen-Facultät Leipzig gekrönte Preisschrift* (1928).

16. Margaret Ryan Papers, in private hands; Otto Kahn to Paul Kahn, June 27, 1927, in possession of Ernst Schulin.

17. "Die Familie Eberstadt"; Charles Edward Strong to Kahn, May 29, 1922, OHK; Lili Deutsch to Paul Kahn, July 25, 1911, in possession of Ernest Schulin.

18. Otto Kahn to Prof. Dr. von Schulze-Gaevernitz, Jan. 24, 1921, OHK.

19. Forbes, *Men Who Are Making America*, 216.

20. Frank, "Profiles: In Tune with the Finite," 23.

21. U.S. House, National Monetary Commission, *Great German Banks*, 2:420–21; Emden, *Money Powers of Europe*, 223; Mosse, "Jewish Emancipation Between *Bildung* and Respectability," 2; Ashton, *German Idea*; Bramsted, *Aristocracy and the Middle-Classes in Germany*; Endelman, *Radical Assimilation in English Jewish History*, 73–77, 93, 114–18, and 125–26; Chapman, *Rise of Merchant Banking*, 67.

22. Juxon, *Lewis and Lewis*.

23. Matz, *Many Lives of Otto Kahn*, 13, suggests he met H. G. Wells, Richard Le Gallienne, Beerbohm Tree, Maxine Elliott, Henry Irving, and Harley Granville-Barker. Kobler, *Otto the Magnificent*, 13, acquaints Kahn with Oscar Wilde, Gilbert and Sullivan, Lillie Langtry, Edward Burne-Jones, James McNeill Whistler, John Singer Sargent, Ellen Terry, and Ignace Jan Paderewski.

24. Kahn to Elizabeth Robins, May 31, 1920, Robins/Fales.

25. Kahn to Chester E. Tucker, Oct. 16, 1926, OHK.

26. Kobler, *Otto the Magnificent*, 13; Ellman, *Oscar Wilde*, 331.

27. Kahn to W. J. Eck, July 1, 1919; Kahn to Pardee, Jan. 1, 1919, OHK; *EW*, Apr. 3, 1925; Kobler, *Otto the Magnificent*, 14.

28. Mosse, *Jews in the German Economy*; Emden, *Money Powers of Europe*, 274–77; Carosso, "Financial Elite"; *Fortune*, Aug. 1931, 82.

29. Perez and Willett, *Will to Win*, 17–19.

30. Carosso, *Investment Banking in America*, 17, 25–26.

31. J. S. Morgan to Drexel, Morgan, Sept. 21, 1880, MG-GH; J. P. Morgan to J. S. Morgan & Co., Oct. 9, 1883, MG-GH; Swaine, *Cravath Firm*, 1:594–607.

32. Adler, *Jacob H. Schiff*, 1:15–16; *Jerseyman* and *NYT*, Oct. 5, 1900; Carosso, "Financial Elite," 81–83.

33. Jacob Schiff to Ernest Cassel, Apr. 26, 1896, AJA Microfilm, r-694.

34. Kobler, *Otto the Magnificent*, 22–23; Roberts, "Conflict of Loyalties," 4.

35. Carosso, *Investment Banking in America*, 92.

36. Jacob Schiff to [Cassel], Apr. 4, 1903; Jacob Schiff to Max Bonn, Nov. 18, 1903; Cyrus Adler note, Sept. 3, 1926, AJA Microfilm, r-694.

37. "Statement by Max Bonn" and Jacob Schiff to Cassel, Apr. 4, 1903, AJA Microfilm, r-694; Warburg, *Long Road Home*, 9; Kuhn, Loeb, *Century of Investment Banking*, 52; Perez and Willett, *Will to Win*, 17; Grunwald, "Windsor Cassel," 125; Adler, *Jacob H. Schiff*, 1:2–30; Carosso, "Financial Elite," 75–76; Roberts, "Conflict of Loyalties," 3.

38. Jacob Schiff to Ernest Cassel, Apr. 26, 1896, AJA Microfilm, r-694; Warburg, *Reminiscences*; Warburg, *Long Road Home*.

39. Landes, "Bleichröders and Rothschilds," 107 (in Europe, the Rothschilds had *yichos*, the Bleichröders did not). Houses of peddler origins in the United States included Goldman, Sachs & Co., Lehman Brothers, and J. & W. Seligman & Co. In contrast, August Belmont arrived in New York in 1837 as an agent of the

Rothschilds, and the Speyers had come directly from their own Frankfurt banking family. See Supple, "Business Elite," 151–53; Carosso, "Financial Elite," 71–76, and *Investment Banking in America*, 9–11.

Chapter Two

1. Supple, "Business Elite," 166.

2. *Jerseyman*, Mar. 18, 1898, Aug. 19, 1898, July 21, 1899, Nov. 17, 1899, Apr. 6, 1900, June 8, 1900, Oct. 1, 1900, Nov. 9, 1900, Dec. 7, 1900, Mar. 29, 1901, Dec. 19, 1902, May 1, 1903, and Oct. 21, 1904; *NYT*, Oct. 3, 1900; Adler, *Jacob Schiff*, 1:18–19.

3. Kahn, *Reflections*, 399–420, and *Of Many Things*, 107–51. Interviews with Kahn (as well as Jacob Schiff) helped to shape Kennan, *E. H. Harriman*. More recent revisions in sympathy with Harriman include Mercer, *E. H. Harriman*, Klein, *Union Pacific* and *Life and Legend of E. H. Harriman*.

4. Kennan, *E. H. Harriman*, 1:108–38; Adler, *Jacob H. Schiff*, 1:121–23; Trottman, *History of the Union Pacific*, 262–63.

5. Carosso, *Morgans*, 363.

6. Adler, *Jacob H. Schiff*, 1:94.

7. J. S. Morgan & Co. to J. P. Morgan, Jan. 12, 1894, and J. P. Morgan & Co. to J. P. Morgan, Apr. 13, 1894, MG-GH; Klein, *Union Pacific*, 24–25; Kennan, *E. H. Harriman*, 1:123; Kahn, *Of Many Things*, 107.

8. Kennan, *E. H. Harriman*, 1:124–25; Adler, *Jacob H. Schiff*, 1:51–54, and Carosso, *Investment Banking In America*, 33.

9. Adler, *Jacob H. Schiff*, 1:51–54; and Carosso, *Investment Banking in America*, 33.

10. Kahn, *Of Many Things*, 107–13; Birmingham, *"Our Crowd,"* 186.

11. Kennan, *E. H. Harriman*, 1:1–24; Klein, *Life and Legend*, 27–38.

12. Eaton, *Miracle of the Met*, 31; Jaher, "Style and Status," 258–84.

13. Eaton, *Miracle of the Met*, 102; *NYT*, Feb. 16, 1892; Kahn, *Of Many Things*, 114, 115.

14. Kahn, *Reflections*, 399–400, and *Of Many Things*, 111, 115, 125.

15. Klein, *Union Pacific*, 52; Kahn, *Of Many Things*, 118, 133, 139.

16. Jacob H. Schiff to Samuel Rea, Dec. 1, 1899, AJA Microfilm, r-694; Kahn, *Of Many Things*, 125–26, 145; Winkler, *First Billion*, 100; Klein, *Life and Legend*, 128.

17. Kahn, *Of Many Things*, 120–23.

18. Carosso, *Investment Banking in America*, 93, 113–14, and *Morgans*, 471; Swaine, *Cravath Firm*, 1:648, 715–19, 721–22, 734; Klein, *Life and Legend*, 220–38; *EP*, Nov. 1, 1901; New York Senate and Assembly, *Life Insurance Companies*, 701, 1033–34; *NYT*, Apr. 17, 1897, Jan. 3, 1898, May 23, 1901, Oct. 30, 1903, Apr. 11, 1900, Aug. 31, 1903, Sept. 1, 1903, Apr. 29, 1905, May 17, 1905.

19. Carosso, *Investment Banking in America*, 93, and *Morgans*, 471; Swaine, *Cravath Firm*, 1:622, 648–50, 715–35; 2:44–69; Adler, *Jacob H. Schiff*, 1:152–74, 211–42; *NYT*, Oct. 30, 1903, Apr. 11, 1900, Aug. 31, 1903, Sept. 1, 1903, Apr. 29, 1905, May 17, 1905.

20. *Jerseyman*, May 8, 1903, Feb. 10, 1905; *NYT*, Aug. 16, 1903; author's interview with Margaret Ryan, Sept. 1985.

21. Morgenthau, *All in a Lifetime*, 101–2.

22. George Haven to Hyde, Feb. 25, 1904, MOA.

23. Buley, *Equitable Life Assurance Society*, 1:514–26, 594.

24. Ibid., 1:598–603; Carosso, *Investment Banking In America*, chap. 5; *NYT*, Feb. 1, 1905.

25. Hyde to Kahn, May 3, 1909, Jan. 11, 1910, and n.d. (ca. 1910); Hyde to Kahn, Feb. 18, 1932, OHK.

26. Upton Sinclair, *Metropolis*, 94; Gabriel Astruc to Hyde, n.d. (ca. 1906), JHH/NYPL; Adler, *Jacob H. Schiff*, 1:19–20, 75–80.

27. *American*, Apr. 5, 1905; Buley, *Equitable Life Assurance Society*, 1:603, 633–34; Kahn, "Grand Opera," address at Century Opera, ca. 1914, OHK.

28. Eliott Gregory to Hyde, Jan. 10, 17, 20 and Feb. 5 and 9, 1906, JHH/NYPL.

29. Gregory to Hyde, Jan. 10, 17, 20 and Feb. 5 and 9, 1906, JHH/NYPL; Gregory to Hyde, Mar. 1, 1906, MOA.

30. Gregory to Hyde, Jan. 10 and 30, Feb. 5 and 9, 1906, JHH/NYPL; CMOC board minutes, MOA.

31. CMOC minutes, Jan. 15 and 27, 1907, MOA.

32. Kolodin, *Metropolitan Opera*, 185–87; Krehbiel, "Salome of Wilde and Strauss"; Mayer, *The Met*, 90; Henderson, *Modern Musical Drift*, 8, 13; "Kahn, Morgan, and Salome," *Saturday Review*, May 30, 1964, 60.

33. *Daily Tribune*, Jan. 31, 1907; MORECo minutes, Jan. 30, 1907, MOA.

34. Goelet, *Old Order Changeth*, 25.

35. CMOC Minutes, Mar. 1, Apr. 12, and June 1, 1907; Gregory, Hyde, and Kahn to R. L. Cottenet, May 30, 1907, MOA; Mosse, *Nationalism and Sexuality*, 14; Henderson, *Modern Musical Drift*, 116–17.

36. Adler, *Jacob H. Schiff*, 1:43–50; Kahn, *Of Many Things*, 114–15.

37. Matz, *Many Lives of Otto Kahn*, 37; Kahn, *Of Many Things*, 144; *EP*, Feb. 27, 1907; *Daily Tribune*, Feb. 28, 1907.

38. Simmel, *Philosophy of Money*.

39. Eliot Gregory to Hyde, Feb. 9, 1906, JHH/NYPL; CMOC minutes, Feb. 27, 1908; MOC minutes, Apr. 3, 1908; Gregory to Hyde, Jan. 15, 1908, MOA; Kolodin, *Metropolitan Opera*, 181; "Kahn, Morgan and 'Salome,'" *Saturday Review* 47 (May 30, 1964), 60.

40. Rawlin L. Cottenet to Hyde, Nov. 20, 1906, and Gregory to Hyde, June 10, 1908, MOA; *NYT*, Feb. 27, 1906, Feb 12, 1908; *WSJ*, Nov. 24, 1908; *World*, Dec. 6, 1908.

41. Gregory to Hyde, Jan. 15, 1908, MOA.

42. Gregory to Hyde, June 10 and 15 1908, MOA.

43. *NYT*, Oct. 21, 1909; *American*, June 1909 (partially dated clipping), OHK; author's interview with Margaret Ryan, Sept. 1985.

44. Samuels, *Bernard Berenson*, 178, 128; Gatti-Casazza, *Memories of the Opera*,

46; Mahler, *Gustav Mahler*, 157–59; Waterbury, "Mrs. Otto H. Kahn," 67; author's interview with Margaret Ryan, Sept. 1985.

45. Interview with Margaret Ryan, Sept. 1985.

46. Gregory to Hyde, Dec. 2, 1909, MOA; Kolodin, *Metropolitan Opera*; Horowitz, *Wagner Nights*.

47. Mahler, *Gustav Mahler*, 157–59; Blaukopf, *Mahler: A Documentary Study*, plate 296; Blaukopf, *Mahler's Unknown Letters*, 41; Gregory to Hyde, Dec. 2, 1909, MOA;.

48. Comparative Financial Statements, MOA; Clarence Mackay to Kahn, Oct. 20, 1910, OHK, regarding Toscanni's salary and the consensus that the Met "policy should be in the direction of decreasing expenses rather than increasing."

49. Dizikes, *Opera in America*, chap. 28; Cone, *Oscar Hammerstein's Manhattan Opera Company*, chaps. 18–20 and appendix 4; Swaine, *Cravath Firm*, 2:79–85; Gregory to Hyde, Mar. 1, 1906, MOA; Henry Russell to Kahn, Apr. 30, 1913 and Aug. 26, 1913; Kahn to Russell, June 16, 1913; Paul Cravath to Kahn, Nov. 15, 1912, July 9 and 19, 1914; Kahn to Henry D. Clayton, Apr. 9, 1914, OHK. In the latter, Kahn writes, "The Metropolitan Opera is not now and never was, an 'opera trust,'" and asks for this remark to be added to the Congressional Record.

50. Hermand, "Commercialization of Avant-Garde Movements," 74–75.

51. Edward Robinson to Kahn, Apr. 5, 1910, OHK; *NYT*, Mar. 4, Mar. 19, June 26, Aug. 7, and Aug. 24, 1910.

52. Kahn to Percival Farquhar, Sept. 18, 1910, OHK; *Denver Post*, Nov. 4, 1910.

53. Matz, *Many Lives of Otto Kahn*, 153–55; Taylor, *Beaverbrook*, 44; Koss, *Rise and Fall of the Political Press in Britain*; Saunders, *Regent's Park Villas*, 1–35; Samuel, *Villas in Regent's Park and Their Residents*, 23–24.

54. Lili Deutsch to Paul Kahn, July 23 and Nov. 22, 1911, Ernst Schulin, private collection; Max Aitken to Kahn, Nov. 20, 1911, OHK.

55. Kahn to Max Aitken, Nov. 11, Dec. 2 and 6, 1911, and Feb. 1, 1912; Kahn to Bonar Law, Dec. 1, 1911; Aitken to Kahn, Feb. 12, 1912, Beaverbrook C/186–87; J. W. D. Barron to Kahn, Feb. 2, 1912; Kahn to Barron, Jan. 30, 1912, OHK; *Manchester Courier*, Jan. 3, 1912; *Manchester Weekly Citizen*, Feb. 3, 1912; Koss, *Rise and Fall of the Political Press in Britain*, 22, 34, 94.

56. Kahn to Aitken Feb. 15, 1912, OHK; Aitken to Kahn, Feb. 26, 1912, Beaverbrook C/186–87.

57. Swaine, *Cravath Firm*, 2:69, 180–84; Carosso, *Investment Banking In America*, 137; Paul Cravath to Kahn, July 7, 1910; Robert Lovett to Kahn, June 30, 1911; Norman R. Pendergast to Kahn, Aug. 16 and 25, 1911; Frank Taussig to Kahn, Feb. 12 and 13, 1912, OHK.

58. Aitken to Kahn, Feb. 26, Mar. 9 and 14, Apr. 3, 1912; Jan. 22, Apr. 24, Aug. 18, 1913; Kahn to Aitken, Apr. 1, 1912, OHK.

59. Crawford Livingston to Kahn, Dec. 11, 1913 and Jan. 10, 1914; Thomas W. Joyce to Kahn, May 26, 1913; Kahn to Aitken, June 13, 1912 and Cassel to Kahn, Jan. 3, 1913; Walter Damrosch to Kahn, May 20 and 22, 1913; Hyde to Kahn, July 28, 1913; F. E. Holliday to Kahn, July 9, 1912; Dippel to Kahn, June 28 and Aug.

18, 1913; J. H. Thomas to Kahn, Jan. 30, 1912; Max Reinhardt to Kahn, Jan. 21, 1913; Aitken to Kahn, Mar. 10, 1913; Cravath to Kahn, Nov. 15, 1912 and Feb. 13, 1913; Kahn to Harold McCormick, Mar. 25, 1912, and McCormick to Kahn, Mar. 27, 1912; Russell to Kahn, Apr. 30, 1913; Russell to Kahn, June 28, 1913; Maurice Wertheim to Kahn, Jan. 13 and Feb. 8, 1911; Cravath to Kahn, Nov. 15, 1912; Russell to Kahn, June 28, 1913, OHK; *NYT*, Aug. 13, 1913, Oct. 7, 1913, Nov. 2, 15, 1913, May 14, 1914, July 12, 1914.

60. *NYT*, Apr. 1, 1914.

Chapter Three

1. Addie Kahn to Kahn, July 18, 1914, Aug. 6, 14, and 19, 1914; affidavit by Kahn, June 1914, OHK; *American*, Aug. 8, 1914.

2. Carosso, *Investment Banking in America*, 197; E. C. Grenfell to Kahn, Aug. 13, 1914, OHK.

3. Watson, *Strange Bedfellows*, 205; Van Vechten, *Sacred and Profane Memories*, 104–5.

4. Carosso, "Chapter Two Typed Notes," VPC/PML.

5. Norman Hapgood to Kahn, June 8, 1914; Max Reinhardt to Kahn, Jan. 21, 1913; "American Miracle Co.," folder, 1914, OHK. See also Cheney, *New Movement in the Theatre*.

6. Kahn to Henry Payne Whitney, Oct. 19, 1914; Kahn to William Churchill, Dec. 1, 1914; Alfred A. Seligsberg to Kahn, Sept. 14, 1915; Gatti-Casazza to Kahn, Aug. 22, Sept. 10 and 27, and Oct. 11, 1914; Kahn to Gatti-Casazza, Sept. 10, 1914; Maurice Leon to Kahn, Dec. 11, 1914; John Brown to Kahn, Oct. 8, 1914; Kahn to Clarence Mackay, Nov. 25, 1914; Henry Russell to Kahn, Nov. 6, 1914; Maurice Leon to Kahn, Dec. 11, 1914, OHK; *Chicago Tribune*, Aug. 30, 1914; *Examiner*, Aug. 30, 1914; *Chicago Herald*, Aug. 30, 1914.

7. Carosso, *Investment Banking in America*, 197; Adler, *Jacob H. Schiff*, 2:241–43.

8. Mortimer L. Schiff to Kahn, May 28, 1910, OHK.

9. Adler, *Jacob H. Schiff*, 2:185.

10. Kahn to Max Aitken, Dec. 1915, and Aitken to Kahn, Dec. 18, 1914, OHK. See also Jacob Schiff to Max Warburg, Jan. 28, 1915, JHS/AJA.

11. Kahn to Lord Victor Paget, Dec. 14, 1914; Kahn to I. F. Marcossen, Mar. 28, 1917; J. B. Elwell to Kahn, Dec. 26, 1914; Kahn to Elwell, Dec. 28, 1914, OHK. Also see Brubaker, *Citizenship and Nationhood in France and Germany*, 21–34.

12. Max Aitken to Kahn, Dec. 18, 1914; F. M. Ponsonby to C. Arthur Pearson, Feb. 6, 1915; Pearson to Kahn, Feb. 8 and 28, 1915; Kahn to Pearson, Feb. 26, 1915; F. B. Henson to James Herbert, Oct. 1, 1915, OHK. Jacob Schiff and Felix Warburg were benefactors of the New York Association for the Blind ("The Light-house"). See Jacob Schiff to Edward R. Hewitt, June 27, 1906; Schiff to Winifred Holt, Dec. 28, 1908; Holt to Felix Warburg, Oct. 25, 1907, Dec. 6, 1980 and July 26, 1910; Warburg to Holt, Sept. 18, 1906, Feb. 20, 1908, Dec. 7, 1909, and July 18, 1910; minutes, Nov. 26, 1912, Lighthouse.

13. Jacob Schiff to James H. Wilson, Oct. 22, 1914, JHS/AJA; *NYT*, Nov. 22, 1914.

14. Rudolf Hecht to Kahn, July 13 and Nov. 5, 1915; Kahn statement, Jan. 2, 1919, OHK.

15. Kahn to Lord Victor Paget, Dec. 14, 1914, OHK; Kahn, *Right above Race*, 7, 17, 39, 49, 55–56, 60–61.

16. Rudolf Hecht to Kahn, July 13, 1915; Paul Kahn to Kahn, Oct. 12, 1915; Kahn to Maximilian Harden, Oct. 27, 1915; Kahn to Oswald Garrison Villard, Aug. 11, 1915; Herman Waldeck to Rudolf Hecht, Sept. 13, 1915; James Herbert to Kahn, Sept. 8, 1915, OHK.

17. Carosso, "The Morgans as Private International Bankers (1854–1934)," 108.

18. E. C. Grenfell to Jack Morgan, Aug. 17, 1914; Morgan to Grenfell, Sept. 20, 1914, JPMJr/PML.

19. Henry P. Davison to Morgan, Dec. 11, 1914; Davison to Lamont, Dec. 11, 1914; Lamont to Davison, Dec. 12, 1914; J. P. Morgan to Grenfell, Apr. 9, 1919, JPMJr/PML.

20. Morgan to Harjes, Sept. 20, 1914; J. P. Morgan to Grenfell, Sept. 5, 1914; Morgan to James J. Hoyt and Morgan to Kahn, Aug. 29, 1914; J. P. Morgan to Mrs. Henrietta E. Shelton, Nov. 2, 1914, JPMJr/PML.

21. J. P. Morgan, Jr., to Vivian Smith, Mar. 24, 1909; J. P. Morgan, Jr., to J. P. Morgan & Co., Oct. 9, 1909; J. P. Morgan, Jr., to J. P. Morgan, Sr., Jan. 24, 1903; J. P. Morgan, Jr., to Charles E. Dawkins, Mar. 7, 1905; J. P. Morgan, Jr., to J. S. Morgan & Co., Jan. 30, 1907; J. P. Morgan, Jr., to Walter S. M. Burns, Jan. 16, 1908; J. P. Morgan, Jr., to Vivian Smith, Mar. 23, 1908; Morgan, Grenfell & Co. to J. P. Morgan, Mar. 10, 1913; J. P. Morgan to Morgan Grenfell & Co., Mar. 10, 1913; J. P. Morgan to E. C. Grenfell, Mar. 11, 1913; Leslie to J. P. Morgan, July 24, 1913, JPMJr/PML.

22. J. S. Morgan to Drexel, Morgan, Sept. 21, 1880, MG-GH; J. P. Morgan, Jr., to J. P. Morgan, Nov. 13, 1903, J. P. Morgan, Jr., to C. E. Dawkins, Feb. 26, 1904; J. P. Morgan, Jr., to George W. Perkins, Nov. 19, 1908; J. P. Morgan, Jr., to J. P. Morgan, Sr., Mar. 17, 1905; J. P. Morgan, Jr., to Charles Steele, Apr. 30, 1906; J. P. Morgan, Jr., to J. P. Morgan, Sr., Mar. 17, 1905; J. P. Morgan, Jr., to Charles Steele, Aug. 3, 1906; J. P. Morgan, Jr., to E. C. Grenfell, Aug. 21 and 31, 1906, and Jan. 11, 1907, J. P. Morgan, Jr., to Vivian Smith, Feb. 27, 1907; J. P. Morgan, Jr., to E. C. Grenfell, Jan. 5, 1909; J. P. Morgan to E. C. Grenfell, Mar. 11, 1913, JPMJr/PML. See also Swaine, *Cravath Firm*, 1:715–16, and *NYT*, Mar. 29 and 30, 1905.

23. J. P. Morgan, Jr., to George W. Perkins, Nov. 19, JPMJr/PML.

24. Nicholson, *Dwight Morrow*, 188–89. The full text of Ezekiel 36:22 reads, "Therefore say unto the house of Israel, thus saith the Lord GOD; I do not this for your sakes, O house of Israel, but for mine holy name's sake, which ye have profaned among the heathen, whither ye went." Additionally illuminating was the reaction of Morgan partner Thomas Lamont, when a report in the *New York World* criticized the Morgans' role in New York City's financial crisis. In a pointed response, Lamont lashed out at Kuhn, Loeb. They had been foisted upon the Morgans at the insistence of the U.S. government when in fact, Lamont argued, the house of Morgan had done most of the work and had not needed Kuhn, Loeb

to manage the syndicate. He also suspected that "our friends, K.L. & Co.," had planted the story. See Thomas Lamont to Grenfell, June 2, 1915, 111/11, TWL/H-B.

25. Jacob Schiff to Kahn, Aug. 19, 1915, OHK.

26. Adler, *Jacob H. Schiff*, 2:252–53; Carosso, *Investment Banking in America*, 203–5; Burk, *Britain, America and the Sinews of War*, 67–76.

27. U.S. Senate Special Committee, *Munitions Industry Hearings*, 8304–6; Walter E. Sachs Oral History, 2:38–39, CUOH; Jacob Schiff to Max Warburg, Sept. 22, 1915, JHS/AJA; Max Warburg to Jacob Schiff, Oct. 10, 1915, AJA Microfilm, r-694; *NYT*, Sept. 15, 17, 22, 23, and 29, 1915; Thane, "Cassel, Sir Ernest Joseph" and "Financiers and the British State."

28. Lamont, *Henry P. Davison*, 193–97; Carosso, *Investment Banking in America*, 204–6; Burk, *Britain, America and the Sinews of War*, 134; Seibert & Co., *Business and Financial Record of World War Years*, 97.

29. Frank A. Vanderlip, Circular, Nov. 27, 1915 (copy in author's possession); Wilkins, *Maturing of Multinational Enterprise*, 21; Scheiber, "World War I as Entrepreneurial Opportunity."

30. Frank A. Vanderlip to James Stillman, Oct. 8 and 29, Nov. 19 and 27, and Dec. 17, 1915; John A. Garver to Vanderlip, Nov. 1, 1915; American International Corporation, "Annual Statement," Dec. 6, 1916, FAV/CU; Vanderlip, Circular, Nov. 27, 1915 (copy in author's possession); Kahn to Jacob Schiff, Aug. 26, 1915, OHK.

31. James H. Hyde to Kahn, Apr. 29, 1915, OHK; Silver, *Esprit de Corps*, 5–13, and "The Germans, Destroyers of Cathedrals," *New York Times Current History* 2 (Aug. 1915): 1004–12.

32. Kahn to James H. Hyde, Mar. 4, 1915; Alice Franc to Otto Kahn, ca. May 10, 1915; James Herbert to Franc, May 11, 1915; Robert H. Hibbard to Herbert, May 11, 1915; Hibbard to The Creditors of Miss Isadora Duncan, ca. Nov. 1915; Max Rabinoff to Herbert, Sept. 19 and Dec. 3, 1915; Edward Goodman to Kahn, June 17, 1915; Kahn to Goodman, June 18, 1915; Kahn to Mrs. Granville Barker, Sept. 27, 1915; Washington Square Players, announcement, OHK; Blair, *Isadora*, 242–50; Money, *Anna Pavlova*, 203–32.

33. Kahn to Henry Russell, Oct. 13 and Dec. 1, 1915; Russell to Kahn, Dec. 17 and 31, 1915; Enclosure, Kahn to Paul D. Cravath, Jan. 26, 1916, OHK; *NYT*, Jan. 26, 1916; Buckle, *Diaghilev*, 301–3.

34. Enclosure, Kahn to Paul D. Cravath, Jan. 26, 1916; Kahn to Adolph S. Ochs, Jan. 18, 1916, OHK; Hines, *Collaborative Form*.

35. Silver, *Esprit de Corps*, 113–14; Garafola, *Diaghilev's Ballets Russes*, 96; Scheiber, "World War I as Entrepreneurial Opportunity," 487.

36. Henry Russell to Kahn, Jan. 19, 1916; Kahn to Baron Burian, Mar. 14, 1916, OHK; Garafola, *Diaghilev's Ballets Russes*, 203.

37. Henry Russell to Kahn, Jan. 19, 1916; Kahn to Dalimiers Feb. 17, 1916; Kahn to Adolph Ochs, Dec. 27, 1916; Kahn to Charles A. Ellis, Aug. 21, 1916, OHK.

38. J. P. Morgan to Herman Harjes, June 27, 1916, and Harjes to Morgan, June 29, 1916, cables, JPMJr/PML.

39. Gatti-Casazza to Kahn, Sept. 6, 1915; Henry Russell to John Brown, Nov. 5, 1915; William Asch to Kahn, Dec. 21, 1916; Russell to Kahn, Jan. 19, 1916; Kahn to James H. Hyde, Feb. 14, 1916; Kahn to Countesse Greffuhle, May 16, 1916; Kahn to Charles A. Ellis, Aug. 21, 1916, OHK.

40. Kahn to Countesse Greffuhle, May 16, 1916; Kahn to Lieut. M. R. Hely Hutchison, May 2, 1916; Kahn to George Bakhmetieff, Oct. 2, 1916, OHK.

41. Grunwald, "Windsor Cassel," 159–61; Kahn to Max Aitken, June 26, 1916, Beaverbrook.

42. Kahn to Jacob H. Schiff, Aug. 9, 1916, OHK; *NYT*, Aug. 23, 1916. In January 1916, rumors that Kuhn, Loeb wanted to control the Winchester Repeating Arms Company left the British Munitions Ministry "most anxious" that Winchester, which was scheduled to provide Britain with 200,000 Enfield rifles beginning March, should "not pass into unsuitable hands or into the hands of Kuhn, Loeb & Co." Thomas Lamont of the New York firm replied, "We would be surprised if Kuhn Loeb & Co. would act in this matter for the enemy." U.S. Senate Special Committee, *Munitions Industry Hearings*, 25:7670–71, 7680, 7690.

43. Seibert & Co., *Business and Financial Record of World War Years*, 97; Jacob Schiff to M. M. Warburg, Oct. 11, 1916, JHS/AJA.

44. Kahn to Mortimer Schiff, Oct. 10 and 27, 1916; Kahn to Hauser, Oct. 9, 1916; Mortimer Schiff to Kahn, Sept. 10, 1916; Kahn to Jacob Schiff, Sept. 7, 1916; Jacob Schiff to Kahn, Sept. 10, 1916; Kahn to Poniatowski, Sept. 29, 1916; Kahn to Allan Forbes, Oct. 2, 1916; Willard Straight to Kahn, Oct. 4, 1916, OHK.

45. Kahn to M. Percy Peixotto, Aug. 13, 1918; Kahn to Henry Say, Oct. 30, 1916; E. H. Paul to Edward L. Bernays, June 25 1918, OHK; U.S. Senate Special Committee, *Munitions Industry Hearings*, 28:8748.

46. Carosso, "Chapter Five Typed Notes," 41–42 and nn. 87–91, VPC/PML; U.S. Senate Special Committee, *Munitions Industry Hearings*, 30:8537–8.

47. Seibert & Co., *Business and Financial Record of World War Years*, 97.

48. U.S. Senate Special Committee, *Munitions Industry Hearings*, 28:8723. Henry P. Davison and Thomas W. Lamont to J. P. Morgan and Herman Harjes, Nov. 7, 1916; J. P. Morgan & Co. to J. P. Morgan, Nov. 10, 1916; J. P. Morgan & Co. to Morgan, Grenfell & Co., Nov. 11, 1916; Davison to J. P. Morgan, Nov. 15, 1916; J. P. Morgan to Herman Harjes, Nov. 15, 1916, JPMJr/PML.

49. Kahn to Jerome Hanuaer, Nov. 21, 1916, OHK; U.S. Senate Special Committee, *Munitions Industry Hearings*, 28:8970. See also J. P. Morgan to Harjes, Nov. 15, 1916; Davison to Lamont and Grenfell, Nov. 18, 1916; Davidson to Lamont and Morgan, Nov. 21, 1916; J. Ridgely Carter to J. P. Morgan, Nov. 20, 1916, JPMJr/PML.

50. U.S. Senate Special Committee, *Munitions Industry Hearings*, 28:8959–60; Carosso, "Chapter Four Typed Notes," VCP/PML.

51. U.S. Senate Special Committee, *Munitions Industry Hearings*, 28:8744; Link, *Papers of Woodrow Wilson*, 3:315–16.

52. Kahn to Aitken, June 26, 1916, OHK; U.S. Senate Special Committee, *Munitions Industry Hearings*, 28:8722, 8727.

53. Kahn, *Right above Race*, 93, 97, 105, 108, 121, and 124; *NYT*, May 21, 1917, June 2 and 8, 1917, Aug. 3, 1917.

54. Kahn to Max J. Bonn, Jan. 17, 1918, OHK; Leopold Hirsch to Kahn, June 7, 1917, OHK.

55. [Davidson?] to Baird, May 22, 1918, 84/7/32, Bonar Law; Kahn, *Reflections*, vii and 352–54.

56. Kahn to Woodrow Wilson, Apr. 6, 1917; Joseph P. Tumulty to Kahn, Apr. 9, 1917; Metropolitan Opera, Board of Directors, draft statement, n.d., OHK.

57. *NYT*, Oct. 13, 1918; Brownlee, *The War, The West and the Wilderness*, 145.

58. Mackay to Kahn, Oct. 11, 20, and 30, 1917; Kahn to Mackay, Oct. 18 and 22, 1917; Herman A. Weinstein to Kahn, Nov. 5, 1917, and Kahn to Weinstein, Nov. 9, 1917, OHK. See Kolodin, *Metropolitan Opera*, 270–71, and *NYT*, Nov. 2, 3, 14, and 18, 1917.

59. Kahn to Weinstein, Nov. 19, 1917, OHK; Gatti-Casazza, *Memories of the Opera*, 180–83; Kolodin, *Metropolitan Opera*, 270, 283; *NYT*, May 8, 1914, Nov. 3, 13, 14, 18 and 19, 1917, Feb. 19 and 21, 1918, Apr. 28 and 30, 1918, Nov. 12, 1918.

60. Kahn to Mortimer Schiff, Aug. 7, 1917; Kahn to Octave Homberg, July 30, 1917; Kahn to André Tardieu, July 6, 23, and 27, 1917; Kahn to Peixotto, Aug. 27, 1917; C. Grant Forbes to Charles A. Stone, Nov. 14, 1917; Kahn to P. Chabert, Sept. 6, 1918, OHK.

61. Paul Cravath to Kahn, Nov. 9, 1917; Kahn to Max J. Bonn, Jan. 17, 1918, OHK; Kahn, *Reflections*, 265.

62. "Confidential Memorandum to the President," enclosed with Kahn to Edward M. House, Sept. 5, 1918, EMH/S-YU.

Chapter Four

1. Jacob Schiff to Max Warburg, Aug. 26, 1919, AJA Microfilm, r-694; Adler, *Jacob H. Schiff*, 2:185.

2. Kahn, *Reflections*, 4, 335, 338; *NYT*, Aug. 23, 1920; Kahn to Max Warburg, Sept. 24, 1920, OHK.

3. *Amerikan Magyer Nepsava*, New York edition, Aug. 16, 1922.

4. H. Crouch Batchelor to Kahn, June 30, 1921; Kahn to Batchelor, Dec. 20, 1921; Kahn, "Statement," Jan. 2, 1919, OHK. See also Silverman, *Reconstructing Europe after the Great War*.

5. Shaw, "Preface to Plays," viii.

6. One of the top executives of Amerada Petroleum, a wildcat developer, said that Hanauer was "the coldest-blooded member of Kuhn, Loeb & Co." J. B. Brody to T. J. Ryder, July 10, 1924, FSP.

7. Kahn to Leonard Keesing, June 21, 1921; Kahn to Isaac F. Marcossen, Kahn to E. B. Franken, Sept. 7, 1921; Kahn to George Lewis, Sept. 20, 1921. OHK; *NYT*, Dec. 7 and 8, 1913, and Aug. 5 and 6, 1921.

8. Kahn, *Reflections*, 27–28, 297–98, 336; Kahn to B. Attolico, Nov. 13, 1919, OHK.

9. Eskimo, "Opera Hats"; Kahn to Gero von Schulze Gaevernitz, Feb. 6, 1925; Kahn to Rudolph Hecht, Dec. 21, 1920, OHK; Eisenstein, *Immoral Memories*, 141.

10. Jack Morgan to Lamont, Nov. 16, 1915; Jack Morgan to A. L. Lowell on Mar. 2, 1920, JPMJr/PML.

11. Kahn to de Neuflize, Oct. 11, 1919, OHK.

12. Chernow, *House of Morgan*, 215–16; Grenfell to Lamont, June 2, 1921 and Oct. 9, 1922, 111/13; Lamont to J. P. Morgan & Co., May 22, 1922, 111/14, TWL/H-B; Charles A. Sawyer, "Memorandum for Mr. Cravath, Mr. Kahn's Citizenship Re: Conference Mar. 16, 1922 with Mr. Charles Blumenthal," OHK.

13. Kahn to Gatti-Casazza, Aug. 25, 1919, OHK; Kolodin, *Metropolitan Opera*, 301–2.

14. Kahn, *Of Many Things*, 219; Kahn to L. Boemare, Oct. 27, 1920; *NYT*, Aug. 26, 1920, Aug. 3, 1922 and Kahn to B. Attolico, Nov. 13, 1919, OHK.

15. Kahn, *Reflections*, 331–43; Kahn to B. Attolico, Nov. 13, 1919; Kahn to L. Boemare, Oct. 27, 1920; Kahn, "The Resumption of Trade Relations with Germany," Nov. 11, 1919; Kahn to Mortimer Schiff, June 22 and May 1, 1923; Kahn to Bainbridge Colby, June 14, 1920; Colby to Kahn, June 18, 1920; Kahn to Frederick Strauss, Nov. 1, 1920; Leonard Wood to Kahn, Sept. 24, 1920; Kahn to Wood, Sept. 30, 1920; James W. Wadsworth to H. R. Winthrop, Oct. 31, 1920; Kahn to Warren G. Harding, Oct. 13, 1921, OHK; *NYT*, Feb. 19, 1920, Oct. 4, 1921, Aug. 3, 1922; Leffler, "Origins of Republican War Debt Policy," 587; Frieden, "Sectoral Conflict and Foreign Economic Policy," 73.

16. Swaine, *Cravath*, 2:306; Kahn to Robert Horne, Sept. 17, 1921, and Kahn to William Wiseman, Apr. 3, 1922, OHK; Harjes to Lamont, May 15, 1922, and Lamont to H. H. Harjes, May 17, 1922, 112/18, TWL/H-B.

17. Kahn to R. Rosenbacher, Dec. 13, 1920; Kahn to Felix Deutsch, Sept. 26, 1921; Kahn to Wiseman, Apr. 3, 1922; Kahn to Max Warburg, May 29, 1922; Max Warburg to Kahn, May 23, 1922; Kahn to Louis Thomas, Apr. 5, 1923, OHK; Teichova and Cottrell, *International Business and Central Europe*, 336, 417; Swaine, *Cravath Firm*, 2:306.

18. Jacob Schiff to Ernest Cassel, Dec. 15, 1897, and Jacob Schiff to James H. Hill, May 25, 1896, AJA Microfilm, r-693; Adler, *Jacob H. Schiff*, 2:345, 353.

19. Max Warburg to Kahn, May 23 and 31, 1922; Kahn to Max Warburg, May 29, 1922; Felix Warburg to Kahn, June 17, 1922; Kahn to S. Rachmann, Aug. 14, 1922; Max Reinhardt to Kahn, Oct. 22, 1922, Kahn to W. Regandez, July 7, 1922, and Kahn to Leopold von Popper, July 8, 1922, OHK; Reinhardt, *Genius*, 28.

20. Grenfell to Lamont, Oct. 9, 1922, 111/13, and Nov. 28, 1922, 111/15, TWL/H-B; Burk, *Britain, America, and the Sinews of War*, 140.

21. Kahn to Mortimer Schiff, Apr. 7, 1923 and May 1, 1923, OHK.

22. Kahn to Karl Popper, June 8, 1923; Kahn to Mortimer Schiff, Apr. 7, 1923 and May 1, 1923, OHK.

23. Adler, *Jacob H. Schiff*, 1:214–19; Jacob Schiff to Baron Takahashi, Feb. 10,

1920, JHS/AJA; Kuhn, Loeb to Kahn, Oct. 12 and 16, 1923, Kahn to Mortimer Schiff, Oct. 12, 1923; see also Kahn to Erastus Brainerd, Mar. 11, 1919; K. Shoda to Kahn, Nov. 1, 1920; Kahn to I. F. Marcossen, Dec. 29, 1921, OHK; Kahn, *Reflections*, 435; Chernow, *House of Morgan*, 233–34; and Lamont, *Across World Frontiers*, 232.

24. Chernow, *House of Morgan*, 235–36, 741 n. 8; Lamont diary, Jan. 18, 21, 22, 1924, 172/26, TWL/H-B.

25. Kahn to Mortimer Schiff, Sept. 20, 1923; Kahn to James deConlay, June 28, 1923, OHK; Elliot, "Mussolini, Prophet of the Pragmatic Era in Politics," 190.

26. J. P. Morgan & Co. to Lamont, July 22, 1924 176/18; Morgan Grenfell to J. P. Morgan & Co., cable 24/4896, July 22, 1924, 176/18; Grenfell to Lamont, July 29, 1924, 176/20, TWL/H-B; Schuker, *End of French Predominance in Europe*, 295–331.

27. Frank B. Kellogg to Kahn, June 28, 1924; Kahn to Kellogg, June 29, 1924; Cravath to Kahn, [July 27, 1924]; Kahn to Kuhn, Loeb, July 29, 1924; [Kuhn, Loeb] to Kahn, n.d. [received July 31, 1924]; Kahn to Kuhn, Loeb, July 31, 1924; Kahn to Cravath, Aug. 5, 1924; Kahn to Mortimer Schiff, Aug. 5, 1924, OHK.

28. Kahn to Mortimer Schiff, Aug. 5 and 21, 1924, OHK.

29. Kahn to Mortimer Schiff, July 16 and Aug. 5, 1924, OHK.

30. Charles Steele, W. H. Porter, D. W. Morrow, Thomas Cochran, R. C. Leffingwell, George Whitney to Morgan, Grenfell, Oct. 2, 1924, 177/21, TWL/H-B.

31. J. P. Morgan and Thomas Lamont to J. P. Morgan & Co., Oct. 3, 1924, 177/22, TWL/H-B.

32. Kahn, *Of Many Things*, 411–14.

33. Chas. Steele et al. to Morgan, Grenfell, Oct. 2 and 4, 1924; J. P. Morgan to J. P. Morgan & Co., Oct. 3, 1924. JPMJr/PML.

34. Lamont to J. P. Morgan & Co., May 22, 1922, 111/14 TWL/H-B; William Wiseman to Kahn, Mar. 4, 1922, OHK; *NYT*, Jan. 14, 1920. Some insight into the opportunism of Blair & Co. as well as Dillon, Read can be found among correspondence and other documents in the folder, "Negotiations with Kuhn, Loeb," FSP.

35. Kahn to Mortimer Schiff, Aug. 21, 1924. Perez and Willett, *Clarence Dillon*, 28–38; McNeil, *American Money and the Weimar Republic*, 71–73.

36. Kahn, *Reflections*, 381.

37. Kahn to Prof. Dr. von Schulze-Gaevernitz, Jan. 3, 1921, OHK.

38. Kahn, *Of Many Things*, 27, 73–76, and *Reflections*, 374.

39. *Chauve Souris* program, 1923.

40. Sayler, *Our American Theatre*, 220–32, 312.

41. Seldes, *7 Lively Arts*, 260–63.

42. Kahn to John Murray Anderson, Sept. 2, 1920; Hugh Anderson to Kahn, Jan. 15, May 18, July 5, 1923; John Murray Anderson to James T. Dartt, May 28, 1929; Theatre Guild files, 1923, 1927; Lawrence Langner to Kahn, May 27, 1924; Cravath to Kahn, Dec. 22, 1922, and Oct. 29, 1923; Otto Kahn to Roger Kahn, Aug. 26, 1924; Kahn to George Gershwin, Nov. 18, 1927; Alex A. Aarons to Kahn,

May 13 and 27, 1926, Oct. 20, 1926, July 24, 1928; Joseph P. Bickerton to Aarons, May 13, 1926; Joseph J. Klein to Aarons, May 28, 1926; Kahn to Alex A. Aarons, July 25, 1928, OHK; Hutchinson, "Roger Wolfe Kahn's Band Shorts of 1927"; *NYT*, Feb. 8, 1924; Kahn, *Of Many Things*, 71.

43. Kahn, *Of Many Things*, 25, 27; Pater *Renaissance*, 192.

44. Kahn to Olin Downes, Nov. 18, 1920; Kahn to Leonard Keesing, June 21, 1921; Kahn to Edward Steinam, June 7, 1921; Kahn to Isaac Marcossen, July 1, 1921, OHK.

45. Moore, *You're Only Human Once*, 95.

46. Ibid., 89.

47. Jeritza, *Sunlight and Song*, 138, 143–44, 154–55, 161; Gatti-Casazza, *Memories of the Opera*, 215; Mayer, *The Met*, 150; Kolodin, *Metropolitan Opera*, 302–3; Tuggle, "From The Metropolitan Opera Archives: Acquisitions 2: Maria Jeritza and Tosca"; *NYT*, Nov. 5 and 20, 1921; Jan. 19, 1922.

48. Moore, *You're Only Human Once*; Kahn to Gatti-Casazza, Mar. 15, June 3, and Aug. 9, 1927; Gatti-Casazza to Kahn, July 27, 1927, OHK.

49. Pat Russell to Kahn, ca. Mar. 1928, and Aug. 9, and 26, 1928 and Kahn to Pat Russell, Aug. 11 and 12, 1928, OHK; Kahn to Giggen [Margaret Kahn], Mar. 8, 1925 (copy in author's possession); Paris, *Louise Brooks*, 72.

50. Grace Moore, *You're Only Human Once*, 134; Nichols, *All I Could Never Be*, 115.

51. Betty Callish to Kahn, Feb. 22, 1920, OHK.

52. Kahn to Cravath, Feb. 2, 1922; Edward Zielger to Kahn, Jan. 5, 1922, OHK.

53. Gray, *Margaret Sanger*, 173; NYT, Nov. 14 and Dec. 10, 1921; *Birth Control Review*, May 1924, 156; Addie Wolff Kahn to Margaret Sanger, July 15, 1927, Aug. 30, 1928, and Apr. 16, 1931; Margaret Sanger to Mrs. Kahn, Aug. 1, Sept. 8, 1928, Oct. 3 and 5, 1928, Apr. 14, 1931, Nov. 13, 1931 and Nov. 3, 1932; S. J. Lawson to Sanger, May 27, 1930, Sanger to Edwin R. Embree, Apr. 17, 1929; Clara McGraw to Sanger, Jan. 22, 1930; McGraw to Rudolph I. Coffee, Mar. 1930; Alice Palache, memorandum, Jan. 11, 1932, MS/LC.

Chapter Five

1. Benedict, "Otto H. Kahn—Maecenas," 11; Gilbert, "Otto H. Kahn"; Frank, "Profiles: In Tune with the Finite," 23; Salpeter, "Otto the Magnificent," 386; Bogard and Bryer, *Selected Letters of Eugene O'Neill*, 189.

2. Jencks, *What Is Post-Modernism*, 29.

3. Paige, *Selected Letters of Ezra Pound*, 54.

4. Josephson, *Life among the Surrealists*, 297.

5. Anderson, *Out without My Rubbers*, 66. Of the broader literature, see Baxandall, *Painting and Experience in Fifteenth-Century Italy*; Burke, *Italian Renaissance*; Seigel, *Bohemian Paris*; Mayer, *Persistence of the Old Regime*; Zolberg, *Constructing a Sociology of the Arts*; Boime, "Entrepreneurial Patronage in Nineteenth-Century France"; Santirocco, "Poet and Patron in Ancient Rome," 56–62.

6. Edward Said, *Beginnings: Intention and Method*, 13.

7. Bel Geddes, *Miracle in the Evening*, 180–81, and Norton, "Geddes, Norman Bel," 233.

8. Bel Geddes to Kahn, Feb. 6 and Mar. 2, 1917; Kahn to Bel Geddes, Feb. 14 and Mar. 19, 1917, OHK.

9. Bel Geddes to Kahn, Oct. 13, 1917; Kahn to Bel Geddes, Oct. 22, 1917, OHK.

10. Bel Geddes to Kahn, Nov. 26, 30, and Dec. 6, 1917; Kahn to Bel Geddes, Nov. 27 and Dec. 5, 1917; Bel Geddes, *Miracle In the Evening*, 184–85.

11. Kahn to Charles Henry Meltzer, Aug. 9, 1918, OHK.

12. Bel Geddes to Kahn, Dec. 20, 1917; Kahn to Bel Geddes, Dec. 21, 1917, OHK.

13. Paul Robeson to Kahn, n.d., filed Mar. 13, 1923, OHK; Duberman, *Paul Robeson*, 53.

14. Kahn to Robeson, Mar. 12, 1923, OHK; Duberman, *Paul Robeson*, 53, 55, 585–86; Sheaffer, *O'Neill*, 109; Gelb and Gelb, *O'Neill*, 513, 522–23.

15. Kenneth Macgowan to Kahn, Feb. 6, 17, and 28, 1924; Kahn to Kenneth Macgowan, Feb. 19, 1924; Kahn to Helen Freeman, May 6, 1924; Hannah Deutsch to Kahn, Jan. 28, 1930; Kahn to Hannah Deutsch, Feb. 5, 1931, OHK; Sheaffer, *O'Neill*, 134–38; Duberman, *Robeson*, 57–62; Deutsch and Hanau, *Provincetown*, 104, 107–10.

16. James Weldon Johnson to Kahn, Jan. 20 and Sept. 23, 1925, and Kahn to Johnson, Jan. 22, 1925, OHK; Sheaffer, *O'Neill*, 136–37, 141–44; Duberman, *Robeson*, 64–67, 70, 73–81; Kahn, *Of Many Things*, 69–70; Deutsch and Hanau, *Provincetown*, 100; *Boston Globe*, Nov. 18, 1924; Kellner, *Letters of Carl Van Vechten*, 74–75.

17. Eslanda Robeson to Kahn, n.d., filed June 22, 1925, OHK; Duberman, *Paul Robeson*, 44, 83, 596; Van Vechten Papers Catalogue (marginalia), CVV/NYPL; Berger, "Jazz: Resistance to the Diffusion of a Culture Pattern," 462.

18. Kahn to Carl Van Vechten, June 19 and June 25, 1925; Kahn to Eslanda Robeson, June 29, 1925; Eslanda Robeson to Kahn, n.d., filed July 30, 1925; Paul Robeson to Kahn, July 1, 1925, OHK; Duberman, *Paul Robeson*, 89, 119, 596.

19. Crane to Kahn, Dec. 3, 1925, OHK.

20. Ibid.

21. Ibid.; [Meinhardt] to Crane, Dec. 5, 1925, including marginalia, OHK; Weber, *Letters of Hart Crane*, 11, 27–33, 225, 138; Pater, *Renaissance*, 111, 113; Jones, "The Groves of Isadora."

22. Crane to Kahn, Sept. 19, 1926, OHK; Lewis, *Letters of Hart Crane and His Family*, 40, 167–71, 173–75, 179–81, 219–22, 310; Fuchs, "Poet & Patron"; Brown, *Robber Rocks*, 196.

23. Crane to Kahn, July 31, 1926 and Sept. 12, 1927; Kahn to Crane, Jan. 6, 1926; "Crane, Hart" [summary of donations and loans], ca. 1930, OHK; Weber, *Letters of Hart Crane*, 232.

24. Rhodes, "Reassessing 'Uncle Shylock,' " 787–803; Mayer, *Outsiders*.

25. Eslanda Robeson to Kahn, n.d., filed July 3, 1925, n.d., filed July 30, 1925,

n.d. [Aug. 21, 1925], and Sept. 17, 1925, OHK; Duberman, *Paul Robeson*, 85, 596.

26. Kahn to Eslanda Robeson, Sept. 28 and Nov. 2, 1925; Eslanda Robeson to Kahn, Oct. 9 and Nov. 17, 1925, OHK; Duberman, *Paul Robeson*, 90–91.

27. Duberman, *Paul Robeson*, 87–88; E. H. Paul to Kahn and Secretary to Mrs. Eslanda G. Robeson, Dec. 18, 1925, OHK.

28. Duberman, *Paul Robeson*, 98–103, 601.

29. Secretary to Adolph Goldhammer, Jan. 26, 1923; OHK. He had been loaned $1,000.

30. Margaret Anderson to Kahn, Mar. 15, 1922 and Sept. 15, 1922; Kahn to Anderson, Sept. 19, 1922, OHK.

31. Kahn to Marc Connelly, Mar. 27, 1930, OHK.

32. E. H. Paul to Kahn, Jan. 28, 1925 and Feb. 2, 1925, OHK.

33. See Duberman, *Paul Robeson*, 68–69, 102–18, 589.

34. Eslanda Robeson to Kahn, Jan. 21, Mar. 12, and May 23, 1929, and Kahn to Eslanda Robeson, Feb. 1, 1929, and June 15, 1929, OHK. Her book, *Paul Robeson: Negro*, was published in 1930 by Victor Gollancz, Ltd., London.

35. Eslanda Robeson to Kahn, May 23, 1929, OHK.

36. Kahn to Eslanda Robeson, June 15, 1929, OHK.

37. Eslanda Robeson to Kahn, Oct. 7, 1929, OHK; Duberman, *Paul Robeson*, 122. It cost the Robesons $8,000 to settle the suit with Caroline Dudley Reagan.

38. Eslanda Robeson to Kahn, Oct. 7, 1929, OHK.

39. Bruce Bromley to Kahn, Jan. 31, 1931, OHK.

40. Eslanda Robeson to Kahn, Dec. 21, 1931 and May 28, 1932; Kahn to Eslanda Robeson, Jan. 2, 1932 and May 30, 1932, OHK.

41. Duberman, *Robeson*, 85; Bel Geddes, *Miracle in the Evening*, 182.

42. Bel Geddes to Kahn, Apr. 2, 1918, and Kahn to Bel Geddes, Mar. 25, 1918, OHK; Bel Geddes, *Miracle in the Evening*, 201–2, 205–6; Matz, *Many Lives of Otto Kahn*, 200.

43. Bel Geddes to Kahn, Dec. 9, 1919, and Kahn to Bel Geddes, Dec. 12, 1919, OHK; Bel Geddes, *Miracle in the Evening*, 212–16.

44. Bel Geddes to Kahn, Nov. 13, 1921, and Kahn to Bel Geddes, Nov. 15, 1921, OHK; Bragdon, "Towards a New Theatre"; Bogard and Bryer, *Selected Letters of Eugene O'Neill*, 183–84; 171–82; Sayler, *Our American Theatre*, 149–68; Bel Geddes, *Miracle in the Evening*, 247–53, 269.

45. Reinhardt to Kahn, n.d. (enclosed with Kahn to Ziegler, Jan. 21, 1924); Rudolf Kommer to Kahn, Jan. 18 and Mar. 2, 1923, and Jan. 12, 1925; Kahn to Morris Gest, Feb. 8, 1926; Bel Geddes to Kahn, May 24, 1923; Kahn to Bel Geddes, Jan. 25, 1924; Kahn to Bel Geddes, Nov. 5, 1924, OHK; "The Miracle" program, 1925.

46. Kahn to Edward Ziegler, Feb. 10, 1924; Kahn to Jesse Lasky, Mar. 31 and July 1, 1924; Bel Geddes to Kahn, June 19 and Aug. 18, 1924, OHK; Bel Geddes, *Miracle in the Evening*, 313–19. Bel Geddes' letters to Kahn neglected to mention the incident with the columnist.

47. Bel Geddes to Kahn, Feb. 6, 1925 and Dec. 23, 1925; Kahn to Bel Geddes,

Feb. 6, 1925; and Kahn to Richard G. Herndon, Sept. 30, 1925 and Oct. 13, 1925, OHK.

48. Herndon to Kahn, Dec. 2, 1925; Kahn to Herndon, Dec. 3, and 14, 1925; Bel Geddes to Kahn, Dec. 23, 1925; Kahn to Bel Geddes, Dec. 16, 1925; Kahn to Maurice Wertheim, Feb. 27, 1926, OHK.

49. Lewis, *Hart Crane and His Family*, 452.

50. Paul, *Hart's Bridge*, 168; Weber, *Letters of Hart Crane*, 225, 233.

51. Weber, *Letters of Hart Crane*, 244, 240–42, and Paul *Hart's Bridge*, 168.

52. Anderson, *My Thirty Years War*, 227–28.

53. Kahn to Crane, Apr. 8 and Apr. 13, 1926; Crane to Kahn, Apr. 10, 1926 and n.d., filed May 11, 1926, OHK; Weber, *Letters of Hart Crane*, 247, 254, 262, 265, 273–74.

54. Weber, *Letters of Hart Crane*, 247, 248, 250, 259, 267, 268, 271.

55. Crane to Kahn, Sept. 21, 1927, OHK.

56. Crane to Kahn, Sept. 12, 1927, OHK; Weber, *Letters of Hart Crane*, 304–9.

57. Crane to Kahn, Mar. 18, July 31, and Sept. 19, 1926, OHK.

58. Kahn to Crane, Sept. 19, 1927, OHK.

59. Giles, *Hart Crane: The Contexts of the Bridge*, 215; Fuchs, "Poet & Patron," 48; Josephson, *Life among the Surrealists*, 297–98.

60. Weber, *Letters of Hart Crane*, 233.

61. Kahn to David Gray, Sept. 24, 1928, OHK.

62. Cited in Kobler, *Otto the Magnificent*, 92.

63. Weber, *Letters of Hart Crane*, 233.

64. Kahn to Hart Crane, Nov. 1, 1926, OHK.

65. Brown, *Robber Rocks*, 196; Weber, *Letters of Hart Crane*, 310.

66. Kahn to James Dartt, Dec. 29, 1927, OHK; Weber, *Letters of Hart Crane*, 247.

67. Giles, *Hart Crane: The Contexts of the Bridge*, 128; Baker, "Commercial Sources for Hart Crane's *The River*," 45–55; Forbes, *Men Who Are Making America*; Bogard, *Contour in Time*. In a similar vein, when Ford's anti-Semitic newspaper, the *Dearborn Independent*, was called to Kahn's attention in 1924 by Jacob Landau of the Jewish Telegraphic Agency, Kahn decided to give no comment (Kahn to Landau, Nov. 11, 1924, OHK). Edison admired Otto Kahn's writings on economics, and in 1918 the inventor hung an autographed picture of Kahn in the library at his laboratory. While Edison sometimes agreed with his friend Henry Ford on the subject of Jews as a race and thought a number of Jews were "crooks," he also said that Otto Kahn was an exceptional Jew—"a good man." Thomas A. Edison to Meadowcroft, n.d.; Meadowcroft to Kahn, Nov. 15, 1918, and Kahn to Edison, Nov. 17, 1918, TAE/ENHS; Shands, "The Real Thomas Edison," 85.

68. Kahn, *Of Many Things*, 17, 19.

69. Bel Geddes to Kahn, July 11, 1930; Bel Geddes, "Minutes of Meeting with Pennsylvania Railroad Company," July 27, 1930; Meinhardt to Kahn, Sept. 28, 1926; Crane to Kahn, Sept. 9, 1930 and Apr. 24, 1931; Kahn to Henry Allen Moe, Oct. 2, 1930; Kahn to Frank Trumbull, June 29, 1916; Kahn to Harris, Oct. 4, 1921, Apr. 4, 1922, and June 13, 1923; Harris to Kahn, Mar. 5, 1926; George S.

Viereck to Kahn, Nov. 19, 1926; Kahn to Viereck, Nov. 20, 1926, OHK; Hart Crane to Waldo Frank, May 22, 1926, HCP; Brown, *Robber Rocks*, 196; Harris, *My Life and Loves*, 1023.

70. Kahn to Frank Harris, June 13, 1923; George S. Viereck to Kahn, Nov. 19, 1926; Kahn to Viereck, Nov. 20, 1926, OHK.

71. Bogard and Bryer, *Selected Letters of Eugene O'Neill*, 209.

72. Partially suggestive of the cohort in mix and breadth: Kahn to Max Eastman Nov. 23, 1921; Waldo Frank to Kahn, Mar. 8, 1929; Kahn to Waldo Frank, Mar. 9, 1929; Kahn to Carl Van Vechten, Mar. 3, 1929; Kahn to Alexander Woolcott, Aug. 10, 1925 and Sept. 11, 1924; Mike Gold to Kahn, filed July 3, 1928; Gold to Kahn, July 18, 1928; Kahn to Gold, July 2, 1928; Kahn to James Weldon Johnson, Sept. 28, 1925, OHK; Davidson, *Between Sittings*, 193–98; Bennett, *Journal*, 947–52. For a contrary opinion on New York's internationalism, see Douglas, *Terrible Honesty*, 5.

73. Frank, *Salvos*, 51.

74. Kahn, *Of Many Things*, 21.

Chapter Six

1. Meinhardt to Kahn, Oct. 29, 1929; Kahn to Paul Einzig, Apr. 7, 1929, OHK.

2. Galbraith, *Great Crash*, 4.

3. *NYT*, Apr. 24 and 25, 1926; Kahn, "The Stock Market and the Public," pamphlet, Apr. 1926, OHK; Meinhardt to Kahn, June 26, 1926, enclosure, OHK.

4. Chernow, *Warburgs*, 309–10; U.S. Senate, Committee on Banking and Currency, *Stock Exchange Practices: Hearings*, 1007–9, 1285.

5. Kahn to Paul Einzig, Apr. 7, 1929, enclosure, OHK.

6. Ibid.; U.S. Senate, Committee on Banking and Currency, *Stock Exchange Practices: Hearings*, 1007, 1009.

7. Matthew Brush to Kahn, Oct. 30, 1929, and Kahn to Lady Diana Cooper, Nov. 23, 1929, OHK; U.S. Senate, Committee on Banking and Currency, *Stock Exchange Practices: Hearings*, 963.

8. Kahn to Diana Cooper, Nov. 23, 1929; Kahn to Arthur Brisbane, Nov. 19, 1929, OHK.

9. S. J. Woolf, "Kahn Talks of Our Cultural Future," 3, 20; Erwin Panofsky cited in Basil S. Yamey, *Accounting and Art*, 9–11.

10. S. N. Melamed to Kahn, Nov. 2 and 25, 1929; Kahn to Melamed, Nov. 4 and 27, 1929, OHK.

11. M. Eleanor Fitzgerald to Kahn, Nov. 6 and Dec. 19, 1929; Kahn to Fitzgerald, Nov. 7 and Dec. 12, 1929; Arthur L. Carnes to Kahn, Dec. 9 and 11, 1929; Kahn to Carnes, Dec. 9 and 11, 1929; Howard S. Cullman to Carnes, Nov. 27, 1929; Cullman to Kahn, Oct. 8, 1929; Experimental Theatre, Inc., "Notice to Subscribers," Dec. 19, 1929; Clarence Mackay to Kahn, Dec. 19, 1929; Kahn to Mackay, Dec. 21, 1929, OHK; *NYT*, Dec. 15, 1929.

12. Gertz, *Odyssey of a Barbarian*, 266; Viereck to Kahn, Nov. 12 and 13, 1929, OHK.

13. Gold to Kahn, ca. Feb. 15, 1930, OHK.

14. Paris, *Louise Brooks*, 175; Gilmer, *Horace Liveright*, 102–3.

15. Viereck to Kahn, Nov. 11, 12, and 13, 1929; Kahn to Viereck, Nov. 13, 1929, OHK.

16. Viereck to Kahn, Nov. 13, Dec. 17 and 28, 1929, OHK.

17. Kahn to Viereck, Nov. 14, 1929, OHK.

18. Viereck to Kahn, Nov. 18, 1929, OHK.

19. Viereck to Kahn, Dec. 27 and 30, 1930; "List of Stocks George Sylvester Viereck," OHK.

20. Kahn to Le Maréchal Lyautey, Aug. 6, 1926; Kahn to Viereck, May 3, 1927; Max Warburg to Otto Kahn, Jan. 21, 1927; Kahn to Jakob Goldschmidt, Dec. 24, 1927; Mortimer Schiff to Kahn, Aug. 24, 1928; Kahn to Kuhn, Loeb, Sept. 1, 1928; Kahn to Wiseman, June 16, 1929; Kahn to Ferdinand Eberstadt, June 8, 1929, OHK; U.S. Senate, Committee on Banking and Currency, *Stock Exchange Practices: Hearings*, 1377; Swaine, *Cravath Firm*, 2:441–43; Perez and Willett, *Will to Win*, 41–45.

21. Kahn to Dr. Joseph Chapiro, Feb. 26, 1929 and May 10, 1929; Kahn to Kuhn, Loeb, Apr. 25, 1929; Wiseman to Kuhn, Loeb, May 7, 1929; Wiseman to Kahn, June 15, 1929; George Deutsch to Kahn, Sept. 26, 1929; Kuhn, Loeb to Kahn, June 10, 1929, OHK.

22. Kahn to Thomas Lamont, June 7, 1929; Kahn to Owen Young, June 6, 1929; Kahn to Kuhn, Loeb, Apr. 25, 1929, OHK.

23. James Murphy to Kahn, Jan. 9, 1930, OHK; more generally, Willett, *Art and Politics in the Weimar Period* and *Theatre of the Weimar Republic*; Cook, *Opera for a New Republic*.

24. Theodore D. Burton to Kahn, Dec. 8, 1925 and Mar. 17, 1926; Kahn to Burgermeister Boettger and Dr. Epstein, Dec. 26, 1929; Kahn to Gold, May 15, 1930 (Kahn apparently subsidized Gold's European tour); William Guard to Kahn, Dec. 31, 1930; Kahn to Karl Lion, Dec. 21, 1921; Kahn to Henry Russell, Dec. 24, 1929; Kahn to Diana Cooper, Nov. 23, 1929, OHK; von Sternberg, *Fun in a Chinese Laundry*, 131.

25. Kahn, *Right above Race*, 67, 69, 97, 123. See also Karl Lion, Dec. 21, 1921; Kahn to Henry Russell, Dec. 24, 1929; Kahn to Diana Cooper, Nov. 23, 1929, OHK.

26. Schumpeter, *Business Cycles*, 334; Kahn to Norman Bel Geddes, Feb. 14, 1931; James N. Rosenberg to Kahn, Mar. 18, 20, and 27, 1930, OHK.

27. Kolodin, *Metropolitan Opera*, 355 (the actual losses for the 1929–30 Met season amounted to more than $53,000, but the sale of U.S. bonds made the adjusted deficit $14,743); "Little Cinema Theatres, Inc. Balance Sheet," Mar. 31, 1930; Kahn to John Brown, Apr. 16, 1930; Doris Kirchner Earl to Kahn, May 9, 15, and 24, 1930; Kahn to Doris Kirchner Earl, May 13 and 19, 1930; Doris Troutman Basshe to Kahn, Apr. 22, 1930, OHK.

28. Kahn, "Some Aspects of the Depression," pamphlet, June 30, 1930; James G. Dartt to T. J. Ross, June 30, 1930; Ross to Dartt, July 8, 1930; Kahn to Lee, Mar. 24, 1929, OHK.

29. Kahn, "Some Aspects of the Depression," pamphlet, June 30, 1930, OHK.

30. Ibid.; Kahn to Rudolf Kommer, Sept. 16 and 18, 1930; Kommer to Kahn, Sept. 16, 1930; Kahn to Mortimer Schiff, Oct. 5, 1930; Kahn to Robert Kahn, Sept. 26, 1930, OHK.

31. Schumpeter, *Business Cycles*, 334–35.

32. Kahn to Lennox Robinson, June 20, 1931; Kahn to Max Bonn, July 23, 1931; Kahn to Henry Hurwitz, Nov. 10, 1930; Kahn, "A Few Thoughts on the Great Depression," broadside, Sept. 8, 1931, OHK.

33. Kahn to Mortimer Schiff, Apr. 22, 1931; Kahn to Lili Deutsch, May 19, 1931, OHK.

34. Kahn to Mortimer Schiff, May 15, 1931; Mortimer Schiff to Kahn, May 19, 1931, OHK.

35. Kahn to Jacques de Neuflize, June 20, 1931, OHK.

36. Kindleberger, *Financial History of Western Europe*, 374, 378; Heiber, *Weimar Republic*, 183; Chernow, *Warburgs*, 328.

37. Kahn to Otto Schiff, June 28, 1931; Kahn to Hiram W. Johnson, Jan. 5, 1932; Winthrop W. Aldrich to Otto Kahn, Aug. 19, 1931, OHK.

38. Wigmore, *Great Crash*, 236.

39. Kahn to Lili Deutsch, July 30, 1931, OHK.

40. Kahn, "A Few Thoughts on the Great Depression," broadside, Sept. 8, 1931, OHK.

41. Kahn to Gatti-Casazza, Aug. 5, 1931; Ivy Lee to Kahn, Sept. 16, 1931 and enclosure, "Confidential: European Financial Situation," OHK.

42. Wigmore, *Great Crash*, 236.

43. Lili Deutsch to Kahn, Sept. 28, 1931; George Deutsch to Kahn, Sept. 29 and Oct. 7, 1931, OHK.

44. Eberstadt, "Die Familie Eberstadt."

45. Meinhardt to Kahn, Oct. 23, 1931. See also Dartt to Mrs. Charlotte K. Fraser (widow of Kahn's former superintendent at the Long Island estate), Dec. 1, 1931, OHK.

46. Kahn to Felix Kahn, May 6, 1931; Kahn to Kuhn, Loeb, July 31, 1931; James G. Dartt to Charles Levy, July 31, 1931; Felix Kahn to Kahn, Aug. 25, 1931, OHK.

47. "Stocks Held in Felix E. Kahn's Account," Dec. 14, 1931 (the stocks loaned by Otto Kahn were valued at $93,600 at that time); George Deutsch to Kahn, Oct. 7, 1931, OHK.

48. Otto Kahn to Felix Kahn, Feb. 16, 1933. Also see Kahn to Eugene J. Kahn (cousin), June 12, 1931; Raymond Pollack to Hedwig Pollack (Kahn's sister), May 7, 1932; Hedwig Pollack to Kahn, May 28, 1932; Kahn to Hedwig Pollack, May 30, 1932, OHK.

49. *NYT* and *HT*, Oct. 27, 1931.

50. Kahn, "Grand Opera," address, circa 1914; Kahn to R. Fulton Cutting, May 18, 1928; James Dartt to Price, Waterhouse, Dec. 12, 1931, OHK; "Comparative Statement, 1898–1947," MOA.

51. Conrad, *Song of Love and Death*, 248.

52. [Description of New Opera Site Proposed], Nov. 18, 1925; Cravath to Kahn, Dec. 28, 1925; Kahn to R. Fulton Cutting, Jan. 5, 1926, OHK.

53. Kahn to R. Fulton Cutting, Jan. 5, 1926, OHK.

54. R. Fulton Cutting to Kahn, Jan. 12, 1926; Kahn to Cutting, Jan. 14, 1926; "Statement released in morning papers of January 16, 1926 through Ivy Lee's office," OHK.

55. Kahn to Cravath, Apr. 10, 1928; "Wolab Realty" and "Metropolitan Opera" files, 1927–28, OHK.

56. B. W. Morris, "Re: Metropolitan Opera House," June 25, 1927; R. Fulton Cutting to Otto Kahn, Jan. 26, 1928; Kahn, "Statement for the Press," [unpublished draft], Feb. 1928, OHK; *NYT*, Feb. 21, 1928 and (New York) *Tribune*, Feb. 20, 1928.

57. Kahn, "Memorandum," Apr. 7, 1931, OHK.

58. Kolodin, *Metropolitan Opera*, 257–58.

Chapter Seven

1. Kahn to Bernard Fay, Dec. 16, 1931, OHK.

2. Quoted in Wigmore, *Great Crash*, 315.

3. *Fortune*, Mar. 1930, 89–90, 116–19; *Fortune*, Sept. 1932, 32–36; Born, *International Banking*, 274.

4. Max Ewing to J. C. Ewing, May 24, 1930, Ewing/B-YU.

5. Schwarz, *Interregnum of Despair*, 85.

6. This reading is informed by Cameron and Hoffman, *Guide to Theatre Study*, 55–59; Wilshire, *Role Playing and Identity*, 103; Burns, *Theatricality*, 145; Berger and Luchman, *Social Construction of Reality*, 75.

7. *NYT*, Dec. 22, 1931 and Jan. 5, 1932; *EP*, Jan. 5 and 6, 1932.

8. *NYT*, Dec. 22, 1931 and Jan. 5, 1932; *EP*, Jan. 5 and 6, 1932.

9. *NYT*, Jan. 6, 1932.

10. Clurman, *Fervent Years*, 65–67, 75; Goldstein, *Political Stage*, 17–21, 83–84; Leiter, *Encyclopedia of the New York Stage*, 552–53.

11. Kahn, *Reflections*, 371.

12. Max Eastman to Kahn, July 6, 1933; Kahn to Sergei Eisenstein, Dec. 27, 1930; Eastman, *Love and Revolution*, 527–32; Sinclair, *Mammonart*, 50, and *Autobiography*, 266.

13. Wilson, *Ideology and Economics*, 62–63, 87–88.

14. Francis Walston Welsh to Kahn, Apr. 4, 1930, and Kahn to Welsh, Apr. 7, 1930, OHK.

15. Gold to Kahn, n.d., ca. Oct. 1–12, 1932, OHK.

16. John W. Davis to Kahn, Jan. 6, 1932; Matthew Brush to Kahn, Dec. 22, 1931; F. Kelley to Kahn, Dec. 24, 1931; Paul Cravath to Kahn, Jan. 8, 1932; Beaverbrook to Kahn, Dec. 23, 1931; Henry A. Vernet to Kahn, Jan. 29, 1932; Kahn to Vernet, Feb. 9, 1932, OHK.

17. Wigmore, *Great Crash*, 331–32; *EP*, Jan. 6, 1932.

18. Gulbenkian to Kahn, Feb. 24, 1932; Kahn to Gulbenkian, Mar. 4, 1932, OHK; Coty, *Tearing Away the Veils*.

19. Gulbenkian to Kahn, Feb. 24, 1932; Kahn to Gulbenkian, Mar. 4, 1932, OHK.

20. Otto Schiff to Kahn, Mar. 10, 1932; Kahn to Otto Schiff, Mar. 23, 1932; Kahn to Robert Kahn, Mar. 21, 1932, OHK.

21. Kahn to Otto Schiff, Mar. 23, 1932; Kahn to Leonard Keesing, Apr. 5, 1932, OHK.

22. McCormick, "The Discovery That Business Corrupts Politics," 247–74.

23. Andrew F. Kelley to Kahn, Sept. 1931, OHK; Kahn, *Reflections*, 190–98, 224–25, 244.

24. Olson, *Herbert Hoover and the Reconstruction Finance Corporation*, 33–56; Schwarz, *Interregnum of Despair*, 91.

25. Kahn, *Reflections*, 37–119; *Of Many Things*, 220–321, and "A Few Thoughts on the Great Depression"; Schwarz, *Interregnum of Despair*, 106–41; Ratner, *Taxation and Democracy in America*, 443–50.

26. Kahn to Cong. Henry Rainey (D-Ill.), Mar. 22, 1932, OHK.

27. Kahn to Garet Garrett, Mar. 17, 1932; *NYT*, Apr. 1, 2, and May 1, 1932.

28. Carosso, *Investment Banking in America*, 324.

29. Ivy Lee to Kahn, Apr. 25, 1932, OHK; Carosso, *Investment Banking in America*, 322–27; Galbraith, *Great Crash, 1929*, 67; *NYT*, Apr. 6, 23, 1932.

30. Kahn to William Bird, May 3, 1927, and Edward Ziegler to Bird, May 17, 1927, Pound/B-YU; Paige, *Selected Letters of Ezra Pound, 1907–1941*, 215–16, 233.

31. Pound, "Canto XVIII," *Cantos (1–95)*, 80; William Bird to Ezra Pound, Mar. 16 and 22, Apr. 23, and Nov. 26, 1927, Pound/B-YU.

32. Kahn read "the first rumble" in mid-summer and promised to help interest an American publisher. Kahn to Pound, Aug. 5, 1931, Pound/B-YU.

33. Pound to Kahn, Nov. 19, 1931, Pound/B-YU.

34. Pound to Kahn, Mar. 4, 1932, OHK; Stock, *Life of Ezra Pound*, 260.

35. Pound to Kahn, Mar. 4, 1932; Kahn to Pound, Mar. 17, 1932, Pound/B-YU.

36. *NYT*, Mar. 4, 24, and 25, 1932.

37. Erskine, *My Life in Music*, 130–31; *NYT*, Sept. 26, 1929.

38. H. R. Winthrop to Kahn, Mar. 11, 1932, OHK.

39. Clurman, *Fervent Years*, 63–64; Waldau, *Vintage Years of the Theatre Guild*, and Eaton, *Theatre Guild*.

40. Zora Neale Hurston to Kahn, Dec. 26, 1931; Corn to Hurston, Dec. 28, 1931; B. M. Steigman to Kahn, Mar. 31, 1932; Kahn to Steigman, Apr. 2, 1932; Harold Clurman to Kahn, Apr. 11, 1932; Waldo Frank to Kahn, Mar. 12, 1932; Kahn to Frank, Feb. 20 and Mar. 14, 1932, OHK.

41. Clurman, *Fervent Years*, 75–76.

42. Waldo Frank to Kahn, May 12, 1933, OHK.

43. Kahn to Clurman, Apr. 12, 1932; Antheil to Kahn, Mar. 18, 1932 and n.d. [ca. Feb. 22–25, 1932], OHK; Clurman, *Fervent Years*, 75–76.

44. Wilde, *Complete Works*, 975.

45. Weber, *Letters of Hart Crane*, 366–412.

46. Clurman, *Fervent Years*, 78.

47. Kahn to Ingersoll, May 3, 1932; Kahn, "A Plain Statement of Presidential Preference," pamphlet, Aug. 26, 1928; William E. Borah to Kahn, Oct. 31, 1929; Kahn to Borah, Nov. 1, 1929, OHK; Kahn, *Of Many Things*, 262–65; *NYT*, Oct. 26, 27, 28, and 30, 1929.

48. Kahn to Bernard Baruch, May 9 and 15, 1930; Baruch to Kahn, May 13, 1930; Kahn to *New York Times*, Nov. 6, 1930 (unpublished); William Ziegler, Jr., to Kahn, May 2, 1932; Kahn to William Ziegler, May 3, 1932; Frederick M. Warburg to Kahn, Nov. 9, 1932; Kahn to Robert F. Wagner, Apr. 20, 1932, OHK.

Chapter Eight

1. Kahn to Henry Russell and Kahn to Percy Peixotto, May 30, 1932; Kahn to Louis Sobol, May 20, 1932; Kahn to Lennox Robinson, July 27, 1932, OHK; *NYT*, May 29, 1932.

2. Kahn to Otto Schiff, July 8, 1932; Kahn to William Forbes Morgan, Jr., July 7, 1932; Kahn to W. F. Morgan, Jr., Nov. 9, 1932, OHK; Ratner, *Taxation and Democracy in America*, 452.

3. C. Kahn to Harry van Heukelom, Sept. 28, 1932, OHK; *NYT*, Oct. 15, 1932.

4. Kahn to Edward Percy Howard, Oct. 21, 1932; Kahn to Lennox Robinson, Oct. 25, 1932; Kahn to Harry van Heukelom, Sept. 28, 1932; Mutke to Matthew Brush, Sept. 16, 1932; Norman Bel Geddes to Kahn, Oct. 24, 1932; Mutke to Bel Geddes, Oct. 26, 1932; Kahn to Bel Geddes, Dec. 9, 1932, OHK.

5. Lee Simonson to Kahn, Nov. 13, 1932; Shaw Desmond to Kahn, Nov. 6, 1932, OHK.

6. Horace Liveright to Kahn, Nov. 1, 1932; Dudley Field Malone to Kahn, Oct. 17, 1932; Meinhardt to Kahn, Dec. 27, 1932; Henry Russell to Kahn, Oct. 18, 1932; Brush to Kahn, Sept. 16, 1932, OHK; Gilmer, *Horace Liveright*, 224, 233.

7. Kahn to Mrs. Paul M. Warburg, Jan. 25, 1932; Kuhn, Loeb to Kahn, June 30, 1932; Kahn to Waldo Frank, Jan. 3, 1933; Percy Peixotto to Kahn, May 28, 1932; Kahn to Peixotto, May 30, 1932; Kahn to Max Steuer, July 3, 1933; Kahn to Diana Bourbon, June 22, 1932, "Suggested Letter to Mr. Pecora," n.d.; Kahn to Henry Russell, May 30, 1932, OHK; Chernow, *Warburgs*, 330; Klein, *Union Pacific*, 285.

8. Kahn, *Reflections*, 422–23; Carosso, *Morgans*, 642, 848–49; Williams, *Modern Tragedy*; Westbrook, *Wall Street in the American Novel*.

9. Mike Gold to Kahn, n.d., and Kahn to Gold, Oct. 15, 1932, OHK; League of Professional Groups for Foster and Ford, *Culture and the Crisis*.

10. Swaine, *Cravath Firm*, 2:537–40; *Fortune*, Apr. 1937, 87–96; see also Dartt to Kahn, [Dec. 24, 1932]; Kahn to Dartt, [Dec. 24, 1932]; Kahn to Horatio Stuart, June 8, 1933, OHK.

11. Bryant, *Encyclopedia of American Business History*, 20; U.S. Senate, Committee on Banking and Currency, *Stock Exchange Practices: Hearings*, 1276–93; Kahn to Felix Warburg, June 7, 1932, OHK.

12. Kahn to Deems Taylor, Mar. 30, 1932; Cravath to Kahn, May 3, 1932; Cravath to Taylor, May 3, 1932; Taylor to Cravath, Apr. 29, 1932, OHK.

13. John Erskine to Kahn, Nov. 23, 1932; Kahn to Erskine, Nov. 28, 1932; Edward Ziegler to Kahn, Sept. 16, 1932, OHK; Erskine, *My Life in Music*, 150; Mayer, *The Met*, 175.

14. Cravath to Kahn, Feb. 17, 1933, OHK; *NYT*, Feb. 10, 1933; Eaton, *Miracle at the Met*, 248.

15. Kahn to Cravath, Feb. 21, 24, 25, 1933, OHK.

16. Kahn to Cravath, Feb. 21, 1933, and Apr. 24, 1933, OHK.

17. Cravath to Kahn, Feb. 17, 1933; Cravath to Kahn, Nov. 21, 1933, OHK; Mayer, *The Met*, 105, 242, 250, 395.

18. Kahn to Cravath, Nov. 17, 1933; Cravath to Kahn, Nov. 21, 1933, OHK; *NYT*, Dec. 7, 1933.

19. Kolodin, *Metropolitan Opera*, 26; *NYT*, Mar. 3, 1933.

20. Conrad, *Song of Love and Death*, 257.

21. *NYT*, May 19, 1933; Vanderbilt, *Farewell to Fifth Avenue*, 280–82.

22. Kolodin, *Metropolitan Opera*, 371.

23. See Will Marion Cook to Kahn, Oct. 16, 1925; Kahn to Cook, Oct. 19, 1925, Jan. 26, 1926; H. S. Meinhardt to Kahn, May 10, 1932; Jasper Deeter to Kahn, Mar. 22, 1928 and Nov. 24, 1928; Kahn to Deeter, Mar. 29, 1928; John Murray Anderson to Kahn, Nov. 3, 1926; Cal Conrad to Kahn, Feb. 10 and 16 and Mar. 4, 1928; Tillman Falice, Jr., to Kahn, Nov. 15, 1928, OHK; Lewis, *When Harlem Was in Vogue*, 207.

24. Quoted in Mayer, *The Met*, 182.

25. Kahn to Gatti-Casazza, July 5, 1920, and Gatti-Casazza to Kahn, July 23, 1920, OHK; MORECo, minutes, Mar. 24, 1915, and Feb. 14, 1922, MOA.

26. Kolodin, *Metropolitan Opera*, 377.

27. Viereck to Kahn, Feb. 8, 1933; Kahn to Viereck, Feb. 20, 1933; Viereck, "Germany's Self Determination" and Viereck to Kahn, Dec. 8, 1933, OHK ("I am trying hard to suggest a Concordat, or some kind of minority rights for the Jews in Germany. . . . I would like to secure for the Jews the largest measure of justice attainable in this imperfect world"). See also Johnson, *George Sylvester Viereck*, 188.

28. Kahn to Jos. Geissinger, Mar. 22, 1933; Felix Wittmer to Kahn, May 6, 1933, OHK.

29. Henry Hurwitz to Kahn, Apr. 26, 1933; Kahn to Hurwitz, May 1, 1928, OHK. One cannot say for sure whether Kahn used the term "men of liberal convictions" to exclude communists from his sympathies.

30. Kahn to E. R. A. Seligman, May 4, 1933; Seligman to Kahn, May 8, 1933, OHK; *Fortune*, Sept. 1932, 32–36.

31. Jonah B. Wise to Kahn, May 18, 1933; Alvin Johnson to Seligman, Apr. 23, 1933; Seligman to Kahn, Apr. 26 and May 8, 1933; Kahn to Seligman, May 4 and 11, 1933; Dudley D. Sicher to Kahn, June 16, 1933, OHK.

32. Gay, *Freud, Jews and Other Germans*, 105.

33. Kahn to Walter Russell, Oct. 18, 1921; Kahn to H. Crouch Batchelor, Dec.

20, 1921; Kahn to Landau, Nov. 11, 1924; Kahn to Prof. D. Schor (Paris), Sept. 11, 1928; Kahn to John Simons, Aug. 16, 1927; Gulbenkian to Kahn, Feb. 24, 1932; Kahn to Gulbenkian, Mar. 4, 1932, OHK.

34. "An Evening with Groucho Marx," Carnegie Hall, May 21, 1972. Variant versions include Gottfried, *Jed Harris*, 21–22.

35. Kahn to Jewish Chronicle, Dec. 7, 1927, OHK.

36. Mike Gold to Kahn, ca. June 5–22, 1928; Kahn to Gold, June 26, 1928, OHK.

37. Kahn to Joseph Chapiro, Sept. 28, 1933, OHK.

38. Kahn to Frank, July 3, 1933; Frank to Kahn, July 1, 1933, OHK.

39. Kahn to Joseph Chapiro, Sept. 28, 1933; Robert de Bruce to Kahn, Mar. 28, 1933; Kahn to de Bruce, Apr. 10, 1933; Kahn to Felix Wittmer, May 5, 1933, OHK.

40. Kahn to George Antheil, July 20, 1933 and Oct. 5, 1933; Antheil to Kahn, Sept. 24 and Oct. 4, 1933, OHK.

41. Frank to Kahn, May 12, 1933; Kahn to Frank, May 22, 1933; Charles R. Walker to Kahn, May 27, 1933; Kahn to Walker, May 31, 1933, OHK. *Professor Mamlock*, the play by Wolf, was produced in 1937 by the Jewish Theatre unit of the Federal Theatre Project. Leiter, *Encyclopedia of the New York Stage*, 651.

42. Em Jo Basshe to Kahn, Oct. 20, 1933, OHK.

43. Max Kahn to Otto Kahn, Oct. 22, 1933; Otto Kahn to Benedict Getzoff, Sept. 12, 1933; Otto Kahn to Max Kahn, Nov. 11, 1933; Kahn to Joseph Chapiro, Sept. 28, 1933; S. Zacharias to Kahn, Aug. 7, 1933; Rosie Graefenberg to Kahn, Aug. 3, 1933, OHK.

44. Felix Warburg to Paul Baerwald, June 14, 1933, AJA. See Kahn's file of Kuhn, Loeb cables, 1929, OHK, regarding North German Lloyd.

45. Edith Mutke to Kahn, June 24 and Dec. 1, 1933; Mutke to Eppstein, Oct. 6, 1933, OHK; *NYT*, June 25, 1933. See also Warburg, "Transfer of the Warburg Institute," 13–16.

46. Laugwitz, "Robert Kahn and Brahms"; Levi, *Music in The Third Reich*, 45; Warburg, "Transfer of the Warburg Institute." See also Otto Kahn to Robert Kahn, June 9, 1933, OHK.

47. Gay, *Freud, Jews and Other Germans*, 246–47.

48. Otto Kahn to Robert Kahn, June 9, 1933, OHK; Laugwitz "Robert Kahn and Brahms."

49. Stern, *Dreams and Delusions*, 178.

50. Robert Kahn to Otto Kahn, Oct. 31, 1933; Otto Kahn to Robert Kahn, Nov. 15, 1933, OHK; Laugwitz, "Robert Kahn and Brahms."

51. Otto Kahn to Robert Kahn, Nov. 15, 1933, OHK; *NYT*, Sept. 29, 1933.

52. Cravath to Kahn, Dec. 1, 1933; Kahn to Cravath, Dec. 4, 1933, OHK.

53. Kahn to Walter Winchell, Dec. 28, 1933, OHK.

Chapter Nine

1. Kahn to Otto Schiff, Mar. 3 and 15, 1933; Kahn to Francesco Ruspoli, Mar. 17, 1933, OHK.

2. Kahn to Francesco Ruspoli, Mar. 17, 1933, OHK.

3. Carosso, *Investment Banking in America*, 321–36.

4. Frank Deutsch to Kahn, Apr. 26, 1933; Kahn to Frank Deutsch, Apr. 27 and May 8, 1933, OHK.

5. *WSJ*, Apr. 28, 1933; Eichengreen, *Golden Fetters*, 331; Feis, *1933*, 126–31; Warburg, *Long Road from Home*, 118–21.

6. Kahn to Frank Deutsch, May 8, 1933, OHK.

7. Williams, *Modern Tragedy*, 87–97.

8. Franklin Delano Roosevelt to Kahn, May 12 and 22, 1933; Kahn to Roosevelt, May 23, 1933, OHK.

9. Wilson, *American Earthquake*, 486; Perez and Willett, *Clarence Dillon*, 102; Croce, *Fred Astaire and Ginger Rogers Book*, 25.

10. Teichmann, *Smart Aleck*, 135.

11. *Newsweek*, July 8, 1933, 21.

12. Ibid., 17.

13. Pecora, *Wall Street under Oath*, 18, 40, 56, 96.

14. Ibid., 4–5.

15. U.S. Senate, Committee on Banking and Currency, *Stock Exchange Practices: Hearings*, 340, 443; Schwarz, *Economic Regulation of Business and Industry*, 4:2618; Carosso, *Investment Banking in America*, 337; Chernow, *Morgans*, 367; *Newsweek*, July 8, 1933, 21.

16. *Newsweek*, July 8, 1933, 21.

17. *Time*, July 10, 1933, 46. For *Death and the Miser*, the sixteenth-century painting by Jan Provoost, see Yamey, *Art and Accounting*, which is a source for several of my collateral remarks. Kahn was spared direct examination on the very embarrassing story of Paramount Pictures, though exhibits highlighting Kuhn, Loeb's loans to studio chief Adolph Zukor are to be found in the hearings' record.

18. U.S. Senate, Committee on Banking and Currency, *Stock Exchange Practices: Hearings*, 959–64.

19. Ibid., 964–65.

20. Ibid., 969–70.

21. Ibid., 970.

22. Ibid., 969–78.

23. Ibid., 157–60, 978–94.

24. Ibid., 1001–2.

25. Ibid., 1003–11.

26. Ibid., 1011.

27. Ibid., 1012–17.

28. Ibid., 1119–21.

29. Ibid., 1119–21, 1134.

30. Leff, *Limits of Symbolic Reform*, 58–59, 67–69. When questioning Kahn, Pecora ignored another common tax sheltering strategy: the "incorporated pocketbook" or personal holding company, in which Kahn's family members were the only stockholders. Kahn's practice of writing off personal loans to artists was also overlooked.

31. U.S. Senate, Committee on Banking and Currency, *Stock Exchange Practices: Hearings*, 1151–53; Kahn to Max Steuer, July 3, 1933; Kahn, "Suggested Letter to Mr. Pecora," n.d. [July 1933; not sent], OHK.

32. U.S. Senate, Committee on Banking and Currency, *Stock Exchange Practices: Hearings*, 1150–54; Leff, *Limits of Symbolic Reform*, 61.

33. Kahn to J. R. Bowie, Oct. 11, 1933, OHK; and Kahn, *Reflections*, 400.

34. U.S. Senate, Committee on Banking and Currency, *Stock Exchange Practices: Hearings*, 1197–1206.

35. Ibid., 1206–7.

36. Ibid., 1208–13; and Carosso, *Investment Banking in America*, 357, 349.

37. U.S. Senate, Committee on Banking and Currency, *Stock Exchange Practices: Hearings*, 1215–16.

38. Ibid., 1230–35.

39. Ibid., 1236–37.

40. Ibid., 1243–47, 1279–87. The committee counsel was continuing a motif from the examination of previous witnesses. The Allegheny Corporation (Pennroad's competitor) had been discussed during the Morgans' testimony. Both companies were attempts to recapture some of the power which had been lost under antitrust regulation, as Kahn indirectly admitted. A decision in recent weeks by the U.S. Circuit Court of Appeals had held the Pennroad was legitimate under antitrust law.

41. Ibid., 1287–88, 1291–92.

42. Ibid., 1301–2.

43. Ibid., 1305–15.

44. Ibid., 1305–17.

45. Ibid., 878–81.

46. Ibid., 1318–26.

47. S. M. Melamed to Kahn, June 29, 1933; Henry Russell to Kahn, July 5, 1933; Aldrich to Kahn, July 10, 1933; Baruch to Kahn, July 13, 1933, OHK.

48. Kahn to Max Steuer, July 3, 1933 and enclosures, OHK.

49. Kuhn, Loeb to Kahn, Aug. 25 and 30, 1933; Kahn to Kuhn, Loeb, Aug. 24, 26, 29, and 30, 1933, OHK.

50. Kahn to Walter Lippmann, Oct. 21, 1933, OHK.

51. Carosso, *Investment Banking in America*, 370, 376, 443; Leuchtenberg, *Franklin D. Roosevelt and the New Deal*, 59.

52. Carosso, *Investment Banking in America*, 352; and Pecora, *Wall Street under Oath*, 45.

53. Conrad, who met Kahn on a transatlantic crossing during 1928, borrowed $5,000 for *Keep Shuffling*. See Conrad to Kahn, Feb. 10, 16, and 25, Mar. 4, and June 2, 1928, OHK. "The Continental" was the closing number of *The Gay Divorcee* (RKO, 1934).

Chapter Ten

1. Kahn to Walter Wanger, Jan. 2, 1934; Kahn to Pecora, Jan. 18, 1934; Kahn to Duncan U. Fletcher, Jan. 3, 1934; Fletcher to Kahn, Jan. 5, 1934, OHK.

2. Kahn to Grace Moore Parera, Feb. 20, 1934, OHK.

3. Jacob Landau to Kahn, Jan. 2, 1934; Horace M. Kallen to Kahn and Kahn to Kallen, Jan. 8, 1934; Friedrich Weil to Kahn, Jan. 22, 1934; Fred Neter to Kahn, Jan. 23, 1934, OHK.

4. Kahn to Gilbert Seldes, Mar. 12, 1934; Kahn to Harold M. Groves, Mar. 12, 1934, OHK; *Motion Picture Daily*, Mar. 30, 1934.

5. Kahn to Kommer, Mar. 5, 1934; Kahn to Grace Moore Parera, Feb. 20, 1934; Kahn to Eddie Cantor, Feb. 8 and Mar. 5, 1934; Archibald Flower to Kahn, Mar. 13, 1934; Kahn to Flower, Mar. 26, 1934, OHK; Gilbert, "Broadway Mourns 'First Angel.' "

6. Kahn to William J. Donovan, Mar. 27, 1934, OHK.

7. Em Jo Basshe to Kahn, Mar. 26 and 27, 1934; Private Secretary to Basshe, Mar. 26 and 28, 1934, OHK.

8. Edward M. M. Warburg to Kahn, Mar. 24, 1934; Kahn to Warburg, Mar. 28, 1934, OHK.

9. Kahn to John Simons, Mar. 29, 1934; Ona B. Talbot to Kahn, Mar. 27, 1934, OHK.

10. *WT*, Mar. 29, 1934; *HT* and *NYT*, Mar. 30, 1934; *Time*, Apr. 9, 1934, 63–64.

11. *WT*, Mar. 29, 1934; *American*, *EJ*, *HT*, and *NYT*, Mar. 30, 1934; *Time*, Apr. 9, 1934, 63–64.

12. Liebling, "Music World Mourns Kahn as Best Friend"; Gabriel, "Kahn Known as Courtliest 'First Nighter' "; *EJ*, Mar. 30, 1934.

13. *EJ*, *HT*, and *WT*, Mar. 30, 1934; *CSM*, Mar. 31, 1934.

14. *NYT*, Mar. 30, 1934.

15. Berens, "Wall Street Mourns Passing of Otto Kahn."

16. Brisbane, "Today."

17. *NYT*, Apr. 17, 1934.

18. *HT*, Mar. 31, 1934.

19. *NYT*, May 16, 1949; Mayer, *The Met*, 237–38; Matz, *Many Lives of Otto Kahn*, 235.

20. Mayer, *The Met*, 238, 315.

21. Caro, *Power Broker*, 1013.

22. Eaton, *Miracle at the Met*, 395.

23. Ibid., 375.

24. Willett, *Theatre of the Weimar Republic*, 198; Reinhardt, *Genius*, 244–50, 284–309; Eisenstein, *Immoral Memories*, 149.

25. Houseman, *Run Through*, 334.

26. Waldau, *Vintage Years of the Theatre Guild*, 240.

27. Payne, *Fourth Estate*, 89–90.

28. Eisenstein, *Immoral Memories*, 141.

29. Sinclair, *World to Win*, 88, 93, 387, 397.

30. *NYT*, Apr. 17, 1934; Kahn to Waldo Frank, May 31, 1933, OHK.

31. Kirstein, *By With To & From*; and Weber, *Patron Saints*.

32. Jane Heap to Otto Kahn, May 28, 1926, OHK.

33. *WT*, Mar. 30, 1934.

34. *Time*, Apr. 9, 1934, 63–64; *NYT*, Mar. 30 and Apr. 2, 1934; *HT*, Mar. 31, 1934.

35. *DN*, Apr. 3, 1934.

36. Kahn, *Of Many Things*, 25.

37. Pater, *Renaissance*, 197.

38. Salpeter, "Otto the Magnificent," 386–87.

39. Viereck to Kahn, Nov. 13 and 18, 1929; Kahn to Viereck, Nov. 14, 1929, OHK.

40. Pater, *Renaissance*, 197.

Bibliography

Manuscripts and Special Collections

Boston, Massachusetts
Baker Library, Harvard Business School
   James Hazen Hyde Papers
   Thomas W. Lamont Papers
Cincinnati, Ohio
American Jewish Archives, Hebrew Union College
   Jacob H. Schiff Papers
   Felix M. Warburg Papers
London, England
Guildhall Library, Special Collections
   Morgan Grenfell Papers
House of Lords Records Office
   Beaverbrook Papers
   Bonar Law Papers
Marleybone Library
   Archives Department
Science Museum, Imperial College
   F. S. Pearson and Sons Archive
Morristown, New Jersey
Morristown Public Library
   Local History and Newspapers Collections
New Haven, Connecticut
Beinecke Library, Yale University
   Hart Crane Papers
   Max Ewing Papers
   Ezra Pound Papers
Sterling Library, Yale University
   Edward M. House Papers
   Walter Lippmann Papers
   Paul M. Warburg Papers
   William Wiseman Papers
New York, New York
Fales Library, New York University
   Elizabeth Robins Papers
Leo Baeck Institute
   Genealogie der Familie Eberstadt aus Worms by Christof P. A. Eberstadt

Lighthouse, Inc.
  Lighthouse, Inc., Archive
Metropolitan Opera
  Metropolitan Opera Archives
Oral History Research Office, Butler Library, Columbia University
  Charles Ascher, Reminiscences
  Benjamin Buttenweiser, Reminiscences
  Walter Sachs Interview
Pierpont Morgan Library
  Vincent P. Carosso Collection
  J. P. Morgan Jr. Papers
Rare Books and Manuscript Division, New York Public Library
  James Hazen Hyde Papers
  Carl Van Vechten Papers
Special Collections, Butler Library, Columbia University
  Frank A. Vanderlip Papers
Princeton, New Jersey
Firestone Library, Princeton University
  Otto H. Kahn Papers
Washington, D.C.
Manuscript Division, Library of Congress
  Jo Davidson Papers
  Margaret Sanger Papers
West Orange, New Jersey
General File, Edison National Historical Site
  Thomas A. Edison Papers

Government Documents

New York State Senate and Assembly. Joint Committee. *To Investigate and Examine into the Business and Affairs of Life Insurance Companies Doing Business in the State of New York.* 7 vols. Albany, 1907.

U.S. House. *Investigation of Financial and Monetary Conditions in the United States.* 62nd Cong., 3rd sess. 3 vols. Washington, D.C.: Government Printing Office, 1913.

U.S. House. National Monetary Commission. *The Great German Banks and Their Concentration in Connection with the Economic Development of Germany, by Jacob Riesser.* 61st Cong., 2nd sess., 1909. Washington, D.C.: Government Printing Office, 1911.

U.S. Senate. Committee on Banking and Currency. *Stock Exchange Practices: Hearings.* 7 parts. 73rd Cong., 1st sess. Washington, D.C.: Government Printing Office, 1933.

U.S. Senate. Committee on Finance. *Sale of Foreign Bonds or Securities in the United States: Hearings.* 72nd Cong., 1st sess. 4 parts. Washington, D.C. Government Printing Office, 1931–32.

U.S. Senate. Special Committee Investigating the Munitions Industry. *Munitions Industry Hearings*. 40 parts. 73rd and 74th Congs. Washington, D.C.: Government Printing Office, 1934–43.

Other Unpublished Sources

Anderson, Joyce Meeks. "Otto H. Kahn: An Analysis of His Theatrical Philanthropy in the New York City Area from 1909 to 1934." Ph.D. diss., Kent State University, 1983.

DFG-Projektteam (Historisches Seminar, Albert-Ludwigs-Universitäät, Freiburg). *Die Revolution von 1848/49 in Baden*.

Eberstadt, Christof P. A. "Die Familie Eberstadt." Erlangen, Germany, ca. 2001.

Moulton-Gertig, Suzanne. "The Berlin Hochschule Composers during the Twilight Years of the Weimar Republic and the Advent of the Third Reich." Originally delivered as a paper at a meeting of the American Musicological Society, Tucson, Arizona, 1996. Available at Music Vistas, an electronic publication of the Lamont School of Music, University of Denver, Denver, Colorado. ⟨http://www.du.edu/lamont/BerlinComposers.html⟩.

Tuggle, Robert. *From The Metropolitan Opera Archives: Acquisitions II: Maria Jeritza and Tosca*. ⟨http://www.metopera.org/history/week2D980111.html⟩.

Books and Collected Editions

Adams, Samuel H. *Alexander Woolcott: His World and Life*. New York: Reynal & Hitchcock, 1945.

Adler, Cyrus. *Jacob H. Schiff: His Life and Letters*. 2 vols. Garden City, N.Y.: Doubleday, Doran, 1928.

Aldcroft, Derek. *From Versailles to Wall Street*. Berkeley: University of California Press, 1977.

Allen, Frederick Lewis. *The Lords of Creation*. New York: Harper & Row, 1935.

Amory, Cleveland. *Who Killed Society?* New York: Harper & Brothers, 1960.

Anderson, John Murray. *Out without My Rubbers*. New York: Library Publishers, 1954.

Anderson, Margaret. *My Thirty Years War*. New York: Horizon Press, 1969.

Antheil, George. *Bad Boy of Music*. Garden City, N.Y.: Doubleday, Doran, 1945.

Arnheim, Rudolf. *Art and Visual Perception: A Psychology of the Visual Eye*. Expanded and rev. ed. Berkeley: University of California Press, 1974.

———. *New Essays on the Psychology of Art*. Berkeley: University of California Press, 1986.

Ashton, Rosemary. *The German Idea: Four German Writers and the Reception of German Thought*. Cambridge: Cambridge University Press, 1980.

Augustine, Dolores L. *Patricians & Parvenus: Wealth and High Society in Wilhelmine Germany*. Oxford: Berg Publishing, 1994.

Baker, Houston A., Jr. *Modernism and the Harlem Renaissance*. Chicago: University of Chicago Press, 1987.

Banham, Martin, ed. *The Cambridge Guide to Theatre*. Enlarged ed. Cambridge: Cambridge University Press, 1992.

Baruch, Bernard. *My Own Story*. New York: Henry Holt, 1957.

——. *The Public Years*. New York: Holt, Rinehart and Winston, 1960.

Baxandall, Michael. *Painting and Experience in Fifteenth-Century Italy*. 2nd ed. Oxford: Oxford University Press, 1988.

Behnken, Eloise M. *Thomas Carlyle: Calvinist without Theology*. Columbia: University of Missouri Press, 1978.

Bel Geddes, Norman. *Miracle in the Evening: An Autobiography*. Ed. William Kelley. Garden City, N.Y.: Doubleday, 1960.

Bell, Daniel. *The Cultural Contradictions of Capitalism*. New York: Basic Books, 1978.

Bender, Thomas. *New York Intellect*. New York: Alfred A. Knopf, 1987.

Bennett, Arnold. *The Journal of Arnold Bennett*. New York: Literary Guild, 1933.

Bennett, Benjamin. *Modern Drama and German Classicism*. Ithaca: Cornell University Press, 1978.

Berger, Peter L., and Thomas Luchmann. *The Social Construction of Reality*. New York: Doubleday, 1966.

Bergreen, Laurence. *As Thousands Cheer: The Life of Irving Berlin*. New York: Viking, 1990.

Berman, Art. *Preface to Modernism*. Urbana: University of Illinois Press, 1994.

Berman, Marshall. *All That Is Solid Melts into Air: The Experience of Modernity*. New York: Penguin Books, 1988.

Berman, Russell A. *Cultural Studies of Modern Germany: History, Representation and Nationhood*. Madison: University of Wisconsin Press, 1993.

Birmingham, Stephen. *"Our Crowd": The Great Jewish Families of New York*. New York: Harper & Row, 1967.

Blackbourn, David. *The Long Nineteenth Century: A History of Germany, 1780–1918*. New York: Oxford University Press, 1998.

Blackbourn, David, and Richard J. Evans, eds. *The German Bourgeoisie*. London: Routledge, 1991.

Blair, Fredrika. *Isadora: Portrait of the Artist as a Woman*. New York: McGraw-Hill, 1986.

Blastenbrei, Peter. *Mannheim in der Revolution 1848/49*. Mannheim: Verlagsbüro v. Brandt, 1997.

Blaukopf, Herta, ed. *Mahler's Unknown Letters*. Trans. Richard Stokes. Boston: Northeastern University Press, 1987.

Blaukopf, Kurt, ed. *Mahler: A Documentary History*. New York: Oxford University Press, 1976.

Bogard, Travis. *Contour in Time: The Plays of Eugene O'Neill*. New York: Oxford University Press, 1972.

Bogard, Travis, and Jackson R. Bryer, eds. *Selected Letters of Eugene O'Neill*. New Haven: Yale University Press, 1988.

Boime, Albert. "Entrepreneurial Patronage in Nineteenth-Century France." In *Enterprise and Entrepreneurs in Nineteenth- and Twentieth Century France*, ed.

Edward C. Carter III et al., 137–207. Baltimore: Johns Hopkins University Press, 1976.

Bordwell, David, Janet Staiger, and Kristin Thompson. *The Classical Hollywood Cinema: Film Style and Mode of Production to 1960*. New York: Columbia University Press, 1985.

Born, Karl Erich. *International Banking in the 19th and 20th Centuries*. Leaminton Spa, Warwickshire: Berg Publishers, 1983.

Boyer, Paul. *Purity in Print: The Vice Society Movement and Book Censorship in America*. New York: Charles Scribner's Sons, 1968.

Bramsted, Ernest K. *Aristocracy and the Middle Classes in Germany: Social Types in German Literature, 1830–1900*. 1937. Rev. ed., Chicago: University of Chicago Press, 1964.

Braudel, Fernand. *The Wheels of Commerce*. Trans. Sian Reynolds. New York: Harper & Row, 1982.

Brooks, John. *Once in Golconda: A True Drama of Wall Street, 1920–1938*. New York: Harper & Row, 1969.

Brown, Susan Jenkins, ed. *Robber Rocks: Letters and Memories of Hart Crane, 1923–1932*. Middletown, Conn.: Wesleyan University Press, 1969.

Brownlee, Elliot. *Federal Taxation in America: A Short History*. Cambridge: Cambridge University Press, 1996.

Brownlee, Kevin. *The War, The West, and the Wilderness*. New York: Alfred A. Knopf, 1979.

Brubaker, Rogers. *Citizenship and Nationhood in France and Germany*. Cambridge, Mass.: Harvard University Press, 1992.

Bryant, Keith, Jr., ed. *Encyclopedia of American Business History and Biography: Railroads in the Age of Regulation, 1900–1980*. New York: Facts on File, 1988.

Bryer, Jackson R., ed. *"The Theatre We Worked For": The Letters of Eugene O'Neill to Kenneth Macgowan*. New Haven: Yale University Press, 1982.

Buckle, Richard. *Diaghilev*. New York: Atheneum, 1984.

Buckler, William E. *Walter Pater: The Critic as Artist of Ideas*. New York: New York University Press, 1987.

Buell, Frederick. *National Culture and the New Global System*. Baltimore: Johns Hopkins University Press, 1994.

Buley, R. Carlyle. *The Equitable Life Assurance Society of the United States, 1859–1964*. 2 vols. New York: Appleton-Century-Crofts, 1967.

Burk, Kathleen. *Britain, America and the Sinews of War, 1914–1918*. Boston: George Allen & Unwin, 1985.

———. *Morgan Grenfell, 1838–1988: The Biography of a Merchant Bank*. Oxford University Press, 1989.

Burke, Kenneth. *A Grammar of Motives*. New York, Prentice-Hall, 1945.

Burke, Peter. *The Italian Renaissance: Culture and Society in Italy*. Princeton: Princeton University Press, 1986.

Burns, Elizabeth. *Theatricality: A Study of Convention in the Theatre of Social Life*. New York: Harper & Row, 1972.

Burns, Rob, ed. *German Cultural Studies: An Introduction*. Oxford: Oxford University Press, 1995.

Cameron, Kenneth M., and Theodore J. Hoffman. *A Guide to Theatre Study*. New York: Macmillan, 1974.

——. *The Theatrical Response*. New York: Macmillan, 1969.

Carlson, Marvin. *Theories of the Theatre: A Historical and Critical Survey*. Ithaca: Cornell University Press, 1993.

Caro, Robert A. *The Power Broker: Robert Moses and the Fall of New York*. New York: Vintage Books, 1975.

Carosso, Vincent P. *Investment Banking In America: A History*. Cambridge, Mass.: Harvard University Press, 1970.

——. *The Morgans: Private International Bankers, 1854–1913*. Cambridge, Mass.: Harvard University Press, 1987.

Carringer, Robert L. *The Making of Citizen Kane*. Berkeley: University of California Press, 1985.

Casillo, Robert. *The Genealogy of Demons: Anti-Semitism, Fascism, and the Myths of Ezra Pound*. Evanston: Northwestern University Press, 1988.

Cassis, Youssef, ed. *Finance and Financiers in European History, 1880–1960*. Cambridge: Cambridge University Press, 1990.

Chapman, Stanley. *The Rise of Merchant Banking*. London: Allen & Unwin, 1984.

Cheney, Sheldon. *The Art Theater*. New York: Alfred A. Knopf, 1925.

——. *The New Movement in the Theatre*. New York: Mitchell Kennerley, 1914.

——. *The Theatre: Three Thousand Years of Drama, Acting and Stage Craft*. New York: David McKay, 1929.

Chernow, Ronald. *The House of Morgan: An American Banking Dynasty and the Rise of Modern Finance*. New York: Atlantic Monthly Press, 1990.

——. *The Warburgs: The 20th Century Odyssey of a Remarkable Jewish Family*. New York: Random House, 1993.

Christaller, Walter. *Central Places in Southern Germany*. Trans. Carlisle W. Baskin. Englewood Cliffs, N.J.: Prentice-Hall, 1966.

Cleveland, Harold van B., and Thomas F. Huertas. *Citibank, 1812–1970*. Cambridge, Mass.: Harvard University Press, 1985.

Clurman, Harold. *The Fervent Years*. New York: Alfred A. Knopf, 1945.

Cone, John Franklin. *Oscar Hammerstein's Manhattan Opera Company*. Norman: University of Oklahoma Press, 1964.

Connelly, Marc. *Voices Offstage*. Chicago: Holt, Rinehart & Winston, 1968.

Conrad, Peter. *A Song of Love and Death: The Meaning of Opera*. New York: Poseidon Press, 1987.

Cook, Susan C. *Opera for a New Republic: The Zeitopern of Krenek, Weill, and Hindemith*. Ann Arbor: UMI, 1988.

Cookson, William. *A Guide to the Cantos of Ezra Pound*. New York: Persea Books, 1985.

Cooper, Diana. *Autobiography*. 1958–69. Reprint, New York: Carroll & Graf, 1985.

Coty, Francois. *Tearing Away the Veils: The Financiers Who Control the World.* Trans. Eugene N. Sanctuary. New York: N.p., 1940.

Coughlin, Charles E. *A Series of Lectures on Social Justice.* Royal Oak, Mich.: The Radio League of the Little Flower, 1935.

Cowley, Malcolm. *Exile's Return: A Literary Odyssey of the 1920s.* New York: Viking, 1964.

———. *The Portable Malcolm Cowley.* Ed. Donald W. Faulkner. New York: Penguin, 1991.

Craig, Edward. *Gordon Craig: The Story of His Life.* New York: Alfred A. Knopf, 1968.

Croce, Arlene. *The Fred Astaire and Ginger Rogers Book.* New York: Outerbridge and Lazard, 1972.

Croly, Herbert. *Willard Straight.* New York: Macmillan, 1947.

Dark, Sidney. *The Life of Sir Arthur Pearson.* London: Hodder & Stoughton, n.d.

Davidson, Jo. *Between Sittings: An Informal Autobiography.* New York: Dial Press, 1951.

Deutsch, Helen, and Stella Hanau. *The Provincetown: A Story of the Theatre.* New York: Farrar & Rinehart, 1931.

Dizikes, John. *Opera in America: A Cultural History.* New Haven: Yale University Press, 1992.

Douglas, Ann. *Terrible Honesty: Mongrel Manhattan in the 1920s.* New York: Farrar, Straus & Giroux, 1995.

Duberman, Martin Bauml. *Paul Robeson.* New York: Alfred A. Knopf, 1988.

Duncan, Isadora. *My Life.* New York: Liveright, 1927.

Eastman, Max. *Love and Revolution: My Journey through an Epoch.* New York: Random House, 1961.

Eaton, Quaintance. *The Miracle of the Met.* New York: Meredith Press, 1968.

Eaton, Walter Prichard. *The Theatre Guild: The First Ten Years.* New York: Brentano's, 1929.

Edel, Leon. *Writing Lives: Principa Biographia.* New York: Norton, 1985.

Eichengreen, Barry J. *Golden Fetters: The Gold Standard and the Great Depression, 1919–1939.* New York: Oxford University Press, 1992.

Eisenstein, Sergei. *Immoral Memories.* Ed. and trans. Herbert Marshall. Boston: Houghton Mifflin, 1965.

Ellman, Richard. *James Joyce.* New York: Oxford University Press, 1959.

———. *Oscar Wilde.* New York: Vintage Books, 1987.

Emden, Paul H. *Money Powers of Europe in the Nineteenth and Twentieth Centuries.* New York: Appleton-Century, 1938.

Endelman, Todd M. *Radical Assimilation in English Jewish History, 1656–1945.* Bloomington: Indiana University Press, 1990.

Erickson, Erik H. *Childhood and Society.* New York: W. W. Norton, 1963.

———. *Identity and the Life Cycle.* New York: W. W. Norton, 1980.

Erskine, John. *My Life in Music.* New York: William Morrow, 1950.

Evreinoff, Nicolas. *The Theatre in Life.* Trans. Alexander I. Nazaroff. New York: Benjamin Blom, 1927.

Eyck, Erich. *A History of the Weimar Republic.* 2 vols. Cambridge, Mass.: Harvard University Press, 1962.

Fahl, Steffen. *Tradition der Natürlichkeit: zu Biographie, Lyrikvertonung und Kammermusik des spätromantischen Klassizisten Robert Kahn.* Series: Berliner Musik Studien 15. Sinzig: Studio Publishing House, 1998.

Feis, Herbert. *1933: Characters in Crisis.* Boston: Little, Brown, 1966.

Ferguson, Thomas. "Industrial Conflict and the Coming of the New Deal: The Triumph of Multinational Liberalism in America." In *The Rise and Fall of the New Deal Order, 1930–1980,* ed. Gary Gerstel and Steve Fraser, 3–31. Princeton: Princeton University Press, 1989.

Fitzgerald, F. Scott. "The Rich Boy." In *Babylon Revisited and Other Stories,* 152–87. New York: Charles Scribner's Sons, 1971.

Forbes, Bertie C. *Men Who Are Making America.* 5th ed. New York: B. C. Forbes, 1921.

Frank, Waldo. *In the American Jungle, 1925–1936.* 1937. Reprint, Freeport, N.Y.: Books for Libraries Press, 1968.

———. *Memoirs.* Ed. Alan Trachtenberg. Amherst: University of Massachusetts Press, 1973.

———. *The Rediscovery of America.* New York: Charles Scribner's Sons, 1929.

———. *Salvos: An Informal Book About Books and Plays.* New York: Boni and Liveright, 1924.

———, ed. *The Collected Poems of Hart Crane.* New York: Liveright, 1933.

Frisby, David. *Fragments of Modernity: Theories of Modernity in the Works of Simmel, Kracauer and Benjamin.* Cambridge, Mass.: MIT Press, 1986.

———. *Simmel and Since: Essays on Georg Simmel's Social Theory.* London: Routledge, 1992.

Fussell, Paul. *The Great War and Modern Memory.* London: Oxford University Press, 1975.

Galambos, Louis. *The Public Image of Big Business in America, 1880–1940: A Quantitative Study in Social Change.* Baltimore: Johns Hopkins University Press, 1975.

Galambos, Louis, and Joseph Pratt. *The Rise of the Corporate Commonwealth.* New York: Basic Books, 1987.

Galbraith, John Kenneth. *The Great Crash, 1929.* Boston: Houghton Mifflin, 1955.

Garafola, Lynn. *Diaghilev's Ballets Russes.* New York: Oxford University Press, 1989.

Gatti-Casazza, Giulio. *Memories of the Opera.* 1941. Reprint, London: John Calder, 1977.

Gay, Peter. *Freud, Jews and Other Germans: Masters and Victims in Modernist Culture.* Oxford: Oxford University Press, 1978.

———. *Weimar Culture: The Insider as Outsider.* New York: Harper Torchbooks, 1970.

Gay, Ruth. *The Jews of Germany: A Historical Portrait.* New Haven: Yale University Press, 1992.

Gelb, Arthur, and Barbara Gelb. *O'Neill*. New York: Harper, 1962.

Gerber, David A., ed. *Anti-Semitism in American History*. Urbana: University of Illinois Press, 1986.

Gershwin, Ira. *Lyrics on Several Occasions*. New York: Alfred A. Knopf, 1959.

Gertz, Elmer. *Odyssey of a Barbarian: The Biography of George Sylvester Viereck*. Buffalo: Prometheus Books, 1978.

Giddens, Anthony. *The Consequences of Modernity*. Stanford: Stanford University Press, 1990.

Gilbert, Clinton W. *The Mirrors of Wall Street*. New York: G. P. Putnam's Sons, 1933.

Gilder, Rosamond, et al., eds. *Theatre Arts Anthology: A Record and a Prophecy*. New York: Theatre Arts Books, 1950.

Giles, Paul. *Hart Crane: The Contexts of the Bridge*. Cambridge: Cambridge University Press, 1986.

Gilman, Sander, and Steven T. Katz, eds. *Anti-Semitism in Times of Crisis*. New York: New York University Press, 1991.

Gilmer, Walker. *Horace Liveright: Publisher of the Twenties*. New York: David Lewis, 1970.

Goelet, Robert. *The Old Order Changeth*. New York: Country Life Press, 1940.

Goffman, Erving. *Behavior in Public Places*. New York: Free Press, 1963.

——. *Frame Analysis*. Cambridge, Mass.: Harvard University Press, 1974.

——. *The Presentation of Self in Everyday Life*. Garden City, N.Y.: Doubleday Anchor, 1959.

Gold, Mike. *Jews without Money*. New York: Liveright, 1930.

Goldstein, Joshua S. *Long Cycles: Prosperity and War in the Modern Age*. New Haven: Yale University Press, 1988.

Goldstein, Malcolm. *George S. Kaufman: His Life, His Theater*. New York: Oxford University Press, 1979.

——. *The Political Stage: American Drama and the Theatre of the Great Depression*. New York: Oxford University Press, 1974.

Gombrich, E. H. *Aby Warburg: An Intellectual Biography*. 2nd ed. Chicago: University of Chicago Press, 1986.

Gottfried, Martin. *Jed Harris: The Curse of Genius*. Boston: Little, Brown, 1983.

Gray, Madeline. *Margaret Sanger: A Biography of the Champion of Birth Control*. New York: R. Marek, 1979.

Griffith, Linda. *When the Movies Were Young*. New York: Dover, 1969.

Grossman, Barbara W. *Funny Woman: The Life and Times of Fanny Brice*. Bloomington: Indiana University Press, 1991.

Gulbenkian, Nubar. *Portrait in Oil: The Autobiography of Nubar Gulbenkian*. New York: Simon & Schuster, 1965.

Habermas, Jürgen. "Modernity—An Incomplete Project." In *The Anti-Aesthetic*, ed. Hal Foster, 3–15. Port Townsend, Wash.: Bay Press, 1983.

Hampton, Benjamin. *History of the American Film Industry*. New York: Convici-Fried, 1931. Reprint, New York: Dover, 1970.

Hare, A. Paul. *Social Interaction as Drama: Applications from Conflict Resolution.* Beverly Hills: Sage Publications, 1985.

Harlow, Alvin F. "Kahn, Otto Herman" [Feb. 21, 1867–March 29, 1934]. In *Dictionary of American Biography* Suppl. 1, Vol. 11:19–20. New York: American Council of Learned Societies, 1944.

Harris, Frank. *Contemporary Portraits.* 4th ser. New York: Brentano's, 1923.

——. *My Life and Loves.* Ed. John F. Gallagher. New York: Grove Press, 1963.

Harris, José, and Pat Thane. "British and European Bankers, 1880–1914: An 'Aristocratic Bourgeoisie'?" In *The Power of the Past: Essays for Eric Hobsbawm*, ed. Pat Thane et al., 215–34. Cambridge: Cambridge University Press, 1984.

Harris, Leon. *Upton Sinclair: American Rebel.* New York: Thomas Y. Crowell, 1975.

Harvey, David. *The Condition of Postmodernity.* Oxford: Basil Blackwell, 1989.

Hecht, Ben. *Charlie: The Improbable Life and Times of Charles MacArthur.* New York: Harper & Row, 1954.

——. *A Child of the Century.* New York: Simon & Schuster, 1954.

Heiber, Herbert. *The Weimar Republic.* Trans. W. E. Yuill. Oxford: Blackwell, 1993.

Heilbut, Anthony. *Exiled in Paradise: German Refugee Artists and Intellectuals in America from the 1930s to the Present.* Boston: Beacon Press, 1983.

Helburn, Theresa. *A Wayward Quest.* Boston: Little, Brown, 1960.

Hemenway, Robert E. *Zora Neale Hurston: A Literary Biography.* Urbana: University of Illinois Press, 1977.

Henderson, W. J. *Modern Musical Drift.* New York: Longmans, Green, 1904.

Herf, Jeffrey. *Reactionary Modernism: Technology, Culture and Politics in Weimar and the Third Reich.* Cambridge: Cambridge University Press, 1984.

Hines, Thomas Jensen. *Collaborative Form: Studies in the Relations of the Arts.* Kent, Ohio: Kent State University Press, 1991.

Horowitz, Joseph. *Understanding Toscanini.* Minneapolis: University of Minnesota Press, 1987.

——. *Wagner Nights: An American History.* Berkeley: University of California Press, 1994.

Houseman, John. *Run Through.* New York: Simon & Schuster, 1972.

Hulderman, Bernhard. *Albert Ballin.* Trans. W. J. Eggars. London Cassell, 1922.

Hynes, Samuel. *The Edwardian Turn of Mind.* Princeton: Princeton University Press, 1968.

Ingham, John N. *Biographical Dictionary of American Business Leaders.* Westport, Conn.: Greenwood Press, 1983.

Iser, Wolfgang. *Walter Pater: The Aesthetic Moment.* Trans. David Henry Wilson. Cambridge: Cambridge University Press, 1987.

Jaher, Frederic. "Style and Status: High Society in Late Nineteenth-Century New York." In *The Rich, the Well Born, and the Powerful: Elites and Upper Classes in History*, 258–84. Urbana: University of Illinois Press, 1973.

Jencks, Charles, ed. *The Post-Modern Reader.* London: Academy Editions, 1992.

——. *What Is Post-Modernism.* London: Academy Editions, 1986.

Jeritza, Maria. *Sunlight and Song: A Singer's Life.* New York: D. Appleton, 1924.

Johnson, Arthur. *Winthrop W. Aldrich: Lawyer, Banker, Diplomat*. Boston: Graduate School of Business, Harvard University, 1968.

Johnson, Niel M. *George Sylvester Viereck: German-American Propagandist*. Urbana: University of Illinois Press, 1972.

Jones, Charles A. *International Business in the Nineteenth Century: The Rise and Fall of a Cosmopolitan Bourgeoisie*. New York: New York University Press, 1987.

Jones, Robert Edmond. "The Groves of Isadora [1947]." In *Theatre Arts Anthology*, ed. Rosamund Gilder et al., 189. New York: Theatre Arts Books, 1950.

Josephson, Matthew. *Life among the Surrealists*. New York: Holt, Rinehart & Winston, 1962.

———. *The Robber Barons: The Great American Capitalists, 1861–1901*. 1934. Reprint, New York: Harcourt, Brace & Jovanich, 1962.

Juxon, John. *Lewis and Lewis: The Life and Times of a London Solicitor*. New York: Ticknor & Fields, 1984.

Kael, Pauline, et al. *The Citizen Kane Book*. Boston: Little, Brown, 1971.

Kahn, Otto. *Of Many Things: Being Reflections and Impressions on International Affairs, Domestic Topics, and the Arts*. New York: Boni & Liveright, 1926.

———. *Reflections of a Financier*. London: Hodder & Stoughton, 1921.

———. *Right above Race*. New York: The Century Company, 1918.

Kaplan, Marion A. *The Making of the Jewish Middle Class: Women, Family, and Identity in Imperial Germany*. New York: Oxford University Press, 1991.

Katz, Esther, ed. *Margaret Sanger Papers, Microfilm Edition*. Bethesda, Md.: University Publications of America, 1996, 1997.

Katz, Jacob. "German Culture and the Jews." In *The Jewish Response to German Culture from the Enlightenment to the Second World War*, ed. Jehuda Reinharz and Walter Schatzberg, 85–99. Hanover, N.H.: University Press of New England, 1985.

Keller, Morton. *In Defense of Yesterday: James M. Beck and the Politics of Conservatism, 1861–1936*. New York: Coward-McCann, 1958.

———. *The Life Insurance Enterprise, 1885–1910: A Study in the Limits of Corporate Power*. Cambridge, Mass.: Harvard University Press, 1963.

Keller, Phyllis. *States of Belonging: German-American Intellectuals and the First World War*. Cambridge, Mass.: Harvard University Press, 1979.

Kellner, Bruce. *Carl Van Vechten and the Irreverent Decades*. Norman: University of Oklahoma Press, 1968.

———. *Letters of Carl Van Vechten*. New Haven: Yale University Press, 1987.

Kelly, George A. *The Psychology of Personal Constructs*. Vol. 1: *Theory of Personality*. New York: W. W. Norton, 1955.

Kennan, George. *E. H. Harriman*. 2 vols. Boston: Houghton Mifflin, 1922.

Kennedy, Joseph P., ed. *The Story of Films as Told by the Leaders of the Industry*. New York: A. W. Shaw, 1927.

Keynes, John Maynard. *Two Memoirs*. New York: Augustus Kelley, 1949.

Kimball, Robert, ed. *The Complete Lyrics of Cole Porter*. New York: Da Capo Press, 1992.

Kindleberger, Charles. *A Financial History of Western Europe*. London: George Allen & Unwin, 1984.

——. *The World in Depression, 1929–1939*. Berkeley: University of California Press, 1975.

Kirstein, Lincoln. *By With To & From: A Lincoln Kirstein Reader*. Ed. Nicholas Jenkins. New York: Farrar, Straus & Giroux, 1991.

Klein, Maury. *The Life and Legend of E. H. Harriman*. Chapel Hill: University of North Carolina Press, 1999.

——. *Union Pacific: The Rebirth, 1894–1969*. New York: Doubleday, 1989.

Knox, Paul, and John Agnew. *The Geography of the World Economy*. London: Edward Arnold, 1989.

Kobler, John. *Otto the Magnificent: The Life of Otto Kahn*. New York: Scribners, 1988.

Kolodin, Irving. *The Metropolitan Opera, 1883–1966*. New York: Alfred A. Knopf, 1966.

Koss, Stephen E. *The Rise and Fall of the Political Press in Britain*. Chapel Hill: University of North Carolina Press, 1981.

Kotz, David M. *Bank Control of Large Corporations in the United States*. Berkeley: University of California Press, 1978.

Krooss, Herman. "Speyer, James Joseph." *Dictionary of American Biography*, Supplement 3, 728–29. Philadelphia: American Council of Learned Societies, 1973.

Krutch, Joseph Wood. *The American Drama Since 1918: An Informal History*. New York: Random House, 1939.

——. *Modern Drama: A Definition and an Estimate*. Ithaca: Cornell University Press, 1953.

Kuhn, Loeb & Co. *A Century of Investment Banking*. New York: privately printed, 1967.

——. *Investment Banking through Four Generations*. New York: Kuhn, Loeb, 1955.

Kushner, Tony. *The Holocaust and the Liberal Imagination: A Social and Cultural History*. Oxford: Basil Blackwell, 1994.

Lamont, Thomas. *Across World Frontiers*. New York: Harcourt, Brace, 1951.

——. *Henry P. Davison: The Record of a Useful Life*. New York: Harper & Brothers, 1933.

Landes, David. "Bleichröders and Rothschilds: The Problem of Continuity in the Family Firm." In *The Family in History*, ed. Charles E. Rosenberg, 95–114. Philadelphia: University of Pennsylvania Press, 1975.

Langner, Lawrence. *The Magic Curtain*. New York: E. P. Dutton, 1951.

Lash, Scott, and Jonathan Friedman. *Modernity and Identity*. Oxford: Blackwell, 1992.

Le Gallienne, Eva. *At 33*. New York: Longmans, Green, 1940.

League of Professional Groups for Foster and Ford. *Culture and the Crisis: An Open Letter to the Intellectuals of America*. New York: Workers Library Publishers, 1932.

Lebo, Harlan. *Citizen Kane: The Fiftieth Anniversary Album*. New York: Doubleday, 1990.

Leff, Mark. *The Limits of Symbolic Reform: The New Deal and Taxation*. Cambridge: Cambridge University Press, 1984.

Leiter, Samuel L. *The Encyclopedia of the New York Stage, 1930–1940*. New York: Greenwood Press, 1989.

Leuchtenberg, William E. *Franklin D. Roosevelt and the New Deal*. New York: Harper & Row, 1963.

Levi, Erik. *Music in the Third Reich*. New York: St. Martin's Press, 1994.

Levine, Lawrence. *Highbrow/Lowbrow: The Emergence of Cultural Hierarchy in America*. Cambridge, Mass.: Harvard University Press, 1988.

Lewis, David Levering. *When Harlem Was in Vogue*. New York: Vintage Books, 1982.

Lewis, Thomas S. W. *Letters of Hart Crane and His Family*. New York: Columbia University Press, 1974.

Lewisohn, Ludwig. *The Modern Drama: An Essay in Interpretation*. New York: B. W. Huebsch, 1915.

Lindenberger, Herbert. *Opera: The Extravagant Art*. Ithaca: Cornell University Press, 1984.

Link, Arthur, et al., eds. *The Papers of Woodrow Wilson*. Vol. 3. Princeton: Princeton University Press, 1983.

Lowenthal, David. *The Past Is a Foreign Country*. Cambridge: Cambridge University Press, 1985.

Lukács, Georg. *Essays on Thomas Mann*. Trans. Stanley Mitchell. New York: Grosset & Dunlap, 1964.

———. *The Theory of the Novel*. Trans. Anna Bostock. Cambridge, Mass.: MIT Press, 1971.

Macgowan, Kenneth, and Robert Edmund Jones. *Continental Stagecraft*. New York: Harcourt, Brace, 1922.

Magill, Roswell. "Cravath, Paul D." *Dictionary of American Biography*, Supplement 2, 130–31. Philadelphia: American Council of Learned Societies, 1944.

Mahler, Alma. *Gustav Mahler: Memories and Letters*. Trans. Basil Creighton. Ed. Donald Mitchell. Rev. and enlarged ed. New York: Viking, 1969.

Maier, Charles S. *Recasting Bourgeois Europe*. Princeton: Princeton University Press, 1975.

Mann, Klaus. *The Turning Point: Thirty Five Years in This Century*. 1942. Reprint, New York: Markus Weiner, 1984.

[Mannheimer Bettfedernfabrik, Kaufmann GMBH & Co.] *150 Jahre Mannheimer Bettfedernfabrik, Kaufmann GMBH & Co*. Mannheim: privately printed, 1976.

Manning, Philip. *Erving Goffman and Modern Sociology*. Stanford: Stanford University Press, 1992.

Martin, Albro. *Railroad Triumphant: The Growth, Rejection, and Rebirth of a Vital American Force*. New York: Oxford University Press, 1992.

März, Eduard. *Austrian Banking and Policy: Creditanstalt at a Turning Point, 1913–1923*. Trans. Charles Kessler. London: Weidenfeld & Nicolson, 1981.

Mason, Hamilton. *French Theatre in New York: A List of Plays, 1899–1939*. New York: Columbia University Press, 1940.

Matz, Mary Jane. *The Many Lives of Otto Kahn*. New York: Macmillan, 1963.

May, Henry F. *The End of Innocence*. New York: Oxford University Press, 1979.

Mayer, Arno J. *The Persistence of the Old Regime: Europe to the Great War*. New York: Pantheon Books, 1981.

Mayer, Hans. *Outsiders: A Study in Life and Letters*. Trans. Denis M. Sweet. Cambridge, Mass.: MIT Press, 1984.

Mayer, Martin. *The Met: One Hundred Years of Grand Opera*. New York: Simon & Schuster, 1983.

McNeil, William C. *American Money and the Weimar Republic*. New York: Columbia University Press, 1986.

Mellor, Roy E. H. *Nation, State, and Territory: A Political Geography*. London: Routledge, 1989.

Mercer, Lloyd J. *E. H. Harriman: Master Railroader*. Boston: Twayne, 1985.

Meryman, Richard. *Mank: The Wit, World and Life of Herman Mankiewicz*. New York: William Morrow, 1978.

Mitchell, W. J. T., ed. *The Language of Images*. Chicago: University of Chicago Press, 1980.

———. *On Narrative*. Chicago: University of Chicago Press, 1980.

Money, Keith. *Anna Pavlova: Her Life and Art*. New York: Alfred A. Knopf, 1982.

Morgenthau, Henry. *All in a Lifetime*. Garden City, N.Y.: Doubleday, 1922.

Mosse, George L. *German Jews: Beyond Judaism*. Bloomington: Indiana University Press, 1985.

———. "Jewish Emancipation between *Bildung* and Respectability." In *The Jewish Response to German Culture from the Enlightenment to the Second World War*, ed. Jehuda Reinharz and Walter Schatzberg, 1–16. Hanover, N.H.: University Press of New England, 1985.

———. *Nationalism and Sexuality: Respectability and Abnormal Sexuality in Modern Europe*. New York: H. Fertig, 1985.

Mosse, Werner E. *Jews in the German Economy: The German-Jewish Economic Elite, 1829–1935*. Oxford: Claredon Press, 1987.

Mosse, Werner E., and A. Paucker, eds. *Juden in Wilhelminischen Deutschland*. New York: Leo Baeck Institute, 1976.

Mosse, Werner E., et al., eds. *Revolution and Evolution: 1848 in German-Jewish History*. Tubingen: J. C. Mohr, 1981.

Moulton, Harold G. *Financial Organization and the Economic System*. New York: McGraw-Hill, 1938.

Nadel, Stanley. *Little Germany: Ethnicity, Religion, and Class in New York City, 1845–80*. Urbana: University of Illinois Press, 1990.

Nichols, Beverley. *All I Could Never Be*. New York: E. P. Dutton, 1952.

Nicolson, Harold. *Dwight Morrow*. New York: Harcourt, Brace, 1935.

Norton, Elliot. "Geddes, Norman Bel." *Dictionary of American Biography*, Supplement 6, 232–34. Philadelphia: American Council of Learned Societies, 1980.

Olson, James Stuart. *Herbert Hoover and the Reconstruction Finance Corporation,*
    1931–1933. Ames: Iowa State University Press, 1977.
O'Neill, Eugene. *The Unknown O'Neill: Unpublished or Unfamiliar Writings of Eugene*
    O'Neill. Ed. Travis Borgard. New Haven: Yale University Press, 1988.
Ortolani, Benito, ed. *Pirandello's Love Letters to Marta Abba.* Princeton: Princeton
    University Press, 1994.
Paige, D. D., ed. *The Selected Letters of Ezra Pound, 1907–1941.* London: Faber &
    Faber, 1950.
Paley, William S. *As It Happened: A Memoir.* Garden City, N.Y.: Doubleday, 1979.
Paris, Barry. *Louise Brooks.* New York: Alfred A. Knopf, 1989.
Pater, Walter. *The Renaissance.* 1873. Reprint, New York: Modern Library, n.d.
Paul, Sherman. *Hart's Bridge.* Urbana: University of Illinois Press, 1972.
Payne, George Henry. *The Fourth Estate and Radio, and Other Addresses.* Boston:
    Microphone Press, 1936.
Pecora, Ferdinand. *Wall Street under Oath.* New York: Simon & Schuster, 1939.
Percival, John. *The World of Diaghilev.* New York: Harmony Books, 1971.
Perez, Robert C., and Edward F. Willett. *Clarence Dillon: A Wall Street Enigma.*
    Lanham, Md.: Madison Books, 1995.
———. *The Will to Win: A Biography of Ferdinand Eberstadt.* Westport, Conn.:
    Greenwood Press, 1989.
Perry, Robert L. *The Shared Vision of Waldo Frank and Hart Crane.* Lincoln:
    University of Nebraska Press, 1966.
Petrie, Graham. *Hollywood Destinies: European Directors in America, 1922–1931.*
    London: Routledge & Kegan Paul, 1986.
Poggi, Jack. *Theater in America: The Impact of Economic Forces, 1870–1967.* Ithaca:
    Cornell University Press, 1968.
Poggioli, Renato. *The Theory of the Avant-Garde.* Trans. Gerald Fitzgerald.
    Cambridge, Mass.: Harvard University Press, 1968.
Postlewait, Thomas. *Prophet of the New Drama: William Archer and the Ibsen*
    Campaign. Westport, Conn.: Greenwood Press, 1986.
Pound, Ezra. *The Cantos (1–95).* New York: New Directions, 1956.
Puffett, Derrick, ed. *Salome.* Cambridge: Cambridge University Press, 1989.
Rae, John W., and John W. Rae, Jr. *Morristown's Forgotten Past: The Gilded Age.*
    Morristown, N.J.: John W. Rae, 1979.
Rank, Otto. *Art and Artist: Creative Urge and Personality Development.* Trans. Charles
    F. Atkinson. New York: Alfred A. Knopf, 1932.
Ratner, Sidney. *Taxation and Democracy in America.* 1942. Reprint, New York:
    Octagon Books, 1980.
Raynor, Henry. *Music and Society since 1815.* New York: Schocken Books, 1976.
Redmond, George F. *Financial Giants of America.* 2 vols. Boston: Stratford,
    1922.
Reed, Howard Curtis. *The Preeminence of International Financial Centers.* New York:
    Praeger, 1981.
Reid, Benjamin. *The Man from New York: John Quinn and His Friends.* New York:
    Oxford University Press, 1968.

Reinhardt, Gottfried. *The Genius: A Memoir of Max Reinhardt*. New York: Alfred A. Knopf, 1979.

Reinharz, Jehuda, and Walter Shatzberg, eds. *The Jewish Response to German Culture from the Enlightenment to the Second World War*. Hanover, N.H.: University Press of New England, 1985.

Reitlinger, Gerald. *The Economics of Taste: The Rise and Fall of the Objets d'Art Market since 1750*. New York: Holt, Rinehart & Winston, 1965.

Ricoeur, Paul. *Time and Narrative*. 2 vols. Trans. Kathleen McLaughlin and David Pellauer. Chicago: University of Chicago Press, 1984.

Ripley, William Z. *Railroad Finance and Reorganization*. New York: Longmans, Green, 1915.

———. *Main Street and Wall Street*. Boston: Little, Brown, 1927.

Rischbieter, Henning, ed. *Art and the Stage in the 20th Century: Painters and Sculptors Work for the Theatre*. Trans. Michael Bullock. Greenwich, Conn.: New York Graphic Society, 1968.

Roberts, Priscilla M. "A Conflict of Loyalties: Kuhn, Loeb and Company and the First World War, 1914–1917." In *Studies in the American Jewish Experience II*, ed. Jacob R. Marcus and Abraham J. Peck, 1–31, 168–83. Lanham, Md.: University Press of America and American Jewish Archives, 1985.

Roland, John. *A Beginner's Guide to the Cantos of Ezra Pound*. Salzburg: University of Salzburg Press, 1995.

Romasco, Albert U. *The Poverty of Abundance: Hoover, the Nation, the Depression*. New York: Oxford University Press, 1965.

Rosenbaum, Eduard, and A. J. Sherman. *Das Bankhaus M. M. Warburg & Co., 1798–1938*. Hamburg: Hans Christian Verlag, 1976.

Rostow, W. W. *The Stages of Economic Growth*. Cambridge: Cambridge University Press, 1960.

Rubin, David C., ed. *Autobiographical Memory*. New York: Cambridge University Press, 1986.

Rudlin, John. *Jacques Copeau*. Cambridge: Cambridge University Press, 1984.

Said, Edward. *Beginnings: Intention and Method*. New York: Basic Books, 1975.

Samuel, Enid C. *The Villas in Regent's Park and Their Residents*. London: St. Marleybone Society Publications Group, 1959.

Samuels, Ernest. *Bernard Berenson: The Making of a Legend*. Cambridge, Mass.: Harvard University Press, Belknap Press, 1987.

Sarlós, Robert Károly. *Jig Cook and the Provincetown Players: Theatre in Ferment*. Amherst: University of Massachusetts Press, 1982.

Sarris, Andrew. *The Films of Josef von Sternberg*. New York: Museum of Modern Art, 1966.

Saunders, Ann. *Regent's Park from 1086 to the Present*. 2nd ed. London: Bedford College, 1981.

———. *The Regent's Park Villas*. London: Bedford College, 1981.

Sayler, Oliver M. *Our American Theatre*. New York: Benjamin Blom, 1923.

———, ed. *Max Reinhardt and His Theatre*. New York: Brentano's, 1924.

Schanke, Robert A. *Shattered Applause: The Lives of Eva Le Gallienne*. Carbondale: Southern Illinois University Press, 1992.

Schleier, Merrill. *The Skyscraper in American Art: 1890–1931*. New York: Da Capo, 1986.

Schorer, Mark. *Sinclair Lewis: An American Life*. London: Honeymoon, 1961.

Schuker, Stephen A. *The End of French Predominance in Europe*. Chapel Hill: University of North Carolina Press, 1976.

Schulzinger, Robert D. *The Wise Men of Foreign Affairs: The History of the Council on Foreign Relations*. New York: Columbia Univeristy Press, 1984.

Schumpeter, Joseph. *Business Cycles*. 1939; reprint, abridged, New York: McGraw-Hill, 1964.

Schwarz, Bernard. *The Economic Regulation of Business and Industry: A Legislative History of U.S. Regulatory Agencies*. 10 vols. New York: Chelsea House, 1973.

Schwarz, Jordon A. *The Interregnum of Despair: Hoover, Congress, and the Great Depression*. Urbana: University of Illinois Press, 1970.

———. *The Speculator: Bernard A. Baruch in Washington, 1917–1965*. Chapel Hill: University of North Carolina Press, 1981.

Seibert, Herbert D., & Co., Inc. *The Business and Financial Record of World War Years*. 1939. Reprint, New York: Arno Press, 1975.

Seigel, Jerrold. *Bohemian Paris: Culture, Politics, and the Boundaries of Bourgeois Life, 1830–1930*. New York: Penguin Books, 1987.

Seltsam, William H., ed. *Metropolitan Opera Annals: A Chronicle of Artists and Performers*. New York: H. W. Wilson, 1947.

Shaw, George Bernard. "Preface to Plays: Pleasant and Unpleasant." 1898. Reprinted in *Arms and the Man*. New York: Dover, 1990.

Sheaffer, Louis. *O'Neill, Son and Artist*. Boston: Little, Brown, 1973.

Sheehan, James J. *German Liberalism in the Nineteenth Century*. Chicago: University of Chicago Press, 1978.

Shell, Marc. *Money, Language and Thought:*. Berkeley: University of California Press, 1982.

Shi, David E. *Matthew Josephson: Bourgeois Bohemian*. New Haven: Yale University Press, 1981.

Silver, Kenneth E. *Espirit de Corps: The Art of the Parisian Avant-Garde and the First World War, 1914–1925*. Princeton: Princeton University Press, 1989.

Silverman, Dan P. *Reconstructing Europe after the Great War*. Cambridge, Mass.: Harvard University Press, 1982.

Simmel, Georg. *The Conflict in Modern Culture and Other Essays*. Trans. K. Peter Etzkorn. New York: Teachers College Press, 1968.

———. *The Philosophy of Money*. Trans. Tom Bottomore and David Frisby. 2nd enlarged ed. London: Routledge, 1990.

———. *The Sociology of Georg Simmel*. Trans. and ed. Kurt H. Wolff. New York: Free Press, 1950.

Sinclair, Upton. *The Autobiography of Upton Sinclair*. New York: Harcourt, Brace & World, 1962.

————. *Mammonart*. Pasadena, Calif.: N.p., 1925.

————. *The Metropolis*. New York: Moffat Yard, 1908.

————. *A World to Win*. New York: Viking, 1946.

Skildelsky, Robert. *John Maynard Keynes: The Economist as Savior, 1920–1937*. New York: Penguin Books, 1992.

————. *John Maynard Keynes: Hopes Betrayed, 1883–1920*. New York: Penguin Books, 1983.

Sobel, Robert. *The Great Bull Market: Wall Street in the 1920s*. New York: Harper & Row, 1968.

Sontag, Raymond J. *A Broken World, 1919–1939*. New York: Harper & Row, 1971.

Soule, George. *Prosperity Decade: From War to Depression, 1917–1929*. New York: Holt, Rinehart & Winston, 1947.

Stanislavsky, Constantin. *An Actor Prepares*. Trans. Elizabeth Hapgood. New York: Theatre Arts Books, 1936.

————. *Building a Character*. Trans. Elizabeth Hapgood. New York: Theatre Arts Books, 1949.

————. *Creating a Role*. Trans. Elizabeth Hapgood. New York: Theatre Arts Books, 1961.

Stern, Fritz. *Dreams and Delusions: National Socialism in the Drama of the German Past*. New York: Vintage Books, 1987.

Sternberg, Josef von. *Fun in a Chinese Laundry*. New York: Collier Books, 1965.

Stevens, Holly, ed. *Letters of Wallace Stevens*. New York: Alfred A. Knopf, 1966.

Stimpson, Catherine R. "Introduction." In Jane Kramer, *Whose Art Is It?*, 1–35. Durham, N.C.: Duke University Press, 1994.

Stock, Noel. *The Life of Ezra Pound*. New York: Pantheon Books 1970.

Stone, Gregory P., and Harvey A. Farberman, eds. *Social Pyschology Through Symbolic Interation*. 2nd ed. New York: John Wiley & Sons, 1981.

Stone, Lawrence. *The Past and the Present Revisited*. London: Routledge & Kegan Paul, 1987.

Strauss, Lewis L. *Men and Decisions*. Garden City, N.Y.: Doubleday, 1962.

Swaine, Robert. *The Cravath Firm and Its Predecessors, 1819–1948*. 2 vols. New York: N.p., 1948.

Tambling, Jeremy. *Opera, Ideology and Film*. New York: St. Martin's Press, 1987.

Taylor, A. J. P. *Beaverbrook*. London: Hamish Hamilton, 1972.

Teichmann, Howard. *Smart Aleck: The Wit, World and Life of Alexander Woolcott*. New York: William Morrow, 1976.

Teichova, Alice, and P. L. Cottrell. *International Business and Central Europe, 1918–1939*. New York: St. Martin's Press, 1983.

Thane, Pat. "Cassel, Sir Ernest Joseph." *Dictionary of Business Biography*, ed. David J. Jeremy, 1:604–14. London: Butterworths, 1984.

Trachtenberg, Alan, ed. *Hart Crane: A Collection of Critical Essays*. Englewood Cliffs, N.J.: Prentice-Hall, 1982.

Trachtenberg, Marc. *Reparations in World Poltics: France and European Economic Diplomacy, 1916–1923*. New York: Columbia University Press, 1980.

Trottman, Nelson. *History of the Union Pacific*. New York: Ronald Press, 1923.

Unterecker, John. *Voyager: A Life of Hart Crane*. New York: Farrar, Straus & Giroux, 1974.

Van Rensselaer, Mrs. John King. *The Social Ladder*. New York: H. Holt, 1924.

Van Vechten, Carl. *Sacred and Profane Memories*. New York: Alfred A. Knopf, 1932.

Vanderbilt, Cornelius, Jr. *Farewell to Fifth Avenue*. London: Victor Gollancz, 1935.

Vanderlip, Frank A. *From Farm Boy to Financier*. New York: Appleton-Century, 1935.

Vater, Harold G. *The Drive to Industrial Maturity*. Westport, Conn.: Greenwood Press, 1976.

Vevier, Charles. *The United States and China, 1906–1913: A Study in Finance and Diplomacy*. New Brunswick, N.J.: Rutgers Unviersity Press, 1955.

Von Eckardt, Wolf, et al., eds. *Oscar Wilde's London: A Scrapbook of Vices and Virtues, 1880–1900*. Garden City, N.Y.: Anchor Books, 1987.

Waldau, Roy S. *Vintage Years of the Theatre Guild, 1928–1939*. Cleveland: Press of Case Western Reserve University, 1972.

Warburg, Frieda Schiff. *Reminiscences of a Long Life*. New York: N.p., 1956.

Warburg, James P. *The Long Road Home: Autobiography of a Maverick*. New York: Doubleday, 1964.

Wasko, Janet. *Movies and Money: Financing the American Film Industry*. Norwood, N.J.: Albex Publishing, 1982.

Watson, Steven. *Strange Bedfellows: The First American Avant-Garde*. New York: Abbeville Press, 1991.

Watzinger, Karl Otto. *Geschichte der Juden in Mannheim, 1650–1945: mit 52 Biographien*. Stuttgart: W. Kohlhammer, 1987.

Weber, Brom, ed. *The Letters of Hart Crane, 1916–1932*. Berkeley: University of California Press, 1965.

Weber, Nicholas Fox. *Patron Saints: Five Rebels Who Opened America to a New Art, 1928–1943*. New York: Alfred A. Knopf, 1982.

West, Nathanael. *The Complete Works of Nathanael West*. New York: Farrar, Straus and Cudahy, 1957.

Westbrook, Wayne W. *Wall Street in the American Novel*. New York: New York University Press, 1980.

Wiebe, Robert. *Businessmen and Reform: A Study of the Progressive Movement*. Chicago: Triangle, 1968.

———. *The Search for Order*. New York: Hill & Wang, 1967.

Wigmore, Barry. *The Great Crash and Its Aftermath*. Westport, Conn.: Greenwood Press, 1985.

Wilde, Oscar. *The Complete Works of Oscar Wilde: Stories, Plays, Poems & Essays*. New York: Harper & Row, 1989.

Wilkins, Mira. *The Maturing of Multinational Enterprise*. Cambridge, Mass.: Harvard University Press, 1974.

Willett, John. *Art and Politics in the Weimar Period: The New Sobriety, 1917–1933*. New York: Pantheon Books, 1978.

———. *The Theatre of the Weimar Republic*. New York: Holmes & Meier, 1988.

Williams, Raymond. *Culture and Society: 1780–1950*. New York: Columbia University Press, 1983.

———. *Keywords*. New York: Oxford University Press, 1978.

———. *Modern Tragedy*. Stanford: Stanford University Press, 1966.

Wilshire, Bruce. *Role Playing and Identity: The Limits of Theatre as Metaphor*. Bloomington: Indiana University Press, 1982.

Wilson, Edmund. *The American Earthquake: A Documentary of the Twenties and Thirties*. New York: Farrar, Straus & Giroux, 1958.

———. *The Shores of Light: A Literary Chronicle of the 1920s and 1930s*. New York: Farrar, Straus & Giroux, 1952.

Wilson, Joan Hoff. *American Business and Foreign Policy, 1920–1933*. Boston: Beacon Press, 1971.

———. *Ideology and Economics: U.S. Relations with the Soviet Union, 1918–1933*. Columbia: University of Missouri Press, 1974.

Winkler, John K. *The First Billion: The Stillmans and the National City Bank*. Babson Park, Mass.: Spear & Staff, 1951.

Winkler, Max. *Foreign Bonds: An Autopsy*. Philadelphia: Roland Swain, 1933.

Wulf, Joseph. *Musik im Dritten Reich: Eine Dokumentation*. [Gütersloh]: S. Mohn, 1963.

Yamey, Basil S. *Art and Accounting*. New Haven: Yale University Press, 1989.

Zagona, Helen Grace. *The Legend of Salome and the Principle of Art for Art's Sake*. Genve: Libraire E Droz, 1960.

Zolberg, Vera L. *Constructing a Sociology of the Arts*. Cambridge: Cambridge University Press, 1990.

Signed Articles in Newspapers and Periodicals

Abrahams, Paul. "American Bankers and the Economic Tactics of Peace: 1919." *Journal of American History* 56 (1969): 572–83.

Anderson, John. "Kahn Generous Drama Patron." *New York Evening Journal*, March 30, 1934.

Aronsfeld, C. C. "Jews in Victorian England." *Leo Baeck Institute Yearbook* 7 (1962): 312–29.

[Artists, Writers, Musicians, and Philosophers of France]. "The Germans, Destroyers of Cathedrals." *New York Times Current History* 2 (August 1915): 1004–12. Translated extracts from *Les Allemands destructeurs de cathédrales et de trésors du passé; mémoire relatif aux bombardements de Reims — Arras — Senlis — Louvain — Soissons, etc., accompagné de photographies et de pièces justificatives.* Paris: Hachette, 1915.

Augustine-Perez, Dolores L. "Very Wealthy Businessmen in Imperial Germany." *Journal of Social History* 22 (1988): 299–321.

Baker, John. "Commercial Sources for Hart Crane's 'The River.' " *Wisconsin Studies in Contemporary Literature* 6 (1965): 45–55.

Berens, Julius G. "Wall Street Mourns Passing of Otto Kahn, Leading 'Old School' Financier." *New York American*, March 30, 1934.

Bender, Thomas. "Wholes and Parts: The Need for Synthesis in American History." *Journal of American History* 73 (June 1986): 120–36.

Benedict, Libbian. "Otto H. Kahn — Maecenas." *Reflex* (November 1927): 11–19.

Berger, Morroe. "Jazz: Resistance to the Diffusion of a Culture-Pattern." *Journal of Negro History* 32 (October 1947): 461–94.

Bottomley, William L. "A Selection from the Works of Delano & Aldrich." *Architectural Record* 54 (July 1923): 3–31.

Bragdon, Claude. "Towards a New Theatre." *Architectural Record* 52 (September 1922): 171–92.

Brisbane, Arthur. "Today." *New York American*, March 30 and 31, 1934.

Caro, Robert A. "Annals of Biography: The City Shaper." *New Yorker* (January 5, 1998): 38–55.

Carosso, Vincent P. "A Financial Elite: New York's German-Jewish Investment Bankers." *American Jewish Historical Quarterly* 56 (September 1976): 67–88.

———. "The Morgans as Private International Bankers (1854–1934)." *Congresso Internazionale di Storia Americana* (1976): 103–12.

Cassis, Youssef. "Bankers in English Society in the Late Nineteenth Century." *Economic History Review*, 2nd ser., 38/42 (1985): 210–29.

———. "Merchant Bankers and City Aristocracy." *British Journal of Sociology* 39 (1988): 114–26.

Chapman, Stanley D. "Aristocracy and Meritocracy in Merchant Banking." *British Journal of Sociology* 37 (1986): 180–91.

Cheney, Sheldon. "The Painter in the Theatre." *Theatre Arts Magazine* 6 (July 1922): 191–99.

Colby, Bainbridge, et al. "Kreuger & Toll Company International Match Corp.; To Debenture Holders, Shareholders, and Other Security Holders." *New York Times*, April 23, 1932.

Crane, Hart. "Two Letters on 'The Bridge.' " *Hound and Horn* 7 (July–September 1934): 678–82.

Cruikshank, Herbert Knight. "The Great Kahn." *Theatre Magazine* (November 1929): 26, 80.

Cushing, Edward. "The Americanism of the Metropolitan Opera House: Reflections on the Statement of Otto H. Kahn." *Brooklyn Eagle*, October 25, 1925.

Cushing, Henry. "The New Wall Street." *World's Work* 32 (June 1916): 215–23.

Davidson, James West. "The New Narrative History: How New? How Narrative." *Reviews in American History* 12 (September 1984): 322–34.

Donoghue, Denis. "Seeking the Source of the Blaze." *New York University Magazine* 2 (winter 1987): 53.

Downer, Edgeworth. "Understanding Millionairedom." *New York Morning World*, August 1, 1918.

Downes, Olin. "Kahn's Bold Fight Saved the Opera." *New York Times*, March 30, 1934.

Elliot, W. Y. "Mussolini, Prophet of the Pragmatic Era in Politics." *Political Science Quarterly* 41 (1926): 161–92.

Eskimo [pseudonym]. "Opera Hats." *New Yorker* (February 28, 1925): 23.

Flutterbye, Mme. [pseudonym]. "In the Mayfair with Mme. Flutterbye." *New York Evening Journal,* March 30, 1934.

Frank, Waldo [Searchlight]. "Profiles: In Tune with the Finite." *New Yorker* (February 20, 1926): 23.

Frieden, Jeff. "Sectoral Conflict and Foreign Economic Policy, 1914–1940." *International Organization* 42 (1988): 59–90.

Fuchs, Miriam. "Poet & Patron: Hart Crane & Otto Kahn." *Book Forum* 6 (1982): 45–51.

Gabriel, Gilbert W. "Kahn Known as Courtliest 'First Nighter.'" *New York American,* March 30, 1934.

Gilbert, Douglas. "Broadway Mourns 'First Angel' Who Gave of Wealth Unstintedly." *New York World-Telegram,* March 31, 1934.

———. "Otto H. Kahn. The Impressions of an Unprejudiced Newspaper Man." *New York Telegram* reprint, January 1, 1931.

Glass, J. P. "The Finding of Otto Kahn in London." *New York Evening World,* April 3, 1925.

Gould, Bruse. "Erskine, Antheil to Write Opera On Kahn's Order." *New York Evening Post,* September 26, 1929.

Grunwald, Kurt. "Windsor Cassel — the Last Court Jew." *Leo Baeck Institute Yearbook* 14 (1969): 119–61.

Hawley, Ellis. "The Discovery and Study of Corporate Liberalism." *Business History Review* 52 (1978): 311–20.

Hendrick, Burton J. "The Jewish Invasion of America." *McClure's Magazine* 30 (March 1913): 125–65.

Hermand, Jost. "Commercialization of Avant-Garde Movements at the Turn of the Century." *New German Critique* 29 (1983): 71–83.

Hutchinson, Ron. "Roger Wolfe Kahn's Band Shorts of 1927." *Vitaphone Project — Vitaphone News* (summer-fall 1999). http://www.geocities.com/ppicking/vitaphone44.html.

Josephson, Matthew. "A Letter to My Friends." *Little Review* (spring-summer 1926): 17–19.

Krehbiel, H. E. "The Salome of Wilde and Strauss." *New York Daily Tribune,* January 23, 1907.

Krondatieff, N. D. "The Long Waves in Economic Life." *Review* 2 (spring 1979): 519–62.

Laugwitz, Burkhard. "Robert Kahn and Brahms." Trans. Reinhard G. Pauly. *Musical Quarterly* 74 (1990): 595–611.

Leffler, Melvyn. "The Origins of Republican War Debt Policy, 1921–1923: A Case Study in the Applicability of the Open Door Interpretation." *Journal of American History* 59 (1972): 585–601.

Liebling, Leonard. "Music Mourns Kahn as Best Friend." *New York American,* March 30, 1934.

Lisle-Williams, Michael. "Beyond the Market: The Survival of Family Capitalism in the English Merchant Banks." *British Journal of Sociology* 35 (June 1984): 241–71.

———. "Merchant Banking Dynasties in the English Class Structure: Ownership, Solidarity and Kinship in the City of London, 1850–1960." *British Journal of Sociology* 35 (September 1984): 332–62.

Loree, Lenor F. "Introduction of Otto H. Kahn." *Chamber of Commerce of New York State Bulletin* (November 1929): 181–83.

Ludwig, Emil. "Society in the Old World and New." *New York Times Magazine,* November 3, 1929.

McCormick, Richard L. "The Discovery That Business Corrupts Politics: A Reappraisal of the Origins of Progressivism." *American Historical Review* 86 (April 1981): 247–74.

Macgowan, Kenneth. "Imported and Domestic: Some Words As to the Wares on Display for the Coming Season." *Theatre Arts Magazine* 7 (October 1923): 265–74.

Manson, George J. "The Foreign Element in New York City." *Harper's Weekly* (Supplement) (August 4, 1888): 231–46.

Maurois, Andre. "Europe Watches Detroit and Moscow." *New York Times Magazine,* January 12, 1930.

Moody, John, and George K. Turner. "Masters of Capital in America." *McClures* 36 (January 1911): 334–52.

Nelson, S. A. "Little Stories of Wall Street." *New York Tribune,* February 17, 1907.

Nemo [pseudonym?]. "Can Ca-U Can? Khan Kahu to be the Tory Candidate." *Manchester Weekly Citizen,* February 3, 1912.

Rhodes, Benjamin D. "Reassessing 'Uncle Shylock': The United States and the French War Debt, 1917–1929." *Journal of American History* 55 (March 1969): 787–803.

Rickey, John. ["Kahn's Estate"]. *New York Times,* December 13, 1936.

Ruhling, Nancy A. "The Castle on the Hill." *Newsday,* December 11, 1994.

Rürup, Reinhard. "Jewish Emancipation and Bourgeois Society." *Leo Baeck Institute Yearbook* 14 (1969): 67–91.

St. John, A. "Men in Wall Street's Eye: Introducing Mr. Otto H. Kahn." *Barron's,* July 2, 1923.

Salpeter, Harry. "Otto the Magnificent." *Outlook* 149 (July 4, 1928): 386–87, 398.

Santirocco, Matthew S. "Poet and Patron in Ancient Rome." *Book Forum* 6 (1982): 56–62.

Saylor, Oliver M. "The Year Ahead with Europe as Preceptor." *Theatre Arts Magazine* 6 (October 1922): 267–75.

Scheiber, Harry N. "World War I as Entrepreneurial Opportunity: Willard Straight and the American International Corporation." *Political Science Quarterly* 84 (1969): 486–511.

Schmidt, James. "The Concrete Totality and Lukács' Concept of Proletarian *Bildung*." *Telos* 24 (summer 1975): 2–40.

Shands, A. L. "The Real Thomas Edison." *The Haldeman-Julius Monthly* 8 (August 1928): 83–89.

Sharp, Michael. "Theme and Free Variation: The Scoring of Hart Crane's The Bridge." *Arizona Quarterly* 37 (1981): 197–213.

Sinclair, John F. "Idealism Is the Characteristic Spiritual Quality of Americans, Says Otto Kahn." *Kansas City Star*, April 13, 1928.

Slattery, Charles V. "Mingled Financial Keenness with Intelligent Love for Various Arts." *New York American*, March 30, 1934.

Solon, Leon V. "The Residence of Otto H. Kahn, Esq. New York." *Architectural Record* 46 (August 1919): 99–114.

Supple, Barry E. "A Business Elite: German Jewish Financiers in Nineteenth Century New York." *Business History Review* 31 (summer 1957): 143–78.

Taylor, Tom. "The Transition to Adulthood in Comparative Perspective: Professional Males in Germany and the United States at the Turn of the Century." *Journal of Social History* (summer 1988): 636.

Thane, Pat. "Financiers and the British State: The Case of Sir Ernest Cassel." *Business History* 28 (1986): 80–99.

Trowbridge, Helen. "Otto H. Kahn." *T.P.A. (Travelers Magazine)* (ca. 1925): 13–14.

Warburg, Eric M. "The Transfer of the Warburg Institute to England in 1933." *Warburg Institute Annual Report* (1952–53): 13–16.

Waterbury, Florence. "Mrs. Otto H. Kahn." *Archives of Asian Art* 3 (1948–49): 67.

Wineapple, Brenda. "Mourning Becomes Biography." *American Imago* 54 (1997): 437–51.

Winerip, Michael. "For Sale: A Blighted 'Xanadu.' " *New York Times*, June 21, 1988.

Wolff, Joseph. "Idealism in Wall Street." *American Weekly Jewish News*, August 9, 1918, 390.

Woolf, S. J. "Kahn Talks of Our Cultural Future." *New York Times Magazine*, November 24, 1929.

Wright, Preston. "Discoveries in Humans." *Grand Rapids Herald*, May 17, 1925.

Young, James C. "The Human Show in the Broker's Office; There Is Drama When the Prices Dance in Light above the Board." *New York Times Magazine*, December 1, 1929.

Zeck, Gregory R. "The Chan's Great Continent: Otto Kahn and *The Bridge*." *Markham Review* 7 (1978): 61–65.

Index

DeMille, Cecil B., 175, 177
Deutsch, Elisabeth Franziska "Lili"
    (sister), 41, 89, 207, 209–12, 221,
    271–72
Deutsch, Felix (brother-in-law), 41,
    100–101, 198, 230
Deutsch, Franz "Frank" (nephew),
    209, 271
Deutsch, George (nephew), 210
Deutscher Press Club (N.Y.), 259
Deutsches Bank, 43, 45
Deutsches Theater, 42
Deutsche Unionsbank, 33
Diaghilev, Sergei, 109
Dichotomies, 12–15, 23, 307
Die Meistersinger von Nürnberg (Wag-
    ner), 22, 267
Die tote Stadt (Korngold), 130
Dillon, Clarence, 142, 273
Dillon, Read & Co., 142, 143, 198,
    273
Don Carlo (Verdi), 303
Dow Jones Industrial Index, 190, 202,
    207, 209, 229, 233
Downes, Olin, 218, 252
Dresdner Bank, 102
Dubuque, Sioux City Railroad, 59
Duggan, Stephen, 265
Duncan, Augustin, 160
Duncan, Isadora, 2, 108, 164
Duveen, Joseph, 87

Eastman, Max, 227
Eberstadt, Edward F. (uncle), 46
Eberstadt, Falck "Ferdinand" (grand-
    father), 30–32, 50, 143
Eberstadt, Ferdinand (cousin), 143,
    198
Eberstadt, Sarah Zelie Seligmann
    (grandmother), 31–32
Economic Consequences of the Peace, The
    (Keynes), 203
Economic regulation and legislation,
    15, 71, 79–80, 87, 88, 91, 225–26,
    231, 269

Edison, Thomas A., 103, 185
Edward, Prince of Wales, 31, 44, 45
Einzig, Paul, 190
Eisentstein, Sergei, 7–8, 9, 129, 227,
    304, 305
Embourgeoisment, 8, 11, 20–21, 25–
    26, 35, 38, 41, 84–85, 95, 186, 221
Emergency Committee in Aid of Dis-
    placed German Scholars, 265
Emperor Jones (Greunberg), 20, 256
Emperor Jones (O'Neill), 20, 161, 162,
    167, 256
Eppstein, Paul, 265
Equitable Life Assurance Company
    (ELAS), 70–72
Equitable Trust Company, 68, 195,
    196, 212
Erie Railroad, 59
Eroica (Beethoven), 308
Erskine, John, 238, 252, 254
Evening Journal (N.Y.), 297, 301
Evening Post (N.Y.), 73

Family Group (Hals), 87
Farrar, Geraldine, 75, 122, 145, 146,
    150, 258
Father Duffy Memorial Committee,
    298
Featherbedding, 30, 32
Federal Reserve Bank, 229, 251, 281
Federal Reserve Board, 116, 222
Federation for the Support of Jewish
    Philanthropic Societies, 267
Feldberg, Germany, 266
Fields, Dorothy, 21
Fiesta (Gold), 193
Financial Times (London), 190
First National Bank, 140–42
Fish, Stuyvesant, 62, 63
Fitzgerald, Eleanor, 161
Fitzgerald, F. Scott, 13
Flecther, Duncan, 276, 291, 292, 296
Fleming, Robert, 53
Florence, Italy, 95
Folkine, Michel, 144

Forbes, B. C., 185
Ford, Henry, 185, 201
Fortune, 223, 242, 260
Four Saints in Three Acts (Stein and
    Thomson), 258, 297
Fox Movietone, 188
France, 97, 104–6, 108, 114–18, 130,
    132, 206
Francophilia, 71, 73, 126, 146
Franco-Prussian War, 119
Frank, Waldo, 42, 163, 184–85, 240–
    41, 243, 255, 262, 263
Frankfurt, Germany, 18, 33, 34, 45,
    48, 51, 84, 115
Frankfurt Assembly, 28
Franz Josef (emperor of Austria), 111

Gabriel, Gilbert, 300–301
Gaieties of 1919, 147
Gailbraith, John Kenneth, 189
Galleria del Accademia (Venice), 149
Garbo, Greta, 296
Garden, Mary, 145, 154
Garrick Theatre, 193
Gatti-Casazza, Guilo, 83, 84, 109, 122,
    130, 145, 150, 159, 174, 175, 219,
    254, 258
Geistgemeinschaft, 200
General Electric Company, 107
George V (king of England): corona-
    tion of, 88
German Americans, 14, 29, 46–45,
    99, 101–4, 106, 120. *See also* World
    War I
German External Loan (1924), 140–
    42
German Jews, 9, 15, 27, 32, 36–37,
    95, 101–4, 118, 120, 125, 135–
    36, 201, 259–61, 264–68. *See
    also* Anglo-German Jewry; Anti-
    Semitism; Morgan, Jack; New York,
    N.Y.; World War I
Germany: economic change in, 23,
    32–34; Hoover Moratorium
    (1931) and, 206; hyperinflation

(1923) in, 134; municipal finance
    proposals, 115, 116, 117, 118; Naz-
    ism in, 24, 36, 141, 200–201, 204,
    207, 210, 230, 259–61, 297, 305–
    6; reparations and, 130, 138; revo-
    lutions of 1848–1849 and, 28–29,
    31–33; World War I and, 98–101,
    115–18, 120, 124, 130. *See also*
    Buildung; Dawes Plan; Dillon, Read
    & Co.; Kuhn, Loeb & Co.; M. M.
    Warburg & Co.; Postwar interna-
    tionalism; *Sittleichkeit*; Warburg
    Institute
Gershwin, George, 1, 147, 148, 151,
    161, 170, 256
Gest, Morris, 144, 173, 175
Gibbs, Henry Hucks, 89
Gilbert, Douglas, 300
Gilly, Dinh, 97
Gilmore, Frank, 298
Gish, Lillian and Dorothy, 146
Glass, Carter, 271, 277
Glorifying the American Girl (film), 274
Gluck, Alma, 151
Goelet family, 48
Goethe, Johann Wolfgang von, 26, 38,
    120, 200
Gold, Mike, 9, 193, 194, 200, 228, 249
Goldberg, Rube, 5
Goldman, Sachs, 234
Goldschmidt, Jakob, 198
Gold standard, 271
Gorky, Maxim, 55
Gould, Jay, 58, 63
Grace, W. R. & Co, 107
Great Britain, 95, 98–99, 100, 101,
    114, 117, 118
Great Depression: impression manage-
    ment and, 188–89, 192, 202, 208,
    222–23, 226, 228–29, 273–76
Greenwich Village Theatre, 161
Greffuhle, Countess, 111
Gregory, Eliot, 74, 78, 81, 83
Grenfell, E. C., 94–95, 97. *See also* Mor-
    gan, Grenfell & Co.

Index

Index

—representations of: caricatures, 22, 146; literary and theatrical, 1, 2, 4–8, 5, 6, 7, 8, 25, 26, 155, 185, 192, 305–6
—Senate testimony (Pecora, 1933) and, 258, 270–92; aftermath of, 291–93; on bankers' practices and services, 277–79, 281, 288; on bull and bear pools, 286–87; on Chile, 282–83; on competitive bidding, 278–79, 281; critique of 1920s, 281, 287–88, 290; on Federal Reserve Bank, 279; on financial disclosure, 280, 290; on Kuhn, Loeb partnership, 278, 279, 280, 281, 282–83, 289–91; on need for regulation, 287, 290; on Pennroad Corp., 289–90; on speculation, 286–87; on taxes, 284–86, 291; preparations for, 258, 270, 272, 273, 276, 284; press coverage of, 273, 276, 291; rhetorical strategies in, 258, 277, 279, 281, 283–91
—Senate testimony (foreign bonds, 1931–1932) and; on Germany, 224; on Kuhn, Loeb partnership, 225–26; press coverage of, 226; rhetorical strategies of, 224–26, 228; on war debts and reparations, 224–25
See also Cosmpolitanism; Crane, Hart; Harriman, Edward H.; Metropolitan Opera; Salome; World War I
Kahn, Paul (brother), 40, 42, 101
Kahn, Robert (brother), 39, 40, 41, 210, 265–67
Kahn, Roger Wolfe (son), 68, 147–48
Kant, Immanuel, 120
Karlsruhe, Germany, 16, 28, 42
Katz, Irving, 36
Kaufman, George F., 146. See also Animal Crackers
Kellogg, Frank, 138
Keynesianism, 204, 221
Kindleberger, Charles P., 206, 207

Kipling, Rudyard, 92
Kirstein, Lincoln, 307
Kobler, John, 9
Korngold, Erich Wolfgang, 130
Kountze family, 82
Krehbiel, Henry E., 76
Kreuger & Toll, 191, 234
Krupps munitions group, 199
Kubla Khan (Coleridge), 2
Kuhn, Abraham, 49, 53
Kuhn, Loeb & Co.: assets of, in 1929, 191; call loans and, 190; 1932 election and, 247; foreign bonds and securities and, 67, 72, 97–98, 104, 114–17, 126, 130, 131, 135–43, 198–99, 207–8, 281–83; generational succession at, 18, 53–54, 105, 126–27, 132, 223; Great Depression and, 190–91, 202, 205–7, 209, 211, 251; history and clients of, 9, 15, 18–19, 48, 49–54, 66–67, 103; investment trusts and, 9, 15, 49–51, 65, 143, 191, 202, 252, 281, 289; Kahn's death and, 299–300; neutrality in World War I and, 98–101, 104–7, 114, 118; offices of, 13, 50, 51, 67, 97, 135, 157, 160, 162, 163, 165, 184, 192, 212, 241, 276, 285, 299–300; partners of, 18–20, 49–51, 53–54, 90–91, 127, 142, 143, 276; repurchase agreements (buybacks) and, 251; RFC and, 232; stature of, 9, 18, 48, 53, 58–60, 66–67, 79, 97, 225, 274; Union Pacific and, 58–60

LaGallienne, Eva, 44, 177
LaGallienne, Richard, 44
Lamont, Thomas W., 131, 136–41, 199, 300, 301
Landenburg, Seligmann, 34
Landesbank of Rhine Province, 206
Langner, Lawrence, 13
Lanny Budd novels, 305–6
Laparra, Raoul, 299

Mercury Theatre, 304
Methodology, 4–5, 10–17
Metropolis, The (Sinclair), 72, 227
Metropolitan Magazine, 71
Metropolitan Opera (N.Y.): African
    Americans and, 256; Committee to
    Save Opera at the Metropolitan
    Opera House and, 253, 254; Con-
    ried Metropolitan Opera Company
    and, 69–70, 74–76; finances of, 75,
    76, 81, 83, 86–87, 96–97, 130,
    212–18, 238–39, 251–53, 255,
    302, 304; German opera and, 70,
    83, 96, 121–23, 130, 150, 200,
    219; Kahn and, 1, 5–6, 13, 20, 70,
    73–78, 81–83, 86–87, 121–23,
    147, 149–51, 159, 174, 175, 181–
    82, 194, 202, 212–21, 252–59,
    260, 261, 267, 274, 302–3; lease
    and, 69, 76, 82, 217; Lincoln Cen-
    ter and, 254, 303–4. *See also* New
    York, N.Y.; *Salome*
Metropolitan Opera Association, 237,
    254
Metropolitan Opera Company, 13, 81,
    92, 96–97, 194, 212–15, 217–18,
    237
Metropolitan Opera Guild, 303
Metropolitan Opera House, 2, 6, 46,
    59, 63, 68–70, 108, 121, 154; new
    house proposals and, 2, 6, 213–18,
    237–38, 254, 303; radio broadcasts
    and, 147, 212; women's patronage
    of, 255, 303
Metropolitan Opera Real Estate Com-
    pany (MORECO), 70, 74–75, 78,
    121, 213–18, 238
Metropolitan Secuirities Company, 67
Mexico, 58
Millionaires, 1–2, 13–14, 62, 71, 144,
    235, 255, 301, 307
Mills, Ogden, 233
Ministry des Beaux Arts (France), 112
Miracle, The (Vollmoeller), 92, 95, 133,
    175, 187

Miracle at Verdun (Chlumberg), 305
Missouri Pacific Railroad, 67, 92, 232
Mitchell, Charles, 135, 141, 269, 270,
    273, 284, 294
Mittleuropa, 126
M. Kahn Söhn, 32, 33, 41
M. M. Warburg & Co. (Hamburg), 19,
    51, 97, 136, 198, 206, 211
Modernity and modernisms: actors in
    networks and, 9, 11–12, 157; after-
    life fantasies and, 305–6; artistic
    ambitions and temperaments in, 8,
    9, 20, 21–22, 64–65, 108, 157,
    175, 181, 186, 263, 264; authen-
    ticity in, 308–9; avant-gardism and,
    64–65, 87, 106, 111, 200; capital-
    ist, 1, 10, 13–16, 18–21, 26–28,
    32–34, 43, 47, 80, 189, 192, 305;
    cinema and, 4–5; cultural capitals
    in, 16, 20, 44, 46–47, 55, 96, 108,
    112–13, 193, 200, 305; cultural
    marketplace and brokerage in, 10–
    11, 20, 21–23, 81–83, 149–52,
    155–56, 161–67, 178, 183, 184–
    86, 193, 228, 235–36, 303–5, 306–
    8; cultural nationalism and, 20, 73,
    150, 175, 187; death metaphors in,
    248–49, 277; difficulties of new-
    ness and, 65, 109, 266; family life
    and, 27–28, 30–32, 41, 85, 149–
    50, 152; hybrids of, 20, 24, 144–
    48; idioms of money in, 1–2, 192;
    impulses and insurgences of, 20,
    70, 76, 78, 219, 240, 258; liberal
    expectations and, 24, 36, 129, 266,
    270, 272; literary, 23; memory in,
    304–5; optimism and, 24, 185,
    192, 200–201, 220–23, 227; per-
    formative values in public life and,
    79–80, 135, 189, 219–20, 224,
    226, 228, 274–76, 293–94; privacy
    and, 10–11, 79–80, 149–50; rup-
    tures in, 10, 11, 28–29, 95–97,
    101, 125, 135–36, 188–89; sex-
    uality in, 10–11, 44, 76, 82–83,

San Francisco earthquake (1906), 75, 76

Sanger, Margaret, 154

San Simeon castle, 4

Sarnoff, David, 267

Satterlee, Louisa Morgan, 76

Saylor, Oliver, 146

Schiff, Jacob H., 18–19, 47, 50–54, 56, 58, 60, 64, 66, 74, 79, 80, 88, 90, 98–101, 103, 104, 105, 114–15, 123, 125, 127, 132, 248

Schiff, Mortimer L., 18–19, 53–54, 97, 98, 104–6, 116, 127, 132, 137, 139, 141, 204, 205–6, 212

Schiff, Otto, 239

Schiff, Therese Loeb (Mrs. Jacob H.), 53

Schiller, Friedrich von, 26, 120

Schoenberg, Arnold, 265

Schreker, Franz, 130, 265

Schumpeter, Joseph, 205

Scotti, Antonio, 5

Securities Act of 1933, 272, 274, 286

Securities Exchange Act of 1934, 292, 296

Seldes, Gilbert, 147, 297

Seligman, E. R. A., 48, 261

Seven Arts, 243

Seven Lively Arts, The (Seldes), 147

Shakespeare, William, 26, 44, 196

Shanewis (Cadman), 173, 159

Shaw, George Bernard, 126

Sherman Anti-Trust Act, 87

Sherry's Resaurant (N.Y.), 71

Showboat, 170

Shubert brothers, 144

Siemens & Halske, 199

Sifton, Claire, 227

Sifton, Paul, 227

Simonson, Lee, 174

Sinclair, Upton, 72, 227, 305–6

Sittleichkeit, 26, 43, 54

Skyscrapers (Carpenter), 219

Smith, Al, 243

Smoot-Hawley Tariff, 202

Socialism, 227

Sombart, Werner, 92

Southern Pacific Railroad, 79

Spartacus League, 124

Speyer, Edgar, 45, 49, 113

Speyer, James G., 48, 49, 68, 74

Speyer & Co. (N.Y.), 45, 48, 49, 54, 103, 142

Stanislavsky, Constantin, 226, 294

Stebbach, Germany, 26

Stein, Gertrude, 258

Steinam, Edward, 248–49

Steiwer, Frederick, 286

Sterling Crisis (1931), 209

Sternberg, Josef von, 200

Stettheimer, Florine, 258

Stettinius, Edward R., 114

Stimpson, Catherine R., 11

Stock market crash (N.Y., 1929), 143, 188, 189–94, 202, 289

Stone and Webster, 107

Strange Interlude (O'Neill), 273

Strasberg, Lee, 226

Strauss, Lewis, 127

Strauss, Richard, 76, 78, 130, 133, 150, 258, 259

Stravinsky, Igor, 92

Sumurûn (Reinhardt), 159

Sun (N.Y.), 78

Syndicates, 34, 79–80

Taboo (Wiborg), 160

Tate, Alan and Carolyn, 178

Taxation, 120, 166–67, 208, 231–33, 284–86, 291, 297

Taylor, Deems, 252

Tempest, The (Giorgione), 149

Temple Emanu-El (Manhattan), 56, 308

Thanhouser Film Corp., 92

Theater Union, 263–64

Theatre Arts (magazine), 146, 175, 187

Théâtre des Champs-Elyées, 72, 92

Théâtre du Vieux-Colombier, 112

Théâtre français de États-Unis, 112